Sounds, Screens, Speakers

Sounds, Screens, Speakers

An Introduction to Music and Media

CHARLES FAIRCHILD

BLOOMSBURY ACADEMIC
NEW YORK · LONDON · OXFORD · NEW DELHI · SYDNEY

BLOOMSBURY ACADEMIC
Bloomsbury Publishing Inc
1385 Broadway, New York, NY 10018, USA
50 Bedford Square, London, WC1B 3DP, UK

BLOOMSBURY, BLOOMSBURY ACADEMIC and the Diana logo are trademarks of
Bloomsbury Publishing Plc

First published in the United States of America 2019

For legal purposes the Acknowledgments on p. xix constitute an extension
of this copyright page.

Cover design: Avni Patel
Cover image: Paolo Monti, *servizio fotografico* (Milan, 1957)

A catalog record for this book is available from the Library of Congress.

ISBN: HB: 978-1-5013-3624-9
PB: 978-1-5013-3623-2
ePDF: 978-1-5013-3626-3
eBook: 978-1-5013-3625-6

Typeset by Deanta Global Publishing Services, Chennai, India
Printed and bound in the United States of America

To find out more about our authors and books visit www.bloomsbury.com and
sign up for our newsletters.

CONTENTS

LIST OF FIGURES

ACKNOWLEDGMENTS

The author and publisher gratefully acknowledge the permission granted to reproduce the copyright material in this book:

Forman, Murray. (2014) "Music, Image, Labor: Television's Prehistory." From *One Night on TV Is Worth Weeks at the Paramount: Popular Music on Early Television*. Durham, NC: Duke University Press, 17–51. Used with the permission of Duke University Press.

Garofalo, Reebee. (1999) "From Music Publishing to MP3: Music and Industry in the Twentieth Century." *American Music*, 17(3): 318–54. © 1999 by the Board of Trustees of the University of Illinois. Used with the permission of the University of Illinois Press.

Horning, Susan. (2000) "Chasing Sound: The Culture and Technology of Recording Studios in Postwar America." *Icon*, 6: 100–18. Republished by permission of the publisher.

James, David. (2015) "Introduction: Rock 'N' Film." In David E. James, *Rock 'n' Film: Cinema's Dance with Popular Music*. New York: Oxford University Press, 1–22. By permission of Oxford University Press, USA.

Every effort has been made to trace copyright holders and to obtain their permission for the use of copyright material. The publisher apologizes for any errors or omissions in the above list and would be grateful if notified of any corrections that should be incorporated in future reprints or editions of this book.

Overview:

All media are social media: Concepts, materials, methods

Media create social relationships. This is what they are designed to do. They are meant to connect you to someone else by engaging your senses and then accessing your emotions and knowledge. Importantly, they do this by capturing your time and attention. In this sense all media are social media, always.

This book is about the social relationships created through the mediation of music. Specifically, it is about the kinds of social relationships created through music in which the music industry has had a strong financial interest since the late nineteenth century. It is within these relationships in which the ability of an audience to pay attention becomes a kind of currency with its own kind of value. It is this ever-changing "attention economy" that you will be exploring throughout this book in a time period encompassing just over the course of the twentieth century. Just as importantly, this book is also about the various kinds of *social conflict and anxiety* over what were the "right" or "wrong" sorts of social relationships people were supposed to have through music. These conflicts and anxieties have been a remarkably persistent feature of our collective public culture for a very long time.

This book is divided up chronologically into four overlapping time periods each tracking significant historical changes in one broad area of interest. These eras are defined by significant changes in one or more areas of the music industry:

- Part One: The early recording industry, 1875 to 1940.

The first section examines the evolution of the experience of recorded sound, comparing and contrasting the era of early sound recording with the culture of sheet music that preceded it.

- Part Two: Bigger, better, louder, longer, 1930 to 1970

The second section examines how technologies of sound recording and sound reproduction shaped the evolution of the relationship between music and radio, music and film, music and television, and music and the evolution of the recording studio.

- Part Three: New forms of media, new kinds of fame, 1960 to 2000

The third section changes tack and begins to examine the evolution of the musical celebrity from its status as an "entertainer" or "artisan" to that of "artist." Importantly, this section examines how images of artists changed in parallel with the increasingly sophisticated technologies used to record and distribute their music.

- Part Four: Clouds, crowds, and idols, 1980 to 2015

The final section of this book examines the evolution of music listening and music consumption in light of the transition to digital which began in the early 1980s and was largely complete by 2015.

Each chapter will have the following structure:

- Background and topics (economic and cultural change)

Each chapter will begin with a kind of "setting of the scene." You will read about the kinds of social and cultural change that shaped how the music industry worked and decided what its priorities were. The purpose of this is to try to understand something of the circumstances in which people experienced the introduction of new forms of musical experience. This will help us see why some people reacted the ways they did to new technologies and contexts for understanding music.

- Explore and report (task-based work; listening and viewing exercises)

You will be asked to complete a range of analytical tasks in each chapter. These will include examining different kinds of sound recordings, analyzing imagery and photos of people making or consuming music, or trying to understand how different forms of music consumption were sold to new audiences.

- Focus (case studies and illustrative examples)

Each chapter will have one example of the kinds of circumstances of musical experience we are talking about. These sections are meant to spark ideas for your own independent research work.

- Independent research work

You will have the opportunity to pursue a given research topic in each chapter in considerable depth.

- References and further readings

You will be given a range of resources to help you start to plan your own research project. These are the sources used to write this book.

- Key readings

There are five "key readings" included in this book and one available on the internet. These are placed strategically throughout the text to act as core background for the writing and analysis tasks you are asked to develop. Each reading gives you a model for understanding the methods and materials you are expected to use. There are a series of questioning exercises set for each reading to take advantage of their contents.

Concepts

It is important to understand right from the start that, while this book follows a general chronological arc, it is not a simple chronology of the relationships that have been forged between music and media. Instead, the main focus of this book is to help you develop analytical methods for understanding the evolution of these relationships over time. As such, the case studies are not meant to be comprehensive explanations of the subject matter of each chapter, but illustrative examples of how different kinds of social relationships have developed through music in various circumstances.

In order to make sense of the many, many ways in which music and media relate to one another and are integrated in our everyday experience of music, there are a few key historical ideas you should understand before you start using this book:

- Music has been centrally involved in the introduction, development, and acceptance of almost all new forms of media since the late nineteenth century.

- Across the entire twentieth century, the music industry has always worked across many forms of media simultaneously to engage audiences and capture their attention.

- The figure of the music celebrity has grown to become a dominant feature across many different areas of popular culture including film, television, and the internet.

These ideas establish the importance and centrality of music to many of the larger changes across popular culture in the twentieth century. In order to make sense of these complex and large-scale changes, everything in this book will relate back to the relationship between four seemingly simple things: Production—Distribution—Consumption—Mediation.

- Production: the circumstances in which sounds are produced, shaped, and fixed;
- Distribution: the ways in which sounds are moved from place to place.
- Consumption: particular ways in which people experienced and understood those sounds.
- Mediation: the material and experiential forms and actions that link musicians to audiences.

Throughout this book, we will look at each of these concepts in very particular ways. First, we will see how all four of these elements are always intimately tied together. In short, when the forms and practices of any one part of the music production, distribution, consumption, and mediation chain change, so will all of the others. Second, we will look at some of the practices people engage in when they produce, distribute, consume, and mediate music. For example, we will look at what exactly people had to do to make sound recordings at different points in history. These practices started with people singing into large horns sticking out of big wooden boxes covered in carpets or other sound-dampening devices. More recently studio recording has seen musicians using sophisticated directional microphones in multiroom recording studios capturing sound with nearly no extraneous noise. Similarly, we will look at how the early, heavy, fragile shellac discs were transported by hand and used in stores, concert halls, and radio stations. More recently, we will see how digital sound files coursed through global electronic networks of copper wires and fiber optic cables and changed the very act of music listening in dramatic ways. Finally, we will examine how people have used, shared, and experienced the sounds that were encoded on those discs and within those digital files. We will read about how the actual sensory experience of recorded music has changed and how these changes have affected the kinds of relationships musicians and audiences are able to forge with one another.

It is crucial to understand that it is mediation that is the glue that holds the production, distribution, and consumption of music together. It establishes the necessary practical links between these three elements that allow the music industry to exploit and capitalize on all kinds of music and musical experiences. Mediation also produces the socially, culturally, and personally meaningful connections between musicians and their audiences. Just as importantly, mediation is a task undertaken by people who occupy specific occupations in various industries related to the production and marketing of music through media. These people are often referred to as "cultural intermediaries" and include people such as radio DJs or the hosts of television programs or the curators of playlists on streaming media platforms.

The concept of mediation can often be quite abstract. So we need to clarify what we mean by it right from the start. Mediation is a way of making various forms of connection and understanding between audiences, the music, and the people who make and sell that music. Think of it as all that stands in between us and "The Music." It is in between the production and consumption of music that we can see the primary role of media to facilitate relationships between musician and audiences. Perhaps most important are the meanings produced and attributed to music through the processes of mediation. Given this, we will focus on how mediation shapes and produces musical meaning and what forms these musical meanings take. To do this we will analyze a wide range of media forms which will be our primary materials for analysis. We will also use a range of distinct methods to perform these analyses.

Central to these relationships is an important idea in the advertising, marketing, and public relations industries: the attention economy. Those who work in the entertainment industry know very well that their industry survives mostly on their ability to capture the attention, interests, and expectations of a large number of people over time to form them into lasting and profitable consumer relationships. But there are only so many things most of us can pay attention to. Further, our culture is far more crowded with more competing messages and forms of communications than it has ever been before. There are exponentially increasing demands made on people's time and attention produced by increasingly pervasive forms of media that have changed the dynamics of the economics of advertising. To put it bluntly, the more taxed public attention gets, the less it is available, and the more valuable it becomes. Therefore, as we progress through the twentieth century, we will see how media and mediation have become increasingly complex and important in our understanding of the value and meaning of music.

Materials and methods

In order to understand the range and character of the social relationships and meanings produced through music, we need to know what kinds of materials we will be studying. The range of such materials is very broad and diverse. These materials are not confined to musical sounds. They will include all aspects of a media production. For example, we will look at how the sounds we hear have been fixed into recordings or shaped into radio or television broadcasts.

But we will also examine how people were made aware of those recordings or broadcasts. Did they learn about them from newspapers or fan magazines? How did advertisements for sound recordings, radio broadcasts, or playback equipment explain or describe what was on offer? We need to answer these questions to see what ideas or values people may have associated with the many different forms of musical experience they sought and consumed.

To answer these questions we will need to look very closely at a variety of the elements associated with a mediated form of musical experience. This might include elements such as the imagery associated with musical experiences. This might include photographs from fan magazines, or an artist's clothing, posture, bearing, and physical gestures. It will include the means through which that media production was made. For example, when we examine the early history of short musical films we will note the camera angles and movements used to make these films. This is because these elements of a media production can tell us a good deal about how producers tried to engage the attention and senses of their audiences. What we will develop throughout this book is an integrated and coherent method for analyzing the social relationships produced through music when it is mediated in specific ways.

It is very important to understand that this book is not a comprehensive history of the social and economic relationships it examines. Instead, it presents sixteen interrelated case studies that offer a wide range of starting points for your own reading, writing, and research. As part of this, there is a constant motivation and encouragement for you to make use of the extraordinary amount of useful and relevant materials freely available online. Numerous references and suggestions for use have been made to such materials throughout this book.

Focus: Analytical example

It is worth presenting a brief example of the kind of analysis we will be engaging in throughout this book as a kind of model for the kinds of analysis you will be asked to complete. You can regard this example as a kind of sample or template for the kinds of materials and methods that will be used throughout this book to help us understand the many complex relationships between music and media.

First, we need to choose an object of analysis and the purpose for doing so. For this sample analysis we will examine an article from *The Guardian* from 2006 in which the journalist Simon Hattenstone interviews Paris Hilton on the occasion of the release of her first album. You can find it here:

https://www.theguardian.com/music/2006/jul/08/popandrock

or by simply entering the following into a search engine: "Guardian Paris Hilton Hattenstone."

This article is useful for analysis because of the mere fact that Paris Hilton had an album to release. It was something of a surprise at the time that this album was being taken so seriously by *The Guardian*, a publication respected by many for its long tradition of high-minded arts coverage. There are several reasons for this. They tasked one of their highest-profile writers on popular culture to produce what was, for this publication at this time, a fairly lengthy article about someone, Hilton, who was not considered a musician at all. Our purpose, then, is to see what this article could tell us about what the music industry was like in 2006.

In order to understand what this article can tell us about the music industry circa 2006 there are several things we need to do:

1 Understand the backgrounds of the subject of the article, the author of the article, and the publisher of the article. Think of this as a sort of factual inventory.

2 Understand the purpose of the article in terms of how the writer and publication addressed their audience and presented the subject. Think of this as establishing an interpretive framework.

3 Present a clear argument with argument to support it to achieve this purpose. In this case, I want to explain what this article can tell us about the music industry. The main point of this analysis is to explain the simple, perhaps confounding, fact that Paris Hilton released an album.

The subject

As you may or may not be aware, Paris Hilton is described as "an American businesswoman, socialite, television and media personality, model, actress, singer, and DJ," at least according to her Wikipedia page. Indeed, if you want a concise encapsulation of the conventional wisdom about a musician or celebrity, start by engaging in a critical and contextually aware reading of their Wikipedia page and a skeptical perusal of their social media accounts. In this case, if we read Wikipedia carefully we can learn that Hilton was born into a very wealthy family and has used her wealth and public profile to exploit a wide range of media forms to increase her wealth and fame. These forms included fashion and modeling, so-called lifestyle brands, reality television, perfumes, books, film appearances, and others.

We can also learn that the release of her album, entitled simply *Paris*, came at a particularly important moment in her trajectory as a celebrity. She revealed publicly that she was beginning work on an album in 2003, not long after a reality television show starring her and her friend Nicole Ritchie began airing on MTV. It was one piece of a multiyear roll-out of Paris Hilton-branded media products, including her own lifestyle brand and two books of photographs and aphorisms that acted as fashion templates and lifestyle advice, respectively. We can contextualize this album as one in a string of media events that accessorize Hilton's presence as an officially "Famous Person."

The author

Simon Hattenstone is a high-profile British journalist who has a long professional relationship with *The Guardian*, the publisher of this article. Importantly, his writing from the period circa 2006 was the writing of a celebrity journalist, not a music critic or music journalist. In this sense, this article is an accurate representation of his celebrity profiles from this period. He writes in a very direct and personal style. He often writes his profiles as if they are simple descriptions of his experiences of meeting famous people. This article reflects these stylistics priorities.

The publisher

The Guardian is a British publication founded in 1821 as the *Manchester Guardian*. It took on its shorter name in 1959. Of particular interest here is the fact that this publication's arts and music journalism has been widely regarded as high-quality, internationally influential writing that has some role in shaping the wider public perceptions of musicians and artists in the English-speaking world.

The address

Understanding the way in which content is shaped to appeal to a particular audience is largely an interpretive act, as opposed to a factual or empirical one. You need to ask: "Who are they addressing and how?" In this case, the publication and its author directed this article, not to Hilton's presumed fans which are largely assumed to be young women around her age (25 in 2006) or probably slightly younger. Instead, the article is clearly directed to an older audience. We can see this in the tone and writing style produced by Hattenstone. For example, Hattenstone's opening salvo describes "the posse of hairdressers, personal assistants, dressers, and publicists" standing between him and his interviewee. Upon meeting Hilton, he describes how he "can see reflections of myself" in her sunglasses. "For a moment I wonder," he continues, "if this is a postmodern joke. Is it Paris Hilton in front of me, or somebody masquerading as Paris Hilton?"

His description of Hilton continues in such a manner that it is a pretty short interpretive trip to discern who his audience is meant to be. He describes Hilton as if the reader has heard the name, but knows very little else about her. For example, he describes her career up to 2006 at some length:

> She is both chaste slut and voracious nun; the inaccessible heiress living the impossible dream and the self-made chav-next-door. She is best known as the girl who is famous for being famous. And yet she has done so much—there is Paris the television star (of The Simple Life, a reality show in which "the heiress to the $360 m Hilton fortune" tries to get down and dirty with normal people doing normal jobs); Paris the author (of Confessions Of An Heiress, an etiquette manual for the born-loaded); Paris the perfumer; Paris the model; Paris the socialite; Paris the property magnate (she is building hotels and casinos); Paris the nightclub owner; Paris the clothing and jewellery designer; Paris the movie star (National Lampoon's Pledge This! and House Of Wax). And now there is Paris the pop star.

Here, Hattenstone is clearly explaining Hilton to an audience that may not be very familiar with her and her career. That audience also can easily be assumed to want a concise, capsule presentation of her. Importantly, he appears to be both entirely credulous about the claims Hilton and her publicists and sponsors have made about her, but also supremely self-aware about his role in the publicity machine in which he is acting as a momentary, but crucial, cog.

But he takes his analysis much further. For example, he provides telling passages claiming Hilton's status as "the ultimate postfeminist" in which he uses well-known feminist writers such as Naomi Wolf to bolster his claims. He also provides confronting passages of conversation extracted from the sex tape a former boyfriend of Hilton's released around this time doing so to support his claims for Hilton as a feminist icon.

My conclusion from his opening paragraphs is that Hattenstone is trying to write an analytical "think piece" about Hilton, one that purports to explain her as a confusing and strange phenomenon to an audience that is expected to be interested in an explanation of the larger issues at stake here, such as "What kind of celebrity is Paris Hilton?" Or "What does Paris Hilton's fame mean for the wider culture?"

And for us, music is a central part of her celebrity as it is presented in this article.

The purpose

There are a great many topics of interest that appear in this article. We could analyze the assumptions about class and gender that shaped this representation of this one female celebrity. We could examine how celebrity journalists try to make distant and often ambiguous personalities feel more direct, real, and intimate. We could examine Hattenstone's writing style as part of a long tradition of first-person writing about music and musicians. However, we will work to figure out what we can learn about the music industry from this article.

First, we need to acknowledge perhaps the most basic fact of the article. In 2006, Paris Hilton was not a professional musician. Her musical background was only casually invoked when Hattenstone notes that "she used to sing on her own karaoke machine at home" and that she played the violin and piano as a child. Further, with the benefit of hindsight we can see quite easily she has not pursued a music career of any significance since 2006. Instead, we need to see her as a media personality who has occasionally added different types of music-related activity to her suite of media products and branding enterprises. This means that this album was not meant to explore Hilton's unique form of self-expression as an artist or some distinct aesthetic reflection of our world through music. It was, like everything else Hilton was producing in this part of her career, a device for harvesting the time, attention, and money of some part of the wider public. Interestingly, we can see this through the way music is discussed in this article. In a 3500-word article the entirety of the musical discussion lasts only a few short sentences:

> Her first album is an appealing confection of bubblegum pop, stomp-rock, disco and hip-hop-lite. She has surrounded herself with the best money can buy—top producer-writers (J. R. Rotem, Scott Storch, Dr. Luke, Greg Wells, Kara DioGuardi) to complement her light, breathy vocals. The album, *Paris*, is full of self-affirming anthems about gorgeousness, attitude, all things hot and boys left begging.

For our purposes, this is probably the most important and revealing passage in the article. What this tells us is that, in this case, the music industry values the profile of an artist at least as much as the music they produce. Even the shallowest of internet searches on a topic such as "celebrity novelty recordings" will tell us that this is nothing new. Albums have long been used as ancillary marketing devices for people with little or no musical background such as actors or athletes. Just as importantly, Hilton's links with MTV through her television show *The Simple Life*, gave her immediate access to a large and desirable audience that could be presumed to have some interest in musical celebrities. This audience was clearly presumed to at least have a passing interest in her album.

Second, the ways in which albums are often produced is of some relevance here. We can deduce from this passage that Hilton probably had very little to do with the writing or production of this album, having only been describing by this very, very compliant journalist as only "part-writing" a few of the lyrics. The fact that she has been supplied with the labor, reputations, and knowledge of a range of well-known and successful songwriters and producers suggests that the album was substantially complete by the time Hilton added her "breathy" vocals. This was in fact a very common way of making albums in the early 2000s. It was most common in music-based reality television shows such as *American Idol* where the winner of the competition would record the vocals of the debut single only hours after winning the competition. This tells us the song was ready and waiting for the lucky performer blessed with the greatest number of the television audience's votes. Albums and songs are often produced in their entirety and then simply "given" to a celebrity, whether they are a musician or not.

The purpose of this analysis is to try to understand how the broad term "the media" shapes our understanding and experience of music. In this case, there is one final point that is important to understand. When we are analyzing an article such as this, we are working backward, so to speak, by inferring and deducing conclusions from what is, by definition, a finished product. Importantly, the product is not simply the article, but the representation of the musician, artist, or celebrity that is its subject. Therefore, we have to recognize the enormous amount of work that has taken place to put this very carefully crafted image before us. In fact, Hattenstone tells us something about this labor in his very first paragraph when he describes the large number of assistants that he must pass by on his way to meet Hilton. But it goes much deeper than this. We read the words of the highly trained, very experienced journalist, words that were shaped and finished by the editors at *The Guardian* who would have approved this lengthy article in the first place. We also must include the publicists who work for Hilton and her record company. They have shaped this encounter as much as Hattenstone has by telling him what he can and can not ask and by shaping Hilton's answers by working with her to craft a media strategy to govern exactly these kinds of encounters. Beyond this, we can see the work of Hilton's stylists in her hair, make-up, clothes that greet us in the image at the top of the article, not to mention the photographer who made an image that was acceptable for publication. Finally, there is Hilton herself who, at the age of twenty-five was already an experienced and knowledgeable media performer who, with her substantial team, worked to produce this relatively small piece of her larger image. This tells us that in some cases, music can simply act as a "must-have" accessory to broaden and expand the already voluminous attention that is routinely paid to the media production that is "Paris Hilton."

Throughout this book, we will examine many similar kinds of examples. While our terms might vary from case to case, the underlying principles and concepts set out in this chapter will remain relevant and useful.

Key reading: Overview chapter

Garofalo, Reebee. (1999) "From Music Publishing to MP3: Music and Industry in the Twentieth Century." *American Music*, 17/3, 318–54.

The first key reading for this book is the only reading that relates broadly to all of the topics we will address. In it, the media scholar Reebee Garofalo examines the popular music industry in the twentieth century through a small collection of interconnected concepts. These concepts, together with Garofalo's pithy and concise argument, provide us with a very sturdy framework of ideas that should prove very useful for many parts of this book. We have reprinted this article in full so you can find it easier to make immediate and repeated use of it as a central resource of fact and argument as you work your way through the rest of this book.

However, the first thing we need to do is come to a clear understanding of this rather lengthy piece of writing in order to make effective use of it. Second, given its length and complexity, you will need to develop a strategy for managing all of the information Garofalo presents in order to make good sense of it and then make good use of it.

To do this, we have to understand Garofalo's argument and how he supports it. To do this read the first two pages of the article to find Garofalo's main argument and the ways in which he means to organize the evidence he offers to support his argument.

1 This sentence is Garofalo's main argument: "Like any culture industry in a market economy, the role of the music business is transform its cultural products into financial rewards" (p. 318).

This is the main argument primarily because it is the one claim that can act as an overarching idea for everything that follows. In short, every further claim, fact, and observation can be linked directly back to this idea.

Importantly, you need to critically engage with this argument by understanding that it is a very particular kind of claim. Can you give examples of other ways one might define the purpose of the music industry that might compete or contrast with Garofalo's claim?

2 What topic areas does Garofalo establish and prioritize in his introduction? How are these related to each other?

3 What relevance do Garofalo's "historical phases" have for understanding and using his five topic areas to make sense of the mass of information contained in this article?

Now, you will need to use these three things in order to take useful notes from the rest of the article. (It is almost always more effective to take notes by hand if possible.) To do this you will need to integrate Garofalo's argument, relationships, and historical phases. First, write each historical phase on a separate sheet of paper. Then, write each of the five topic areas underneath. Each time you feel you've identified a fact, event, or claim that fits most strongly in one topic area, make a note with the page number. Then, use your three lists to write a summary of each of the five topics areas while still recognizing the extent to which they are interconnected with each other.

Now, identify the ways in which Garofalo has organized his article based on the claims he makes. There are two main places where he gives us clues. Our first important clue comes when he describes that the most important thing we need to understand is how the music industry has changed from "a nation-based mass cultural phenomenon" to an industry that is part of a much larger "global system of interactive, transnational cultural flows" (p. 318). He argues that in order to understand this trajectory of change we need to "trace the uneven relationship between cultural development, technological advancement, professional organization, political struggle, and economic power" (p. 318). In this passage, Garofalo has given the reader a set of loose interconnected categories they can use to organize everything that appears in his article.

His second clue comes on the next page. Explain why Garofalo might think it important to identify three historical phases each "dominated by a different type of organization" (p. 319). These are music-publishing houses, recording companies, and transnational entertainment corporations. Garofalo uses these three phases to place his five topic areas in their specific set of historical circumstances and link his various examples back to his main argument. In each case, he argues that the dominant form of musical production, which includes both the central technologies used to distribute music and the economic forms that facilitated this, shaped both the cultural and economic priorities of the music industry.

Finally, write five short summaries of about 250–300 words each that capture how each topic area has evolved over the course of the twentieth century, according to Garofalo. This summary is a tool you can return to periodically throughout their reading of this book for help understanding events or media forms that stray outside the bounds of Garofalo's article. Given the interconnections between the topic areas, each of your summaries will be fairly different. Some will be much more obvious and straightforward than others. It is probably best to start with "technological advancement" and follow that with "cultural development." The goal of doing this is to help you understand the underlying forces shaping and connecting the events Garofalo describes in such historical detail. Importantly, you are not making an argument or assessing the material. You are simply trying to understand it by describing it concisely and clearly.

Here is an example

Cultural development: By the late nineteenth century, a long-term trajectory of change in the economic and cultural status of both Western popular music and European art music had begun to emerge. According to Garofalo, movable type helped secularize music and allow a much wider range of people to consume it through what he calls the "relative democracy of the marketplace" (p. 320). However, while sheet music was relatively more democratic, Garofalo argues that the era of the publishing houses tended to discriminate against forms of music not reliant on scores or sheet music for its production and distribution. This meant that sheet music sales favored music that is amenable to notation, a fact that often favored the centrality of melody over rhythm and notation over improvisation. Sound recording changed all of this, greatly enhancing precisely those musical traditions Garofalo says were excluded from the previous economic order, those based on rhythm and improvisation. From the 1920s to the 1960s, such forms of music grew to become culturally dominant in most places in the world. Further, as the many material forms in which this music could be experienced expanded and the quality of those musical experiences provided improved, popular music grew to achieve the status of "art." By the end of the twentieth century, Garofalo claims that popular music from English-speaking countries, especially the United States and the United Kingdom, were culturally dominant in most places in the world. They dominated in the form of a small number of global superstars whose music would come to experience unprecedented popularity.

KEY READING

From Music Publishing to MP3: Music and Industry in the Twentieth Century

Reebee Garofalo

Like any culture industry in a market economy, the role of the music business is fundamentally to transform its cultural products into financial rewards. This process, of course, has been significantly influenced by the technological advances that have determined the production, dissemination, and reception of music. To understand the trajectory of popular music in the twentieth century from its beginnings as a nation-based, mass cultural phenomenon to its current state as part of a global system of interactive, transnational cultural flows, one must trace the uneven relationship between cultural development, technological advancement, professional organization, political struggle, and economic power. Since technological advances and the economic power that drives them have been historically centered in industrialized nations (primarily Great Britain, Western Europe, and the United States), these countries have tended to provide the models for the relationship between popular music and the industry that produces it. Given that two world wars were fought on European soil, with devastating material consequences, at key points in the development of the mass media, the industrialization of popular music has been defined disproportionately by the dominant and often controversial practices of the United States. It is also the case that the pivotal musical moment of the twentieth century in terms of cultural redefinition and structural change in music industry—the eruption of rock and roll—was centered in the United States in the 1950s, and expanded to Great Britain in the 1960s. More recently, however, the relationship between corporate capital and musical culture has transcended national boundaries, as the music industry has become an increasingly global phenomenon.

"From Music Publishing to MP3: Music and Industry in the Twentieth Century" by Reebee Garofalo. From *American Music*, 17:3 (Fall 1999), pp. 318–53. Copyright 1999 by the Board of Trustees of the University of Illinois. Used with permission of the University of Illinois Press.

In broad strokes, the history of the music industry can be seen in three phases, each dominated by a different kind of organization:

1   Music-publishing houses, which occupied the power center of the industry when sheet music was the primary vehicle for disseminating popular music;

2   Record companies, which ascended to power as recorded music achieved dominance; and

3   Transnational entertainment corporations, which promote music as an ever-expanding series of "revenue streams"—record sales, advertising revenue, movie tie-ins, streaming audio on the Internet—no longer tied to a particular sound carrier.

Because the centrality of record companies has predominated in the second half of the twentieth century, this phase of development remains the popular conception of the music industry, even though its structure has shifted markedly in recent years. Consequently, the prevailing view of the popular music industry is that of record companies at the center, with radio, music videos, live concerts, booking agencies, management firms, indeed musicians themselves, playing various supporting roles. Because some of the major changes in popular music in the twentieth century can be traced to the technological developments that enabled record companies to displace publishing houses as the power center of the music business, the tendency is to use the terms "music industry" and "recording industry" synonymously. Initially, however, they were quite separate and there was little contact between the two.

Throughout the early development of sound recording, sheet music was the main vehicle for the mass dissemination of music and music publishers were at the center of the music business. At this time, the centerpiece of middle-class home entertainment was the piano. From the turn of the twentieth century until the end of World War I, the number of pianos and player pianos manufactured in the United States alone averaged about 300,000 annually.[1] Recording started as a sideline business, initially given to spoken-word comedy, instrumental brass-band releases, and other novelty selections. It is not surprising, then, that the publishers initially regarded the revolution in technology that would eventually transform the production and consumption of popular music as little more than a supplement to their earnings from sheet music. They were too busy enjoying the fruits of a very lucrative, centuries-old relationship with this earlier form of music software.

Music publishing: The origins of an industry

When Johann Gutenberg invented movable type around 1450, he laid the foundation for the modern music-publishing industry. After his hometown of Mainz was sacked by invading armies shortly after the introduction of his invention, the fledgling printing industry was dispersed, first to France and Italy, and then to England. This was a period of significant social upheaval, involving the establishment of merchant cities throughout Europe, the concomitant expansion of a new middle class, and a growing secularization of church-based cultures. In this process, according to Russell Sanjek, "control of the duplicating process had moved from the hands of the church into those of the entrepreneur. Literature was becoming secularized to meet the demands of its new audience, and music, too, would soon be laicized as its principal patron, the church, was replaced by the public consumer."[2] Operating under an exclusive contract with the city of Venice, Ottaviano dei Petrucci prepared his first publication, a collection of 96 popular songs (mostly French chansons), which qualified him for the title, the Father of Music Publishing.[3]

In the new mercantile economy, the dependency of feudal relations and the elitism of the patronage system were gradually replaced by the relative democracy of the marketplace. As sites of manufacturing and central distribution points for merchant ships and caravans from distant lands, medieval cities served as host for diverse cultures. Slowly a pan-European body of literary and musical works appeared. As the financial interests of merchant bookseller-publishers expanded, they began to join forces to lobby for legal protection.

The first copyright law was enacted in Britain in 1710, when Parliament passed the Statute of Anne, the basis for legal protection of intellectual property in the English-speaking world. While the law included an author's copyright and protections for consumers (by limiting the term of copyright and creating a "public domain"), it clearly favored the stationer's guild, which enjoyed royal sanctions granting an effective monopoly on publishing in return for cooperation in ferreting out and suppressing seditious literary or musical material. In this reciprocal arrangement, booksellers fared considerably better than authors or composers. It wasn't until the end of the eighteenth century, according to Finkelstein, "that composers were able to actually make an important part of their living from the printing and sale of their music."[4] This coincided with the growth of a domestic market for pianos and the establishment of the instrument as a cultural status symbol throughout Europe.

By the nineteenth century, music-publishing interests had begun to turn their attention toward international copyright systems because, as Dave Laing has pointed out, "music, more than other arts, easily crossed national linguistic and cultural boundaries."[5] Britain enacted its first International Copyright Act in 1838 and extended its provisions to include music in 1842. In the latter half of the nineteenth century there ensued a number of multilateral meetings across the continent among members of the music trade which culminated in the Berne Convention of 1886. Berne was essentially a treaty that provided for reciprocal recognition of copyright among sovereign nations. Seven of the initial nine signatories to the Berne Convention were European. Since 1886 the convention has been amended six times essentially to keep pace with the emergence of new technologies: Berlin (1908) incorporated photography, film, and sound recording; Rome (1928) added broadcasting; Brussels (1948), television. By 1993 there were almost 100 signatories to the Berne Convention.[6] Significantly, the United States did not sign on until 1988, more than 100 years after the founding convention.

At the time of Berne, U.S. popular music was only just beginning to come into its own, primarily through blackface minstrelsy and the works of Stephen Foster, which became popular throughout Europe. In the balance of trade, the United States would still have been showing a net loss on the import/export ratio of cultural products; it was not yet in the interest of the United States to embrace reciprocal arrangements with foreign publishers. Within a short time, however, U.S. music publishers would consolidate their operations into the most efficient music machine the world had yet seen—Tin Pan Alley.

At a time when European art music was considered to be superior to popular selections, U.S. music publishers derived their income from the manufacture and sale of classical scores, many of which were in the public domain, and, increasingly, through original popular compositions. In the United States, sheet music retailed for about thirty to forty cents a copy and, for the major publishers, sales in the hundreds of thousands of copies were not unheard of. Charles K. Harris's "After the Ball," written and published in 1892, "quickly reached sales of $25,000 a week," and, according to Charles Hamm, "sold more than 2,000,000 copies in only several years, eventually achieving a sale of some five million."[7] During this period, the previously scattered conglomeration of U.S. publishing houses, who would dominate mainstream popular music until the Second World War, were beginning to converge on the area of New York City that came to be known as Tin Pan Alley, after the tinny output of its upright pianos. Tin Pan Alley anticipated many of the practices of the music business in later years—and therefore provides the clearest model for how business would be conducted.

While it is noteworthy that in less than twenty years leading up to the turn of the century, Tin Pan Alley centralized control of an industry that had been spread throughout major cities across the United States, it is perhaps more important that Tin Pan Alley produced only popular songs. Unlike the older, more traditional music-publishing houses, which issued a broad range of material, the "song factories" of Tin Pan Alley promoted an overwhelmingly successful formulaic pop mentality that yielded "a much more homogeneous style than had ever before been the case in the history of song in America."[8] If the songwriting style of Tin Pan Alley was distinctive, its success was due in equal measure to its aggressive marketing tactics. Tin Pan Alley publishers routinely visited popular venues, offering star performers everything from personal favors to songwriting credits to include a particular song in their acts. Such an investment could be returned many-fold in sheet-music sales.

As was the case with publishing enterprises elsewhere, at this stage in its development Tin Pan Alley turned its attention toward legal protection. While these publishers clearly saw sheet music as their stock-in-trade—and, as a result, never fully embraced records—they saw no reason why their income shouldn't be supplemented with revenues from record sales. Thus, at the end of the first decade of the twentieth century—when it was clear that records were becoming a force to be reckoned with—there ensued a widespread revision of existing copyright laws to accommodate the new medium. In 1909, following the Berlin revision to the Berne Convention, Victor Herbert and John Philip Sousa led the charge for a revision to the U.S. copyright laws which mandated a royalty of two cents for each cylinder, record, or piano roll manufactured, in addition to revenues already derived from live performances. Because the U.S. Copyright Act of 1909 used the language of "mechanical reproduction," these new fees came to be known as a "mechanicals." Comparable laws were passed in Britain in 1911 and elsewhere on the continent at around the same time.

To recover their sources of revenue more efficiently, publishers in the industrialized world, in alliance with composers and songwriters, began to organize themselves into professional associations known in the trade as performing rights organizations. France had anticipated this development, forming the Société des Auteurs, Compositeurs et Editeirs de Musique (SACEM) in 1850. Italy and Austria followed suit before the turn of the century. Three other industrialized music-producing nations came on board before World War I. Publishers in Great Britain formed the Performing Rights Society (PRS), and in Germany, Geselleschaft für Musikalische Aufführungs (GEMA). The Tin Pan Alley publishers established the American Society of Composers, Authors, and Publishers (ASCAP) in 1914. In 1926 these various national societies formed an international confederation, Confédération Internationale des Sociétés Auteurs et Compositeurs (CISAC), headquartered in France.

In general, in their formative stages performing rights organizations were exclusive societies with national monopolies on copyrighted music. Membership in ASCAP, for example, was skewed toward the more "literate" writers of show tunes and semi-serious works such as Richard Rodgers and Lorenz Hart, Cole Porter, George Gershwin, and Irving Berlin. Writers of more vernacular forms, such as the blues and country music, were excluded from ASCAP. As proprietors of the compositions of their members, these organizations exercised considerable power in shaping public taste.

Just as technological advances such as movable type favored industrialized nations, copyright laws kept artistic expression firmly anchored to the European cultural tradition of notated music, in that the claim for royalties was based on the registration of melodies and lyrics, the aspects of music that most readily lend themselves to notation. Artists or countries with musical traditions based on rhythm rather than melody or those that valued improvisation over notation were excluded from the full benefit of copyright protection right from the start. Further, as an extension of literary copyright, musical copyright was based on a conception of authorship, which tended to penalize societies in which composition was conceived as a collective activity.

Recording companies:
The commodification of sound

Although it was clear before the dawn of the twentieth century that the future of the recording industry would be tied to music and entertainment, this was not obvious at first. When Thomas Edison unveiled his legendary "talking machine" in 1877, which is generally considered the birth of recording, the reproduction of music was fourth down his list of intended uses. Edison, as well as most of his competitors, initially saw the phonograph, as he called it, as an office machine, with practical applications in stenography, books for the blind, and teaching elocution. How the fledgling industry gravitated toward music and what they chose to record speaks volumes about the role of the music industry in the production of music.

Edison unwittingly provided a glimpse of the future when he chose to introduce the phonograph by highlighting its novelty value. In countless public demonstrations in Great Britain and the United States, vocalists, whistlers, and local instrumentalists from the audience were invited to make live recordings on the spot, anticipating what would become the dominant use of the invention. Other than the spoken word, it was found that brass reproduced best. Because of the poor sound quality of Edison's early tinfoil cylinders, however, Edison himself dismissed the phonograph as "a mere toy, which has no commercial value"[9] and put the project on the shelf, but only temporarily.

The next steps in the development of sound recording in the United States were taken in Bell Laboratories and eventually consolidated into the North American Phonograph Company, a national combine focused on office technology. It was Louis Glass, manager of North American's West Coast franchise, who pointed the way to the future. Beginning in 1889 Glass placed these "dictating" machines in the Palais Royal Saloon in San Francisco where patrons could listen to a prerecorded "entertainment" cylinder for a nickel. Within a year, these "nickel in the slot" machines were bringing in as much as $1,200 annually. The enterprise earned Glass a place in music history as the Father of the Jukebox.

The Columbia Phonograph Company, North American's District of Columbia franchise, quickly distinguished itself as the leading producer of quality entertainment cylinders. Among those that caught on with the mainstream listening audience were spoken-word comic Irish tales, "coon" songs, which exploited negative stereotypes of African Americans, and brass bands. By 1892 Columbia had issued about 100 recordings of the United States Marine Band, which included Sousa marches and Strauss waltzes, among other favorites.

It was German American immigrant Emile Berliner who first envisaged the contours of the modern music industry full-blown. Berliner had developed a recording process based on a flat disc for a machine he called the gramophone. At its very first demonstration in 1888, Berliner prophesied the ability to make an unlimited number of copies from a single master, the development of a mass-scale home-entertainment market for recorded music, and a system of royalty payments to artists derived from the sale of discs.[10]

During this same time frame, similar developments were being undertaken elsewhere in the industrialized world. The work of Charles and Emile Pathé in Paris paralleled the development of the Edison phonograph. Opening their first phonograph factory in the Paris suburb of Chatou in 1894, Pathé Frères became a full-fledged recording company in 1897. That same year William Barry Owen left his position as head of Berliner's National Gramophone Company in New York and established the Gramophone Company in London to exploit the Berliner European gramophone patents. Deutsche Grammophon, another related company, was set up by Joseph Berliner in Hanover, Germany. Then, in 1901, Emile Berliner founded the Victor Talking Machine Company in the United States.

Even though these companies knew that they were headed for entertainment—not dictation—the fledgling industry faced a number of serious roadblocks—technical, legal, and financial. Because of their limited sound quality, early recordings tended to favor spoken-word and instrumental selections; writers and publishers were not yet entitled to receive royalties from the sale or use of recorded music; and, because cylinders couldn't yet be mass-produced, manufacturing couldn't compete with the consumer demand that already existed for sheet music. In addition, a series of patent wars prevented the industry from progressing smoothly. After the turn of the century, however, the major recording companies determined that pooling their patents would advance the technology, as well as their economic self-interest, far more rapidly and, in the process, provide them with a form of oligopolistic control of the industry.

Emile Berliner delivered on his first prophecy when he made negative discs called "stampers," which evolved into the shellac-based, 78–rpm pressings that went on to become the industry standard until the late 1940s. He then contracted with an enterprising machinist named Eldridge R. Johnson, who developed a competitive twenty-five-dollar machine, creating the possibility of a home-entertainment market for records. To realize his second prophecy, Berliner judged correctly that he would need someone with more musical ability than himself to coordinate talent and recording. A single demonstration of the "beautiful round tones" of Berliner's disc was enough to lure Columbia's Fred Gaisberg—in effect, the first a&r (artist and repertoire) man/producer—to Victor.

If Berliner was the industrial visionary, Gaisberg provided the cultural input. Because recording artists weren't yet paid royalties and received no credit on records or in catalogues, Gaisberg had relatively little trouble persuading popular Columbia artists to record for Victor. Neither was he limited to performers in the United States. Gaisberg had already set up the first recording studio in London in 1898 before he moved from Columbia to Victor. Then in the early 1900s Victor acquired 50 percent ownership of the British Gramophone Company.[11] Through the efforts of William Barry Owen, Gaisberg was soon recording in every music capital in Europe and Russia.

Because of an elitist bias toward high culture, European classical music was considered to be the hallmark of good taste and opera singers occupied the highest rung on the entertainment ladder. Accordingly, the British Gramophone Company catalogue included songs and arias in every European language and many Asian languages as well. Gaisberg also made recordings at the Imperial Opera in Russia. In 1902 Italian tenor Enrico Caruso recorded ten arias in a hotel room in Milan for Gramophone, helping to establish the company as a serious outlet for classical as well as popular music. Eldridge Johnson imported these higher priced "Red Seal" recordings for sale in the United States and then began a domestic Red Label series of his own, which featured the stars of the Metropolitan Opera in New York.[12] Producer C. G. Childs placed a jewel in the crown of the new series when he signed Caruso to an exclusive Victor contract by offering him the unprecedented provision of a royalty on records sold, thereby fulfilling the last of Berliner's 1888 prophecies.

In the 1910s the recording industry extended its tentacles into the most lucrative markets of the world, through pressing plants in the most important areas and through a network of subsidiaries elsewhere. The two largest and most powerful companies, U.S. Victor and British Gramophone, furthered their mutual interests by dividing portions of the globe cooperatively. Victor had the Americas, North and South, and what they called the Far East; Gramophone operated factories in Europe, Russia, and India. After the outbreak of World War I the assets of Deutsche Grammophon were confiscated by the German government as enemy property, forcing a split between the British and German companies. By this time, however, Germany's Lindström company had become an international player and Pathé was not far behind.[13]

By this time, it was clear that records would become a powerful cultural force. In 1909, the United States alone manufactured more than 27 million discs and cylinders, with a wholesale value of nearly $12 million.[14] Comparable figures from around the world were equally impressive. One observer estimated German record production at 18 million copies (including exports) in 1907, Russian sales at 20 million copies in 1915, and the British and French markets at 10 million units each in the same time frame.[15] It was figures such as these which caused the publishers to stand up and take notice.

While the economic vision of the major record companies was nothing short of world domination, their cultural strategy at this time was seemingly more democratic. All of the major companies not only exported their own domestic products internationally, they also recorded and distributed local artists in the countries where they operated, "so that by the early 1910s, Icelandic, Estonian, Welsh and Breton record buyers, the ethnic minorities of the Russian Empire, the twenty largest immigrant groups in the United States, and the most important groups of the Indian subcontinent were all supplied by recordings of their own musical traditions."[16] Given the history of European colonialism and patterns of racism in the United States, however, it is likely that this broad range of cultural products resulted more from considerations of cost effectiveness than a commitment to cultural diversity.

It is also the case that there were (and are) pronounced biases in the way that the music industry conceived of itself and its world. Africa (with the occasional exception of South Africa) and certain other locales are conspicuously absent in much of the writing about the early internationalization of the music industry. Even within the industrialized world, there was internal class and race stratification. Record companies were slow to learn the cultural lesson that while the European classics brought prestige to their labels, the steady income—indeed, the future of the recording industry—was tied more to popular appetites. Victor's prestigious Red Seal series never accounted for more than 20 percent of the sales of the popular black-label recordings.[17] While the record companies grappled with the tension between an elite conception of culture and the financial realities of popular taste, many rich sources of musical culture went beneath their notice, particularly within regions that were insufficiently penetrated by capital and/or populations that were too poor to be thought of as consumers.

Significant cultural blind spots notwithstanding, by the 1910s the recording industry was clearly in an ascending phase, one which, with numerous fits and starts, would continue. The addition of a mechanical royalty to the copyright laws in the early twentieth century was timely in that it opened the door for collaborations between publishers and recording companies which had not existed previously. Companies in Great Britain and the United States were particularly well served, as a lucrative market for musical theater albums was discovered among American soldiers and native Britons during World War I when Gramophone issued a recording of the songs from *Business as Usual,* a popular musical revue. This was followed by recordings of two of Irving Berlin's shows, *Watch Your Step* and *Cheep,* with equal success. Victor emulated the success of its British partner by recording the best-known stage entertainers in the United States. Columbia and Edison soon followed suit.

It should be noted that there were distinctions between the new copyright laws which differentially affected the standing of record companies in different countries. While both the U.S. and British revisions added mechanical rights to already existing performing rights, enabling publishers to extend their reach to a new medium, the British law also included language that was later used to argue for an additional right, referred to somewhat confusingly as a "performance right," which enabled record companies to claim a copyright that inheres in the recording itself "as if such contrivances were musical works."[18] The performance right allows a record company to recover a royalty when a record is used for a public performance, as in a jukebox or on the radio. In Great Britain, Phonographic Performance Ltd. (PPL) was set up to administer these payments and the International Federation of the Phonographic Industry (IFPI) was established to lobby other governments for similar provisions in their domestic laws.

While a number of countries adopted copyright provisions similar to Great Britain's, others—such as France and the United States—did not acknowledge a copyright in records as such.[19] Performance rights were hotly debated in the 1976 revision to the U.S. Copyright Law, but even at that late date Congress decided that the issue required further study. Consequently, no provision was included in the final legislation; indeed, Section 114 (a) states explicitly that the owner's rights "do not include any right of performance," effectively killing the measure. The failure to adopt a performance right has serious consequences, particularly for recording artists with a signature sound, which were made clear in the report of the House Judiciary Committee on the 1976 legislation. "Mere imitation of a recorded performance would not constitute a copyright infringement," said the committee, "even where one performer deliberately sets out to simulate another's performance as exactly as possible."[20]

In addition to the complexity of performing rights, performance rights, and mechanicals, the 1928 Rome revision to the Berne Convention introduced the concept of "moral rights," which granted an author the right to be properly identified and guarded against any editing or other alteration of a work that would compromise its integrity. As with other provisions of Berne, however, the moral rights provision was optional. Again, the United States was significant among the countries that opted out of this provision, even after it signed on to Berne.

Amid the growing complexity of the music industry, it appeared as though the market for recorded music was virtually unlimited. Gross revenues in the

United States hit an all-time high of $106 million in 1921, with comparable growth being reported elsewhere in the industrialized world. The expiration of the original talking-machine patents in the mid-teens enabled a number of new companies to enter the record business. Unsated consumer demand in the areas of blues and country music—known at the time as race and hillbilly—even allowed for the formation of some Black-owned indies such as Black Swan, Sunshine, Merritt, and Black Patti. Pathé opened a branch in New York and Lindström started OKeh Records. At this point, however, the U.S. record market stalled—even as record sales were still climbing in other countries. Two years after the advent of commercial radio broadcasting in 1920, annual record revenues in the United States declined immediately and then plummeted to an all-time low of $6 million in 1933, at the height of the Great Depression. By this time the depression had adversely affected all record-producing nations. To avoid bankruptcy, British Gramophone merged with the Columbia Graphophone Company (the European arm of U.S.-based Columbia) to form Electric and Musical Industries (EMI). In the United States, the major radio networks acquired their first record divisions; RCA merged with Victor in 1929 and CBS bought Columbia Records in the mid-thirties. As is often the case in the music business, technological advances have a way of changing existing power relationships and influencing cultural choices. The introduction of radio—a new medium that not only delivered live music with better sound quality than records, but did so free of charge—initially lessened the appeal of records.

Radio broadcasting: Empires of the air

Radio was one of those developments that clearly resulted from an international process of shared knowledge, beginning with the discovery of electromagnetic waves by the German scientist Heinrich Hertz in the early 1890s. Italian inventor Guglielmo Marconi developed the first practical applications of "Hertzian waves" in the field of telegraphy and set up shop in Britain and the United States by the beginning of the twentieth century. Canadian Reginald Fessenden led the way from telegraphic to telephonic transmissions, but could not compete with the dramatic broadcasts of phonograph music from the Eiffel Tower (1908) or Caruso from the Metropolitan Opera in New York (1910), engineered by Lee de Forest, an American whose country was determined to dominate the new technology.

Owing to the ascending economic power and military might of the United States following World War I, it disproportionately reaped the benefits of commercial broadcasting (as well as the major technical advances of the next thirty years). During World War I the commercial development of radio was temporarily halted by the Allies in order to devote all further research and application to the war effort. Since this pooling of resources effectively meant a moratorium on patent suits, the war years encouraged technical advances at a crucial period in the development of radio which might not otherwise have been possible. Once the war was over, it was clear that there was a future for radio, and Marconi, headquartered in Britain, set his sights on nothing less than a worldwide monopoly on wireless communication. But the U.S. government felt otherwise.

Because President Woodrow Wilson saw mass communication as a key element in the balance of world power, he found the prospect of a British-dominated monopoly on radio unacceptable. Once the president of American Marconi understood his position, he dryly told his stockholders in 1919, "We have found that there exists on the part of the officials of the [U.S.] Government a very strong and irremovable objection to [American Marconi] because of the stock interest held therein by the British Company."[21] When all was said and done, the operations and assets of American Marconi had been transferred to a new entity—the Radio Corporation of America (RCA)—a holding company for American Telephone and Telegraph (AT&T), who manufactured transmitters, General Electric (GE) and Westinghouse, who made receivers, and the former stockholders of American Marconi.

With future developments in radio firmly in U.S. hands, the advent of broadcasting internationally proceeded according to a number of different models. In their pathbreaking study of the international music industry, Roger Wallis and Krister Malm identified three main types—public service, purely commercial, and government controlled—which are derived from archetypes of the historical development of radio.[22] In practice none of these ideal types exist in pure form, and many systems were hybrids from the start or changed over time. In France, for example, some early radio stations were operated by the government, while others were owned by schools or private companies. In Germany, a somewhat independent system of educational and entertainment programs was nationalized by the Nazis in 1933 so as to better exploit the value of radio as a unifying political force.

Britain's BBC is generally considered the archetypal public-service system. According to the BBC website, "John Reith, the BBC's founding father, looked westwards in the 1920s to America's unregulated, commercial radio, and then east to the fledgling Soviet Union's rigidly controlled state system. Reith's vision was of an independent British broadcaster able to 'educate, inform and entertain' the whole nation, free from political interference and commercial pressure."[23] By the time a schedule of daily broadcasts that included drama, news, and children's programs, as well as classical and popular music, went "on the air" over London's 2LO station, more than one million ten-shilling listening licenses had been issued to help insure the independence of the enterprise. Still, BBC radio has hardly been free from government intervention in the censorship of popular music.

Telephonic broadcasting began earlier in both the United States and the Soviet Union. During the Bolshevik Revolution of 1917, radio stations were considered important assets for the new society. Because of the sheer size of the new federation, the lack of infrastructure, high levels of illiteracy, and the diversity of nationalities, Lenin reasoned quite correctly that radio would provide the most effective means of communicating with the masses. "Every village should have radio," opined Lenin. "Every government office, as well as every club in our factories should be aware that at a certain hour they will hear political news and major events of the day. This way our country will lead a life of highest political awareness, constantly knowing actions of the government and views of the people."[24] Control of Soviet radio was placed in the hands of the People's Commissariat for Posts and Telegraphs and, in 1921, the agency began a series of daily broadcasts called the "Spoken Newspaper of the Russian Telegraph Agency." Because individual receivers were too expensive for private use, loudspeakers were installed in public areas for reception.

Although broadcasting in the United States was conceived as a commercial enterprise from the start, it began with the same lofty rhetoric as the BBC regarding education and raising the general level of culture. In the United States, the tension between such elite notions of culture and the dictates of popular taste played itself out in a pivotal debate between the more dignified old guard programmers and a new breed of unabashedly commercial advertisers.

A regular schedule of broadcasting began in the United States in November of 1920 when the Westinghouse station KDKA went live from the roof of their Pittsburgh factory, reporting the results of the Harding/Cox presidential election. Within two to three years, nearly 600 stations were licensed to operate, with few precedents to guide their development. The existing legislation, designed primarily to govern maritime telegraphy, did not anticipate the impact of commercialized telephonic broadcasting. Issues such as programming, financing, organization, ownership, networking, interference, and advertising were worked out in practice and over time as they arose.

Though U.S. legislation was premised on a system of independent stations, radio quickly became concentrated in the hands of two giant corporations, the Columbia Broadcasting System (CBS) and National Broadcasting Company (NBC), a subsidiary of RCA that operated the Red and Blue networks. By the 1930s coast-to-coast network broadcasting was a reality and NBC and CBS already owned 50 of the 52 clear channels—stations with large transmitters positioned to broadcast over great distances with minimal interference—as well as 75 percent of the most powerful regional stations. In terms of ownership patterns, U.S. radio developed as a very private enterprise. Programming, however, was a different matter.

Consistent with radio's educational mission, news and dramatic series had been staples of broadcasting from the beginning, but the bulk of radio programming consisted of music.[25] While the old-line programmers favored concerts of classical or semi-classical music to nourish the cultural sensibilities of the middle-class audience, the advertisers paid more attention to popular tastes. They tended more toward "dialect" comedy and popular song. In this, they were closer to the inclinations of Tin Pan Alley than those of the programmers, and the popular publishing houses, acting through ASCAP, were quick to reap the benefits.

The advent of commercial advertising placed musical broadcasts within the public-performance-for-profit provision of the 1909 Copyright Act. By the end of 1924 "ASCAP income from 199 radio licenses was $130,000, up from the previous year's $35,000 but far from the million predicted when the drive to collect from broadcasters began in the summer of 1922."[26] By 1937 ASCAP's take from radio had jumped to $5.9 million. Considering ASCAP's demands excessive, the broadcasters began an adversarial relationship with the publishers, which led to the formation of a rival performing rights organization in 1939—Broadcast Music Incorporated (BMI)—and which continued well into the 1960s.

No sooner had the broadcasters come to terms with ASCAP than they ran afoul of the American Federation of Musicians, who went to war over the use of "canned music" on radio. Training their sights on the record companies, the AFM struck the recording studios, a strategy intended to hurt record production and, at the same time, keep musicians working on radio. The AFM scored a short-term victory, as the demand for new releases outstripped the supply that the record companies had stockpiled. The strike ended when the record companies agreed to pay a royalty on record sales which was used to finance the Performance Trust Fund for out-of-work musicians. Still, it was inevitable that records would one day replace live musicians on radio.

If the political economy of radio seemed far removed from the average listener, its social functions often touched people deeply. During the Depression, wrote Erik Barnouw, radio won "a loyalty that seemed almost irrational. Destitute families that had to give up an icebox or furniture or bedding still clung to the radio as to a last link with humanity."[27] This reality was hardly wasted on President Franklin D. Roosevelt, the first "radio president," whose popular "Fireside Chats" provided him with a national following throughout his tenure in office.

Not unlike the Bolsheviks or the Nazis, Roosevelt immediately grasped the ideological potential of radio; in 1942 he authorized the Armed Forces Radio Service to keep U.S. troops stationed abroad informed and entertained, and to mount a direct challenge to the opposing ideology promoted by the likes of Axis Sally and Tokyo Rose. By 1945 the AFRS had expanded to a network of 150 outlets that crisscrossed the globe, with weekly shipments of news and music programming being distributed from its Los Angeles Broadcast Center. In this way a steady diet of U.S. military reportage as well as a sizable dose of U.S. popular culture were broadcast around the world.[28]

On the homefront, the tension between high and popular culture in music programming had taken a turn toward the popular in one of the most interesting national prime-time experiments of the period—*Your Hit Parade* on NBC. Tapping into audience responses for programming decisions, the sponsor directed B. A. Rolfe and his thirty-five-piece orchestra to play only popular dance music with "no extravagant, bizarre, involved arrangements," so as to insure the "foxtrotability" of every selection programmed.[29] In focusing solely on musical selections that were popular among the listening audience, *Your Hit Parade* was the first show to confer power in determining public taste on the consumer. Their "listener preference" letters foreshadowed the more "scientific" methods of rating that would eventually determine official popularity charts and format radio programming.

The tension between the "elevated" cultural tendencies of radio's old guard programmers and the straight commercial entertainment favored by the advertisers continued for years. Ultimately, the balance of power in programming favored the advertisers. As a result, radio has tended to follow the popular tastes of consumers, a tendency that had unanticipated consequences as rock and roll emerged in the early 1950s.

Technological advances and structural change

A number of advances in audio technology that came into widespread usage in the 1940s set the stage for the emergence of rock and roll and major structural changes in the music industry. Among these were the inventions of magnetic tape and the transistor, and the advent of microgroove recording.

The concept and equipment for magnetic recording were first patented by the Danish engineer Valdemar Poulsen in 1898, but it was the Germans who perfected it. The German magnetophone developed by Telefunken and BASF used plastic tape coated with iron oxide, which could be magnetized by amplified electrical impulses to encode a signal on the material. Playback simply reversed the process. Aside from the obvious technical advantages of editing, splicing, and better sound reproduction, magnetic tape recording was also more durable, more portable, and less expensive than the existing technologies. The Nazis used the new technology to increase propaganda broadcasts during World War II, but there was no immediate application to the music industry, as the studios and manufacturing plants of Deutsche Grammophon (now owned by Seimens) in Berlin and Hanover had been destroyed by saturation bombing. As Germany rebuilt after the war, Deutsche Grammophon became the first company to use magnetic tape exclusively.

Among the spoils of the war, magnetic tape was one of the items that was "liberated" from the Nazis. In the United States, the main beneficiary was the Minnesota Mining and Manufacturing Company (3M), who came up with a tape that surpassed the sound quality of the German product and marketed it under their Scotch Tape trademark. Simultaneously, tape-recorder manufacturers were able to reduce recording speeds from thirty inches per second (ips) to fifteen ips and then to seven-and-a-half ips, without seriously compromising sound quality. The amount of material that could be recorded on a standard tape thus quadrupled. The advantages of tape were immediately apparent to recording companies and radio stations, who invested in the technology as soon as it became available.

A welcome companion to the new recording technology was the transistor, introduced by U.S.-based Bell Telephone in 1948. Until the transistor, the amplification needed for radio broadcasting and electronic recording was tied to cumbersome and fragile vacuum tubes—a component based on Lee de Forest's audion, capable of generating, modulating, amplifying, and detecting radio energy. The transistor was capable of performing all the functions of the vacuum tube but in a solid environment. As such, it could be made smaller, required less power, and was more durable than the vacuum tube, which was soon replaced. This advance encouraged decentralization in broadcasting and recording, which aided independent production. On the consumption side, the transistor made possible truly portable radio receivers. Teenagers, who were soon to become an identifiable consumer group, could now explore their developing musical tastes in complete privacy.

The same year that the transistor was unveiled, a team of scientists working at CBS labs under the leadership of Dr. Peter Goldmark and William Bachman invented "high fidelity." Developed out of their interest in classical music, this breakthrough yielded the "microgroove" or "long-playing" 33–rpm record (the LP), which increased the number of grooves per inch on a standard record from eighty-five to three hundred. Not to be outdone, RCA responded with a similar product that played at 45 rpm. In what became known as the "battle of the speeds," the competition between the two giant firms produced vinylite discs of excellent sound quality and maximum durability. The 45, whose size caught the fancy of jukebox manufacturers, soon became the preferred configuration for singles. The LP became the industry standard for albums. Because these records were lighter and less breakable than shellac-based 78s, they could be shipped faster and more cheaply. Particularly because of these technological advances, records emerged as a relatively inexpensive medium, which held out the very real possibility of decentralization in the recording industry.

Two policy decisions in the United States also had implications for the further development of popular music and the music industry. Owing to a shellac shortage during the war, which caused a cutback on the number of records that could be produced, the major U.S. labels made a strategic decision to abandon the production of African American music. This decision, coupled with technological advances favoring decentralization, created the conditions in the 1940s under which literally hundreds of small independent labels—among them Atlantic, Chess, Sun, King, Modern, Specialty, and Imperial—came into existence in the United States.

Another important policy decision—leading to the development of television—enabled these fledgling labels to gain a permanent foothold in the industry. The concept of transmitting images over distances had been around since the nineteenth century. As early as 1926 John Logie Baird experimented with a mechanical television system that became the basis for the BBC's first televisual transmissions. The current system of electronic television was first proposed by Scottish inventor A. A. Campbell-Swinton in 1908. It was developed in earnest in the United States at Westinghouse by Vladimir K. Zworykin, a refugee from the Bolshevik Revolution, using a cathode-ray tube invented by Karl Ferdinand Braun in Germany in 1897. In 1935 RCA decided to sink $1 million into the development of the new medium. One year later the BBC began its first regular public television broadcasts.

Television became a viable consumer item in the United States in the late 1940s. By 1951 there were nearly 16 million television sets in operation and RCA had already recovered its initial investment. Television signaled the death knell for network radio, as the new visual medium quickly attracted most of the national advertising. Interestingly, this had the effect of strengthening local independent radio, which emerged as the most effective vehicle for local advertisers—at a time when the number of radio stations in the United States had doubled from about 1,000 in 1946 to about 2,000 in 1948.

Local radio in the late forties and early fifties was a very loosely structured scene. Independent deejays—or "personality jocks" as they were called—were in control. As they replaced the live-entertainment personalities who dominated radio in the thirties and early forties, they became, for a time, the pivotal figures in the music industry. Relying on their own inventiveness for popularity, independent deejays often experimented with alternatives to the standard pop fare of network radio. In most cases the key to their musical success turned out to be rhythm and blues—the direct precursor of rock and roll—produced by independent labels.

The relationship between local radio and record companies also contributed to a major structural change in the music business. In the era of network radio, music was performed live by studio orchestras. In its search for cheaper forms of programming, however, independent radio turned to recorded music. The dawn of a new age was apparent when WINS in New York announced in 1950, over the strong objection of the American Federation of Musicians (AFM), that it would be programming records exclusively from then on. Since recorded music was now the rule for radio, record companies routinely supplied free copies of new releases to deejays in the hope that they could turn them into hits. Eventually, this practice cemented the reciprocal arrangement between radio and record companies that has defined the music industry ever since: inexpensive programming in return for free promotion.

Records became not only the staple of all radio programming but also the dominant product of the music industry as a whole, eclipsing sheet music as the dominant medium for music. Record companies thus displaced publishing houses as the power center of the music industry. Further, with technological advances favoring decentralization in recording and a climate of experimentation in radio, it became possible for small independent labels to challenge the few giant corporations that had monopolized the music business until this time. The stage was set for the emergence of rock and roll.

Cultural transformation and structural change

The eruption of rock and roll in the 1950s changed the popular music landscape permanently and irrevocably, signaling the advent of broader social change to come. It was a pivotal moment for a number of reasons. Economically, the music enhanced the fortunes of "untutored" artists, upstart independent record companies, and wildly eccentric deejays, turning the structure of the music business on its head. The vintage rock-and-roll years coincided with a period when the fortunes of the U.S. music industry nearly tripled; revenues from record sales climbed from $213 million in 1954 to $603 million in 1959. In this expansion, rock and roll jumped from a 15.7 percent share of the pop market in 1955 to a 42.7 percent share in 1959. During the same time period, independent record companies went from a 21.6 percent share of the pop market in 1955 to a 66.3 percent share of a pop market that was roughly three times larger in 1959. Rock and roll was clearly a threat to established music business interests economically. But it was a threat to the whole society culturally and politically.

As a rhythm-dominant music that placed a high aesthetic value on repetition and improvisation, rock and roll represented a hybrid form that favored African ways of making music over European. As such, it created a space for African American artists in mainstream culture that had not previously existed. Further, as a music steeped in regional accents, slurred syllables, and urban slang, it foregrounded working-class sensibilities in opposition to elite notions of culture and Tin Pan Alley's white, middle-class orientation. Finally, it was the first music marketed directly to youth; its performers were roughly the same age as its audience. This, coupled with the rebellious tone of the music, created the first publicly identified generation gap in society at large.

Despite various efforts to tame the music in the late fifties, rock and roll became even more highly politicized in the 1960s, as baby boomers came of age and the music became identified with radical youth movements throughout the world. By this time the music associated with the "British Invasion," its name now shortened to "rock," had made a major contribution, elevating the music to the status of art, even as it became more closely linked with alternative and oppositional tendencies. A whole new broadcast medium— FM rock radio—and a burgeoning rock press opened up to accommodate these new sounds. But, just as the radical movements of the sixties depended in part on the affluence provided by imperialist practices, popular music was inextricably bound to the capitalist interests that produced it. "From the start," said Michael Lydon in 1970, "rock has been commercial in its very essence. . . . [I]t was never an art form that just happened to make money, nor a commercial undertaking that sometimes became art. Its art was synonymous with its business."[30]

The 1960s may have been experienced by artists and audiences as a period of political awakening and cultural development, but for the music industry it was a period of commercial expansion and corporate consolidation. Far from disappearing, as the activists of the 1960s would have had it, capitalism simply became hipper. There was a new wisdom among corporate executives in the music industry. As it became clear that the key to profitability lay in manufacturing and distribution, record companies began contracting out most of the creative functions of music-making. Far from resisting the creative impulses of offbeat artists or upstart independent labels, the major companies now signed acts directly, made label deals, entered into joint ventures, or contracted for distribution.

There ensued a period of unprecedented merger mania. Steve Chapple and I identified three types of mergers: horizontal, vertical, and conglomerate.[31] In reality, of course, such ideal types were often hybrids as in the amalgamation of Warner-Reprise, Elektra-Asylum, and Atlantic in the creation of the Warner Communications empire. By the early 1970s a couple of dozen associated labels—in addition to extensive holdings in film and television, *Mad* magazine, sixty-three comic books, and a piece of *Ms.* magazine—were operating under the new corporate umbrella. CBS integrated vertically to control production and marketing from recording to retail sales. In addition to its own labels, recording studios, pressing plants, national distribution, and a publishing division, CBS, Inc. owned the Columbia Record and Tape Club, Pacific Stereo and the Discount Records chain, Fender Guitars, Leslie Speakers, Rhodes Pianos, and Rogers Drums. In Britain EMI had acquired an analogous set of holdings.

RCA, CBS, and EMI, which had purchased Capitol in 1955, had long been divisions of multinational electronics conglomerates. In the early 1970s they were joined by another electronics-related multinational corporation. Seimens and the Dutch conglomerate Philips had begun to merge their recording interests in the early sixties. In 1971 they combined to form PolyGram, which included MGM and Mercury. In 1980 they added British Decca. The structure of this multinational "Big Five"—four electrics giants plus Warner Communications—formed the basis for the new international music industry in the 1980s, as the business of music became an increasingly global phenomenon.

Meanwhile, the predominance of electronics firms in the music field created an issue, which seemed particularly antithetical to the prevailing ideology of popular music—namely, the connection between music and the military. Advances in electronic communication had always developed according to their military applications. It was no different in the sixties and seventies. The connection became apparent to the Rolling Stones when they discovered that their label had channeled profits from their records into precisely this kind of research and development. Said Keith Richard: "We found out . . . that all the bread we made for Decca was going into making little black boxes that go into American Air Force bombers to bomb fucking North Vietnam. . . . That was it. Goddamn, you find you've helped to kill God knows how many thousands of people without even knowing it. I'd rather the Mafia than Decca."[32]

While popular music maintained a strong connection to the women's movement and the antinuclear movement throughout the 1970s, it was a time when the idealism of the sixties began to fade. Adding to the loss of innocence, it was here that the popular David and Goliath tale of small independent labels successfully challenging the majors for market share ended. While the indies may still have entered the business to fill a void in the market, their larger function became providing research and development for the majors. When Robert Stigwood's RSO label and Neil Bogart's Casablanca demonstrated from the bottom-up that a fortune could be made in disco, PolyGram simply stepped in and acquired a controlling interest in both labels. Warner engineered a similar acquisition when Seymour Stein's Sire demonstrated the commercial potential of new wave. Far from being in competition with the majors, the independents had now become part of the same corporate web.

Rock and its effects on national cultures

As early as 1969, with only eleven countries providing data, IFPI reported that the revenues from the international sale of recorded music had surpassed $2 billion. By 1978 the figure had jumped to more than $10 billion, with twenty-two countries reporting.[33] The fact that three of the five international firms that shared more than 70 percent of this windfall—through subsidiaries, licensing, and/or distribution—were U.S.-owned (and a fourth, British) was cause for concern among many smaller nations around the world, who feared that their national cultures might be overrun.

Earlier in the century, Great Britain itself had experienced the problem. In 1949 Tin Pan Alley had made such an impact on Britain that only 19 percent of the music on the BBC was British. By 1958, at the height of early rock and roll, that figure had declined to 14.8 percent.[34] In the rock explosion of the fifties and sixties, British and U.S. popular music were exported to every corner of the globe. As early as 1977 both CBS and RCA were reporting that more than 50 percent of their sales came from their international divisions.[35] Even in developing countries, the British and U.S. popularity charts provided guidance for local licensees and radio stations regarding which international selections were worth releasing locally.

In this connection, Wallis and Malm noted that the 1970s were characterized by "the almost simultaneous emergence of what could be termed 'national pop and rock music'" in countries throughout the world.[36] This included the adoption of electric instruments and related sound-amplification equipment. In this context, a general debate about culture dating from the sixties turned toward the question of cultural imperialism, particularly on the part of the United States, and to some extent Great Britain, as many nations became more involved in popular music. In Puerto Rico, for example, the rivalry between *salseros* and *rockeros* became so intense that it was often discussed as a referendum on national identity. Socialist countries, with a few notable exceptions such as the German Democratic Republic, tended toward the active suppression of Western popular music and rock-related styles in particular. In these instances rock was perceived as "the music of the enemy," consistent with the cultural imperialism thesis.

A closer look at the roots of rock, however, revealed a more complicated picture. Among its defining characteristics, European melodic and harmonic elements rested on a foundation of Africanisms—rhythm as an organizing principle, bent notes, syncopated phrasing, the call-and-response style—as well as a host of other influences as diverse as Latin American, French Creole, and Hawaiian.[37] "It is difficult to argue, therefore," as Andrew Goodwin and Joe Gore pointed out, "that rock music is 'Western' in quite the same way that Hollywood cinema or British television news are."[38] From this perspective, it would probably be more accurate to describe the emergence of popular West African genres such as Nigerian Afrobeat and Ghanaian Afro-rock as the culture of the African diaspora returning home, rather than a clear-cut instance of cultural imperialism.

Until this time, most governments and national elites tended to steer clear of the popular music sector, considering it to be a commercial product with little or no cultural value. If there were government policies at all, they were usually directed at preserving traditional musics or developing a national art music, which was usually a colonial vestige of European classical music. The developments of the 1970s caused many nations to reevaluate their policies toward popular music. Among the countries visited by Wallis and Malm, "Sweden and Denmark started to give grants to music groups playing national pop and rock. In Tunesia popular Arabic film music was introduced into government supported festivals as was calypso music in Trinidad, reggae music in Jamaica, Welsh-language rock music in Wales and, prior to 1973, *nueva cancion chilena* in Chile. . . . A national pop and rock group, the Afro 70 group, with new electric and electronic instruments, represented Tanzania at FESTAC 77."[39]

Unquestionably, the introduction of Western culture, technology, and organizational forms can exert a transformative influence on traditional cultures. The adoption of electric instruments and amplification can place financial strain on musicians. The establishment of a star system and the introduction of format radio can limit possibilities for exposure. Musics that have developed primarily in live performance and that serve ritual social functions can be packaged and sold to the world as entertainment.[40] The issue, however, is whether or not such changes negate the use value of music. Roots reggae—a product of U.S. rhythm and blues, commercialization, Western technology, and Jamaican mento rhythms— can hardly be described as a music that has been stripped of its cultural power and political edge.

Technology is invariably a double-edged sword. In addition to adding to the coffers of multinational record companies, recording technology also provides small countries with a means of reproducing their own music. Cassette tape is a case in point. It was introduced by Philips in 1963, and later improvements provided the transnational music industry with an efficient format for expansion into remote areas. Cassettes became the preferred configuration for music reception internationally in the mid-eighties. However, precisely because the technology is portable and recordable, it has also been used in the production, duplication, and dissemination of local musics and in the creation of new musical styles. In this way the technology has tended to decentralize control over the production and consumption of music. Decentralized control holds out the possibility that new voices and new musics will find new avenues for expression.

It is important in this regard to consider the social relations of popular music, as distinct from those of other mass media. Most mass cultural products, such as film or video, are generally produced and manufactured in one country and sold as finished products in another. Popular music, on the other hand, is most often exported as a master tape, which is then manufactured locally.[41] This encourages the development of a whole production and distribution infrastructure within the host country. In order to make their facilities cost-effective, multinational recording companies typically get involved in the production of local musics. The employees of the subsidiaries of multinational recording companies are most likely to be residents of the host country. The availability of production facilities, in turn, encourages the development of ancillary small businesses such as clubs and retail outlets, often owned and operated by local residents. With local mentors to turn to, indigenous artists become more aware of their rights and the value of their cultural products.

On a deeper, cultural level, and particularly in those countries with strong musical traditions of their own, there is an interaction between international pop and indigenous musics which simply doesn't exist with other mass cultural forms. "[T]he world had been flooded with Anglo-American music in the fifties and sixties," asserted Wallis and Malm. "This influenced but did not prevent local musicians from developing their own styles, adapted to their own cultures."[42] While the connection between these musics and various rock styles is often obvious, each is also linked—by some combination of language, concrete references, instrumentation, and performance styles—to an indigenous culture. The results, at least as regards music, usually approximate what Wallis and Malm call "transculturation"—a two-way process whereby elements of international pop, rock, and rhythm and blues are incorporated into local and national musical cultures, and indigenous influences contribute to the development of new transnational styles.[43]

In the early 1980s, the potential of this process might have been pushed to a new level, as advances in satellite transmission, which became apparent in the United States with the launching of MTV in 1981, created the possibility of instant national exposure for recording artists and the simultaneous broadcast of performances on a worldwide scale. On the international stage, the wonders of satellite transmission manifested themselves most dramatically in the phenomenon of mega-events—a series of socially conscious international concerts and all-star performances dubbed "charity rock"—that began in 1985 with Live Aid. Given its humanitarian impulse, charity rock provided a moment of opportunity, albeit a limited one, where internationalization itself was a two-way process. While British and American music was disproportionately broadcast to a worldwide audience, the international sounds of artists like Youssou N'Dour and Sly and Robbie also gained greater access to the world market.

The greater acceptance of artists from developing countries prompted the creation of new international marketing structures and promotional vehicles, as non-Western popular musics were incorporated into umbrella categories such as world music or world beat, for sale in industrialized nations. The transnational music industry could have taken this development as a glimpse into a more decentralized and culturally diverse future. But embracing such a vision would have required the industry to challenge some of its own restrictive patterns, such as privileging the English language as a precondition for success in the largest international markets. Instead, the major labels retreated into a formula mentality that pointed the way to a more limiting international culture.

Globalization: Blockbusters, superstars, and revenue streams

Like all capitalist enterprises, the transnational music industry tends toward expansion and concentration. But try as they might to manipulate the market, history has proven that it is seldom one they can predict or control. The triumph of rock and roll in the 1950s is a case in point. And while a handful of major corporations may rule financially, it is important to note that this is not synonymous with controlling the form, content, and style of popular music. The overwhelming success of hip-hop in the face of exclusion, suppression, and outright censorship is testament enough to that. If anything, record companies have relinquished control over form and content in their relentless pursuit of higher profits.

Beginning in the 1980s, the major companies embarked on a strategy that made production significantly more restrictive, making it harder for new artists to enter the business. The precipitating incident was a recession that hit the industry in the early 1980s. From an all-time high of $11.4 billion in 1980, the sales figures from IFPI's two dozen or so reporting countries declined some 18 percent to $9.4 billion in 1983. While recovery began in 1984, the industry as a whole did not fully return to its 1980 level until 1986.[44] In an industry thought to be recession-proof, this was a seismic event; labels responded by laying off personnel, trimming artist rosters, and limiting the number of new releases. Between 1980 and 1986 CBS alone eliminated over 7,000 positions worldwide.[45]

The runaway success of Michael Jackson's *Thriller* pointed the way to recovery. Released in 1983, *Thriller* went on to sell some 40 million units worldwide, generating an unprecedented seven Top Ten singles and a record twelve Grammy Awards in the process. For the major companies, this became the model for success. In the cost-cutting fever generated by the recession, major companies looked to reap greater rewards from fewer artists. If a single artist can move 40 million units, they reasoned, why shoulder the extra administrative, production, and marketing costs of 80 artists moving half a million units each? *Thriller* thus signaled an era of blockbuster LPs featuring a limited number of superstar artists as the solution to the industry's economic woes.

Over the next few years a significant proportion of music industry revenues were generated by a few dozen superstar artists; in addition to Michael Jackson, there were Lionel Richie, Madonna, Prince, Bruce Springsteen, Whitney Houston, Tina Turner, Wham!, Phil Collins, Steve Winwood, Huey Lewis and the News, the Pointer Sisters, Janet Jackson, Anita Baker, and a handful of others. A surprising number of the new superstars were black. This was perhaps the first hint that the greater cosmopolitanism of a world market might produce some changes in the complexion of popular music.

But if it looked like the industry had at least succeeded in becoming more inclusive of African Americans and women, one couldn't help but notice that the only artists outside the British-American axis of popular music who could rival these superstars in terms of sales and cultural impact—Bob Marley, U2, Abba—all sang in English. Even Julio Iglesias, at one point the best-selling artist in the world, had to sing in English to generate hits in the United States. This lesson was hardly wasted on Francophone artist Celine Dion, who made her bid for international stardom on the strength of her first all-English LP, *Unison,* and subsequently cemented her position with the cross-media blockbuster, *Titanic.*

It was at this point that the transnational music companies began to think of themselves more as exploiters of rights than producers of records. Their new mission was to develop as many "revenue streams" as possible. Music-television and cross-media marketing—particularly movie tie-ins— were crucial to this development. All of the above artists had music videos on MTV, many of which were also connected to first-run Hollywood films. The video promoted the movie. The movie sold the record. The label cashed in at every step. Advertising was also institutionalized as a source of revenue; the Beatles' "Revolution" sold sneakers just as Dylan's "The Times They Are A'Changin'" made an accounting firm that much hipper. The music industry had effectively harnessed all the technology and marketing tools at its disposal to create an international roster of superstars who were capable of generating unheard-of profits with less product.

As usual, technology—in this case the compact disc—played a key role in the industry's success story. The CD was introduced in the early 1980s simultaneously by Philips and Sony. In terms of sound quality, resistance to wear, and ease of use, the CD was far superior to the LP. While market penetration was slow at first, because of the added expenditure for new hardware, by 1988 worldwide unit sales of LPs and CDs were roughly on par. Because CDs were priced significantly higher than LPs (even though they cost no more to manufacture), purchases in the new configuration added millions to a label's bottom line. In 1986 "the sale of 53 million CDs generated almost as much income ($930 million) as the 125 million LPs sold ($983 million)."[46] By the end of the decade, the LP had begun its descent into virtual extinction.

The introduction of the CD opened up yet another revenue stream for the major labels—back catalogue. Back catalogue had always been a valuable commodity, as hit records have often boosted sales on previous recordings as well. With the advent of compact discs in the mid-eighties, back catalogue took on an even greater significance as consumers began buying recordings they already owned in the new configuration. The success of reissued artist retrospectives as boxed sets rendered back catalogue even more valuable. By the early nineties, catalogue sales were estimated as high as 40 percent of all album sales, making back catalogue, for many top-selling artists, their most valuable asset.

As always, however, the technology cut both ways. The CD may have captured the market in terms of quality, but cassette tape, because of its greater versatility as a recordable medium, remained the preferred configuration, still outselling CDs two to one until the end of the decade. Cassette technology may have enabled the transnational music industry to penetrate remote corners of the globe, but it was also responsible for the industry's two main financial headaches of the 1980s—piracy and home taping.

In 1982 IFPI estimated piracy at 11 percent of the total market in the United States and Canada, 21 percent in Latin America, 30 percent in Africa, and 66 percent in Asia.[47] The organization had begun to deal with the threat as early as 1971, when they convened the Phonograms Convention, which proposed a three-stage strategy to curb piracy. Stages I and II, which dealt with protecting the major and minor markets, respectively, had made significant progress by the early 1980s. For Stage III, aimed at pirates "mainly . . . situated in the developing world," the genteel system of international conventions was put aside in favor of a more bare-knuckles approach, tying piracy to trade sanctions against the offending nation. By treating music as an "export industry," the more powerful record-producing nations used their economic and political weight to reign in piratical practices elsewhere.[48] This strategy, it should be noted, presupposes an uneven flow of capital and cultural goods, in that developing countries would likely have neither a positive balance of trade in intellectual property nor the economic clout to resist the pressure of industrialized nations. As a result of this approach, musical copyright issues have increasingly been built into trade agreements such as the North American Free Trade Area (NAFTA), the EC's Single European Market program, and the international General Agreement on Tariffs and Trade (GATT).

As regards home taping, IFPI argued that the decline in industry revenues during the recession was directly related to the rising sales of cassette tape recorders and blank tape. There was little hard evidence to support the claim. Nevertheless, IFPI initiated an international campaign to levy a tax on blank tape and equipment that could be used to compensate copyright holders for their loss of income. The industry was not monolithic on this issue. The economic self-interest of hardware manufacturers like Philips, Sony, and Matsushita, who were in the process of bringing digital audio tape (DAT) recorders to market, was quite at odds with that of record companies, who saw blank tape levies as another potential revenue stream. This tension sometimes played itself out among different divisions of the same firm (e.g., Sony, which bought CBS Records in 1988). The hardware manufacturers and record companies finally came to terms in the IFPI-brokered Athens Agreement of 1989. The resulting "memorandum of understanding" provided a blueprint for legislation like the U.S. Audio Home Recording Act of 1992, which imposes levies on digital audio-recording devices and media. The legislation mandates that record companies get 38 percent of the royalty pool, performers 26 percent, and writers and publishers 17 percent each, with the remainder divided among unfeatured musicians and vocalists.[49]

While such legislation appears, at first glance, to confer some measure of recognition on performers (a first in the United States), it is limited in a number of respects. In the first place, only digital hardware and recordable media (i.e., DAT) were subject to the royalty initially. And since the Athens Agreement mandated that all digital recording devices would be equipped with Philips' digital Serial Copy Management System (SCMS), which permits only one digital copy of a digital recording, DAT never caught on as a consumer medium in Europe or the United States. Since the U.S. legislation also included provision for Congress to amend the law as needed to accommodate new technologies, however, it may yet become a significant source of industry revenue, as new configurations like recordable CDs (CD-R and CD-RW) take hold.

Although the rhetoric surrounding intellectual property and the logic of copyright often appears to support the struggling artist, in practice, the result is a very imprecise and uneven system. In the industrialized world, most copyright distribution formulas favor older, more established artists. In 1982, for example, a mere 12 percent of the PRS's 12,000 members shared 80 percent of the Society's earnings.[50] In developing countries, the question of collecting royalties across national boundaries at all presents major problems and internal distribution to artists and writers is even more haphazard.

For all its complaining about lost revenues, the major music corporations quickly resumed a pattern of steady growth following the recession of the early eighties. By 1993 the IFPI family of nations reported $30 billion in worldwide sales. Given the reconfigurations of the global economy, however, full recovery did not come about without some profound structural changes in the ownership patterns of the transnational music industry. Record companies were being bought and sold in a speculative atmosphere that made the merger mania of the late 1960s pale by comparison. In 1988 MCA bought Motown for $60 million. A couple of years later PolyGram purchased A&M and Island for upward of $300 million each. Then MCA shelled out $545 million for Geffen Records.

These huge recording combines were, in turn, bought out by larger multinational corporations. EMI Records remained a division of Thorn EMI (created in 1979), which also controlled Capitol, Virgin, Chrysalis, IRS, and Rhino, among others. The German publishing conglomerate Bertelsmann purchased RCA Records and its affiliated labels when the record division was dumped in the General Electric takeover of RCA. When Sony bought CBS Records (renamed Sony Music) in 1988 for $2 billion, it was the biggest record-company sale in the history of the industry. Those numbers were dwarfed in 1990 when Matsushita forked over $6.6 billion for MCA and its affiliated labels, only to resell the combined companies to Seagrams of Canada five years later. When all was said and done, only one of the Big Five transnational record companies—WEA (Warner/Elektra/Atlantic), a division of Time-Warner—remained in U.S. hands, and in 1991 Time-Warner entered a partnership agreement with Toshiba and C. Itoh to the tune of one billion U.S. dollars.

These new configurations clearly had implications for cultural representation. When Michael Jackson recorded *Thriller* in 1983, Epic Records was U.S.-owned. By the time *Dangerous* was released, the label had become a division of Japanese-owned Sony-CBS, which constructed not so much a supranational cultural identity as a global manufacturing and distribution network, ready to mass market anything that will sell internationally. Queried Simon Frith: "whose culture do Sony-CBS and BMG-RCA represent?"[51]

Even though the world may have been poised to accept a rather broad range of musics pointing toward a more decentralized plan for artist development, the music industry did not alter its marketing strategies in the least. "Instead of investing in and nurturing a wide range of new talents," observed Anthony DeCurtis in 1992, "record companies are betting wildly like drunks at the roulette table, hoping that one big score—whether by an old favorite or a new lucky number—will cover all past debts."[52] Ever since *Thriller,* the music industry has been stuck in a notion of artist development that demands superstardom. Consequently, record companies spent the early nineties ponying up millions for contracts that were as unprecedented as they were unrecoverable.

When Janet Jackson switched from A&M to Virgin in 1991, with only two albums (albeit both number 1) to her credit, she scored a reported $30–million deal. Virgin chairman Richard Branson compared the signing to buying a Rembrandt. Columbia's Don Ienner described Mariah Carey's platinum debut more crassly. "We don't look at Mariah Carey as a dance-pop artist," said Ienner. "We look at her as a franchise."[53] Aerosmith inked a new deal with Columbia in 1991 worth upward of $30 million. That same year, Mötley Crüe re-upped with Elektra for a $25–million guarantee. ZZ Top scored $30 million at RCA. The Rolling Stones topped them with a $40–million, three-album deal at Virgin. And even these contracts couldn't compete with the deals offered to Madonna, Michael Jackson, and Prince (by then known simply as The Artist), each of which were reportedly worth more than $60 million in guarantees.

Interestingly, the biggest superstars failed to sell like superstars. Pearl Jam outsold Michael Jackson. New releases by Madonna and The Artist rose and fell on the charts as never before. The Artist sustained himself with three greatest-hits packages; Madonna with a fifty-dollar "art" book of revealing photographs of herself called *Sex*. But instead of learning from these lessons, in 1996 Warner signed R.E.M. to a five-album, $80–million deal, the largest contract in record-company history.

Into the new millennium

On the eve of the new millennium, corporate shuffling continued unabated. The unexpected demerger of Thorn EMI set the music division afloat, creating a prime target for acquisition. In 1998 Seagrams combined the holdings of MCA (acquired from Matsushita in 1995) and PolyGram (purchased for $10.4 billion) into a single corporate entity called, modestly enough, the Universal Music Group. Among the labels that UMG controls are MCA, Universal (formerly Poly-Gram), Geffen, A&M, Motown, Island, Mercury, London, and Inter-scope. The new mega-firm operates in forty-eight countries and boasts a market share (extrapolating from combined 1997 figures of both corporations) of 23 percent. This kind of merger represents a significant level of concentration in the music industry. The downside, of course, is that as many as 20 percent of the company's 15,500 employees could be fired and literally hundreds of bands could be dropped from its artist roster.[54] No matter. While waiting for the next Michael Jackson to come along, the company will be able to sustain itself on the exploitation of catalogue from its more than forty wholly owned publishing offices.

In this regard, it is interesting to note that corporate capital has expanded its hold over intellectual property rights in at least three critical areas: extending the term of copyright, narrowing the arena for fair use, and creating brand-new intellectual property rights. In the 1990s both the European Community and the United States extended the term of copyright to a point that effectively eliminates the public domain for music written in the twentieth century. In a sweeping revision designed to bring the United States in line with changes in the European Community dating back to 1993, the Sonny Bono Copyright Term Extension Act of 1998 extended U.S. copyrights owned by corporations to ninety-five years and individually held copyrights to the life of the author plus seventy years. While the move was spearheaded by Disney because, under the existing law, Mickey Mouse was about to enter the public domain, such legislation obviously serves the interests of transnational capital, which is becoming better organized on an administrative level.

One of the main avenues through which the international music industry currently seeks to protect its interests is the World Intellectual Property Organization (WIPO), established in 1970 and currently representing 171 member nations. WIPO is charged with developing treaties for protecting the rights of intellectual property owners. These agreements are, in turn, codified in national legislation such as the Digital Millennium Copyright Act of 1998 in the United States, which makes it illegal to circumvent technological measures for protecting sound recordings and other copyrighted material. Seemingly in the interest of creative artists, such measures compel us to revisit the diminishing terrain of fair use. "If data can be protected by code—and it's illegal to break the code," argues Robert J. Samuelson, "then 'fair use' for anything that arrives digitally may vanish."[55]

Extending the reach of corporations even further, the most recent WIPO treaty calls for the creation of a completely new intellectual property right to protect the owners of electronic databases. "The general objective of this right," according to the treaty, "is to protect the investment of time, money, and effort by the maker of a database, irrespective of whether the database is in itself innovative."[56] Depending on how narrowly the treaty is implemented, it may not only be illegal to duplicate a record, it may also be illegal to quote its chart position without permission.

Ironically, it may be the double blade of the technology that makes all of this possible which cuts into corporate control once again. Just as cassettes issued a challenge to centralized control in the seventies and eighties, newer technologies such as the MPEG 1—Audio Layer 3 (MP3) software compression format provides near-CD-quality, downloadable audio over the Internet. MP3 dates back to a 1987 collaboration between Germany's Fraunhofer Institut Integrierte Schaltungen and Dieter Seitzer from the University of Erlangen, whose work yielded a compression/decompression algorithm, or codec, that could shrink sound files to about one-tenth their normal size without sacrificing quality. In 1992 MP3 was approved as a standard by the Moving Picture Experts Group (MPEG), founded by Leonardo Chariglioni in Italy. But it wasn't until modem and computer clock speeds permitted efficient downloads of MP3 files that the technology threatened to turn the music industry on its head. By the late nineties music enthusiasts—indeed, artists themselves—were converting audio CD files to MP3 and posting them on websites for easy, and most often unauthorized, download. Since that time the term "MP3" has become second only to the word "sex" as the most requested item on Internet search engines.

Technologies like MP3 are threatening to the music industry for a number of reasons. In the first place, MP3 holds out the possibility of a business model that links artists directly with consumers, bypassing the record companies completely. And with articulate industry critics like Chuck D and forward-looking artists like Sheryl Crow already on board, MP3 is generating a momentum that the industry can ill afford to ignore. According to *Wired* magazine: "About 846 million new CDs were sold last year. But at least 17 million MP3 files are downloaded from the Net *each day*. That adds up to almost 3 billion in the first six months of 1999."[57] As a result electronic distribution sites like MP3.com and online record labels like Atomic Pop, new home to such artists as Public Enemy and Ice-T, are challenging the status quo.

More upsetting from the industry point of view is the fact that MP3 is an unprotected format, which leaves the industry with no way to regulate its use. Desktop MP3 players such as MacAMP and Winamp (since purchased by America OnLine) have proliferated, enabling users to download and listen to MP3 files on their computers. They have become so successful that MP3 has attracted mainstream computer-industry giants like Microsoft and RealNetworks, who introduced the Windows Media Player and the RealJukebox, respectively, the latter of which was downloaded one million times within ten days of its launch.

It was the introduction of Diamond Multimedia's Rio, a portable MP3 player that moved MP3 beyond the computer desktop, which really caused the industry to stand up and take notice. The Rio is a walkman-like digital player, with no SCMS copy-protection chip, capable of downloading, storing, and playing back 60 minutes of MP3 music. Fearing piracy on a grand scale, the Recording Industry Association of America (RIAA) was quick to bring suit, claiming a violation of the Audio Home Recording Act. Diamond, however, squeezed through a loophole by successfully arguing that the legislation targeted only recording devices and the Rio was a storage device. With the injunction quashed, other portable MP3 players were rushed to market, including Creative Labs' Nomad, Pontis' MPlayer3, and Empeg's Empeg Car, which can hold up to 5,000 songs.

Taking a more proactive stance, the international music industry, as represented by the RIAA, the Recording Industry Association of Japan, IFPI, and the Big Five recording companies, proposed the Secure Digital Music Initiative (SDMI), an open standard that would encode a sound file with a digital "watermark" identifying its owner and origin, as a way of discouraging piracy on the Internet. Interestingly, the person the industry tapped to head up the SDMI project was none other than Leonardo Chariglioni, the founder of MPEG, who certified MP3 in the first place.

With well over 100 organizations participating, SDMI required an enormous amount of collaboration. At the same time, record companies were feeling the pressure to have a commercially viable online presence by the 1999 holiday season, whether it was standardized or not. As a result, individual record companies began making independent deals to advance their own online interests. Universal Music Group and Bertelsman launched GetMusic.com using the Liquid Audio Player for downloading. Free-floating EMI also chose to work with Liquid Audio for secure downloads. Sony formed an alliance with Microsoft using their Media Player software and, together with Warner, merged their jointly owned Columbia House Record Club with the online retail outlet CD Now.

As of this writing, the industry is far from implementing standardized security protocols that work, and new technologies like MP3 show no signs of abatement. While transnational music corporations scramble to protect their bottom lines on new fronts, artists and fans may, at least momentarily, gain some measure of direct access to each other and to sound reproduction possibilities that are becoming increasingly harder to control.

Notes

1 Russell Sanjek, *American Popular Music and Its Business: The First Four Hundred Years,* 3 vols. (New York: Oxford University Press, 1988), 2:296.

2 Ibid., 1:37.

3 Ibid., 1:38.

4 Sidney Finkelstein, *How Music Expresses Ideas* (New York: International Publishers, 1952, 1976), 26.

5 Dave Laing, "Copyright and the International Music Industry," in *Music and Copyright,* ed. Simon Frith (Edinburgh: University Press, 1993), 22.

6 Ibid., 24–5.

7 Charles Hamm, *Yesterdays: Popular Song in America* (New York: W. W. Norton, 1983), 285. In *After the Ball: Popular Music from Rag to Rock* (Baltimore: Penguin Books, 1974), Ian Whitcomb put the figure at 10 million copies over a twenty-year period (4).

8 Hamm, *Yesterdays,* 290.

9 Sanjek, *American Popular Music and Its Business,* 2:365.

10 C. A. Schicke, *Revolution in Sound: A Biography of the Recording Industry* (Boston: Little, Brown, 1974), 41.

11 Interestingly, at this point, the term *gramophone* was dropped from the language in the United States, where *phonograph* became the generic term for all record players. *Gramophone* remained the preferred term in Britain and Germany.

12 As if to compliment the gentility of the series, Johnson then introduced the Victrola, the first "console" record player, which featured an enclosed turntable, tone arm, and playback horn, and a price tag of two hundred dollars.

13 For a more developed discussion of this international structure, see Pekka Gronow, "The Record Industry: The Growth of a Mass Medium," in *Popular Music* 3, ed. Richard Middleton and David Horn (Cambridge: Cambridge University Press, 1983), 55–62.

14 Sanjek, *American Popular Music and Its Business,* 3:23.

15 Gronow, "The Record Industry," 59.

16 Ibid., 60.

17 Sanjek, *American Popular Music and Its Business,* 3:28.

18 See Simon Frith, "Copyright and the Music Business." *Popular Music* 7, no. 1 (1987): 58.

19 In 1971, the United States passed a law that allowed a "limited copyright in sound recordings," but its purpose was to protect record companies against piracy.

20 House Report (Judiciary Committee) No. 94–1476, September 3, 1976, p. 106.

21 Gleason L. Archer, *History of Radio to 1926* (New York: American Historical Society, 1938), 178.

22 Roger Wallis and Krister Malm, *Big Sounds from Small Peoples: The Music Industry in Small Countries* (London: Constable, 1984), 233.

23 "This is London Calling, 2LO calling . . ." BBC website, Dec. 15, 1998.

24 B. H. Rujnnikov, *Tak nachinalos* (Moscow: Iskusstvo, 1987), 169 (trans. Lenny Zeltser).

25 It should be noted that due to a limitation of the 1909 Copyright Act novels and plays could be read on the air without infringing copyright, a loophole that wasn't plugged until 1952; much of the classical music that was performed was already in the public domain, which again required no royalty payments.

26 Sanjek, *American Popular Music and Its Business,* 3:81.

27 Erik Barnouw, *The Golden Web: A History of Broadcasting in the United States, 1933–1953* (New York: Oxford University Press, 1968), 6.

28 Complementing the efforts of the AFRS, it was during this period that the U.S. military and the entertainment industry joined forces in the production of V-discs (Victory discs)—special monthly releases featuring popular recording artists, from Frank Sinatra to Louis Jordan, that were distributed to U.S. soldiers in the field. From 1942 to 1944, eight million V-discs, representing some 400 recordings of more than 640 artists, were distributed. Donating their time and music for free, artists from rival record labels, who might otherwise have been prohibited from recording together for contractual reasons, created a number of "once-in-a-lifetime" sessions for the V-disc program. V-discs were particularly valuable in that they were the only recordings that were permitted during the AFM strike of 1942. To discourage personal gain from this enterprise, most of the V-discs were recalled and destroyed after the war.

29 Sanjek, *American Popular Music and Its Business,* 3:166.

30 Michael Lydon, "Rock for Sale," in *The Age of Rock 2: Sights and Sounds of the American Cultural Revolution,* ed. Lydon (New York: Vintage Books, 1970), 53.

31 For a detailed discussion of the merger movement see Steve Chapple and Reebee Garofalo, *Rock 'n' Roll Is Here to Pay: The History and Politics of the Music Industry* (Chicago: Nelson-Hall, 1977), 82–7.

32 Ben Fong-Torres, ed., *The Rolling Stone Interviews,* vol. 2 (New York: Warner Books, 1973), 292.

33 Michèle Hung and Esteban Garcia Morencos, *World Record Sales, 1969–1990: A Statistical History of the World Recording Industry* (London: International Federation of the Phonogram Industry, 1990), 85.

34 Wallis and Malm, *Big Sounds from Small Peoples,* 261.

35 Part of the surprisingly high international sales figures resulted from international artists like Julio Iglesias, who barely made a dent in the U.S. market, even though he lived in the United States and was the best-selling artist in the world at the time. Disco also tended to transcend national boundaries, but disco was a transnational music right from the beginning. Its global success was based more on the ubiquity of its international connections than a marketing triumph of U.S.-based record companies.

36 Wallis and Malm, *Big Sounds from Small Peoples,* 302.

37 See, for example, Reebee Garofalo, "Crossing Over, 1939–1989," in *Split Image: African-Americans in the Mass Media,* ed. Jannette L. Dates and William Barlow (Washington, D.C.: Howard University Press, 1990); George Lipsitz, "'Ain't Nobody Here but Us Chickens': The Class Origins of Rock and Roll," in his *Class and Culture in Cold War America* (South Hadley, Mass.: J. F. Bergin, 1982); and Portia K. Maultsby, "Africanisms in African-American Popular Music," in *Africanisms in American Culture,* ed. Joseph E. Holloway (Bloomington: Indiana University Press, 1990).

38 Andrew Goodwin and Joe Gore, "World Beat and the Cultural Imperialism Debate," *Socialist Review* 20, no. 3 (July–Sept. 1990): 71.

39 Wallis and Malm, *Big Sounds from Small Peoples,* 219.

40 See Reebee Garofalo, "Whose World, What Beat: The Transnational Music Industry, Identity, and Cultural Imperialism," *The World of Music* 35, no. 2 (1993): 21.

41 Laurence Kenneth Shore, "The Crossroads of Business and Music: A Study of the Music Industry in the United States and Internationally," Ph.D. diss., Stanford University, 1983, 283–84.

42 Wallis and Malm, *Big Sounds from Small Peoples,* 302.

43 Ibid., 300–301.

44 Hung and Morencos, *World Record Sales, 1969–1990,* 85.

45 Simon Frith, "Picking Up the Pieces: Video Pop," in *Facing the Music,* ed. Frith (New York: Pantheon Books, 1988), 93.

46 Ibid., 102–3.

47 Ibid., 117.

48 For a more detailed discussion of this strategy and its implications, see Laing, "Copyright and the International Music Industry," 31–33.

49 Cited in Steve Jones, "Music and Copyright in the USA," in *Music and Copyright,* ed. Frith, 70.

50 *PRS Yearbook,* 1982, reported in Wallis and Malm, *Big Sounds from Small Peoples,* 172.

51 Simon Frith, "Anglo-America and Its Discontents," *Cultural Studies* 5, no. 3 (Oct. 1991): 267.

52 Anthony DeCurtis, "The Year in Music," *Rolling Stone,* Dec. 10–24, 1992, p. 26.

53 "1990 Yearbook," *Rolling Stone,* Dec. 13–27, 1990, 72.

54 Dave Ferman and Malcolm Mayhew, "Merger Could Lead to Band Layoffs," *Boston Globe,* Jan. 2, 1999, D9.

55 Robert J. Samuelson, "Meanwhile Back on the Hill . . ." *Washington Post,* Sept. 17, 1998, A21.

56 WIPO, "Basic Proposal for the Substantive Provisions of the Treaty on Intellectual Property in Respect of Databases to be Considered by the Diplomatic Conference," Geneva, Aug. 30, 1996, notes on Article 1.07.

57 Vito Peraino, "The Law of Increasing Returns," *Wired,* Aug. 1999, 144.

PART ONE

The early recording industry, 1875 to 1940

1

Mediated music, fidelity, and social anxiety

Background and topics

Picture yourself standing next to a piano surrounded by several of your friends. One is playing from a collection of songs she has collected and bound herself. The binding looks expensive. Each song looks like it has been annotated with new markings for dynamics and even a few extra notes here and there (see Figures 1.1 and 1.2; parlor scenes). The choice of songs as well as the ways in which they were performed would have said a lot about your friend. Many would have believed that her true character and qualities as a human being would have been, at least in part, revealed through this pleasurable ritual.

Now imagine a similar scene, only a few years later. The piano is still there, but it is not played nearly as often. Instead, a large rectangular wooden box stands in a prominent place in the same room. Within it is a round platter with a retractable arm with a small needle at the tip. There is a library of heavy, shellac discs sitting on a shelf inside the cabinet (Figure 1.3). Instead of the rich, full sound of the piano, a trebly, tinny, decidedly small sound emerges from this box. But those small sounds call up other worlds entirely. There are pianos, horns, strings, and often marimbas. Occasionally, there is a world-famous opera singer. The music is sometimes surprising, sometimes strange, but always engaging. "Making music" at home is a very different act now. It is almost as if the two social rituals are somehow disconnected.

Of course, they are very much connected. In fact, it is hard to understand what the introduction of sound recording meant to many people without understanding something of the cultures of music-making and listening in the home that preceded the gramophone in the form of sheet music. It is in

FIGURE 1.1 *A typical middle-class parlor piano (ca. 1910s).*

FIGURE 1.2 *A typical parlor scene (ca. 1910s).*

doing so that we can see how, when one part of the chain of music production, distribution, and consumption changes, all of the others follow suit.

Over the next four chapters, we will see how the advent of new audio and visual technologies, such as sound recordings, gramophones, radio, and film, inspired a good deal of excitement and pleasure, but also evoked a good

FIGURE 1.3 *Opera singer Enrico Caruso displays his Victrola phonograph (ca. 1910s).*

deal of social anxiety. While the pleasure people experienced from these technologies is commonly acknowledged and broadly understood by itself, when we try to understand it in relation to the kinds of social anxieties they evoked, we can come to a much better understanding of the kinds of social relationships these technologies created through music.

We will look at three interrelated issues that can help us understand this:

- the massive cultural changes going "in the background" in this time period;
- the new experience of music through sound recording; and
- prevalent conceptions of music in the past that are different than those we hold today.

The key readings for Part One are the collection of gramophone and phonograph advertisements found on pages 64–75 of this chapter. These will help you focus on the idea of "fidelity" which will be a main idea for this chapter especially. The concept of fidelity shaped the arrival of sound recording as a commercial technology primarily used for listening to music. We will address this idea through by examining these advertisements and working through a series of questions and writing activities. The goal of these activities as well as this chapter as a whole will be to understand the links between the new technology, sound recording, with the most widespread technology that immediately preceded it, sheet music. These will be instructive and important to understand. First, we will need to understand how much more significant and larger changes shaped how sound recording was understood and adopted.

Cultural change in the late nineteenth and early twentieth century

In the time period set out for Part One of this book, 1875 to 1940, massive cultural changes happened in the United States and many similar countries around the world. Of particular relevance to our understanding of the music industry will be the changes that enabled modern consumer culture to develop. Consider this list of the new communication technologies that were developed or "perfected" between the 1890s and the 1930s:

- "Advanced" printing techniques: (1850s to 1870s) mass production and distribution of newspapers and magazines creating a pervasive print culture comprised of information from around the world.

- Newspaper photography: (1880s to 1890s) artists' drawings or etchings of events were gradually replaced by photo-engravings, then by "the real thing," a process roughly analogous to sound recording.

- Telegraphy: (invented 1844; widespread use by 1855) the transportation of information across vast distances very quickly using wires.

- Telephony: (1870s) the transportation of actual sounds across vast distances very quickly using wires.

- Sound recording: (invented 1877; widespread use by 1905) the encoding of sound in physical, mostly reproducible forms.

- Sound reproduction: (invented 1887; widespread use by 1905) the mass production of physical carriers of sound.

- Wireless transmission of information: (1900s to 1910s) an extension of telephonic technology, but this time without wires.

- Radio broadcasting: (invented 1906; widespread use by 1920) the use of wireless transmission of sound to present music, talks, and entertainment, was most often live in the first decades of its existence.

- Microphones and amplifiers: (1920s) the electric encoding of sound for recording or transmission and eventual reproduction as live or recorded sounds.

- Moving pictures: (invented 1896; widespread use by 1910; with sound "talkies," ca. 1928) the creation of strips of photographic images which mimicked movement, eventually synched up with sound.

- Television: (1940s) the wireless transmission of sounds and images across vast distances, live by necessity for the first several decades of its existence.

When taken as a whole, these new tools outline a wholesale reordering of the sensory experience of many aspects of culture in a relatively short period of time. It should not be surprising then, that this was accompanied by a good deal of both excitement and dread, both joy and fear. However, it is not simply the emergence of these tools and technologies that affected people so significantly. There were a great many other changes going on that shaped how all these new "cultural technologies" were experienced. In addition to the tangible sorts of change I've just listed, there were also a great many less tangible ones. Across most of the industrialized world, the kinds of social and economic connections that knitted various communities together were becoming unstuck and reformed. The reasons why this was happening were many and extremely complex. However, we can sum them up in a useful way here.

It is important to understand that very large numbers of people around the world were experiencing significant changes in all areas of their lives, including work, family relationships, community life, and the ways in which they ate, dressed, traveled, and felt. As the cultural historian Jackson Lears has explained, the dominant social ethos of the Victorian era, which "enjoined perpetual work, compulsive saving, civic responsibility, and a rigid morality of self-denial" had gradually given way to "a new set of values sanctioning periodic leisure, compulsive spending, apolitical passivity and an apparently permissive . . . morality of self-fulfillment." The name for this new culture is familiar to us: consumer culture.

While these gradual transformations were uneven and took many decades to occur, they were still very widespread phenomena even before the turn of the twentieth century. Instead of feeling like they were part of close economic and cultural networks that were immediate and familiar, many people could see they were becoming part of a very different type of society, a mass consumer society. Lears argues that this left many people with a sense that reality itself was somehow more distant and it was "real life" was "something to be sought rather than merely lived." This was due to increasing urbanization, in which more and more people lived in close proximity to large numbers of people who were not personally known to them. It also stemmed from technological developments in almost all areas of personal life.

Things that have been taken for granted in many wealthier countries of the world for over a century, such as indoor plumbing, central heating, or even canned food, were at that time new modern conveniences. Lears explains that they were thought by some to be symptoms of what was called "over-civilization." The phenomenon of over-civilization was thought to have caused what many regarded as a genuine epidemic of "diseases" such as malaise, ennui, melancholy, nervous prostration, or neurasthenia which was a kind of paralysis of the will. These changes produced various kinds of discomfort and sometimes even panic. Further, the complex interdependent market economy that produced and facilitated such things was said to threaten a highly valued sense of individual autonomy. New types of work were more and more common. Instead of working at home or on a farm in some kind of manual labor, more and more people worked in offices. They were no longer the owners of their labor or time. With all of these new types of more distanced, freer, more individual and anonymous social relationships came a different experience of everyday life, one that felt less real and immediate to a great many people.

From sheet music to the gramophone

If we imagine phonograph to be just one of so many of these kinds of modern conveniences, then it is not hard to see how the experience of music was just one more aspect that contributed to a much wider and deeper sense of unease. Instead of hearing someone you knew playing a familiar kind of music for you, you would listen to a machine make new and strange sounds that came from some distant place made by people you knew very little about.

If we can briefly compare the cultures of music-making that stemmed from sheet music and those that stemmed from sound recording, then we can more easily see why some feared and resented the new medium even as others embraced it wholeheartedly. Importantly, underlying both the enthusiasm and the worry was a common conception of music that we don't completely share with our historical forbears. To put it almost crudely, good music was thought to make you a better person and bad music was thought to make you a bad person. Good music was music that ennobled you and made you accepting of a particular kind of moral uplift. It was almost always Western art music, Christian hymns, or sentimental parlor ballads that were regarded as "good." Given the power of music to affect your morals and outlook, you had to take great care when making it or listening to it. Individual sheet music collections played an important role in this. They were often taken quite seriously and would often encompass multiple volumes that might contain hundreds of pieces.

Like any culture of music-making, the culture of sheet music was one that was defined by various kinds of social protocols and traditions. The performance of what are generally referred to as "parlor songs," mostly brief and straightforward songs that almost always fit into a kind of formula of familiarity and comfort. Parlor songs were mostly written as simplified arrangements for piano and voice and could be about a wide range of themes from sentimental to patriotic or the melancholic and nostalgic. Often, famous operatic arias were adapted and simplified for everyday use as were Christian hymns.

Sheet music culture was very much a middle and upper-middle-class phenomenon and was dominated by the specific classes of people in both Europe and North America. The performance of sheet music in the home was often simply assumed to be something women in particular must do to

FIGURE 1.4 *The cover art for "Goodbye Little Girl, Good Bye" (ca. 1918).*

participate in the expected social rituals of the time, especially courtship and marriage. Singing or playing these songs was about a good deal more than simply enjoying music. Specifically, choices of repertoire and interpretation were more or less explicitly judged to be a reflection of the character of the performer. Beyond that, "good" music was also thought by many to bring a kind of social harmony to the home that was roughly analogous to the musical harmony expressed in those prized bound volumes. As such, great care was often put into managing and editing sheet music collections given their inevitable, if passive, commentary on the collector. The covers for individual songs were often very beautiful and colorful, a result of the new printing techniques of the time (Figures 1.4 and 1.5).

FIGURE 1.5 *The cover art for "He's Got Those Big Blue Eyes Like You, Daddy Mine" (1918).*

The sheet music industry was intensely competitive and while it did not produce what we would call a coherent musical "genre" there was a significant measure of similarity in many of the most commercially successful songs. As the music historian Charles Hamm has found, many songs had similarities that emphasized clear, memorable melodies, especially those found in a song's chorus. Further, most commercially successful songs had a simple verse-chorus structure and the harmonic materials tended to get simpler over time.

Hamm shows how publishers had a set of informal rules that could account for such commonalities. These come from one of the most successful songwriters of the era:

- Watch your competitors; analyze the cause of their success or failure;

- Take note of public demand;

- Avoid slang and vulgarisms; they never succeed;

- Many-syllabled words and those containing hard consonants, wherever possible, must be avoided;

- In writing lyrics be concise; get to your point quickly and then make your point as strong as possible;

- Simplicity in melody is one of the great secrets to success; and

- Let your melody musically convey the character and sentiment of the lyrics.

From these various ideas we can sum up the dominant features of the culture of sheet music as a safe, familiar, and controlled world of social relationships that could be used to regulate the potentially dangerous, but possibly beneficial effects of music.

Fidelity and the gramophone

When a new machine, the gramophone, was tossed into this controlled environment, it sparked a lot of excitement and concern. One of the main concepts around which there was much discussion and debate was "fidelity." It is perhaps most concisely summed up by the famous image of a dog staring into the horn of a phonograph, recognizing "His Master's Voice" (Figure 1.6). Even a simple creature such as a dog can hear the direct correspondence between the recording and the real thing.

The word fidelity essentially means "loyalty." Our contemporary ideas of fidelity are primarily about the extent to which the qualities of a sound recording reproduce the qualities and characteristics of a real sound event. We know a recording is not "real" in the way sound events are. Recordings

FIGURE 1.6 *Francis Barraud (1856–1924) painted his brother's dog Nipper listening to the horn of an early phonograph during the winter of 1898. Victor Talking Machine Company began using the symbol in 1900.*

are most often carefully constructed recreations of the events they captured. They are captured, mixed, mastered, and consumed in ways completely distinct from their origins.

But this was not how historians such as Emily Thompson have interpreted the concept of fidelity in the early years of sound recording. Then, people were most often interested in the extent to which they could hear and then imagine the original sound event in a recording. That is, the sound recording had to be proven to be a loyal representation of a real event. We can see this in the debates and campaigns that surrounded the gramophone in the early twentieth century.

It has been very well documented that sound recording was not originally thought of as an inherently musical medium. Instead, it was thought to be, as the music historian Alexander Rehding has suggested, "an infallible witness and unimpeachable scribe." This was true even of one of its inventors, Thomas Edison. Edison firmly believed that sound recording was best suited to capturing the most important of passing aural events in a thoroughly objective and truthful manner. He thought this attribute was ideal for personal and professional correspondence. We can see this also in the fact that the first commercial sound recording machines, Edison's wax cylinder recorders, were not designed for the mass production of the same recording. They were instead designed for the creation of unique aural documents (Figure 1.7). It was not until the first disc phonographs were invented by

FIGURE 1.7 *Thomas Edison, inventor of sound recording, with his early phonograph (ca. 1877).*

Emile Berliner in 1895 that sound recordings could be endlessly, if somewhat laboriously, reproduced and sold as a mass consumer item (Figure 1.8). It was this development that facilitated the phonograph becoming a musical instrument and taking its place in the parlor alongside the piano.

As the musicologist Mark Katz has explained, there was a tremendous optimism about the potential for a kind of mass musical education with the advent of the commercial phonograph and gramophone. Due to the portability, affordability, and repeatability of recorded music, many imagined that a great new age of music appreciation had come into view. The phonograph was used in homes, schools, and in the wider community to stoke and maintain an interest in and appreciation of "good" music (Figure 1.9).

However, there were also voices of displeasure and foreboding that the phonograph was not simply the pleasure-giving machine so many imagined it to be. These voices argued that sound recording enforced a dangerous musical passivity on the public, allowing them to take part in the great traditions of Western music without much effort at all. The labor necessary

FIGURE 1.8 *Emile Berliner with his disc-based phonograph (ca. 1920s).*

FIGURE 1.9 *Ad for resorts in the US state of Maine; patrons dance to a gramophone (ca. 1908).*

FIGURE 1.10 *Heslop's Phonograph Depot, Brisbane, Australia (1907). Note the musical instruments in the rear.*

FIGURE 1.11 *Harston Music Warehouse, Toowoomba, Australia (1908).*

to inculcate the true appreciation of all that music offered was thought to be perilously marginalized due to the new invention. Further, the skills necessary for the existence and future development of this musical inheritance might be rendered extinct in only a few generations if these circumstances were allowed to persist.

Interestingly, one of the most prominent critics of the new technology was John Philip Sousa, "America's bandleader." As the music historian Patrick Warfield has shown, Sousa wrote his famous article "The Menace of Mechanical Music" in order to appeal to his audience through the anti-modern language of over-civilization I have noted above. Sousa suggested that many in his audience might "recoil from an 'overcivilized' modern existence" in order to seek out more authentic musical experiences free of the pernicious influence of technology. As Warfield suggests, "Sousa's entire career had been spent cultivating a relationship with audiences that consisted of devoted amateurs, [and] the rise of mechanical music threatened to transform these ticket buyers from active performers into passive listeners." Sousa sought, not to erase the influence of sound recording, but to harness it for the ends of professional musicians like himself to maintain the existing social networks that had served him so well up to that point.

FIGURE 1.12 *New Edison Standard Phonograph advertisement (1898).*

There were many others like Sousa who sought to contain the threat of what they derisively called "canned music," motivated by a combination of aesthetic and commercial interests. While we might imagine them to be somewhat hypocritical, especially after Sousa made a deal to advertise for the Victor Talking Machine Company, we should try to understand why this debate was so important and the influence it had on future developments.

Importantly, as you will notice in the gramophone and phonograph ads that follow in the next section, the companies producing these machines responded to criticism by selling the new technology in ways that displayed all the pleasing social rituals and protocols of the parlor piano. They were even sold, not just in furniture shops, but music shops (Figures 1.10 and 1.11). But the phonograph was also sold with a few "modern" twists. We see groups of people listening together, but we are also told, at some length, how technically correct and perfect these machines are. While, without question the phonograph was meant to be seen and understood as an eminently social technology, it was meant to be seen as a modern one as well.

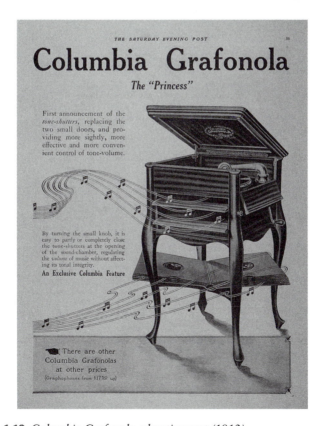

FIGURE 1.13 *Columbia Grafanola advertisement (1912).*

Explore and report: The sound of early recording

First, however, we need understand the qualities of the recordings themselves. If you do a simple internet search for "Berliner Morning on the Farm" you should be led to this page:

http://publicdomainreview.org/collections/morning-on-the-farm-1897/ (It is also probably available on YouTube.)

Here you can listen to and download an early Berliner Gram-O-Phone Company recording called "Morning on the Farm." It was recorded in 1897.

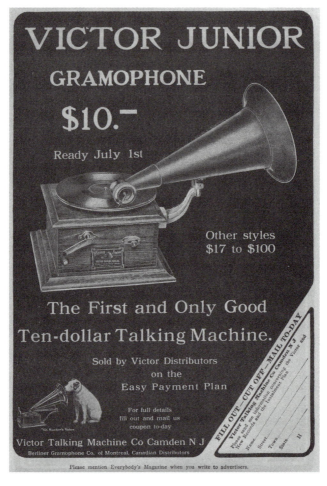

FIGURE 1.14 *Victor Talking Machine advertisement (1909).*

As this recording is in the public domain you can listen to it or download it if you wish. Have a listen.

Without knowing much about the recording, you might imagine it to be a location recording of a farm. We might interpret this as the Berliner company recording familiar sounds that any audience member could be expected to recognize. This would act as a demonstration of the fidelity of the phonograph. Simply put, you couldn't tell the difference between the recording and the real thing. However, this is not a location recording of a farm. It is a recording of a well-known stage performer making animal noises in a studio. It is very interesting to note how the Berliner company's catalogue explained this recording:

FIGURE 1.15 *Columbia Grafanola advertisement (1920).*

This reproduction clearly and accurately brings out the bleating of the sheep, the lowing of the cattle, the crowing of the cock, the cackle of the hens, squeal of the guinea hen and gobble of the turkey, all being answered and accompanied by the cries of the neighboring hawk, crow and various other birds. So real is the arrangement and so exact the imitation that it requires but a slight stretch of the imagination to place one's self in that delightful position, the result of which is the drinking in of copious drafts of fresh air and numerous other pleasures attainable only on the farm.

It is important to understand that it is probably not surprising that the Berliner company emphasized the accuracy of the recording so strongly. Their marketing text is a nearly perfect enactment of the meaning of the term "fidelity" in the early twentieth century. A recording of mostly familiar sounds is concocted in a recording studio to dazzle and distract the listener's imagination. In this instance, the Berliner company worked hard to convince their listeners that the entirely mundane sounds they created were accurately and exactingly reproduced. It is not too surprising then that phonograph companies did the same thing with music.

Now, have a look at the collection of phonograph ads that appear in the following pages. You can also find dozens and dozens of such ads in an image search with any internet browser.

FIGURE 1.16 *Graves Music, Portland, Oregon (1915).*

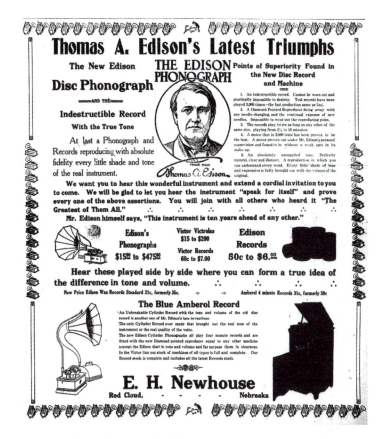

FIGURE 1.17 *Edison Phonograph advertisement (1913).*

Based on the themes of these ads, and remembering the qualities of portability, affordability, and repeatability that defined this technology, write a short "marketing report" making the case for recording and selling "Morning on the Farm." The goal is to convince the president of the Berliner company to put this record out and why they think it will be popular.

Focus: Selling the phonograph

Now we will explore the culture of early sound recording by examining how phonographs were sold. A very important article you should read for extensive background is by Emily Thompson from 1995. It is called "Machines, Music, and the Quest for Fidelity: Marketing the Edison Phonograph in America, 1877–1925." It was published in *The Musical*

FIGURE 1.18 *Edison Phonograph advertisement (1900).*

Quarterly. In this article, Thompson examines the thousands of so-called "Tone Tests" run by Thomas Edison's National Phonograph Company all over the United States in the late nineteenth and early twentieth centuries. You will need this article as background to explore the concept of fidelity and examine how and why those selling phonographs worked so hard to demonstrate the accuracy and legitimacy of their recordings. Further, we will also use this article as a rich and detailed primer in the culture of sound recording consumption in the early twentieth century.

FIGURE 1.19 *An image from the* Victrola Book of the Opera *(1917).*

Note all of the details of the tone test especially, on pages 139 to 161, including publicity, arrangements, directions, protocols, setting, programs, etc. You will need to figure out what the purpose of these elaborate events was, beyond merely selling the phonograph players. The main goal here is to try to understand all of the specific attributes of each performance. The tone tests were meant to reflect the values of so-called "high culture" and "good music." List and interpret all of the many aspects of the tone tests that tell us this is the case. This would include the setting, the venue, the stage set, the performers, the repertoire, and the sequence of events all of which were exactingly prescribed by the Edison company. It is important to understand that Edison didn't simply want to associate his products with such music to sell more machines. Given the strict rules set out for those conducting these events, we can conclude that he probably believed in the widely accepted idea at that time that "good" music made "good" people. Make sure you can dissect the parameters of presentation and the cultural biases they reveal.

Listen to old 78 or cylinder recordings to provide some context for your reading. A very good source of such recordings is the University of California at Santa Barbara Sound Archive (http://cylinders.library.ucsb.edu/index.php). Another is the Library of Congress; National Jukebox (http://www.loc.gov/jukebox/). It would be helpful to listen to old 78 or cylinder recordings in class. Choose and listen to a few recordings and explain your experiences listening to them.

FIGURE 1.20 *Columbia Phonograph Company advertisement (1905).*

Now examine closely Figures 1.14–1.23. They represent a good range of the kinds of images and ideas used to sell gramophones in the early twentieth century. From just these ten images we can see the same range of concerns Thompson recounts and examines in her article. First, many feared that the phonograph would replace or denigrate live music-making and flood the world with bad copies and pale imitations of what they regarded as the real thing. The phonograph companies countered this fear by claiming that their sound recordings and playback machines had perfect fidelity to the originating sound event. But it is important to understand that the predominant understanding of the concept of "fidelity" in the early twentieth century is very different than ours. At this time, "fidelity" meant that sound recordings were meant to transparently reproduce sounds from the real world. There could not have been any expectation that the sound-reproducing abilities

FIGURE 1.21 *Steger and Sons phonograph advertisement (1920).*

of wax cylinders or shellac discs would help exactly reproduce real sounds because that was simply impossible.

We can see this fear addressed in several of these ads. For example, in Figure 1.16, the Edison company makes a big deal out of how the "Edison Diamond Disc Phonograph absolutely recreates the voices and music of the great singers and instrumentalist" claiming it is like "hearing the living person." If you listen to some of the old recordings on the websites noted above, you may notice this claim is somewhat exaggerated. In Figure 1.17, the Edison company makes another argument for the "fidelity" in the form of an aggressive case as to the technical superiority of its products. In Figure 1.18, they appeal to the phonographic "enthusiast" for whom only the best would do. Perhaps not surprisingly, the "best" also included the rather large

FIGURE 1.22 *Victor Victrola advertisement (1908).*

collection of famous opera singers seen in Figure 1.19, all of whom recorded "exclusively for Victor." Compare this to Figure 1.20, in which Madame Fremstad, the "premier soprano of the Metropolitan Opera," lends her image, and ear, to the Columbia Phonograph Company. The text in this ad, as well as those in Figure 1.21, associate the phonograph to music of the European Art Tradition. As with Edison's tone tests described by Thompson, this was a clear strategy to link ideals of musical and artistic "quality" to the technical quality of the phonograph. The Steger phonograph ad in particular even expands these ideals of quality to the cabinet which contained the machine, claiming the "tone chamber of spruce" produced the best sound.

The other fear that phonographs inspired was that the rituals of making music in the home, as described earlier in this chapter, would be obliterated

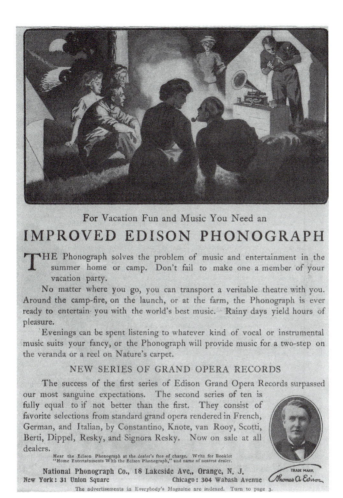

FIGURE 1.23 *Edison Phonograph advertisement (1909).*

by these machines. In Figures 1.14, 1.22, and 1.23 we see the phonograph companies responding. These ads show us people enjoying life lounging at beach or camping in the forest with their phonographs in tow. In Figure 1.22, Victor even suggests that phonograph is an essential ingredient in the "performance" of music at home, allowing you to "pick out your own performers, arrange your own program and enjoy the music, fun and entertainment that every home needs." Look at the posture and arrangement of the people in Figures 1.14 and 1.23. What kinds of scenes are these? Such scenes of a social and communal phonograph were extremely common in this era. They were a clear attempt to push back against criticisms these machines so often attracted.

INDEPENDENT RESEARCH WORK

The culture of listening to record music was very different in the early twentieth century. People generally had very different understandings of what recorded music was, especially in relation to live performance. Research aspects of phonograph listening have been suggested throughout this chapter. This would include how people listened to recorded music, where they did so, and what aspects of their social lives were tied to it. For example, think about why those making phonograph machines made extremely expensive models that look like luxury furniture as well as very inexpensive models that people could carry around with them. Examine a wide range of phonograph advertisements and make a strong, well-reasoned interpretation about what these can tell us about how people used these machines in their everyday lives.

References and further readings

Chanan, Michael. (1995) *Repeated Takes: A Short History of Recording and its Effects on Music*. London: Verso.

Coleman, Mark. (2005) *Playback: From the Victrola to MP3: 100 Years of Music, Machines, and Money*. Cambridge, MA: Da Capo Press.

Gay, Leslie. (1999) "Before the Deluge: The Technoculture of Song-Sheet Publishing Viewed from Late Nineteenth-Century Galveston." *American Music*, 17(4): 396–421.

Hamm, Charles. (1979) *Yesterdays: Popular Song in America*. New York: Norton.

Katz, Mark. (2004) *Capturing Sound: How Technology Has Changed Music*. Berkeley: University of California Press.

Kenney, William. (1999) *Recorded Music in American Life: The Phonograph and Popular Memory, 1890–1945*. New York: Oxford University Press.

Lears, T. J. Jackson. (1981) *No Place of Grace: Antimodernism and the Transformation of American Culture*. New York: Pantheon Books.

Lears, T. J. Jackson. (1983) "From Salvation to Self-Realization: Advertising and the Therapeutic Roots of the Consumer Culture, 1880–1930." In R. Wightman Fox and T. J. Jackson Lears (eds.), *The Culture of Consumption: Critical Essays in American History, 1880–1980*. New York: Pantheon Books, 1–38.

Meyer-Frazier, Petra. (2006) "Music, Novels, and Women: Nineteenth-Century Prescriptions for an Ideal Life." *Women and Music: A Journal of Gender and Culture*, 10: 45–59.

Miller, Bonny. (1994) "A Mirror of Ages Past: The Publication of Music in Domestic Periodicals." *Notes*, 50(3): 883–901.

Rehding, Alexander. (2005) "Wax Cylinder Revolutions." *The Musical Quarterly*, 88(1): 123–60.

Sanjek, Russell. (1996) *Pennies from Heaven: The American Popular Music Business in the Twentieth Century*. New York: Da Capo.

Scott, Derek. (1989) *The Singing Bourgeois: Songs of the Victorian Drawing Room and Parlour*. Milton Keynes: Open University Press.

Scott, Derek. (2008) *Sounds of the Metropolis: The Nineteenth-Century Popular Music Revolution in London, New York, Paris, and Vienna*. New York: Oxford University Press.

Segrave, Kerry. (1994) *Payola in the Music Industry: A History, 1880-1991*. Jefferson, NC: McFarland and Company.

Suisman, David. (2009) *Selling Sounds: The Commercial Revolution in American Music*. Cambridge, MA: Harvard University Press.

Warfield, Patrick. (2009) "John Philip Sousa and 'The Menace of Mechanical Music.'" *Journal of the Society for American Music*, 3(4): 431–63.

Watt, P., D. Scott, and P. Spedding. (2017) *Cheap Print and Popular Song in the Nineteenth Century: A Cultural History of the Songster*. Cambridge: Cambridge University Press.

2

Sound recordings and radio in the "Jazz Age"

Background and topics

For many people, the significant, if not radical, changes of the first few decades of the twentieth century seemed to hit them like a steam train, or perhaps a speeding "motor car." The social and technological changes described in the previous chapter reached a peak of disruption in the 1920s and one word came to symbolize both the optimism and hope of the era and the fear and perceived danger: "Jazz." Jazz was not like the forms of popular music or song that had previously been dominant. Jazz was fast, heavily improvised, and it demanded new ways of making musical sounds and new forms of dancing to those sounds. Importantly, jazz was a form of music and dance created by African Americans and appropriated by others. Jazz spread, prospered, and was attacked as African Americans also spread, prospered, and were attacked. Jazz inspired what seemed like a whole new culture and world view. For some, jazz seemed to relegate the old sentimental and patriotic ballads of the sheet music era to obsolescence. It was the speed and freedom many people heard in jazz that became the metaphor for a time when what was "modern" became the new normal.

To put it mildly, jazz was not universally beloved or acclaimed. There were many people who resented both the sound and speed of the new music and its seemingly mirror reflection of a world that also seemed to be speeding up and getting a lot noisier. For many critics, the unhealthy and threatening aspects of jazz were synonymous with the threat posed by African Americans and the large numbers of newly arriving immigrants to America's major cities. In the same way that sheet music culture was a reflection of wider social forces, so was the culture of listening to jazz, especially in the home.

Brown Bros. Photos

FIGURE 2.1 *Early radio station 8XK, Wilkinsburgh, Pennsylvania (1920).*

There seemed to many people to be a kind of generational battle going on for supremacy in the wider culture. Young people were embracing new kinds of music, new modes of dress, and new ways of socializing with each other.

As noted in the previous chapter, this was a time of change in many spheres of social life. Gender roles were changing with particular visibility and prominence. Many critics of jazz held particular fears about the mixing of young people coming from different communities, especially young white women socializing with young African American men. Fears that the social and economic dominance of Anglo Americans, and especially Anglo American men, was threatened by the actions of their children caused many of their elders, parents, politicians, and community leaders to try to stop them. It was this wider social conflict which shaped the experience of the two mediums that were essential to the Jazz Age: sound recordings and radio.

There are two specific developments we will try to understand in this chapter. First, the advent of radio broadcasting in the early 1920s changed not only how people listened to music, but how people connected with the world through music. Radio was immediately available and it was live. This made it far more exciting than even the best record. Second, radio was a far superior technology than sound recording and as a result it simply sounded a lot better to a lot of people than sound recordings. This fact pushed record companies to improve their technology just as it looked like radio might eclipse them entirely. When radio was combined with the widespread acceptance of improved sound recording, both live and recorded music became very nearly ubiquitous in the homes of many people around the world. Live music was now available at the flip of a switch. Sounds could flood into the home from great distances. With the gramophone and radio in the parlor, the home was no longer the insulated social cocoon many had once imagined it to be. This had profound consequences that are crucial to our understanding of the new mediums.

As with the displacement of sheet music culture with sound recordings, here too we will see how each link in the chain of music production, distribution, and consumption changes in concert with the others. Radio broadcasting and sound recordings brought to widespread attention musical traditions that had previously been confined to specific geographic regions or particular social spheres. Jazz was foremost among these. The new mediums challenged both basic conceptions of the ways in which music was thought to be socially useful and the ways in which various types of music appealed to social groups that did not have much access to them previously.

Jazz and "The Great Migration"

Jazz was born in New Orleans in the late nineteenth century. It was a subtle and complex multicultural amalgam created and dominated by African American performers and composers. This unique musical tradition was forged through a multitude of musical influences. Jazz musicians worked within traditions underpinned by the blues, ragtime, as well as French, Spanish, and Mexican influences. Influences from places in the Caribbean such as Cuba were also important as they had been present in this city and region for decades.

Jazz came to an early form of commercial maturity in a very complex time in American history. In the early decades of the twentieth century, millions of African Americans began moving from the southern states to elsewhere in the United States. The first wave of the so-called "Great Migration" lasted from about 1915 to 1940. Large numbers of African Americans emigrated to cities such as Chicago, Cleveland, New York, Philadelphia, Detroit, and Los Angeles to escape a violent, feudal social and economic caste system in the southeastern states.

Importantly, the late nineteenth and early twentieth century also saw significant immigration to the United States from Europe to many of the same cities in the northeast of the United States. These two phenomena transformed not only the character of these large and influential urban centers, but changed the very self-understanding of American society. The form of modernity embodied in the term "the Jazz Age" was a complex form of global change that established new forms of social, cultural, and economic connection. These connections laid the foundations of the world we live in today.

These changes transformed jazz from being a regional, if not marginal, form of popular music to an international phenomenon. It was literally carried by African Americans leaving the southeastern United States as they settled in large numbers in northern and western cities. These cities were intricately connected to the rest of the world and as a result jazz caught the attention and elicited the excitement of people all over the world. Further, the hostility and segregation African Americans faced in the northern cities meant that these communities developed artistic traditions that were often at a clear remove from other similar traditions produced by others.

Of course, there were many people who were unsettled by these changes. The idea of Americans speaking strange languages and eating unfamiliar foods, like pizza or bagels, seemed wrong somehow. As we will see shortly, the discomfort with the musical forms modernity took motivated an organized resistance to what some imagined to be a dangerous and damaging culture of music-making. First, however we should try to understand a bit more about the place of music in these larger debates about what shape this rapid change would should take. The medium which changed the experience of music in public and at home most substantially was radio.

The advent of radio broadcasting

It is nearly impossible for us today to imagine the impact the introduction of radio broadcasting had on the cultures of music listening in many places around the world. In an age of wonders, it took wonder to another level.

FIGURE 2.2 *Farmer listening to crop reports (1923).*

For what amounted to only a small amount of money for many people, one could build or buy a small box that would let you listen to events taking place ten miles away or two hundred. These events were live. Some were scripted. Some were spontaneous. Some were world-changing. As a result, there grew around radio a whole language of romance and celebration informed by a profound faith in the ability of science and technology to provide social and cultural progress.

As the historian of the medium Susan Douglas has shown, radio seemed magical to many people. Many called the electromagnetic spectrum upon which radio broadcasting depended "The Luminiferous Ether" to make sense of it. Radio was dimly perceived to be part of an all-encompassing medium through which sound traveled. There was an odd almost supernatural quality to radio in these early days. The effects of radio were sometimes described using terms such as "telepathic impact," "the other side of the veil" or "voices borne in on the moonbeams" to describe the crackling sounds and intense feelings of immediate social connection produced by listening to the radio. It is not too much to say that many otherwise sober commentators felt that radio intermingled human voices with the cosmos.

Given this, it should not surprise us that this new medium was hugely intriguing to a lot of people right from the beginning. Between 1913 and 1915, and during the First World War, the public use of the radio spectrum

FIGURE 2.3 *Oregon farm family listening to the radio (July 20, 1925).*

was severely restricted. However, after the restrictions were eased, hoards of new amateur radio operators, many trained by the army for service during the war, started up their own amateur relay stations in their basements and garages around the world. They could not yet broadcast their voices or other sounds, but a rich culture of radio signaling and listening evolved very quickly into a competitive culture of seeing who could pick up broadcasts from the greatest distances.

After the broadcasting of voice and music on radio became possible, the initial torrent of broadcasting activity quickly became a tide. By the early 1920s, huge numbers of public, commercial, and community-based organizations had started their own radio stations. (Reread pages 325 to 329 of the Garofalo article for a helpful contextualization of the advent of radio.) The presence of radio in everyday life became very nearly ubiquitous in many places around the world very quickly. Interestingly, those selling radio often sold it the same way that phonograph companies sold their wares, as inherently social technologies. (Figures 2.2, 2.3, and 2.4)

The question for us now is how did people react to the largely unregulated transmission of live music? There is no question that this caused a great

FIGURE 2.4 *A "radiophone dance" held by an Atlanta social club (May 1920).*

FIGURE 2.5 *Cover of New Orleans newspaper* The Mascot *(November 5, 1890).*

deal of disquiet among those who tasked themselves with regulating what they called "public morals." Specifically, it was the continued blurring of the distinctions between public and private culture through the arrival of real-time musical sound in the home that caused such a strong reaction. This helped pave the way for an attempt to regulate the content of information that could enter your home freely through the radio.

Social regulation and the "music appreciation" movement

The excitement surrounding radio strongly shaped perceptions of the ability of radio to provide both "good" and "bad" music to an unprecedented number of people with a new kind of directness. It should not be surprising that this created a great deal of social anxiety. Given that radio was live, it simply had a much greater impact on those worried about the possible consequences that both "good" and "bad" music might have when it coursed through a genuinely mass, real-time medium. The fear of the contaminating influence on the whole of society was great, not just for those who chose to be "contaminated," but also for those who didn't. A huge volume of complaints was received by the government leading to extensive regulations that sought to transform radio into a more "elevating" and "tasteful" enterprise. This was perceived by some to be a direct line of influence that moved from regulating radio to regulating taste to regulating morals. Music was central to this dubious equation.

This is perhaps not too surprising given how different radio was from sound recordings. First, music was available nearly all the time on radio, on demand. It contrasted quite strongly from those laboriously self-realized sheet music collections or those tinny discs you could only listen to once before resetting the gramophone. Second, you usually had to listen to sound recordings through a horn that had a comparatively limited frequency range. Third, radios had amplifiers and produced superior sound. Finally, radio was immediate. Listeners could suddenly access the sounds of live orchestras and famous dance bands who were performing at that very moment (Figures 2.6 and 2.7). Most people loved the immediate form of social connection it created.

The big radio corporations who increasingly began to define and dominate the new medium boasted about how much better radio was than records. One said the following, "The ordinary record is a pretty poor imitation of the human voice; practically all of them give a pretty disagreeable scratchy noise and even when they don't the enunciation is seldom distinct enough for one to understand the words of a song." All that noise made about how "real" recordings were was suddenly rendered glaringly false. Radio was far more "real" than recordings. Caught between the twin disruptions of radio and the Great Depression, record sales began to collapse.

But radio still had its own problems to face. As Garofalo tells us, radio was managed very differently for different purposes. Some countries were

FIGURE 2.6 *A publicity photo for the National Barn Dance, NBC Radio (1935).*

FIGURE 2.7 *The Victor Salon Orchestra (Victor Talking Machine Company) (ca. 1926).*

dominated by commercial interests, such as the United States, whereas others were dominated by government broadcasting. In most places, however, the medium was gradually regulated. In the United States, the political contests over regulating radio became a strongly symbolic fight over what counted as "acceptable" content. Due to the immense popularity of radio, this was especially true of what authorities deemed to be "acceptable" music.

As a result of the power of those agitating for the legislating of "public morality," the radio broadcasting regulations passed in the United States in 1927 and again in 1932 deemed some content as "obscene" and as such it was unworthy of being broadcast over the nominally "public" airwaves. While this may seem reasonable on the face of it, the definition of what was considered "obscene" was so broad that it effectively banned a great deal of music made by African Americans and working-class white Americans from the most widely experienced form of media of the era. This had a significant effect on what performers and what kinds of music became well-known and popular.

The larger radio broadcasting corporations claimed that their "public service" radio broadcasting was defined by certain "standards" that protected the vulnerable public from dangerously "bad" content, especially "bad" music. This is how one New Jersey station explained what its standards were: "Our Station for Public Service," as they called it, "is an overdue antidote to broadcasters who polluted the airwaves with the stormy clamorous of jazz and thinly cloaked indecencies hurled upon the air from the lips of soaked or half-soaked announcers, to find lodgment in the sanctuaries of the just, as in malodorous dens of the vicious." Over a relatively short period of time "quality" content was enforced, whether it was musical content or otherwise, and amateurs, so celebrated only a few short years earlier as the pioneers of radio, were gradually excluded from broadcasting.

This was a deliberate kind of disciplining of those members of society who were not thought to be the right sort to appear on the radio. Such people were simply not allowed to have unfettered access to this new magical, all-powerful medium.

One important result of these regulations was an emerging hierarchy of two types of radio stations: "Popular" and "Quality." "Quality" stations provided orchestral music and public lectures to listeners. The National Broadcasting Company, the largest and most influential in the new industry, hired famed conductor Arturo Toscanini to conduct the NBC Orchestra, a full orchestra made up of many of the best players of the day. Those we might call the "musical optimists" of the era saw their glasses, not simply as half full, but positively overflowing. *The Etude*, a magazine for both amateurs and professionals alike proclaimed: "Radio has the ability to create a vast new army of music lovers in America. We are now on the threshold of one of the greatest musical awakenings the world has ever known."

Walter Damrosch, the conductor of the New York Symphony, cited letters of praise for broadcast of concerts and performances by the world's great musicians, "from people who pour out their hearts in gratitude for the opportunity to hear for the first time in their lives a wealth of concerts of great music." Damrosch used these letters to press for the creation of a radio show that he was to call the "Music Appreciation Hour." It was broadcast on NBC's national network from 1928 to 1940.

The historian Sondra Hall has shown how Damrosch effused about the opportunity radio offered:

It has been the prerogative of those who lived in or near the great cultural centers and who enjoyed the means to pay for admission to concert halls and opera houses. The great majority remained in ignorance of the music of the masters, untouched by its ennobling influence, barred from participation in its beauties—until the radio suddenly, as if by magic, swept away the barriers and admitted all the people to the charmed circle of music's devotees. Now, for the first time in history, those who live on farms and ranches, in small towns and villages, in mining camps, lumber camps, and other remote places, may come into intimate personal contact with the music of Mozart, Beethoven, and Wagner. A new world has been opened up to them and the response has been phenomenal.

But Damrosch's greatest concern was for the children, for whom he helped create the Music Appreciation Hour, which, in addition to the broadcasts, included workbooks and tests for the children to complete. He said of the enterprise,

> I have found I can demonstrate the tone qualities of the various orchestral instruments and indicate the ways in which the master composers have used them. I have found that I can give my young listeners some perception of the expressive powers of music and a general idea of the evolution of the different musical forms. But while I have imparted a great deal of technical information, my object has always been to create a love for music and an intelligent appreciation of it.

He began his broadcasts with the chipper phrases, "Good morning my young friends. Let me express my happiness that I am to continue my work with you in helping you to understand and love the language of music—the greatest of all languages which translates our emotions into wonderful melodies and harmonies."

He filled his broadcasts with emotive descriptions, such as this about Schumann's *Evening Song*: "This piece, expressing the contentment we feel at the end of the day's work or play, as we sit quietly watching the sunset glow fade into twilight, was composed as a piano duet and has been arranged for orchestra by the French composer Saint-Saens." Toward the end of the program, he concluded optimistically: "What does the future hold for broadcasting of music?" he asked. "The broadcasting companies are exerting themselves to supply quality fine music; more and more commercial sponsors are awakening to the fact that not jazz, not crooners, not the cheap and tawdry emanation from Tin Pan Alley, but the music of the masters is what the public wants."

In many ways, Damrosch was completely wrong. He and the masters of radio and music had won a few battles, but they had not won the war. The crude, rude, awkward side of popular culture relentlessly came to fore in these years. While the guardians of virtue continued to fight, we will see in chapters to come that the subsequent decades would eventually marginalize their ability to legislate public morality. Before we continue this story, we need to understand what exactly this "bad" and "dangerous music" actually sounded like and why some people attacked it.

Explore and report

Before we focus on the attacks on jazz that took place in the 1920s, it is important to understand what this music actually sounded like. Just as importantly, we need to understand the music to which jazz was unfavorably compared when it was attacked. The goal of this exercise, when accompanied by the Focus section to follow, is to try to understand how different kinds of musical gestures or attributes, such as improvisation or syncopation, have come to have specific types of meaning attached to them.

First, go to UCSB Cylinder Audio Archive at http://cylinders.library.ucsb. edu/ index.php and find the following files. They are in the public domain so you can download them. Have a listen.

Band music:

- "The 74th Regiment Band March" by the United States Marine Band (1918)
- "Ace of Diamonds" by the National Promenade Band (1914)

Jazz:

- "Ma Rag Time Baby" by the Peerless Orchestra (1899)
- "Jazzin' Around" by Earl Fullers Famous Jazz Band (1918)

Second, compare the two band pieces and the two "jazz" songs in terms of their sound and their most important or noticeable musical attributes.

The first thing to do is try to make a simple inventory of content. In this case, work to discern and list the instruments being played in each recording. It is worth making a quick internet search for discography databases or websites chronicling early jazz recordings to get a sense of the typical personnel of the standard march band or jazz band. One thing you will probably notice is how all of these ensembles draw from the same small pool of instruments. Ask yourself why this might be the case.

Next, try to work out the structure of each recording. You can do this by setting out a simple chart based simply on timing. Listen closely to see exactly where the piece changes and make a notation on your chart.

Example:

‖ Intro.	Verse	Refrain	Verse	Refrain	
(0:00)	(0:21)	(0:44)	(1:06)	(1:31)	

Finally, try to characterize the actual music. You can do this by listening as closely as you can to the qualities of the sounds you hear. Ask yourself a few questions: What kinds of sounds are present? How do the various instruments relate to one another? Are the musicians playing mostly in unison? Do they clearly "stay together"? Is the music fast, slow, sedate, agitated, etc.? Do any players of instruments seem more prominent than the others? You may realize that all of these pieces have a good deal in common. The question then is, why was band music considered "good" and jazz thought to be "bad"?

Now write two separate letters to your local newspaper from the perspective of someone living the 1920s. In the first, explain why band music is better for your community than jazz. In the second, explain why jazz is not the danger some imagine it to be.

Organize and conduct a class discussion about early sound recording. There are several key points to emphasize. First, make sure you have a clear understanding of how these recordings were made and what their material qualities are. What are the basic characteristics of the wax cylinders and the early discs, or 78s. There are large numbers of very good images of these discs and players available online.

Reminders:

- The phonographic cylinder was not invented to record music;
- It was invented as a business machine to record and transmit correspondence;
- Each cylinder recording was a unique original;
- Cylinders were made in one take, straight through,
- Gramophone discs were the first to allow mass production of sound recordings;
- Most recordings could only be about 2 ½ minutes in length;
- Sounds were literally cut directly onto the cylinder or disc;
- Recordings were often consumed often in public listening machines;
- Sound recording was popular because it was portable, affordable, and repeatable.

Second, be sure that you understand that all of these recordings were made using the same recording techniques and mostly the same instruments. As you work through the Focus section, think about how unremarkable these kinds of jazz sound to us. This is a good way to understand the racist nature of the attacks on jazz.

Finally, guide your discussion toward how central the concept of so-called "hot rhythms," or more simply syncopation and improvisation, were to the criticisms of jazz. Despite the fact that both elements had been part of European art music for centuries, critics of jazz highlighted the supposedly "uncontrolled" and "primitive" nature of jazz specifically through the presence of extensive rhythmic and improvisatory interplay between musicians.

Focus: The devil's music

When we listen to early recordings of jazz today, they may sometimes sound a bit innocent, exuberant, and maybe even a little bit silly. They are often riddled with blatant, corny double entendre and the aurally limited recordings themselves emphasize their rhythmic qualities. However, this should not distract us from the vicious, racist campaigns against this music that were conducted in the 1920s and 1930s. The question for us here is this: given that it is hard for us to hear this music as particularly threatening, what was it that some people were so afraid of?

When we set out to answer this question, we need to remind ourselves that one important quality that sheet music culture sought to cultivate was self-control. The performer controlled the time and space in which the music was created and they controlled the content, and its consequences, or so they thought. We should also remind ourselves that the consequences of music listening were often thought to be potentially quite serious.

With the embrace of radio broadcasting and recorded music, listeners experienced a radical displacement of musical sound from its source. That is why the gramophone and phonograph advertisements mentioned in the previous chapter emphasized both the fidelity and socially harmonious nature of sound recording. With this in mind we can imagine the kinds of anxiety that might get attached to the recording of both old familiar music and new and different music.

Jazz arrived at a historical moment when the kinds of social disruptions of modernity were affecting increasingly larger numbers of people. The focus of the criticism was that jazz would cause people to lose whatever self-control they possessed. Jazz was a kind of bodily intoxicant that affected people all over and this led directly to jazz being a kind of moral intoxicant. The sources of the effects of jazz were its famously "hot rhythms." The syncopated, improvised rhythms of early jazz were said to have some remarkable effects on vulnerable people. Beyond this, the hot rhythms of jazz were feared to

FIGURE 2.8 *King and Carter Jazzing Orchestra, Houston, Texas (1921).*

contest the very possibility of those kinds of universal moral ideals that many authorities thought were embodied in one's individual capacity for self-control, self-improvement, intelligence, and high purpose. They talked about jazz in ways that may shock us today. (Note: the terms "jazz" and "ragtime" were often used interchangeably by some critics.)

Most often, critics claimed that jazz and ragtime were morally corrupting. Music writer Neil Leonard compiled a litany of what seem to us to be extreme reactions to this music. One opponent put it this way: "In Christian homes where purity and morals are stressed, ragtime should find no home. Let us purge America and the divine art of music from this polluting nuisance." Another noted, "Little by little the people have forgotten the noble melodies which used to interest them and have sold themselves body and soul to the musical Satan."

Sometimes, jazz and ragtime were talked about as if they were a kind of infection. The fear of contagion flows directly out of this idea as people began to fear that good, healthy music might become infected by the bad, evil music. One critic noted how ragtime broke out "now and then like a morbid irritation of the skin" while another noted how "the counter of the music stores are loaded with this virulent poison which in the form of a malarious [*sic*] epidemic is finding its way into the homes and brains of youth." Another declared that it was "an evil music that must be wiped out as other bad and dangerous epidemics have been exterminated."

FIGURE 2.9 *The Dixie Ramblers, Omaha, Nebraska (ca. 1923).*

It is important to deduce that this conception of music implies that the listener is no longer in control. No longer does music get produced in safe parlors or upstanding concert halls, but floats around on the air like a virus. Given the newly pervasive presence of radio and records in daily life, this is something we might be able to understand.

There were some who took their opposition to jazz much further, claiming that they had scientific data to prove that jazz and ragtime were not simply metaphorical health hazards, but literal ones. One doctor claimed that jazz "would eventually stagnate the brain cells and wreck the nervous system." Similarly, Dr. E. Elliot Rawlings claimed that jazz "causes drunkenness by sending a continuous whirl of impressionable stimulations to the brain, producing thought and imaginations which overpower the will. Reason and reflection are lost and the actions of the persons are directed by strong animal passions."

These supposed animal passions were most obvious when people danced to jazz as the health hazards of jazz were caused by what appeared to be a loss of bodily control. Critics noted that the new music "had a powerful stimulating effect, setting the blood, nerves and muscles tingling with excitement." Another noted that "I felt my blood thumping in tune, muscles twitching to the rhythm. This ragtime appeals to the primitive love of the dance—a special sort of dance in which the rhythm of the arms and shoulders conflicts with the rhythm of the feet in which dozens of little needles of energy are deftly controlled in the weaving of the whole." Still another, claimed that the "seemingly involuntary gyration of ragtime dancers are such that any unsophisticated visitors from Mars, who did not know their excuse would judge from their looks, their movement and their strident pathetic yells that they were raving lunatics only fit for the Martian equivalent of a straight jacket." Ragtime dancing was often explicitly linked by religious leaders to "tarantism," a form of acute, ecstatic trance or possession often borne of intense grief wherein people would dance and clap or chant rhythmically for hours.

The often energetic dancing seen in dance halls were described thusly by one observer: "It has been discovered that many ragtime songs as well as dances receive their inspiration in the brothel and are tossed upon the market to corrupt the mind of the young." The sheet music to many famous tunes has "title pages picturing contortioned partly clothed dancers in attitudes suggesting inebriated Hottentots."

The Catholic Telegraph of Cincinnati Ohio noted, "The music is sensuous, the embracing of partners is absolutely indecent and the motions can not be described with any respect for propriety in a family newspaper. suffice it to say there are certain house appropriate for such dances, houses which have been closed by law." The orchestra leader of a California hospital noted, "I can say from my own knowledge that about fifty percent of our young boys and girls from age 16 to 25 that land in the insane asylum these days are jazz crazy dope fiends and public dance hall patrons. Where you find one you will find the other."

Educator Alice Barrow went further: "The nature of music and the crowd psychology working together bring to individuals an unwholesome excitement. Boy-girl couples leave the hall in a state of dangerous disturbance. Any worker who has gone into the night to gather the facts of activities outside the dance hall is appalled, first of all perhaps, by the blatant disregard of the elementary rules of civilization. . . . We must expect a few casualties in social intercourse, but modern dance is producing little short of a holocaust."

There is little question that these fears were very often wildly overstated for rhetorical effect. Further, it was only ever a prominent minority that made such claims as jazz remained among the most popular forms of music for decades. However, if we take them seriously as markers of more tangible social anxieties we will be able to understand them more completely. As we have seen in both Chapters 1 and 2 so far, the dominant belief about music in the era of early sound recording was that "good" music would improve your morals, character, and health and "bad" music would damage them. When we set this firmly held belief in a context in which rapid and dramatic social change was affecting nearly every imaginable part of everyday life, from food to clothes to work to family, it is easier to come to a more completed understanding of these groundless and often very hateful fears. For many people, strange music about which they knew very little was suddenly entering their homes. It was available easily and immediately and seemed to possess qualities they had long been told might be dangerous. It would simply take time for these fears to dissipate and this music to become acceptable. As we will see in the next chapter, this didn't really take all that long.

INDEPENDENT RESEARCH WORK

The hostility toward jazz by some people in the early twentieth century may seem strange and extreme to us today. However, as we will see in later chapters, similar kinds of criticism were made about many different kinds of music throughout the twentieth century. In the late twentieth century, three kinds of music were often harshly criticized for their allegedly damaging qualities: punk, heavy metal, and hip hop. All three were the subject of legislation and public campaigns of censorship. Choose one of these forms of music and compare the criticisms made against it with those made about jazz. Write a research essay explaining what you see as the continuities in the social basis for these kinds of criticism of music as well as the content of that criticism. Importantly, think about what these criticisms imply about the function, effect, and power of music more generally.

References and further readings

The Devil's Music: 1920s Jazz. (2000) Boston: WGBH.

Doerksen, Clifford. (2005) *American Babel: Rogue Radio Broadcasters of the Jazz Age.* Philadelphia: University of Pennsylvania Press.

Douglas, Susan. (1989) *Inventing American broadcasting, 1899-1922.* Baltimore: Johns Hopkins University Press.

Douglas, Susan. (2004) *Listening In: Radio and the American Imagination.* Minneapolis: University of Minnesota Press.

Gioia, Ted. (1997) *The History of Jazz.* New York: Oxford University Press.

Gioia, Ted. (1989) "Jazz and the Primitivist Myth." *The Musical Quarterly*, 73(1): 130–143.

Howe, Sondra. (2003) "The NBC Music Appreciation Hour: Radio Broadcasts of Walter Damrosch, 1928-1942." *Journal of Research in Music Education*, 51(1): 64–77.

Jazz. (2001) "Episode 1: Gumbo." Walpole, NH: Florentine Films.

Leonard, Neil. (1962) *Jazz and the White Americans.* Chicago: The University of Chicago Press.

Panetta, Vincent. (2000) "'For Godsake Stop!': Improvised Music in the Streets of New Orleans, ca. 1890." *The Musical Quarterly*, 84(1): 5–29.

Radano, R., and P. Bohlman. (2000) *Music and the Racial Imagination.* Chicago: University of Chicago Press.

Taylor, T., et. al. (2012) *Music, Sound and Technology in America: A Documentary History of Early Phonograph, Cinema and Radio.* Durham, NC: Duke University Press.

Vancour, Shawn. (2009) "Popularizing the Classics: Radio's Role in the American Music Appreciation Movement, 1922–34." *Media, Culture and Society*, 31(2): 289–307.

3

"Microphone singing" and the short musical film

Background and topics

Try to imagine the following. There is a man who is very well-known for his accomplishments in the field of technology. His unprecedented accomplishments were both challenging and exciting to millions of people. He was an inventor who was nicknamed "the dark horse" because so few people knew anything about him. He was notoriously publicity shy. He felt he needed to avoid journalists to focus on his work. Even the publicity agent hired by his investors could not convince him to create a suitable public image. When he completed the remarkable feat he had set out to accomplish, suddenly he became the hottest name in the world. He was flooded with media attention. The somewhat unkind nicknames the press had previously saddled him with were gone, replaced by public adulation. But to his dismay, the press rarely asked him any questions about his greatest achievement, how he did it, or what it might mean to the world. Instead, they pried to get the details of his private life.

Journalists tried to bribe people he worked with, or people who worked for him. He made public declarations against the invasive paparazzi. He publicly demanded that his personal life be left separate from his public and professional endeavors, all to no avail. There was a feeding frenzy to find out who the "real" man was behind the public façade. Perhaps inevitably, rumors and gossip filled the gaps in his public persona and even led to a kind of tragic situation which prevented him from living anything like a normal life. This story, as presented by the cultural historian Charles Ponce De Leon, should sound familiar to us. Celebrities of all stripes, from tech moguls to actors or musicians have had high-profile battles with invasive

FIGURE 3.1 *Bing Crosby and The Rhythm Boys in the film* King of Jazz *(1930).*

media. But this story is about Charles Lindbergh, the first person to fly solo across the Atlantic in 1927. It is important for us to note how some things haven't really changed all that much in our celebrity culture over the last century.

Lindbergh was very much an exemplar of the modern notion of celebrity, the form of celebrity we have inherited. It came to maturity in the time period we have been talking about, the late 1920 to the early 1930s. Whereas historians of celebrity have argued that fame was once bestowed on those whose acts were deserving of the attention, they have also shown how the new celebrity culture expanded to include not only explorers and scientists, but singers, movie stars, and fashion icons. These new celebrities were thought by some to be people less worthy of fame, people for whom fame was its own reward.

The new forms of celebrity these people inhabited were defined by a crucial paradox. The public saw the famous person and their accomplishments very clearly, and yet much of this celebrity phenomenon set about demonstrating to the public the "real" human beings behind their famous personalities or symbolic identities. Most importantly, these new modern celebrities were not defined in public only by their accomplishments, but also by "who they really were" in their real lives. The tone and character of celebrity journalism was defined by this dynamic relationship between the public image and the private person (Figure 3.2)

The question for us is this: Why did it happen when it did? It happened when it did in large part due to the arrival of a new wider and more

FIGURE 3.2 *Cover,* Radio Revue *(December 1929).*

complex world of images and sounds. This was an industrialized world of image production, a world of markets and corporations and new communication mediums. These new public personalities come directly and indirectly from several of the suite of new communication technologies developed or "perfected" between the 1890s and the 1930s that I showed you in the previous chapter. Most important for us in this chapter will be microphones, loud speakers, and film. These new technologies produced an increasingly crowded and complex field of images and sounds experienced in both public and private that each represented new ways to connect with audiences and create new social relationships with them (Figure 3.3). The emergence of this new, modern celebrity was a by-product of the changes we've been examining. Most important among them was the creation of the

FIGURE 3.3 *Kinetoscope Parlor, San Francisco (1894).*

leisure industry in the context of substantially new communications and media environment.

In this new media environment, increasingly intimate sounds and images were widely available in public and entering the home more often. This transformed both the form and content of popular music. Radio both inspired and facilitated the creation of new sound production techniques and technologies. As a result, the transportation of musical sound over greater and greater distances in better and better quality became common and familiar. What we will see in this chapter is how a new kind of popular music star exploited this new environment and these new experiential circumstances to craft a form of musical celebrity that had not been seen before. They were called "crooners" and they inspired the same kinds of excitement and worry that we have seen in previous chapters.

Crooners and their many "musical instruments"

As we will see in the Focus section below, "crooners" were labeled as such because of the quiet, intimate style of singing they perfected. They "crooned" to their audiences through new tools such as the microphone and loud speaker that translated the potential intimacy of the human voice through the new mediums of radio and records. However, there was another new medium that had an equal if not greater impact: film. Crooners such as

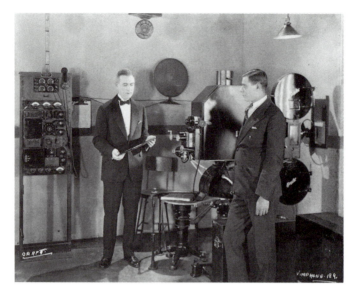

FIGURE 3.4 *Demonstration of the Vitaphone Film Sound System (1926).*

Rudy Vallee and Bing Crosby cleverly pioneered and mastered a multimedia approach to engaging and enticing their audiences like few had done before (Figure 3.4). We need to examine how we got to this point.

As noted earlier, sound recording began as an "acoustic" medium. This means that the sounds to be recorded were etched directly on the surface of the recording medium. Whether disk or cylinder, sounds were sent into a horn attached to the recording device and needles dug into the wax or shellac surface to more or less permanently capture them for playback. Radio, however, did not transport sound through such means. By the mid-1920s, radio used microphones of various types and capabilities. This meant that the sound of someone speaking could be transmitted more closely to its original state by the mid-1920s. However, as common as playing recordings on the radio has been since that time, a complex series of technical and political challenges had to be overcome to make it that way. Nevertheless, by the early 1930s it was possible, but not necessarily common to play recordings over the radio. This was in part due to the objections of musicians fearing losing work, but also due to the demand for genuinely live radio on the part of the public. Most important for us is that fact that radio helped facilitate so-called "electrical recording" which replaced acoustic recording. This had the effect of making sound recordings of higher quality with a wider frequency range that allowed for volume control and the use of speakers, not just headphones.

Whereas previously sound recordings were made wherever a secluded space might have been convenient, such as warehouses or hotel rooms, now

FIGURE 3.5 *Rudy Vallee and His Connecticut Yankees (1931).*

recordings increasingly took place in purpose-built studios that looked and worked very much like radio studios. Further, the very nature of the concept of the sound recording had changed. No longer were gramophone companies simply trying to directly capture and shape the sound of a performance, now they were trying to learn how to shape sounds. The microphone, sound recording, and the radio receiver became the primary "musical instruments" of crooners such as Crosby and Vallee. The exciting directness of radio became all the more engaging when these men sang low and soft as if they were standing right next to their listeners (Figure 3.5).

Explore and report: Crooning and the short film

The use of film made by Crosby and Vallee was every bit as important as the microphone and radio in crafting the intimate relationships each sought with their audiences. Both artists relied quite heavily on the new kinds of celebrity that had emerged in the early twentieth century. They routinely sought to portray themselves as just regular guys and offered their fans what they claimed was a look behind the surface of their celebrity to see "what they were really like." We can see and hear this in their recordings and their films in which an unusually direct address and closeness marks each of these productions very clearly. Each performer appears to be a natural, real person.

In order to understand the reaction to crooning which we will examine in the Focus section below, we need to understand what this music was actually like and how it was experienced. We will focus on recordings and a few of the many short films many of the more prominent crooners made.

First, let's listen to a few songs. Do an internet search for two performers, Al Bowlly and Bing Crosby. YouTube has old films of both performing. There are also many sound recordings of each available. Do a search for Bowlly performing "The Very Thought of You" and Crosby performing "If You Should Ever Need Me." Only look for sounds recordings at this point. Have a listen.

Second, listen again and do your "inventory" on each song (see Chapter 2). What instruments and sound sources are present? How are they used? How do the musicians relate to one another? What is the role of the singer? How prominent is the singer? Are any of the other musicians as central to the performance as the singer? What is the structure of these songs? (Remember to use the chart technique from the previous chapter.) If you compare all of the songs we are examining here, you will find they all share a few key characteristics: simple structures, limited vocal ranges, simple melodies repeated many times, and memorable imagery of mostly the same general type.

Now focus on the vocal and the lyrical sentiments. Given the importance of the singers to these songs, it is important to note the importance of what they are singing as well. (Their lyrics will be available via many easily available lyric websites.) Along with their vocal tone and somewhat theatrical singing display, these singers have very carefully used their voices and delivered them into microphones with great care. Try to link the vocal techniques to the sentiments of the lyrics of both songs.

Both songs are meant to be comforting. Both singers take great care to sing in a smooth, easy way with few if any abrupt changes in dynamics or enunciation. They both hold notes in a similarly smooth and easy way, without much in the way of vibrato or sharp attacks. Each song also places the singer in a passive position in relation to the object of their affection. Each declares that they are both captured by their beloved and are powerless under their spell. Crosby even goes so far as to say we will simply wait until he is needed. He won't "interfere" if the person he is singing to wishes to go their own way.

Now, we also need to understand the important vehicle of the short films crooners made. We find that the typical attributes of the kinds of songs we just listened to are translated in various ways on the screen. Importantly, these films allow us to see how each performer used their facial expressions, bodily movement, and in Crosby's case, a brief vignette, to express the wistful, slightly melancholy sentiments of their songs.

Search for the following films, which should be available on YouTube. Chart the songs out, go through your inventory, and draw as much as you can from the lyrics and their delivery.

- Rudy Vallee: *You're Just Another Memory* (1929).

- Rudy Vallee: *I'm Just a Vagabond Lover* (1929).

- Bing Crosby: *I Surrender Dear* (1931).

In the case of Rudy Vallee, we can see that in both songs, Vallee is the center of attention. He is the center of the scene and the camera stays focused on him throughout each song. (See the publicity photo at the start of this chapter.) This camera use mirrors his centrality to the music. His simple, clear melody does not compete with any of the other instruments. Indeed, most of the band members simply support him by playing the harmonies or repeating the same melodic lines he sings. Further, Vallee's posture is passive in both performances. He looks off wistfully into the distance as he sings that his lovers have left him alone. "Every dream was just a precious token," Vallee sings as he learned that "all your vows were easily broken." Notably, in both films Vallee carries a saxophone throughout and sometimes even chimes in on a clarinet. This was symbolically, but not musically, important because Vallee spent a large portion of his career trying to demonstrate the he wasn't "only" a singer. He wanted to show he had more purpose than the once pejorative tag of singer once implied. We will return to this theme in the Focus section.

The Bing Crosby film is similar, but is a much more complex document of the crooner phenomenon. This is a twenty-minute story of a singer named, well, Bing Crosby of course, who, through many mishaps and cases of mistaken identity, is able win the girl of his dreams. There are a range of important devices this film uses to translate the crooner of the song into the crooner of this story. First and foremost is Crosby's voice. It acts as his primary tool of authentic identification and is demonstrative of his honesty as a person. Second, neither of the secondary male characters, in the form of his sidekick Jerry and his nemesis, The Marquis, represents any real threat to Crosby. Jerry acts as a kind of "wingman," aiding Crosby and offering wry commentary on the events of the film. The Marquis, who begins the film as the fiancée of the female protagonist ends it as a laughing stock. He is a crude comic foil for Crosby's everyday charm and charisma.

Finally, there is the story, which is so simple as to be nearly without purpose. The story is really only a vehicle for the delivery of several of Crosby's songs, and through these, to act as a demonstration of his appeal as just a regular guy. His talents defy their circumstances and eventually allow Crosby to triumph in love and life. (They even get him out of a speeding ticket.) As we examine the crooners more closely in the Focus section, we will return to these themes.

Focus: Crooners versus "real" singers

Crooners were among the most popular musical stars of their era, but they were also subject to a great deal of criticism. As the historian Alison

McCracken has explained, crooning was popular in part because "it combined the intense romanticism of the Victorian ballad with the amorality of the urban novelty song and the emotionalism and sensuality of jazz" while offering "new possibilities for intimacy between singers and their audience, especially a female audience." But it also evoked new kinds of social anxiety: "At a time when a white man's masculinity was defined by his physical vigor and muscularity, radio offered a disturbing artificially amplified male presence, one that competed with traditional patriarchal authority for the attention of the family."

If we wish to understand these concerns, then we need to understand what "real" singing was supposed to be like, that is, we must understand "pre-microphone singing." Before radio and microphones, a particular type of popular singing was predominant in theaters and vaudeville music halls. It was a type of singing that required exaggerated gestures and vocal affects in order to "fill the hall," as it were, or to capture and hold a large audience's attention. This form of singing also implied a certain style of content. It was open, loud, occasionally brash, and often comical because that's what worked in the theatre.

Not surprisingly, the crooners developed an entirely different style of singing. Their skills at introspective, intimate, and "close" singing were developed specifically to exploit the capacities of radio broadcasting and electrical recording, both of which were dependent on the microphone. As a result of these new mediums, a new set of artistic criteria for the measurement of sometimes competing categories of "talent" and "popularity" developed. "Radio singing" demanded different skills from singers as it was in many ways an unforgiving medium. Historian Paula Lockheart quoted a critic of the time noting the conundrum produced by those "baffling, uncertain, unknown quantities" that radio singing demanded, often resulting in a situation where "a voice that in itself is hardly a good voice may be the most popular on the air." He continued, "Somehow the mechanics of radio culls the raucously rough edges from his vocal mannerisms and leaves for the listeners-in only a tender smoothness." The radio itself often had "the same effect on his voice as arduous years of voice training."

Lockheart also quotes one director of a radio station who offered this advice to those wanting to sing on the radio: "The radio voice must sing with the meticulous exactness of a painter in miniatures. The radio voice must not be "breathy" as the impact of the breath column on the microphone may overload the tubes. . . . Clean unexaggerated diction is imperative to prevent hisses and gurgling noises. . . . The artist . . . must be able to pull down volume on forte passages and still achieve power."

But debates about radio singing were about more than mere technique. As Alison McCracken explained in her study of crooning, at this time, singing was also regarded as a healthy activity that was part of a much larger culture of activity and exercise that was meant to improve one's physical and emotional health. For men in particular, singing was meant to be physically strenuous and challenging. It was an activity that they could use to demonstrate their strength, power, and self-control. In many ways, crooners were seen as part of a larger set of changes in popular culture that contradicted these norms and expectations. As McCracken argues, crooners were singled out for criticism because, in an era of economic struggle and cultural change, they were viewed by many to be transgressing traditional gender norms. Their pleading songs and quiet, nakedly emotional voices marked crooners out as less than masculine in both word and deed. Their often abject lyrics, rhetorically placing themselves in total control of the women whose love they sought, seemed to some to have emptied their music of the dignity afforded by self-control. Crooners came to represent a fault line in the new modern popular culture, a fault line not so different from the one represented by jazz.

Specifically, crooners were strongly associated with a new urban popular culture that allowed for new kinds of social relationships between men and women and appeared to encourage a much greater sensuality between them. Further, major cities were increasingly diverse and vaudeville theaters and cabarets catered to audiences seeking to transcend traditional racial and

FIGURE 3.6 *Publicity Photo for Rudy Vallee (1930).*

heterosexual relationships. As such, critics saw crooners as contributing to a culture of cosmopolitan immorality.

Importantly, these criticisms were directed at specific musical attributes. As with the attacks on the pervasive syncopation and improvisation in jazz, critics took crooners to task for *how* they sang as much as *what* they sang. McCracken reports that one high-profile clergyman claimed that the songs crooners sang were "not true love songs; they profane the name. They are ribald and revolting to true men." Such moralists felt it necessary to explain that the low, understated tones used by crooners were often intended as an act of underhanded seduction. They claimed that the very act of crooning acted as something approaching an incantation meant to prevent listeners using their elevated mental and emotional capacities. Voice teachers identified what one called the "devitalized tone" of crooning that robbed "the voice of its ability to express higher emotions and deprives it of its inherent devotional quality." Not only was crooning a moral perversion, it was an artistic perversion as well. Perhaps most disturbing for some was the fact that the intimate sounds crooners produced were not intended to selflessly enlighten or ennoble the public, but to selfishly arouse and excite their emotions and baser instincts.

Despite these sharp and intolerant criticisms, crooners such as Bing Crosby and Frank Sinatra eventually became not only acceptable performers, but very nearly synonymous with American patriotism in popular culture. Specifically, by the early 1940s, Bing Crosby and Frank Sinatra were routinely tasked with selling American democracy at home and overseas. This was a result of how Vallee, Crosby, and their fans reacted to the onslaught of invective directed at them. Both singers worked hard to portray themselves as "natural" musicians and ordinary men. In particular, it was Crosby's careful cultivation of his reputation as just a regular guy that had the greatest impact in blunting the criticisms directed at him and his peers. If we go back briefly, to our analysis of the short musical films Vallee and Crosby made, we can more clearly see now how each film is in many ways a response to the criticism directed at each performer.

One important issue in the early years of the microphone was how the role of singers within popular ensembles had changed. Before the microphone, the singer was often a marginal performer. They did not usually take center stage and were rarely the focal point of the audience's attention. We can see from all three films noted above that the singer is the constant center of attention. Look at how both Vallee and Crosby perform. Crosby, for example, is the focal point not only of the audience's attention, but in particular, female attention. You may notice that as the film starts, Crosby is on stage. In the front of the crowd is a young woman dancing with a much older man. She is staring quite directly and aggressively at the handsome young singer. This visual connection is highlighted by the fact that Crosby is cool and calm, while the woman's older male dance partner is sweating profusely. This is a cheeky encapsulation of the fears many held about figures such as Crosby.

With Vallee, you may notice that in both films he carries a saxophone which he sometimes plays. He also plays the clarinet in "Just Another Memory." Yet, in both cases, his instrumental playing does not stand out at all. He simply joins in and adds to the fullness of the band's sound. This was a calculated part of his image. Vallee routinely emphasized the fact that he was not merely a singer. In fact, he styled himself as an instrumentalist, band leader, and impresario. Further, he relied very heavily on sporting iconography such as college letterman jackets and a cheerleader's megaphone to link himself to traditional ideas of masculinity. The combination of these elements is a clear response to the criticisms of Vallee as a sleazy seducer.

But it was Crosby who most effectively transformed the act of crooning into a safe and pleasing pastime. In fact, the film *I Surrender, Dear* marks the beginning of his attempt to rehabilitate crooning. Expressing themes that would become common in his later films, *I Surrender, Dear* see Crosby innocently cross paths with a young woman he initially mistakes for his sister. He falls immediately in love and gently charms the woman while cleverly getting the best of her fiancée, The Marquis. Despite continually receiving the attentions of other women, Crosby focuses only on this one. He is forced to overcome a whole series of comic blunders and accidents to finally gain her attention. Interestingly, he is forced to repeat the line "Oh no I'm not a masher" several times to the young woman's mother in order to account for his repeated and unwanted presence in their company. He finally wins over his new love by singing to her and she agrees to marry him. Here, Crosby consciously seeks the socially normative and nonthreatening realization of this miniature story as a hedge against the hostile criticism of America's self-appointed moral guardians. As we will see at the start of Chapter 5, Crosby's success at tempering the perceived excesses of the crooner in the 1930s would pay dividends for other similar singers in the 1940s, especially Frank Sinatra.

We can see with the crooners that they were able to construct and inhabit a nascent form of musical celebrity in the early 1920s that they were then able to master by the mid-1930s. Through the use of varied forms of new media, performers such as Bing Crosby and Rudy Vallee were able to construct new, intimate social relationships with their audiences. Further, they were able to use these form of media to respond to and tamp down criticism of their alleged lack of "proper morality." This is a dynamic that we will see repeated in similar ways in later chapters.

INDEPENDENT RESEARCH WORK

The singing style of the crooners was unusual for its time. It was partly dependent on the invention of the microphone. It was also dependent for its success on the invention of amplification in live performance and speakers in radios. Not only could crooners produce intimate sounding performances, but people could listen to those at home more or less in an intimate way. Examine the criticism of the crooners and compare these to criticism of male singers today, especially pop and R&B singers. What commonalities can you find? There has been a long series of criticisms of male pop singers that center around aspects of their expression of gender and sexuality. Write an essay critiquing this tradition of music criticism. How legitimate is it? How is it connected to the actual musical skills or attributes of the music in question?

References and further readings

Giddins, Gary. (2001) *Bing Crosby: A Pocketful of Dreams*. New York: Little, Brown, and Company.

Lockheart, Paula. (2003) "A History of Early Microphone Singing, 1925-1939." *Popular Music and Society*, 26(3): 367–85.

McCracken, Alison. (2015) *Real Men Don't Sing: Crooning in American Culture*. Durham: Duke University Press.

Ponce De Leon, Charles. (2002) *Self-Exposure: Human-Interest Journalism and the Emergence of Celebrity in America, 1890-1940*. Chapel Hill, NC: The University of North Carolina Press.

4

The global gramophone

Background and topics

Between about 1925 and 1935, around the time the crooners began their ascent to top of the music industry in the and United States and the United Kingdom, the gramophone went global. Travelling through existing economic and social networks of colonialism and international trade, gramophone companies worked hard and fast to open every region of the globe to the production and sale of their products. They often competed intensely with one another to go to the farthest reaches of their respective regions and record what to them were the most exotic and strange sounds for sale in local markets as well as back home.

And sell they did. Consumers were transfixed by all kinds of sounds from all over the world. They listened to enormous amounts of music from all over the world, of course, but there was so much more to hear. Many listened to sermons, speeches, poetry, and "comical recitations." Some heard the American orator and politician William Jennings Bryan carefully distinguish between a "revenue tariff" and a "protective tariff." Possibly a few more heard the popular vaudeville performer Cal Stewart recount "Uncle Josh's Trip to Coney Island," in which Stewart inhabited his comical alter ego, Uncle Josh Weathersby, the country rube in the big city.

In this chapter we will look at how recorded music grew to become a pervasive global medium. Also, we will try to gain a sense of the range of music that became available and how new kinds of social relationships between musicians and audiences formed through this. Specifically, we will look closely at what historian Paul Gilroy has called "The Black Atlantic," or the social worlds of people of African ancestry living around the Atlantic Ocean. We will look at the kinds of social and cultural connection fostered by sound recordings among those who shared the persistent oppression and marginalization of the international slave trade and its ongoing aftermath.

FIGURE 4.1 *British colonist plays gramophone for his dog. Lagos, Nigeria (ca. 1920s).*

But first we need to understand the context in which the gramophone industry went global.

In the early twentieth century, the amount of trade around the world reached a new high point. Trade was much more open and countries were more integrated with one another economically than had previously been the case. As the historian Christina Lubinski has noted, "Newly available technologies in transport and communication, such as railroads, steamships and the telegraph, facilitated international travel, communication, and commerce." Further, she argues, "The adoption of free trade and the expansion of Western imperialism led to more exchanges between imperialist countries and their colonies, which were opened up, often forcefully, to international trade."

The gramophone industry was a major beneficiary of these economic and political circumstances. Companies competed fiercely to send their representatives all over the world to seek out all manner of performers and record their work. Historians and archivists have recounted the somewhat exoticized and even romanticized work of young recording engineers who, according to Lubinski, "were regarded as an elite group and traveled around the world to spot new talent and expand the repertoire of the company." For example, Will Prentice, an archivist at the British Library, tells of how a representative of the Gramophone Company of London, Franz Hampe visited the northern Caucasus, Georgia, Armenia, Azerbaijan, Turkestan, and finally made it to several

FIGURE 4.2 *Listening to a phonograph, Hyderabad, India (1891).*

FIGURE 4.3 *Dutch colonial family poses with phonograph. Indonesia (1923).*

towns in present-day Uzbekistan in 1909. According to Prentice, "Hampe faced a round trip of over 5,500 kilometers carrying extremely delicate equipment, through difficult and sometimes dangerous conditions." Even more trying was the experience of Theobald Noble, as Prentice explains, "who recorded for the rival Pathé Company in the same region." Noble "described travelling for eight hours on horseback through the Caucasus Mountains to audition a single choir, only to be ambushed and robbed by bandits on his return journey."

The recordings that resulted from such efforts were sold locally, nationally, and internationally. It is not too much to say that the thousands of recordings these companies produced, distributed, and sold had a profound effect on the musical cultures of almost every region on the globe. The historian Michael Denning argues that there were two important types of consequences to the rise of sound recording around the world: economic and symbolic. The economic consequences of the rise to recording saw the structure and nature of the music industry shift dramatically in a relatively short period of time. The alliances of "concert promoters and sheet music publishers" that dated from the seventeenth century were displaced as "the sale of recordings became the center of the music industry, displacing not only the sale of printed music but even live performance." The shift to recordings saw new players come from the dominant alliances that shaped the music industry, including "instrument manufacturers, instrument companies and royalty collection agencies." These new entities were also part of the symbolic consequences of the rise of recordings. What Denning calls the "economy of prestige and established hierarchies in which certain musics, places, and institutions" defined the cultural value of music was overturned. Instead, Denning demonstrates that "for the first time, the vernacular musics captured on recordings created a new imagination of the constellations of musics around the world," and it was popular music that became an important form of "symbolic currency" around the world. Shortly, we will see one example of how this kind of symbolic currency developed among a diverse range of people of African ancestry across and around the Atlantic Ocean. First, however, we should come to an understanding of the repertoire of recorded music we are talking about.

Explore and report: The recorded repertoire of the global gramophone

It is important to get a direct and clear understanding of the actual music that was recorded in this era. When considered in total, it is a broad, almost impossibly diverse body of recorded sound. However, it is important to realize that nobody really experienced these recordings in this omniscient

FIGURE 4.4 *Romanian family poses with gramophone (1938).*

way. They experienced them locally and personally. They used this new technology for their own reasons and for their own purposes. With the luxury of looking back into the history of recorded sound, we can take a wider and broader view. Our goal here is to assess this body of recorded sound more generally as a whole.

There are a large number of sound archives which have collected and made available a large number of sound recordings taken from wax cylinders and 78s. Here are four:

- UCSB Cylinder Audio Archive

  http://cylinders.library.ucsb.edu/index.php

- Library of Congress-National Jukebox

  http://www.loc.gov/jukebox/

- Library and Archives of Canada—Virtual Gramophone

  https://www.bac-lac.gc.ca/eng/discover/films-videos-sound-recordings/virtual-gramophone/Pages/virtual-gramophone.aspx

- The Great 78 Project

  http://great78.archive.org/

  https://archive.org/details/georgeblood

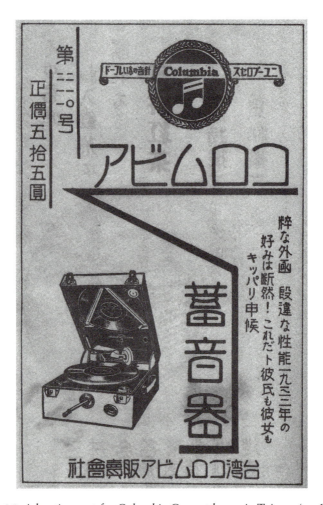

FIGURE 4.5 *Advertisement for Columbia Gramophones in Taiwan (ca. 1940s).*

All of these archives have search functions. Use the advanced search functions, often found under the "Discover" tab, to systematically get a sense of the full range of different types of sound recordings that are available. Search under different genres, especially nonmusical genres such as speeches or recitations. Search under different time periods. Pay special attention to the changes in sound quality in different eras. Search under topics, countries of origin, and primary musical instruments.

Next, listen to as wide a range of recording types as is practical. Keep organized notes about how they sound, how the materials are presented, the length of each recording, and how they address you as a listener. You may notice that a lot of the recordings announce the name of the piece and the performer in an almost theatrical way at the start. Write a series of short reflective journal entries based on your notes for each recording. You will need to do internet searches on the keywords for each recording to make sure you have the required background knowledge and context.

Finally, use your notes as the basis of a short research essay on the nature of the global recording industry in the years 1900 to 1930. The goal is to understand in the broadest and most general sense how sound recording went from being mostly a parlor novelty in 1900 to a global cultural force by 1930. Use the sources listed at the end of this chapter as a starting point for your research. How did the range of materials that were recorded and sold contribute to the popularity of the medium? How did recording company's catalogues reflect various musical worlds that had not been recorded before? What effects did the sound recording boom in the 1920s have on wider understandings of what forms of music were important and valuable around the world?

FIGURE 4.6 *Gramophones from the Primofon, Stockholm, Baltic Exhibition in Malmö (1914).*

Focus: The recorded music of "The Black Atlantic"

The economic and political relations between Europe and Africa have been defined by colonialism for centuries. Even after the formal end to colonialism and the advent of independence for African nations in the 1950 and 1960s, the same kinds of economic and political relationships that defined formal colonialism persisted. These relationships are defined by the exertion of social, cultural, economic, and military power over the indigenous people of a region, nation, or society by foreign invaders. In the specific case we will be examining here, the case of West Africa, the dominant institution in the colonization of West Africa was the Atlantic slave trade. Lasting for about 300 years, roughly from the 1550s to the 1850s, this institution forcibly removed millions of Africans from a wide geographic area to spend their lives in forced labor across the Western Hemisphere.

Despite the obvious and numerous horrors of the slave trade, so voluminously recounted by so many historians, those subjected to enslavement were nevertheless able to spend multiple generations creating a wide range of unique expressive cultures that included new forms of language, literature, mythology, and music. Importantly, one crucial effect of the slave trade was the deliberate and brutal estrangement of those who were enslaved from one another and their own languages and cultures. This demanded that people who were enslaved learn how to communicate and cooperate with one another in new ways in order to survive. One of the ways in which they did so was music. Over the centuries, a variety of forms of music developed in the places such as the southern United States, Cuba, Jamaica, Trinidad, and all across West Africa. Importantly, all of these cultures were linked practically through the slave trade and subsequent forms of trade and migration back and forth across the Atlantic.

Those millions of people who were part of these cultures shared a particular experience of the world in the form of different kinds of racist oppression, exclusion, and marginalization that have proved to be persistent features of the modern world. This experience has produced what scholars of the African diaspora have called "double consciousness." This concept, which originated in the scholar work of the historian W. E. B. DuBois, suggests that there is an inherent and continuous conflict within those who are part of the African diaspora. The conflict stems from an inability to reconcile their history of exclusion and oppression with the demands of being a citizen and a participant in the societies which enslaved their ancestors and continue to oppress them. It also means that people who are oppressed and marginalized because of their race by definition experience modernity both through their own agency, but also through the racist oppression that has long sought to exclude them from the benefits of that same modernity.

The historian Paul Gilroy has argued that this contradictory experience has produced something he calls "The Black Atlantic," that is a distinct experience of modernity by those of African ancestry living in the Atlantic region. Music has been an important part of this experience. From the earliest documentation of the presence of African-derived music in the Caribbean and North America, strong evidence tells us that there have been strong links between West Africa and many locations around the Atlantic for centuries. By the time sound recording arrived in the port towns and regions all around the Atlantic Ocean, there were already complex, vibrant, and geographically dispersed cultures of popular music-making knitting together a huge range of diverse people from West Africa to the Caribbean and North America.

For example, calypso developed in Trinidad from its roots in kaiso, a form of music and dance attributed to communities of the descendants of Ibibio people originally from southwest Nigeria. Calypso was widely performed throughout the Caribbean by the start of the twentieth century as were several other very similar forms such as mento in Jamaica. Mento developed from communities of so-called "Maroons" who lived in towns along the steep mountainous spine of the island. The communities were started by those who had escaped slavery. Cuban *són* was also a very influential and important style of music that developed under similar circumstances. As you may have already guessed, jazz also became an internationally known and practiced style throughout the Atlantic World during this period. It is important to note, however, that outside the United States, the term "jazz" was often used more as a catch-all stylistic ideal rather than the specific form of music we might be familiar with from the work of such performers as Louis Armstrong and King Oliver. During the 1920s and 1930s, the rise of sound recording also saw the emergence of genres of music such as juju in Nigeria and highlife in Ghana and elsewhere. Interestingly, West African forms of calypso as well as *són* and rumba developed in Guinea and Congo in this same period. As I will explain shortly, all of these forms shared a general set of musical commonalities that have had profound influence on the modern world.

The people who made these forms of music were by no means isolated from one another. In fact, members of these and many similar communities traveled back and forth across the Atlantic Ocean as ship workers, sailors, passengers, migrants, and laborers. They brought their knowledge and experience with them and found others with whom they shared a general type of experience, social status, and world view. As the trade links between West Africa, the Caribbean, Europe, North America grew in the early twentieth century, a complex culture of musical interconnection through commercial sound recordings developed in a great many places among those of African ancestry. Interestingly, it developed most effectively in port cities such as New Orleans (United States), Kingston (Jamaica), Havana (Cuba),

FIGURE 4.7 *Markets in Lagos, Nigeria (ca. 1920s).*

Port of Spain (Trinidad), Dakar (Senegal), Conakry (Guinea), Freetown (Sierra Leone), Accra (Ghana), and Lagos (Nigeria). These cities were all tied to major international urban centers such as New York and London (Figures 4.7 and 4.8).

The development of these interconnected forms of music in the port cites of the colonial Atlantic was no accident. As the historian Michael Denning explains, these cities were carefully and specifically managed in such a way as to almost demand the kinds of social solidarity and collaboration among people of African ancestry all across the Atlantic World that was necessary to produce all of these forms of music.

Port cities attracted a diverse range of people from many places around the world representing all social and economic classes. They included working people and local elites, colonial administrators from abroad and their local colonial counterparts, traders and sailors, as well as those brought in as servants or low-wage agricultural workers many of whom were often indentured for years on end. Many residents of port cities during colonialism were there because they were forcibly removed from their land as it was made available to foreign economic interests. Given this, colonial authorities established and enforced strict practices of segregation by class, race, nationality, and gender in order to manage this complex, and in the colonialists view, potentially volatile mix of people. The efforts at control and regulation coercively created critical masses of

FIGURE 4.8 *Portside neighborhood. Accra, Ghana (1929).*

people from common diasporic origins. Denning explains one important consequence of this:

> Throughout this archipelago of colonial ports, young musicians found that they could make a living from music in the proliferating cafes, taverns, shebeens, brothels, cabarets, "black and tans," dance halls, hotels, and vaudeville theaters catering to waterfront transients as well as well-to-do tourists, to young mill workers as well as students and clerks aspiring to middle-class respectability.

This created a trans-oceanic, transnational musical culture of musicians who began increasingly to learn from one another and trade riffs, gestures, and styles, albeit often at a technologically mediated distance. One interesting example is how the style of Cuban music called *són* became popular in Kinshasa, Congo. Congo was colonized first, not by a nation, but by a man, King Leopold II of Belgium. As part of the so-called "scramble for Africa," European political and economic elites divided up large portions of sub-Saharan Africa for their own exploitation. In 1885, Leopold claimed what was called the Congo Free State. He ruthlessly exploited its natural resources at the cost of untold numbers of African lives. Only when the atrocities became too big to be ignored was the state turned into a colony of Belgium in 1908. As the journalist and author Gary Stewart has chronicled, gramophones entered Congo in the early 1900s. South American records were extremely popular, especially those by guitarist Miguel Matamoros and his Trio Matamoros as well as Sexteto Habanero. This was largely because Caribbean music had long been a part of the musical cultures of many West African ports and cities. Stewart relates a circumstance that was probably repeated countless numbers of times in these years. As Stewart suggests, large numbers of Congolese musicians learned their trade by listening to and copying foreign songs and the instrumental performance styles they heard on record. "The coastmen could be observed first hand," he says, "at a neighborhood bar called the Siluvangi." Stewart continues,

> Some of them took the time to show their Congolese friends how to play. Imported records could be listened to over and over while a nascent guitarist or trumpeter played along . . . . Unintelligible English or Spanish lyrics were replaced by words in Kikongo or Lingala or some other local language.

During the period we are examining here, the 1920s and 1930s, the changes wrought on Congolese people by colonialism were immense. Many were forced off from their land and had to move into cities where many locals had no choice but to embrace an international and cosmopolitan form of modernity. Stewart tells us of the musical consequences:

> Musical instruments, guitars and horns, and the new technological marvels, radios, gramophones, and records, were high on the list of desirability. Soon the sounds of Europe, America, and more importantly, Latin America permeated Congolese cities. African rhythms exported on slave ships echoed from the grooves of 78 r.p.m. records, and crackling radio loudspeakers.

While the historical evidence linking various kinds of music around and across and throughout "The Black Atlantic" is strong, we also have available to us another kind of evidence as well: the music itself. Given the extensive range of early recordings from West Africa and the Caribbean now becoming widely available we can compare songs across styles, traditions, and genres. What we find is that there are a set of musical qualities shared among a huge range of styles from a wide range of places and time periods.

The musicologist Veit Erlmann has argued that music of the West African diaspora has a few key characteristics that defines it. First, he argues that these forms of music are defined by particular practices of repetition. Erlmann explains,

> There is a wide spectrum of forms in which repetition occurs, from cyclical recurrence of short patterns to the polyrhythmic interlocking of

several such contrasting cycles and larger call-and-response structures. The most important characteristic, however, of the cyclic structure of African music and the main point where it differs from Western types of repletion lies in the fact that repetition must be thought of as a practice.

We can hear these practices of repetition in a range of songs from a wide expanse of time periods. Yet, despite their differences we can hear all of the elements Erlmann describes in each one.

- "Akuko Nu Bonto"—George Williams Aingo (Ghana, ca. 1927–9).

- "Scrubbs Na Marvellous Boy"—Famous Scrubbs (Sierra Leone, ca. 1950s).

- "Mama Ngai Habanera"—Grand Kalle Et l'African Jazz (Congo, 1960).

We will briefly look at each song. Works by all of these artists should be available on video-streaming platforms. Please look at the discography at the end of this chapter and seek these and similar works so you can hear them directly. There are a few issues we will examine here: the structural commonalities of each song, their expressive commonalities, and what we might call the "social" commonalities, or how the circumstances in which each was created were similar as well.

Very little appears to have been known about George Williams Aingo, despite many recordings of his music having been made for Zonophone records in London in the late 1920s. However, as the liner notes to "Living Is Hard: West African Music In Britain, 1927–1929" tell us, he was part of a community of West African residents of London brought there for both economic and educational opportunity. Members of this community had their recordings exported back to West Africa where some enjoyed careers as musicians. What are important here are the musical attributes of "Akuko Nu Bonto." In short, the song possesses each of the defining features Erlmann describes, cyclical recurrence of short patterns of melody and harmony, polyrhythmic interlocking of rhythms across the ensemble, and larger call-and-response structures. "Akuko Nu Bonto" has all of these attributes, with an eight bar pattern that repeats throughout. Also, the guitar picking pattern, voices, and percussion all play polyrhythmic interlocking rhythms, and the structure of the song alternates between a solo singer and chorus of several vocalists showing us the larger call-and-response structures Erlmann describes.

"Scrubbs Na Marvellous Boy" by Famous Scrubbs holds these musical attributes in common with "Akuko Nu Bonto." However, this song is clearly distinct, offering us a light-hearted, self-referential song in English, probably intended for the polyglot audiences in Freetown portside bars. Enticingly, the ensemble is almost exactly the same, solo vocals sometimes twinned

FIGURE 4.9 *Grupo OK Jazz in a recording session (1961).*

with back-up vocals, a plucked string instrument, in this case a banjo, and a rhythmic pattern tapped out on a bottle. Recorded in the 1950s, this song is a reflection of the influx of Caribbean styles and rhythms across West Africa in the 1930s and 1940s where, as the liner notes to Marvellous Boy tell us, "a sound interchangeably designated 'calypso' or 'highlife' ruled urban dancefloors."

In the 1960s, *són* had become firmly established in West Africa travelling under the catch-all name "rumba." One of the foremost and successful exponents was Grand Kalle Et l'African Jazz. Led by the soaring vocals of bandleader Joseph Kabasele and the crisp solo electric guitar of Dr. Nico Kasanda, their song "Mama Ngai Habanera" highlights the arrival of a particular type of cosmopolitan modernity in West Africa (Figure 4.9). The song explicitly linked the vibrant music scene of colonial Kinshasa and Brazzaville to a wider world through the sought-after electric guitar and horns. Again, we hear the same cyclical patterns of melody and harmony, interlocking rhythmic patterns tethering all of the members of the ensemble together, and a larger structure of call-and-response leading us from beginning to end.

What we can learn from these three songs is an important lesson about how musicians and their audiences were linked together across the Atlantic Ocean in the colonial era. Each song was recorded in a different decade from the others, they were recorded in different countries by people who had no direct contact with one another. The musical materials they made use of reached them through common, but distinct, pathways of migration, trade, and politics. All of these musicians were part of much larger and more forceful tides of history and culture than any one person could navigate alone. However, if we listen carefully these songs tell us about the expressive and social commonalities that linked millions of people across multiple decades and generations in many towns, cites, regions, and countries. We would do well to listen to what they are telling us.

INDEPENDENT RESEARCH WORK

West African popular music has had long-standing and productive connections with France, the United Kingdom, the Caribbean, and the North America. The types of music that have been shaped from these many years of contact are very numerous. Examine the writings of scholars, critics, and historians and choose one tradition (or "genre") of music and examine the cross-Atlantic connections that shaped and produced it. Be sure to listen very closely to the music attributes this music shares with other related styles that preceded and succeeded it. Be sure that you don't simply base your argument on things that sound similar, but also make sure you can point to tangible incidents of contact that might be responsible for the forms of mutual influence that produced that music.

References and further readings

Denning, Michael. (2015) *Noise Uprising: The Audiopolitics of a World Musical Revolution*. London: Verso.

Erlmann, V. (2003) "Communities of Style: Musical Figures of Black Diasporic Identity." In From I. Monson (ed.), *The African Diaspora: A Musical Perspective*. New York: Routledge, 83–99.

Gilroy, Paul. (1993) *The Black Atlantic: Modernity and Double Consciousness*. Cambridge, MA: Harvard University Press.

Gronow, Pekka. (1981) "The Record Industry Comes to the Orient." *Ethnomusicology*, 25(2): 251–84.

Gronow, Pekka. (1983) "The Record Industry: The Growth of a Mass Medium." *Popular Music*, 3: 53–75.

Lubinski, Christina. (2012) "The Global business with Local Music: Western Gramophone Companies in India Before World War 1." *Bulletin of the GHI*, 51: 67–85.

Prentice, W., and N. Steinke. (2013) "How the Great Gramophone Companies Fought to Control Central Asia." *ABC* (Australia). http://www.abc.net.au/radionational/ programs/intothemusic/4842682.

Stewart, Gary. (2000) *Rumba on the River: A History of the Popular Music of the Two Congos*. London: Verso.

Discography

Before The Revolution: A 1909 Recording Expedition In The Caucasus & Central Asia By The Gramophone Company. (2002) London: Topic Records. TSCD921.

Living Is Hard: West African Music In Britain, 1927-1929. London: Honest Jon's Records. HJRLP33.

Sprigs Of Time: 78s From The EMI Archive. London: Honest Jon's Records. HJRLP36.

PART TWO

Bigger, better, louder, longer, 1930 to 1970

KEY READING

Rock 'n' Film: Cinema's Dance with Popular Music

David E. James

Introduction

Forty years after the 1913 premiere of Stravinsky's *Le Sacre du Printemps*, a musical event of even greater significance occurred. On the evening of Thursday July 8, 1954, the test acetate of Elvis Presley's record "That's All Right" was first played on Memphis radio station WHBQ. Both works incorporated musical elements then considered primitive, and responses to both were passionate: riotously mixed for Stravinsky but, on this occasion at least, so uniformly fervent for Elvis that his song was broadcast some eleven times on the show. But their differences in other respects now appear as signal announcements of the distinct cultural regimes that respectively dominated the first and the second halves of the twentieth century in the transatlantic West: a live orchestral performance of European music accompanying a ballet for an haute bourgeois audience in the one case, and in the other the mass dissemination of a recording that amalgamated black and white working-class US musics; an art music constructed in difference from all the new forms of industrial culture over which cinema already presided in the one case, and in the other a vernacular music that would soon replace cinema as the medium in dominance and would invalidate previous cultural hierarchies of high and low.[1]

Rock 'n' roll's emergence coincided with the enormous expansion of industrial culture in the North Atlantic countries and the integration of its various branches. Until then, cinema had been the most prestigious

"Introduction," in *Rock 'n' Film: Cinema's Dance with Popular Music* by David E. James (2016), pp. 1–22. By permission of Oxford University Press, USA.

component and indeed the twentieth century's paramount art form, hierarchically ranked above radio and television, though already locked in struggle with the latter. While initially appearing as a threat to both conglomerated culture and the social status quo, the new form of popular music quickly infiltrated both. Until the emergence of new forms of visuality in the digital revolution at the turn of the next century, music became the fulcrum of the media industries. Technological innovations gave it a unique mobility that allowed an initial cultural product to be activated and redeployed across all other media. Circulating on records and radio, "That's All Right," for example, (p.2) became a regional hit, even as Elvis and his musicians toured the South to promote it and then make more records. Their dissemination, especially in television appearances, made him a national phenomenon, and Hollywood called: "Hollywood is the next move, you know. That's what happens: you get a record and then you get on television and then you go to Hollywood," he remarked, " So I made *Love Me Tender,* then I did *Loving You.*"[2] Initially performed on television on the Ed Sullivan Show, "Love Me Tender" had received enough advance orders by the next day it to make it a gold record and to cause the film to be retitled after it. Elvis went on to make another thirty features in Hollywood, creating a virtually autonomous genre that made him the most valuable movie star of his time.

As popular music threatened its hegemony in conglomerated industrial culture, cinema was forced to compete, sometimes to attack or attempt to contain or take revenge upon upstart rock 'n' roll, but more often to incorporate, enhance, or celebrate it in the creation of hybrid audio-visual forms. Always something of the power of the live music was lost, but much more was gained: the amplification of the sonic component, its visual elaboration in narrative or other spectacular forms, and the reciprocal promotion and dissemination of the two component mediums. As film and as cinema, rock 'n' roll danced in and with the movies.

Rock

When modes of music change, the fundamental laws of the State always change with them. . . . Lawlessness too easily steals in. . . . Little by little this spirit of license, finding a home, imperceptibly penetrates into manners and customs.

PLATO, *The Republic*

Rock 'n' roll had many beginnings and has had many definitions. The origin of the phrase is presently dated to 1916, only three years after *Le Sacre du Printemps,* in the lines "We've been rockin' an' rollin' in your arms/

in the arms of Moses" from "The Camp Meeting Jubilee," performed by an anonymous African American quartet on Little Wonder records.[3] After Trixie Smith's 1922 more fleshly "My Man Rocks Me (With One Steady Roll)," in the 1930s and 1940s the term traveled as a metaphor for both divine and carnal love through religious and secular black music: blues, gospel, boogie woogie, and eventually "rhythm and blues," that replaced the more abrupt "race music" category in *Billboard*'s chart listings in 1949. A frankly erotic jump, "Rock and Roll Blues," written and recorded in 1949 by an African American woman, Erline "Rock and Roll" Harris, was one of a cluster of similar proto–rock 'n' roll songs around the turn of the decade that also included Wynonie Harris's (p.3) "Good Rockin' Tonight" (1948) and Ike Turner's "Rocket 88" (1951), the latter recorded by Sam Phillips at Sun, his small, independent studio in Memphis. In the early 1950s white groups began recording similar material, most notably Bill Haley, leader of a Western Swing combo, who covered "Rocket 88" in 1951; and then in 1954, as Bill Haley & His Comets, his cover of "(We're Gonna) Rock Around the Clock" became a huge success. Three months later, on July 5, 1954, and again at Sun, Phillips produced Elvis's "That's All Right," his version of a song written and first recorded in 1946 by Delta blues singer Arthur Crudup as "That's All Right, Mama." The record was backed with "Blue Moon of Kentucky," a bluegrass waltz by Bill Monroe, also written in 1946.[4]

These and related musical innovations in the years between the end of World War II and the mid-1950s coincided with fundamental transformations in US society and the music industry. The steady rise of disposable income during the postwar economic boom produced unprecedented freedoms for young people, including African Americans. Panic about juvenile delinquency accompanied the emergence of teenagers as a distinct demographic with their own independent economic power. By early 1956, the average teenager's weekly income equaled the disposable income of the average US family fifteen years earlier, allowing them to spend $75 million annually on records.[5] The migration of African Americans introduced Southern musical culture to Northern urban centers, as did the wider dissemination on mainstream radio of rhythm and blues records, which were not regulated by the American Society of Composers, Authors and Publishers (ASCAP) and hence could be played royalty-free. Radio stations with all-African American on-air personnel, exclusively programming black music, emerged, notably Nat D. Williams at WDIA in Memphis; and the airwaves were integrated by white DJs playing black music, most notably Alan Freed with the "Moondog House" at WJW in Cleveland in 1951, and Dewey Phillips with the "Red Hot & Blue" show on WHBQ in 1952, where "That's All Right" was first broadcast. The increasing numbers of white teenagers listening to such shows quickly led to black and white dancers mixing in theaters and nightclubs in advance of other forms of desegregation. As the popularity of both the 33⅓ rpm 12″ LP and the 45 rpm 7″ single, introduced respectively in 1948 and 1949, grew, so independent record companies outside the majors proliferated.[6] The Fender Telecaster, the first mass-marketed solid-body electric guitar, appeared in 1950, and the transistor radio four years later. These combined social and musical developments produced exchanges between black and white cultures that inspired rapture in many teenagers and consternation in almost everyone else.

The consternation focused on working-class delinquency and especially racial mixing. By mid-1955, less than a year after "That's All Right" and with *Blackboard Jungle* (Richard Brooks, 1955), the first film that included a rock 'n' roll (p.4) record in release, the controversy was at its height. A three-page spread in *Life* emphasizing the music's associations with African Americans and manic dancing pegged the phenomenon:

ROCK N' ROLL

A frenzied teen-age music craze kicks up a big fuss

The nation's teenagers are dancing their way into an enlarging controversy over rock n' roll. In New Haven, Conn., the police chief has put a damper on rock n' roll parties and other towns are following suit. Radio networks are worried over questionable lyrics in rock n' roll. And some American parents, without quite knowing what it is their kids are up to, are worried that it's something they shouldn't be.

Rock n' roll is both music and dance. The music has a rhythm often heavily accented on the second and fourth beat. The dance combines the Lindy and Charleston, and almost anything else. In performing it, hollering helps and a boot banging the floor makes it even better. The over-all-result, frequently, is frenzy.

A QUESTION OF QUESTIONABLE MEANINGS

The heavy beat and honking-melody tunes of today's rock n' roll have a clearly defined ancestry in US jazz going back to Louis Armstrong and Bessie Smith of 30 years ago. Once called "race" records, and later "rhythm and blues," the music was first performed by Negroes and sold mostly in Negro communities.[7]

Accompanying the text was a small photograph of the New Haven police chief in question, followed by much larger ones of the teenagers, mostly white but some black, as they danced in a Los Angeles parking lot, in Brooklyn's Paramount Theater, and at a mock-up of an ice-cream parlor in a San Francisco television studio, along with images of the music that inspired them: the Fats Domino Band in a Los Angeles ballroom and Alan Freed spinning discs. The photo essay succinctly assembled the crucial issues: on the one hand, close on the 1954 Supreme Court decision that mandated public school integration, a musical innovation bringing blacks and whites and their respective cultures together, projecting itself as unruly dance and provocative words, or what a subsequent paragraph referred to as the "frequently suggestive and occasionally lewd" "leerics" that implied even more promiscuous forms of physical abandon; and on the other, the fears of disorder that the errant teenagers aroused in the police and in the media industry. Large numbers of musicians, sociologists, educators, politicians, and parents in the mid-1950s believed that rock 'n' roll led only to lawlessness and license. Its lyrics mocked propriety; its rhythms ignited promiscuous physical liberties; and its attitudinizing occupied the body and the mind, manners and customs.

(p.5) Less circumspect than *Life,* other arbiters addressed the threat of African American culture directly. After six rock 'n' rolling teenagers were arrested in 1956, also in Connecticut, and a hundred more were ejected from a theater, a psychiatrist diagnosed the "cannibalistic and tribalistic" music as a "communicable disease."[8] White resistance to race mixing was especially strong in the South and, the same year, *Newsweek* reported a declaration made by Asa Carter, head of the White Citizens Councils of Alabama, that "rock and roll music is the basic, heavy-beat music of Negroes. It appeals to the base in man [and] brings out animalism and vulgarity."[9]

Even when they avoided racial issues, assessments made by many mainstream musicians also returned to social implications. Not long after Sammy Davis had volunteered that "[i]f rock 'n' roll is here to stay, I might commit suicide," no less an authority on popular music—and veteran of rioting fans—than his pal Frank Sinatra was reported to have declared that "[r]ock 'n' roll smells phony and false. It is sung, played and written for the most part by cretinous goons and by means of its almost imbecilic reiteration, and sly, lewd, in plain fact, dirty lyrics . . . it manages to be the martial music of every side-burned delinquent on the face of the earth."[10] However nostalgic it may seem today, Sinatra's execration typified the consternation. In rock 'n' roll, musical and social delinquencies were intertwined, each the other's cause and manifestation.

For the next thirty years, public discussions of rock 'n' roll were primarily sociological, almost all of them reiterating Sinatra's accusations of amalgamated transgressions.[11] As 1950s disturbances metamorphosed into 1960s cultural rebellion, the associations between music and delinquency were reconstructed. The evolved rock 'n' roll of sixties' youth was understood by its critics as the clarion call of a generation in ungodly, drug-inspired revolt; and as the countercultures disintegrated in the early seventies, heavy metal, glam, reggae, early disco, and other innovations prompted charges of new depravities that flourished until mid-decade, when punk and rap offered even more spectacular forms of deviance. But for its enthusiasts, rock's power was limitless and all-enfolding. A 1967 paean in the *San Francisco Oracle,* for example, proposed that "far from being degenerate or decadent, rock is a regenerative & revolutionary art, offering us our first real hope for the future. . . . rock seems to have synthesized most of the intellectual & artistic movements of our time & culture, cross-fertilizing them & forcing them rapidly toward fruition and function. . . . [and] any artistic activity not allied to rock is doomed to preciousness and sterility."[12] Many believed that the music's domination of other arts made it an autonomous cultural agency. Writing in the same year during the "Summer of Love," Ralph J. Gleason, a San Francisco music critic and one of the cofounders of the magazine *Rolling Stone,* introduced his article on the period's cultural transformation in a mainstream (p.6) journal, *The American Scholar,* with an aphorism of his own coining: "For the reality of what's happening today in America, we must go to rock 'n' roll, to popular music."[13] And the following spring, only days before the Democratic National Convention in Chicago, Jann Wenner, his *Rolling Stone* cofounder, argued that "[r]ock and roll is the *only* way in which the vast but formless power of youth is structured, the only way in which it can be defined or inspected. . . . It has its own unique meaning, its own unique style and its own unique morality."[14]

Wenner's argument was designed to keep rock free of political involvement, safe from a "self-appointed coterie of political 'radicals' without a legitimate constituency."[15] But the radicals also testified to the importance of rock 'n' roll and of black music generally in sowing disruption among the materialism and conformity of the Eisenhower era. Summarizing the importance of black music and black dance, civil rights leader Eldridge Cleaver declared, "The Twist was a guided missile, launched from the ghetto into the very heart of suburbia. The Twist succeeded, as politics, religion, and law could never do, in writing in the heart and soul what the Supreme Court could only write on the books."[16] And white radicals elaborated a similar historical trajectory, repeating all but verbatim the earliest critics' arguments, but positively transvaluing them. Jerry Rubin, Yippie publicist and the immediate target of Wenner's wrath, for example, claimed that "the New Left sprang, a predestined pissed-off child, from Elvis' gyrating pelvis," and that "hard animal rock energy beat/surged through us, the driving rhythm arousing repressed passions." He also recognized the affluence and the new ancillary technologies that allowed those passions' release: "The back seat produced the sexual revolution, and the car radio was the medium for subversion."[17] The synthesis of black and white vernacular music had been ongoing since the melodies and harmonies of British hymns had first been married to African timbres and rhythms in the earliest days of slavery; but the new conjunction of them in rock 'n' roll promoted a cultural revolution and a revolution in the ways in which mainstream US popular music was composed, recorded, performed, and experienced. It transformed the mode of musical production.[18]

Modes of production

Since the 1930s the major source of US popular music had been the Great American Songbook, written almost exclusively by a small group of professional musicians and lyricists based in New York, and disseminated by stage shows, film musicals, radio, and sheet music, the last providing the basis for popular musical performance around the family piano. The market for sheet music collapsed by the late 1950s, and its role in disseminating popular music was superseded by records; rock 'n' roll became popular as recordings that variously combined the two, originally performative, (p.7) black and white folk traditions that had also long been industrialized. Blues was commercially recorded as early as 1920 with Mamie Smith's "Crazy Blues"; and, spurred in fact by race music's commercial success, hillbilly music very soon followed with Vernon Dalhart's hit, "Wreck of Old 97," recorded in 1924 and selling over a million copies. The Brill Building pop music composers continued to be important well into the sixties, but rock 'n' roll was increasingly composed by the individuals and small groups who performed it, live and on records.

After the singer-songwriters of the early 1960s folk boom, and especially as the Beatles began to follow Bob Dylan's conspicuously personal songwriting, the individualist "handicraft" element in rock 'n' roll's composition achieved a greater control over its manufacture and allowed it to claim a personal expressivity parallel to jazz and classical music but unprecedented in popular music.[19] In addition, this organic popular music was largely decentralized, developing provincially in New Orleans, Memphis, and other places in the South, but also in Philadelphia, Los Angeles, and Chicago—and, of course, later in Liverpool and Manchester. And most of it was initially recorded, not by major corporations, but in small, independent studios, with the records distributed by local independent labels. Beginning in 1953, the number of record labels finding a place in the US weekly top ten dramatically increased from 12 to highs of 46 in 1959, and 52 in 1962 and 1963, to reach a highpoint of 53 in 1964, before beginning a decline that accelerated after 1970.[20] Though many independent recording and distribution agencies were eventually assimilated by large corporations, early rock 'n' roll's radical innovations and diversity were most often inaugurated by performers themselves and by producers outside the corporate world. But though never separable from amateur and semi-amateur performance, records were rock 'n' roll's fundamental material realization. They, rather than live performances, were the staple of radio dissemination, and through the 1950s, nightclub, concert, and television live performances aimed to reproduce the record as closely as possible. Records were similarly the basis for many of rock 'n' roll's ancillary cultural products and venues, including album jackets, record players, jukeboxes, and record stores; and in early feature films, artists almost invariably lip-synced to records.

Records replaced sheet music, family listening around the phonograph replaced singing songs around the piano, and, as generationally restricted musical tastes crystallized, younger family members listened individually in different rooms or in coffee bars and similarly youth-oriented venues. But rock 'n' roll's musical simplicity and the relative cheapness of the required instruments allowed such consumption of commodity music to flower easily into amateur and semi-amateur performance and composition. From the beginning, popular practices not administered from above intersected with, nourished, and contested industrial forms of rock 'n' roll, reviving the (p.8) characteristics of pre-capitalist music. So, proposing that rock 'n' roll marked a return to the itinerant minstrelsy of the jongleurs, Jacques Attali emphasized that it entailed

> a resurgence of music for immediate enjoyment, for daily communication, rather than for a confined spectacle. No study is required to play this kind of music, which is orally transmitted and largely improvisational. It is thus accessible to everyone, breaking the barrier raised by an apprenticeship in the code and the instrument. It has developed among all social classes, but in particular among those most oppressed (the workers of the big industrial cities, Black American ghettos . . .). The number of small orchestras of amateurs who play for free has mushroomed. Music is thus becoming a daily adventure and an element of the subversive festival again.[21]

As teenagers themselves became involved in production rather than merely consuming music produced for them by adults, rock 'n' roll's expanded popular musical practices introduced new cultural possibilities. As Jim Curtis observed, "For the first time, teenagers singing for teenagers about being teenagers constituted a major force in American popular music."[22]

The musical practices that emerged in the mid-fifties were never entirely free from industrial encroachment, but nor were they controlled by it. By the mid-sixties, the primacy of amateur innovation and the countercultural ideal of the dissolution of the boundary between performers and audience encouraged the belief that, even if elements of rock 'n' roll continued to be industrialized, popular investment and participation in it and in popular rituals organized around it could transcend alienated social relations to make it a modern *folk* music. Almost anyone could compose a song, perform it, and record it. And any song could be realized by a girl or boy *a cappella* in the shower or with a guitar alone or with friends; as a record played on a phonograph in a bedroom, on a jukebox in a bar, on a radio in a car; by a band in a garage or in a recording studio, and simulated by a band at a concert or covered by a different band on record or in concert, and so on. All these forms of musical production existed before rock 'n' roll, but with rock 'n' roll, the active, performative components multiplied and proliferated, often using industrialization to their own advantage. The multidirectional circulation of innovations and appropriations between the amateur and commercial extremes and in various intermediary modes of production in this expanded musical economy never eliminated the distinctions between producer and consumer, but it did make them much more porous, contradictory, and subject to local popular intervention.

The many reciprocal interactions between folk and the industry among which rock 'n' roll was created reconfigured the concept of the popular: "popular" as an indicator of mass consumption turned like a Mobius strip around the "popular" as a reflection of a newly vitalized role for the working class as (p. 9) cultural producers. In the circulation of music and its associated rituals, individual, subcultural, and commercial modes of production interacted more thoroughly than in any previous epoch, leading critics in the mid-1960s in the United Kingdom to recognize that "teenage culture is a contradictory mixture of the authentic and the manufactured; it is an area of self-expression for the young and a lush grazing pasture for the commercial providers."[23] Tin Pan Alley and the American Songbook's domination of popular song waned, and the consuming public began to have a more comprehensive and generative influence over music than any other form of modern culture. Rock 'n' roll inaugurated new forms of *music,* new *modes of musical production,* and new socio-musical regimes in which multiple modes of musical production, from the completely amateur to the completely industrial, interpenetrated and reciprocally sustained each other. Buoyed and enlivened by the various forms of popular participation during both production and consumption of music and its associated culture, the belief that popular expressivity could command commercially produced music without losing its autonomy and power made it the most important art in the period of resurgent populist politics in the two decades after the mid-1950s. Equivalent forms of popular empowerment were to a degree achieved in other mediums, especially in journalism and underground cinema in the United States; but no other industrialized medium matched music's capacity for popular participation and popular control. No other medium carried such an unalienated utopian promise; but because that utopian center was surrounded and besieged by equally radical and extensive new forms of incorporation, its utopian and dystopian components were inextricably combined.

The interdependency of popular participatory culture and the commodity industrial culture constructed upon it was the comprehensive form of rock 'n' roll's many dualities, assimilating its constituent tensions between black and white, blues and hillbilly, individual and community, male and female, noir rebellion and sunshine fun, and eventually Britain and the United States. All the questions about generational self-expression and the social meaning of music became central to rock 'n' roll's own self-consciousness: debated in its lyrics, enacted in its performance, dissected by its polemicists, and dramatized in other cultural forms. But nowhere was it more crucially an issue than in films about rock 'n' roll, where these innovations were dramatized in different ways, in various modes of film production, in various cinemas.

A cultural gestalt

Rock 'n' roll's early supporters and detractors agreed that the pulsing rhythms inherited from big band swing and juke joints reflected its most immediate function, that of facilitating popular dance. Often denigrated for its emphasis on sonic properties outside the parameters of conventional musicology, (p.10) rock 'n' roll was experienced somatically as much as heard or understood. Its communicative and affective contents were completed, not in the ear or the mind, but in the whole body, especially below the waist, so that dancing was the most fundamental of most fans' performance of rock 'n' roll. As such, it was integrated into a range of associated activities and objects, a total culture in which meaning was produced in the everyday interaction between the sounds themselves and the popular use of them. Music—making it, hearing it, dancing to it, and talking about it—was certainly rock 'n' roll's primary and most essential ritual activity. But the music was lived and its meanings elaborated and performed in multiple private and social practices of everyday life: in dance steps and styles, body language, and posture; in hairstyles, clothes, shoes, accessories, and ornaments; in argot and catch-phrases; in photographs, posters, record covers, magazines, fanzines, and graphic styles; in musical instruments, concerts, records, transistor radios, radio and television shows, and cinema; in soda fountains, high-school hops, youth clubs, and concerts; in hot rods and motorcycles; indeed, in almost anything that its community did or imagined or made, bought, or desired. Far from being merely ancillary to rock 'n' roll, these constellations of subjectivities, rituals, communities, and commodities were intrinsic to it, and all had strong visual components.[24] As popular use of rock 'n' roll interpreted the music and reframed it, it also *recomposed* it. All forms of music have to some degree realized themselves materially and socially in equivalent events and observances; but the elaboration of rock 'n' roll into a complete cultural syntax was immediate and richly inter-articulated. Rock 'n' roll culture was from its inception a social production, made and lived communally, and continually renewing itself environmentally as a total cultural gestalt.

Since its beginning, rock 'n' roll has then been almost as much a complex of visual as of auditory cultural innovations, a field of integrally interdependent sight and sound. Experienced synesthetically, heard in the eyes and seen in the ears, its audio-visuality has been elaborated in the visuality of its musical forms and in the musicality of its visual forms.[25] Rock 'n' roll's visuality developed during its first two decades in many forms of popular culture, especially in three industrialized media: print, television, and cinema.[26] Cinema indeed projected some of its essential elements, even before music realized them. "Live fast, die young, and leave a good-looking corpse," the credo of John Derek's Nick Romano in *Knock on Any Door* (Nicholas Ray, 1949) was echoed by Marlon Brando in *The Wild One* (Laslo Benedek, 1953), by Sinatra himself in *The Man with the Golden Arm* (Otto Preminger, 1955), and then by James Dean in *Rebel Without a Cause* (Nicholas Ray, 1955); all variously dramatized new forms of angst, rebellion, narcissism, generational division, and the determination to run amok at any price.[27] But as well as introducing initial rock 'n' roll iconographies, cinema collaborated in the scandal of its mass emergence; with *Blackboard Jungle*, rock 'n' roll and the (p.11) rock 'n' roll film became global phenomena, and since then musical and cinematic developments have tracked each other, sustaining a synergistic combination of aesthetic, social, and commercial vitality. Cinema has not been merely a supplement to music in rock 'n' roll culture, but one of the means by which it has existed, one of the modes of rock 'n' roll production.

'n' Film

. . . we are made to recognize the tremendous split, in origins and purposes, between the visual, Apollonian arts and the non-visual art of music, the Dionysian. The two creative tendencies developed alongside one another, usually in fierce opposition, each forcing the other to more energetic production.

FRIEDRICH NIETZSCHE, *The Birth of Tragedy*

For a quarter of a century after the early 1930s, the musical was the queen of Hollywood genres, with the films of Busby Berkeley at Warners, Fred Astair and Ginger Rogers at RKO, Jeanette MacDonald and Nelson Eddy's operettas followed by Judy Garland and Mickey Rooney at MGM being among the most prestigious and remunerative of the era. In the 1940s, the Freed unit at MGM took the genre to its Golden Age with the fully integrated singing, acting, and dancing of the Technicolor integrated book musical, culminating in *Oklahoma* (Fred Zinnemann, 1955). With sound, the movies had become the major means of disseminating popular songs, both those composed for Broadway musicals that were subsequently filmed and those written by the studio's own teams of lyricists; by 1990 some 25,000 popular songs had been introduced or reprised in Hollywood films.[28] But no sooner did rock 'n' roll appear than its integration in cinema began, and the rock 'n' roll film emerged as simultaneously a break with the Hollywood musical and a renewal of it, the decline of the one punctually coinciding with the emergence, though on a smaller scale, of the other.[29]

"When is a musical not a musical?" asked Rick Altman, the foremost historian of the film musical, before answering his question with: "When it has Elvis Presley in it."[30] Though at least partly facetious, his axiom flags the rupture between the classic musical and its rock 'n' roll successor. After Elvis appeared in 1954, stellar productions including *High Society* (Charles Walters, 1956), and *Silk Stockings* (Rouben Mamoulian, 1957) extended the musical's Golden Age. And *West Side Story* (Jerome Robbins and Robert Wise, 1961), *My Fair Lady* (George Cukor, 1964) (both symptomatically concerned with working-class delinquency) and other important musicals were produced in the next decade; but by the mid-fifties the genre had essentially run its course. A week after the release of Elvis's second film, *Loving You* (Hal Kanter, 1957), (p.12) Fred Astaire announced as much in *Silk Stockings,* crushing his signature top-hat at the conclusion of his rock 'n' roll parody, "The Ritz Roll and Rock" (added to the film from the 1955 stage show) and retiring from musicals on the film's release.[31] The new musical culture quickly created its own narratives and generic conventions, but rock 'n' roll films were constructed from the three main subgenres of earlier film musicals: the revue, the backstage musical, and the biopic.[32]

Along with operettas and comedies, the revue was one of the most important forms of early musical film. Adopting the format of vaudeville and burlesque stage shows and especially of the Ziegfeld Follies, most studios brought their contracted singing, dancing, comedy, and novelty acts together in films: MGM's *The Hollywood Review Revue of 1929* (Charles F. Reisner, 1929), Warner Brothers' *The Show of Shows* (John G. Adolfi, 1929), Paramount's *Paramount on Parade* (Dorothy Arzner, Otto Brower, and Ernst Lubitsch, 1930), and Universal's *King of Jazz* (John Murray Anderson, 1930). These revues were introduced by a presenter, whose repartee linked the various numbers, implying that they were taking place sequentially in real time and space. *The Hollywood Revue of 1929,* for example, featured large choruses of dancers along with a "Galaxy of Stars," including Joan Crawford, Stan Laurel and Oliver Hardy, and Bessie Love, who earned a nomination for the Academy Award for Best Actress. Separated from each other by curtain falls, their various musical, comedy, and dramatic numbers were linked by interactions among Jack Benny and two other masters of ceremonies, who themselves also performed. All the acts took place on a proscenium stage with the camera mostly placed front and center but capable of switching among long and medium shots and close-ups, and distinctly cinematic special effects enriched many of them. The opening dance routine, the "Palace of Minstrels," for example, featured a large chorus of dancers in elaborate, contrasting black and white costumes with the boys in blackface; it was periodically thrown into negative to reverse the tones, and at one point

Bessie Love appears in miniature out of Jack Benny's pocket. Photography of several dance routines anticipated Busby Berkeley's overhead shots of patterns of female bodies, as well as his pans along lines of faces. Three of the numbers were presented in two-strip Technicolor, including a section from Shakespeare's *Romeo and Juliet* performed by Gilbert and Shearer, and the finale, "Singin' in the Rain," was performed by the entire cast underneath a huge ark and rainbow. Concomitant with their prioritizing audio-visual spectacle, the revues lacked any narrative, apart from that supplied by the presenters. The genre survived its decline after the early 1930s by becoming internalized in the narrative of the second subgenre, backstage musicals; stories about people involved in the production of a revue or some other kind of show brought narrative and spectacle to play upon each other.

(p.13) Like classic musicals generally, backstage musicals contained two distinct filmic modes, a *narrative* that formed a matrix inside which the *spectacle* of songs and dance, called units or numbers, was set. Though song lyrics or other elements within the narrative may organically motivate and justify the spectacle to create an *integrated* musical, the spectacle typically interrupts the narrative and arrests its forward momentum, developing its implications in an entirely different register.[33] Even when they include a heterosexual romance, the narratives of other classic Hollywood genres are linear and are focused on one main protagonist, following the causally linked sequence of his setbacks and successes to a resolution that coincides with the closure of the other narrative elements. But, Rick Altman has argued, the musical typically contains two paired protagonists, a boy and a girl, juvenile and ingénue, representing antithetical values between whom the narrative alternates to create a "dual focus" that is successfully resolved in their marriage and the reconciliation of the values they each represent.[34] In the mid-1930s, preeminently in the sequence of musicals for which Busby Berkeley designed the numbers, the narrative recounts attempts to put on a Broadway show. The performers include a leading boy and girl who fall in love, and their romantic involvements run parallel to their efforts to stage the show, coming to a conclusion in which both are resolved simultaneously. Often, several numbers are stacked together at the end of the film, much like an interpolated revue that provides a dazzling conclusion in which the boy's expression of love to his girl in the show simultaneously completes their commitment to each other in the narrative of the show's production.

Backstage musicals as celebrated as *Footlight Parade* (Lloyd Bacon, 1933), *Stage Door Canteen* (Frank Borzage, 1943), and *The Band Wagon* (Vincente Minnelli, 1953) indicate the genre's enduring stability before the emergence of rock 'n' roll. Effectively inaugurated with *The Broadway Melody* (Harry Beaumont, 1929), the first musical to win the Academy Award for Best Picture and a huge moneymaker for MGM, the backstage musical flowered with *42nd Street* (Lloyd Bacon, 1933), *Gold Diggers of 1933* (Mervyn Le Roy, 1933), and other early 1930s Warner Brothers films, before passing though several permutations. Fred Astaire's late-1930s films with Ginger Rogers at RKO modified the genre in that the narratives do not revolve around putting on a show; the dance routines take place in real-world environments rather than in a theater; they were fully integrated into the plot; and they were filmed as much as possible as a single shot with a stationary camera for, as Astaire insisted, "Either the camera will dance, or I will."[35] But still, Astaire plays a professional dancer, and the films usually end in an especially spectacular number: "The Continental" in *The Gay Divorcee* (Mark Sandrich, 1934), for example. The genre continued in Arthur Freed's MGM "Backyard Musical" series in which younger kids put on a show for a charity of some kind. Starring Mickey Rooney and Judy Garland, and directed in their entirety by Berkeley, these included (p.14) *Babes in Arms* (1939), where Rooney's "Let's put on a show in the barn" was first heard, *Strike Up the Band* (1940), and *Babes on Broadway* (1941). In *Strike Up the Band,* for example, the pair are graduating high-school seniors, with Rooney's character, Jimmy, the drummer for the school's marching band. Hoping eventually to lead a "modern dance orchestra" like Paul Whiteman's, Jimmy uses his band to put on a school dance, and then wins a radio contest sponsored by Whiteman, all the while featuring Garland as his vocalist. The overall narrative, some specific motifs, and the attraction of a new especially rhythmic dance music very clearly anticipate the rock 'n' roll films of the next decade,[36] though the complete absence of intergenerational tension and of delinquency or real sexuality mark a difference, as do the superior production values, especially in Berkeley's sumptuous numbers.

Any backstage musical inevitably generates patterns of similarity and difference between the film itself and the musical show it depicts, and hence implications about the differences between and relations among film, stage show, and even song. *The Broadway Melody,* for example, is quintuply rich in these terms, with the title phrase designating the film, the stage musical whose production it narrates, the title song (which contributed enormously to the film's popularity), the cultural institution that produces the musical, and the physical space in which it occurs: "A million lights they flicker there/A million hearts beat quicker there/No skies of grey on the Great White Way/That's the Broadway Melody." The same polyvalence recurs in films featuring rock songs that are themselves about rock 'n' roll: "Jailhouse Rock" designates the song, the dance number, the event in the county jail, and the film about all of them, while "Ziggy Stardust and the Spiders from Mars" similarly references the song, band, stage show, and film. Such interlaced references produce what Jane Feuer categorized as the "self-reflective musical," and the kind of reflexivity she finds in the classic musical are fundamental to the rock 'n' roll film.[37]

Feuer argues that a recurrent subgenre of backstage musicals involves "kids (or adults) 'getting together and putting on a show,'"[38] and that the show they put on has an ideological function within the film as a whole. Invoking a distinction between "folk art" and "mass art" derived from the best of the early attempts to theorize pop music,[39] she suggests that the depiction of the represented show as "folk art" impedes the audiences' consciousness of the commodity nature of the musical film itself and of the alienated social relations between producer and consumer in capitalist cinema ("mass art"):

> The Hollywood musical as a genre perceives the gap between producer and consumer, the breakdown of community designated by the very distinction between performer and audience, as a form of cinematic original sin. The musical seeks to bridge the gap by putting up "community" as an ideal concept. In basing its value system on community, the producing (p.15) and consuming functions severed by the passage of musical entertainment from folk to popular to mass status are rejoined through the genre's rhetoric. The musical, always reflecting back on itself, tries to compensate for its double whammy of alienation by creating humanistic "folk" relations in the films; these folk relations in turn act to cancel out the economic values and relations associated with mass-produced art. Through such a rhetorical exchange, the creation of folk relations *in* the films cancels the mass entertainment substance *of* the films. The Hollywood musical becomes a mass art which aspires to the condition of folk art, produced and consumed by the same integrated community.[40]

Rather than creating Brechtian or other forms of modernist distanciation, Feuer continues, reflexive devices in the prewar backstage musical films promote a sense of community by narratively including surrogate intradiegetic audiences and emphasizing spontaneity and populist performance. After the late 1940s, the musical becomes increasingly reflexive, and the represented shows often portray the singers and dancers as themselves amateurs and emphasize motifs, settings, and incidents invoking earlier American folk communities, as in *Oklahoma* or *Seven Brides for Seven Brothers,* for example. These form a subgenre within the backstage musical, the folk musical that "reeks with nostalgia for America's mythical communal past even as the musical itself exemplifies the new, alienated mass art."[41]

The structure of the backstage musical was fundamental to the rock 'n' roll film from its beginnings through the 1960s until the emergence of the filmed rock opera in the mid-1970s. Parallel strategies of rhetorically presenting rock 'n' roll *as folk art in the film* as a means of concealing the commodity nature of *the film itself* were facilitated overall by the music's considerable folk elements. In periods when rock 'n' roll claims to be authentic folk music, films about it typically represent it as spontaneous community self-expression, in which the performers are organically linked to the intradiegetic audience and, by implication, to the film's spectators. In so presenting themselves as unmediated extensions of the counterculture, *Woodstock* (Michael Wadleigh, 1970) and other hippie-era festival documentaries similarly conceal their own commodity nature. But films about rock 'n' roll in which the promotion of the ideal of folk authenticity is subordinated to recognition of its commodity nature and industrial production, especially when they focus on recording studios and television, generate different narrative possibilities. Films that are critical of rock 'n' roll, for example, may emphasize an internal distance between themselves and the music; and by depicting rock 'n' roll as itself alienated and the music business as compromised or corrupt, they imply their own superior integrity. *Nashville* (Robert Altman, 1975), for example, presents itself as honorable and so contrary to the degenerate, alienated country music it satirizes. It was preceded by a series of British films, including (p.16) *Expresso Bongo* (Val Guest, 1959), *Privilege* (Peter Watkins, 1967), and *Stardust* (Michael Apted, 1974), that implied their own probity as they dramatized the co-optation of rock 'n' roll by commercial or political interests. Conversely, a series of US films released in 1956–1957, when anxiety about rock 'n' roll was at its height, attempted to justify it, not as authentic folk art, but as an innocuous and viable component of industrial culture: *Don't Knock the Rock* (Fred F. Sears, 1956), *Shake, Rattle & Rock* (Edward L. Cahn, 1956), *Loving You* (Hal Kanter, 1957), and *Mister Rock and Roll* (Charles Dubin, 1957) are important instances. But despite the differences in their analysis of the music, rock 'n' roll backstage musicals were implicitly or explicitly preoccupied with the relationship between the social meaning of the film itself and that of the rock 'n' roll it depicted, and hence the relationship between cinema and popular music generally.

Similar concerns inform the film biography, or biopic, a common subgenre of both classic and rock 'n' roll musicals that replaces the dual narrative of a paired couple with a focus on a single artist. Structurally parallel to the subgenre of films about actors' careers, themselves variants on the Horatio Alger, rags-to-riches movies that began in the early 1920s, the biopic usually dramatizes the "rise to stardom" motif: it narrates a musician's discovery of his or her vocation, struggle for success, eventual attainment of stardom, and either a happy career or a tragic decline. When placed within a narrative of his or her career as a whole, a depiction of a series of performances inevitably involves some appraisal of the musician and the music.[42] The musician may be fictional or real: one of the former, *The Jazz Singer* (Alan Crosland, 1927), inaugurated the feature-length sound film, while *The Jolson Story* (Alfred E. Green, 1946) and its sequel *Jolson Sings Again* (Henry Levin, 1949) are of the latter type, partially fictionalized biographies of its star. After the war, biopics about swing bandleaders became a Hollywood staple with, for example, *The Fabulous Dorseys* (Alfred E. Green, 1947), *The Glenn Miller Story* (Anthony Mann, 1954), and *The Benny Goodman Story* (Valentine Davies, 1956), and as rock 'n' roll displaced swing as the most popular dance music, these segued readily to fictional, semi-fictional, and biographical films about the careers of Buddy Holly, Richie Valens, Ray Charles, Tina Turner, and other rock 'n' roll musicians or groups.[43]

Representation

Adapting its predecessors' motifs and conventions, these three subgenres— revue, backstage musical, and biopic—were the basis of the rock 'n' roll film's reinvention of the musical. Like its precursors, the rock 'n' roll musical narrates the context in which the music is produced, rather than simply using music to embellish narratives set outside it. Its fundamental attractions are the *spectacle* of musical performance and its setting in the *narrative* of (p.17) the performers' back- and offstage lives. The resulting composite film consists of two different modes, each with its specific premises and codes: the essentially documentary nature of the spectacle and the drama of the historical or fictional narrative. The former creates audio-visual compositions that variously depict, amplify, and elaborate musical performance through the mediation of cinema-specific recording technologies and the conventions of editing, special effects, and other cinematic recourses. While letting us hear and see what rock 'n' roll can (be made to) sound and look like, the narrative returns the musicians and the music to their social and historical worlds.

Though any given listener's imagination and capacity for synesthesia ensure that hearing a record is always to some degree also a visual experience, filmic representations of rock 'n' roll performance combine the attenuation of some of its pleasures with the intensification of others. Presence at a live performance enriches the audience/spectator's sensory manifold with multiple forms of audio, visual, somatic, and other pleasures: the auditory presence of music in immediate acoustic space or over a sound system superior to a domestic radio; the excitement attendant on the performance being the chief focus of all senses, rather than being accompanied by or interrupted by other activities; the pleasure of optical, acoustic, and spatial proximity with the artist, intensified by the company and energy of other fans, known and unknown co-enthusiasts who transform a private event into a social ritual; the pleasure of seeing, hearing, and perhaps touching other fans, their bodies, clothes, hair, movements; the pleasure of being seen, heard, or touched by other fans; and perhaps of being seen, of being heard, and even being touched by the performers. Surrogates, initially at least, for being present at an actual musical performance, the audio-visual spectacle that films of rock 'n' roll performance provide is, like other cinematic spectacles, constructed as a play of absence and presence. Replaced by technologies of simulation and illusion, the performers are not actually present; but at the multiple points of photography and audio-recording, editing, printing, publicizing, and finally projection, the apparatuses of cinema reproduce but also transform the original performance, bringing it closer both aurally and optically and providing a presence that may be more powerful than the source event. The musicians appear closer, larger, and in greater detail, and may be heard in high fidelity, clearer, and louder. As Frank Zappa recalled of his seeing—and hearing—*Blackboard Jungle* at the inception of rock 'n' roll film:

> When the titles flashed up there on the screen Bill Haley and his Comets started blurching "One Two Three O'Clock, Four O'Clock Rock. . . ." It was the loudest rock sound kids had ever heard at that time. I remember being inspired with awe. . . . he was playing the Teen-Age National Anthem and it was so LOUD I was jumping up and down. *Blackboard Jungle,* not even considering the story line (which had the old people winning in the end) (p.18) represented a strange sort of "endorsement" of the teen-age cause: "They have made a movie about us, therefore we exist. . . ."[44]

Though teenagers listening to "Rock Around the Clock" hardly appeared in *Blackboard Jungle,* images of fans enjoying the music in rock 'n' roll films generally offer a communal experience in which audiences may participate; the two audiences become one, effectively making the movie theater an extension of the audio-visual space of the high-school prom, the nightclub, and later the stadium. But, whether superior to a live performance or not, the cinematic musical spectacle is simultaneously aural and visual, and its pleasures are fundamentally sexual: the pleasures of seeing and being seen, of hearing and being heard.[45]

Cinematic spectacles in which hearing and seeing are equally fundamental and interdependent raise the issues of the relation between image and sound in their reception, whether they create spectators who also hear or audiences who also see.[46] Though sound in cinema is generally considered supplementary to images, certain conjunct audio-visual filmic events may activate both senses equally, or may even subordinate the image to the sound. But whether or not seeing is ever preempted or directed by hearing, short visual compositions, certainly those the length of a song, may be sonically structured. Sonic events, including bar, line, and stanza divisions, other instrumental rhythmic elements, and shifting relations among voices and instrumentation, may all be used to organize imagery, camera position and movement, editing, and other visual components. As sound inflects and directs the visuals, music becomes an optic through which we see; the audio-visual composition becomes a synesthetic spectacle, a visual music. Over its history, the rock 'n' roll film has created visual languages appropriate, sometimes more and sometimes less, to the music presented within them: forms of rock 'n' roll visuality or rock 'n' roll filmic musicality.[47]

Except in films in the revue format exclusively, the spectacle of musical performance is surrounded by a second form of representation, the narrative of the music's social and historical contexts and the mode of its production. This wider field of representation variously includes the professional and personal lives of the performers themselves, where they come from, where they go, and whom they love; the songwriters, back-up and session musicians, and recording engineers; other artists, those who assist and those who compete; the agents, promoters, distributors, disc jockeys, and corporate executives; the fans who consume the music, and the panoply of social agents who encourage and facilitate this consumption; those who incorporate, regulate, and disseminate the music, expanding its operations in relation with other forms of cultural practice and other branches of the entertainment industries—all the people and apparatuses that comprise the real or imagined world in which rock 'n' roll exists. As they document its fans' use of it, how and what they (p.19) make it mean and how they articulate it with other activities—those immediately adjacent to it like dance, but also everyday life in general—rock 'n' roll films also have the pedagogic function of disseminating and popularizing these practices, or of teaching others how to rock 'n' roll. Though television music shows share these functions, especially in teaching youth how to dress for and dance to rock 'n' roll, cinema's more extensive narrative and documentary capabilities has permitted expression of a fuller panorama of people's interaction with the music. As much as reviewers and other journalistic media and sociological and other academic projects, cinema's stories about rock 'n' roll elaborate and interpret the music's aesthetic and social meanings, its effectivity and affectivity in the lives of individuals and society as a whole. Debating and projecting, attacking and justifying these meanings, cinema makes them sensually present and ideologically resonant. In narrating rock 'n' roll, cinema *theorizes* it.

Such theorizations of rock 'n' roll may be complicated. The spectacle and the narrative may work in concert, each elaborating and proving the other; but, as Zappa's anecdote above illustrates, the two may disagree; the narrative may misunderstand and misrepresent the spectacle. So for Zappa, Haley's performance of "Rock Around the Clock, "represented a strange sort of 'endorsement' of the teen-age cause," even though the story line "had the old people winning in the end." As in this case and as, most dramatically, in Frank Tashlin's *The Girl Can't Help It*, released the next year, such a discrepancy is most common in films whose narrative denigration of rock 'n' roll is countermanded by the music's power, but it can also occur when a narrative makes unjustified claims for the music it depicts. Similarly, whatever narrative possibilities the music offers may change over time so that the music's meanings in the present differ from those it had in the past. In most cases, cinematic representations of rock 'n' roll reflect the values obtaining in the period when the film is made. But whatever meaning a phase of popular music has in its own time is subject to retrospective historical revision, so that within cinema's history of rock 'n' roll runs the history of the changes in the meaning of its past. From 1950s rock 'n' roll, doo-wop, and British beat music, through soul, disco, and punk, to yesterday's crunkcore and Christian black metal, genres and eras of music have multiple meanings: the contested meanings each has in its own time, and the changes in meaning that time brings. A film about music contemporary with it participates in the negotiation of its first meanings, but when it concerns earlier music, a rock 'n' roll film negotiates between the music's own moment and the historical moment of the film's production.

Finally, the representation of the meaning of music in cinema is also shaped by the mode of the film's own production, for just as at a given time music as a whole includes various modes of musical production, cinema includes multiple modes of film production.[48] Most American (p. 20) films, including classic musicals, are commercial projects, manufactured as commodities in the industrial cinema summarily designated as "Hollywood," which comprises the studios where they are produced, the theaters where they are consumed, the television programs where they later play as reruns, and so on, along with all the people and other establishments involved in these processes. But outside and on the edges of the commodity cinema there have been many forms of independent and semi-independent production: documentaries, especially, but also amateur, experimental, and other non-commodity practices that are created and consumed in alternative institutions. Such marginal, independent modes of film production have been especially important for rock 'n' roll.

When rock 'n' roll emerged in the mid-1950s, the US cinema industry was in a state of transition marked, on the one hand, by the crisis caused by the rise of television and by antitrust rulings against the Big Five studios that owned the large exhibition circuits and, on the other, by the emergence of popular semi-amateur filmmaking, much of it documentary-influenced, that became known as the New American Cinema or underground film. Inspired especially by Maya Deren's claims for the superiority of amateur over industrial filmmaking, these new cinemas were framed by the Beat generation's idealization of the spontaneous collective improvisation of jazz. Many of the most important early underground films were either about jazz musicians or attempts to assimilate the formal properties of jazz to its own visual language. *Shadows* (John Cassavetes, 1959) and *Pull My Daisy* (Robert Frank and Alfred Leslie, 1959), two of the inaugural underground films, were the most celebrated forerunners of avant-garde films about rock 'n' roll. In the 1960s, underground film's association with rock continued to grow, and by the mid-1970s many of the underground's screening venues had become dominated by rock 'n' roll films, most of them independently produced, where they effectively substituted for live performance.

Rock 'n' roll's development as popular innovation on the edges of and sometimes against the established music industry paralleled developments in filmmaking, in both cases, producing the interaction of multiple modes of production, an unprecedented variety of forms of musical film in which the multiple modes of rock 'n' roll culture in its first two decades found representation in different modes of film production: feature films from minor—and later—major studios, independent documentaries, and experimental shorts. Since the 1970s, most rock 'n' roll films have been studio productions concerned with mainstream commercial rock 'n' roll, but independent filmmaking has continued to sustain different narrative or documentary modes with different interpretations of the music's meaning.[49] The rock 'n' roll musical as a whole comprises a spectrum of modes of film production representing the spectrum of modes of musical production. At any given time, the different forms of determination operating on different modes of film production (p. 21) frame and establish priorities and limitations on both the spectacle of musical performance and narratives about it. Each form invited music and film to join in different dances.

In contrast to the stable productive methods of the classic musical, the changes in films about rock 'n' roll from the mid-1950s to the mid-1970s reflected both the changes in the music's aesthetic and social meaning and unprecedented innovations in the mode of film production. Accounts of rock 'n' roll produced by the film industry tended to reflect the values of capitalist culture, while those made independently proposed other meanings, reflecting ideological possibilities and constraints of their own means of production, with bottom-up independent productions usually more sympathetic to bottom-up forms of music in which rock 'n' roll originated and in which it has continually renewed itself. With the exception of Frank Tashlin's satire on rock 'n' roll, *The Girl Can't Help It,* made at Twentieth Century Fox, the major studios ignored the new music, and films about it in the 1950s were independently produced by small exploitation studios, especially American Independent Pictures (AIP). Independent production of this kind continued into the 1960s, even as the major studios eventually entered the field with Elvis, primarily at Paramount and MGM, and then the Beatles in the United Kingdom at United Artists. Otherwise, the mid-1960s counterculture baffled the major studios as much as early rock 'n' roll had, and the music was primarily represented in minor cinemas, especially in independently produced documentaries, from *Dont Look Back* (D. A. Pennebaker, 1967) to *Woodstock, Gimme Shelter* (Albert and David Maysles and Charlotte Zwerin, 1970), and beyond. But in the late 1960s, when more than any other band the Rolling Stones seemed to address the political disillusionment that accompanied the disintegration of the counterculture, the band was represented in alternative or avant-garde modes of production. Hollywood was only able to reassert its hegemony as rock 'n' roll's combination of black and white music split again into separate streams, generating blaxploitation on the one hand and films about country music on the other.

These developments in music, in film, and in films about music between the mid-1950s and the mid-1970s coincided with and contributed to shifts in the relative importance of the two mediums and of other components of industrial culture they mobilized. Despite the challenges of television in the mid-1950s, film still retained its position as the most important medium, in many ways as much the model and inspiration for the other arts as it had been since the early years of the century. A decade later, rock 'n' roll and the forms of popular music from which it derived and into which it mutated had replaced cinema as the medium in dominance, especially for youth. Record sales doubled in the period to reach $1.6 billion, and for the first time exceeded the revenues of all other components of industrial culture.[50] Combining the operation of capital and of cultural resistance to it, rock 'n' roll and, as it later (p.22) became, simply "rock" replaced cinema as the most popular, the most democratic art. As its various forms penetrated all aspects of life, it became the chief means by which people in the North Atlantic and eventually the world discovered and performed their aesthetic and social values, the medium in which the culture breathed.

The corpus of rock 'n' roll films, especially as it appears in the alphabetized lists of popular guides, may seem a directionless miscellany, with none of the generic consistency and stability of the classic musical. In fact, cinema's encounter with the new music produced a structured evolution that marshaled innovations in sound-image relations, formal and narrative strategies, generic variations, and new and old modes of production, all responding quite directly to epochal cultural, ideological, and social developments. From the mid-1950s to the mid-1970s, rock 'n' roll films narrated a myth of the contested emergence, maturation, and eventual decline of a fundamentally biracial cultural initiative that accompanied, sustained, and in some ways preceded the utopian politics of the same period. Cinema and rock 'n' roll, musicality in the former and visuality in the latter, engaged in a complex dance: a *pas de deux* of approach, retreat, struggle for mastery, and virtuoso turns, with the one variously elaborating or challenging the other. Cinema offered immense possibilities to rock 'n' roll: the expansion of sonic qualities into visual compositions and narrative embodiments, all with the cultural prestige of what had previously been the century's most important art. Conversely, the music had its own allures for film: the freedom and creativity of youth, the desire and bewitchment that it seemed to embody and which made music the newest and most dangerous of cinema's rivals.[51] In its dreams, cinema found itself dancing with rock 'n' roll.

Notes

1 Béla Bartók believed *Le Sacre du Printemps* (*The Rite of Spring*) to be "one of the best examples of the intensive permeation of art music by genuine peasant music"; "The Relation of Folk Song to the Development of the Art Music of Our Time" (1921) in Benjamin Suchoff, ed., *Béla Bartók: Essays* (New York: St. Martin's Press, 1978), p. 325. In Elvis's second film, *Loving You,* his manager invoked the riots that greeted *The Rite of Spring* in defending him against censorious town elders. In 2005, Augusta Read Thomas received a commission from the Memphis Symphony Orchestra and the Music Library Association for an eight-minute work for orchestra, *Shakin': Homage to Elvis Presley and Igor Stravinsky.*

2 Quoted in Peter Guralnick, *Careless Love: The Unmaking of Elvis Presley* (Boston: Little, Brown, 1999), p. 350.

3 "The Camp Meeting Jubilee" appears on the Document Records' album, *The Earliest Negro Vocal Quartets (1894–1928).* The film *Transatlantic Merry-Go-Round* (Benjamin Stoloff, 1934) included a song called "Rock and Roll," which invoked the earlier nautical use of the phrase; see William H. Young and Nancy K. Young, eds., *The Great Depression in America: A Cultural Encyclopedia* (Westport, CT: Greenwood Press, 2007), p. 506.

4 Of the many histories of rock 'n' roll, I have found Jim Curtis's *Rock Eras: Interpretations of Music and Society, 1954–1984* (Bowling Green, OH: Bowling Green State University Popular Press, 1987) the most useful. For African American popular music from the late 1950s to the early 1970s, Brian Ward's *Just My Soul Responding: Rhythm and Blues, Black Consciousness, and Race Relations* (Berkeley: University of California Press, 1998) is indispensable. Though distinct and mutually exclusive "black" and "white" musical elements cannot be defined, still functional historically specific generalizations do allow distinctions between the more assertive and complex rhythmic tendencies of African and African American music and the harmonically richer European music. Though rock 'n' roll is properly characterized as fundamentally a white assimilation of black musical styles, US and UK popular music from the mid-1950s to the end of the 1960s was characterized by especially open interchanges in both directions. For the theoretical justification of the use of the concepts of black and white music in this period, see Ward, *Just My Soul Responding,* pp. 7–8.

5 According to David Halberstam, by early 1956 the thirteen million US teenagers had a total income of seven billion dollars, 26% more than three years earlier; see *The Fifties* (New York: Villard Books, 1993), p. 473. Jon Savage has traced the history of teenagers from the late nineteenth-century British and US hooligan and the Parisian Apache gangs, through the flappers and the French Zazous and German Pirates based on swing music, to their emergence as a distinct social and marketing demographic in the United States at the end World War II. First appearing in print in 1941, the term "teenager" had become accepted by 1944, when *Seventeen,* a magazine for girls, was launched, and in January 1945 the *New York Times* published "A Teen-Age Bill of Rights"; see Jon Savage, *Teenage: The Creation of Youth Culture* (London: Chatto & Windus, 2007). The term "youth culture" was coined by Talcott Parsons in an essay, "Age and

Sex in the Social Structure of the United States," *American Sociological Review* 7 (1942): 604–616. Parsons proposed that at the offset of adolescence, "a set of patterns and behavior phenomena which involve a highly complex combination of age grading and sex role elements" (p. 606) emerges, different from the kind of responsibility displayed by adult males; this "specifically irresponsible" culture with a "particularly strong emphasis on social activities in company with the opposite sex" (pp. 606–607) was characterized by "a strong tendency to develop in directions which are either on the borderline of parental approval or beyond the pale, in such matters as sex behavior, drinking and various forms of frivolous and irresponsible behavior" (608).

6 See Richard A. Peterson and David G. Berger, "Cycles in Symbol Production: The Case of Popular Music" in Simon Frith and Andrew Goodwin, eds., *On Record: Rock, Pop, and the Written Word* (New York: Pantheon Books, 1990).

7 *Life* 38.16 (April 18, 1955): 166–8.

8 "Rock-and-Roll Called 'Communicable Disease,'" *New York Times*, March 28, 1956, p. 33.

9 "White Council vs. Rock and Roll," *Newsweek*, April 23, 1956, p. 32. On the same page, the magazine also reported that members of the Citizens Council had assaulted Nat King Cole during a performance in his hometown of Montgomery in retaliation for his singing with white women. For extended details of racist attacks on black musicians, see Ward, *Just My Soul Responding*, pp. 95–109.

10 Davis was quoted in Steve Chapple and Reebee Garofalo, *Rock 'n' Roll Is Here to Pay: The History and Politics of the Music Industry* (Chicago: Nelson-Hall, 1977), p. 47; Sinatra was quoted in Gertrude Samuels, "Why They Rock 'n Roll—And Should They?" *New York Times Magazine*, January 12, 1958, p. 18. Linda Martin and Kerry Segrave provide a comprehensive history of what they term "rock-bashing" from the mid-1950s to the mid-1980s in *Anti-Rock: The Opposition to Rock 'n' Roll* (Hamden, CT: Archon Books, 1988).

11 The sociology of classical music had been developed and codified early in the twentieth century most notably by Max Weber in *Die rationalen und soziologischen Grundlagen der Musik* (1921) (tr. *The Rational and Social Foundations of Music* [Carbondale: Southern Illinois University Press, 1958]), but significant attention to popular music and the culture industries generally began with Theodor Adorno and Max Horkheimer. Though based on the standardization and pseudo-repetition he found in 1930s commercial light music, Adorno's analysis of the social function of distraction remains fundamental to the understanding of capitalist entertainment generally, including much popular music: "Distraction is bound to the present mode of production, to the rationalized and mechanized process of labor to which, directly or indirectly, masses are subject. This mode of production, which engenders fears and anxiety about unemployment, loss of income, war, has its 'nonproductive' correlate in entertainment; that is, relaxation which does not involve the effort of concentration at all. People want to have fun." "On Popular Music," rpt. in Frith and Goodwin, eds., *On Record: Rock, Pop, and the Written Word*, p. 310. Despite Adorno being made a *bête noire* in 1990s

affirmative cultural studies, nothing in his analysis of 1930s light music, which lacked rock 'n' roll's social transgressiveness, could be reconstructed as a putative Adornian critique of the later music. In fact, he specifically excepted "youngsters who invest popular music with their own feelings" (p. 314, n. 3) from the processes of distraction. David Riesman understood the immediate antecedents of rock 'n' roll similarly in his 1950 essay "Listening to Popular Music," in which he differentiated between majority and minority attitudes among teenage popular music fans; whereas the former are indiscriminate consumers, the latter group "comprises the more active listeners, who are less interested in melody and tune than in arrangement or technical virtuosity. It has developed elaborate, even overelaborate, standards of music listening." "Listening to Popular Music," in Frith and Goodwin, eds., *On Record*, p. 9. Somewhat later, Stuart Hall and Paddy Whannel formulated distinctions among "folk art," "popular art," and "mass culture," arguing for a continuity between pre-industrial folk art and popular artists such as Charlie Chaplin or Miles Davis, yet for a categorical break between them and mass art where "the formula is everything—an escape from, rather than a means to, originality. . . . Mass art uses the stereotypes and formulae to simplify the experience, to mobilize stock feelings and to 'get them going.'" Stuart Hall and Paddy Whannel, *The Popular Arts* (New York: Pantheon Books, 1965), p. 69.

12 Chester Anderson, "Rock and the Counterculture," *San Francisco Oracle* 1 (1967): 2, 23; in Theo Cateforis, ed., *The Rock History Reader* (New York: Routledge, 2013), p. 96.

13 Ralph J. Gleason, "Like a Rolling Stone," *The American Scholar* 36.4 (Autumn 1967): 555.

14 Jann Wenner, "Musicians Reject New Political Exploiters," *Rolling Stone* 1.10 (May 11, 1965): 22.

15 Wenner, "Musicians Reject New Political Exploiters," p. 1.

16 Eldridge Cleaver, "Convalescence," in *Soul on Ice* (New York: McGraw-Hill, 1968), p. 195.

17 Jerry Rubin, *Do It!* (New York: Ballantine Books, 1970), pp. 17–19.

18 The patterned sounds we know as *music* are generated by and generate psychic, social, and material relations in the minds, bodies, and activities of the people who produce and receive them. Like the *mode of film production* (or *cinema*), any given *mode of musical production* involves the interaction between two apparatuses, the one psychic and somatic and the other institutional and material. The former consists of the physical and mental procedures, skills, and pleasures though which music is created and perceived, and the latter all the agencies and establishments in which the sounds exist and which they bring into existence: musicians, critics, fans, and audiences; performances, concerts and concert halls, musical instruments, records and record players, music schools, radio, and television programs—and films. During the postwar industrialization of popular music, both apparatuses expanded and proliferated exponentially.

19 Cf. "Though all industrial mass production necessarily eventuates in standardization, the production of popular music can be called 'industrial'

only in its promotion and distribution, whereas the act of producing a song-hit still remains in a handicraft stage. The production of popular music is highly centralized in its economic organization, but still 'individualistic' in its social mode of production." Adorno, "On Popular Music," p. 306.

20 See Peterson and Berger, "Cycles in Symbol Production," p. 142.

21 Jacques Attali, *Noise: The Political Economy of Music* (Minneapolis: University of Minnesota Press, 1985), p. 140. Written in 1977, Attali's theorization of transformations in the mode of musical production proposing an emancipatory component in rock 'n' roll at the point of popular production was, however, only one moment in his more comprehensive analysis of its overall industrial recuperation, colonization, sanitization, and banalization, through which it becomes a mechanism of social control: "It creates a system of apolitical, nonconflictual, idealized values. It is here that the child learns his trade as a consumer" (ibid., p. 110). Rick Altman approached similar questions in *The American Film Musical* (Bloomington: Indiana University Press, 1989). He proposed that the ideological accomplishment of the classical film musical narrative reflects the additional social function of the songs, which he calls the musical's "operation role": "the societal practices directly influenced, enabled, or engendered" by a genre (p. 353). Since the songs were deliberately "written for the [unamplified] voice and piano," and also "self-consciously written not to surpass the range and capacities of the average amateur music lover," they provided the basis for various kinds of amateur domestic practice, rather than mere passive consumption. This popular practice was sustained and mediated by the sale of sheet music, so that "for over a quarter-century the musical and the sheet music industry together combined to provide the nation's most powerful defense against mass-mediated passivity" (p. 352). The emergence of "Electronic Reproduction," specifically "the rise of the original-cast recording in the late forties along with the long-playing record" (p. 353) and the mass circulation of recordings, especially of records that were no longer "simply recordings of live performance, but electronically created in studio" (p. 355) ended this period of participatory interchange: "Where once American popular music had provided a liberating impulse working against the very media serving as its vehicle, now that same music fully deserved the criticisms leveled at it by Adorno" (p. 356). For Altman, the decline of the classic musical represented the last stage in the destruction of truly popular music and its commodification. Since the nineteenth century, a growing rift between amateur and professional endangered the previous "situation where composition, listening and performance remain[ed] interchangeable community activities" (p. 348). Altman recognizes that in the 1930s and 1940s, theater and film musicals had enabled and managed a fundamental reciprocity between the production and consumption of music as commodified entertainment and the popular re-creation of the same songs; but, refusing to recognize that rock 'n' roll films also provide the basis for popular practice, he argues that it coincided with and in fact caused the collapse of the formal and structural possibilities of the musicals themselves:

> From the films of Elvis Presley and the teenie-bopper beach blanket shows starring Frankie Avalon and Annette Funicello to the rock concert

documentaries of the seventies ... the musical has slowly destroyed itself by losing its balance between narrative and music, indeed by abandoning the classic syntax whereby narrative is not just an excuse for music, but stands in a particular, structured relationship to that music. This way, in short, lies the musical as illustrated record album. This way lies MTV (p. 121).

22 *Rock Eras,* p. 4.

23 Hall and Whannel, *The Popular Arts,* p. 276.

24 Where earlier sociology attempted to read music's social meaning from its intrinsic formal properties, recent projects modeled on reader-response literary analysis recognize that musical meaning is created in " human-music interaction, "so that "musical affect is constituted reflexively, in and through the practice of articulating or connecting music with other things"; Tia DeNora, *Music in Everyday Life* (Cambridge: Cambridge University Press, 2000), p. 33.

25 Filmmakers and film theorists have explored the musical structuration of film images almost since the beginning of cinema. Around 1912, the painter Léopold Survage made abstract animations based on musical principles, while in the 1920s French critic Émile Vuillermoz suggested orchestrating images "according to a strictly musical process." The history of abstract visual music derives from these ideas, most notably in the work of Oskar Fischinger, but they have also been important for non-abstract filmmakers, especially Sergei Eisenstein. James Tobias has explored the musicality of these and other filmmakers in *Sync: Stylistics of Hieroglyphic Time* (Philadelphia: Temple University Press, 2010), where the Vuillermoz quote appears (p. 19). His foundational definition of musicality proposes that it "comprises those effects of music as they may be performed or presented in other than auditory media: performances that may only mime or otherwise do not produce audible music, or qualities specific to music presented in visual terms." (p. 19).

26 Though the present account focuses on cinema, television enters its story in many ways, being integral to both rock 'n' roll's development (especially in popularizing it outside urban centers) and to cinematic negotiations with it; filmic depiction of rock 'n' roll television and filmic projects initially conceived for the other medium are two of the most important. Beginning in the early 1950s, teen dance shows with popular stars lip-synching to current hits emerged locally before moving to the networks, most importantly *Bandstand,* renamed *American Bandstand* in 1957 and running for thirty-five years. Rock 'n' roll was also popularized in variety shows including *The Steve Allen Show, The Tonight Show,* and *The Ed Sullivan Show.*

27 As early as 1958, Robert Brustein traced an important genealogy of such variously vulnerable, inarticulate, narcissistic, and rebellious figures from the proletarian heroes of 1930s Group Theatre through Brando, Dean, Paul Newman, and Montgomery Clift to Elvis in *Jailhouse Rock* in "America's New Culture Hero: Feeling Without Words," *Commentary* 25 (Fall 1958): 123–129. Brustein saw Elvis as performing such an inarticulate character, and also as being its "musical counterpart": "Beginning by ignoring language, rock and roll is now dispensing with melodic content and offering only animal sounds and

repetitive rhythms. In Elvis Presley, the testament of Stanley Kowalski is being realized," p. 129.

28 Richard Fehr and Frederick G Vogel, *Lullabies of Hollywood: Movie Music and the Movie Musical, 1915–1992* (Jefferson, NC: McFarland, 1993), p. 1.

29 Books about film and rock 'n' roll include David Ehrenstein and Bill Reed, *Rock on Film* (New York: Putnam's, 1982); Rob Burt, *Rock and Roll: The Movies* (Poole, UK: Blandford Press, 1983); Linda J. Sandahl, *Encyclopedia of Rock Music on Film* (Poole, UK: Blandford Press, 1987); R. Serge Denisoff and William Romanowski, *Risky Business: Rock in Film* (New Brunswick, NJ: Transaction, 1991); Marshall Crenshaw, *Hollywood Rock: A Guide to Rock 'n' Roll in the Movies* (New York: Harper-Perennial, 1994); Jonathan Romney and Adrian Wootton, eds., *Celluloid Jukebox: Popular Music and the Movies since the 1950s* (London: British Film Institute, 1995); Kevin Donnelly, *Pop Music in British Cinema* (Berkeley: University of California Press, 2001); Pamela Robertson Wojcik and Arthur Knight, eds., *Soundtrack Available: Essays on Film and Popular Music* (Durham, NC: Duke University Press, 2002); Ian Inglis, ed., *Popular Music and Film* (New York: Wallflower Press, 2003); John Kenneth Muir, *The Rock & Roll Film Encyclopedia* (New York: Applause Theatre & Cinema Books, 2007); and David Laderman, *Punk Slash! Musicals* (Austin: University of Texas Press, 2010). The last of these, *Punk Slash! Musicals,* is a unique consideration of a specific musical form and the moving image culture associated with it. Journalistic overviews of films about rock 'n' roll include Richard Staehling, "The Truth about Teen Movies," *Rolling Stone* 49 (December 29, 1969), 34–47; Thomas Weiner, "The Rise and Fall of the Rock Film," *American Film* 1.2 (November 1975): 25–29 and 1.3 (December 1975): 58–63; Greil Marcus, "Rock Films" in Jim Miller, ed., *The Rolling Stone Illustrated History of Rock & Roll* (New York: Random House, 1976), pp. 390–400; Dave Marsh, "Schlock Around the Clock," *Film Comment* 14 (August 18, 1978): 7–13; Carrie Rickey, "Rockfilm, Rollfilm" in Anthony DeCurtis and James Henke, eds., *The Rolling Stone Illustrated History of Rock & Roll: The Definitive History of the Most Important Artists and Their Music* (New York: Random House, 1992), pp. 111–120; and Howard Hampton, "Scorpio Descending: In Search of Rock Cinema," *Film Comment* 33.2 (March–April 1997): 36–42; Hans J. Wulff, "Rockumentaries. Eine Arbeitsbibliographie," *Kieler Beiträge zur Filmmusikforschung* 5.1 (2010): 158–167; www.filmmusik.unikiel.de/KB5/KB5.1-Biblio.pdf (accessed 9/25/2010) is a bibliography of writings on rock 'n' roll and cinema.

30 Altman, *The American Film Musical*, p. 92.

31 A remake of *Ninotchka* and one the last of Arthur Freed's great MGM musicals, *Silk Stockings* culminates, not in a duet between the two stars, Astaire and Cyd Charisse, but in Astaire's own "The Ritz Roll and Rock." With his trademark top hat and tails, his dance appears to be an appropriation of elements of rock 'n' roll into the more sophisticated form of the musical proper, even though it is not entirely clear whether Cole Porter's lyrics indict or celebrate its appropriation by the "smart set." Astaire sings of how, finding it "much too tame," "they jazzed it up and changed its name"; now "all they do around the clock is the Ritz Roll and Rock," "dowagers and diplomats

behave like alley cats," and "fancy fops and fillies . . . make those hick hillbillies look like squares." Astaire's own skills and his position within the "smart set" appears to signal the superiority of the genre he had served so beautifully, and it wins him Ninotchka.

32 On the rock 'n' roll films and classic musicals, see Barry K. Grant, "The Classic Hollywood Musical and the 'Problem' of Rock 'n' roll," *Journal of Popular Film & Television* 13.4 (Winter 1986): 195–205. Grant notes the importance of rock 'n' roll's rising popularity and industry convergence in producing conglomerates dealing in both films and records whose interests were served by the promotion of the new music, but argues that rock 'n' roll films often forced the music to fit earlier conventions, with the result that in them "rock 'n' roll changed more than did the musical film" (p. 199). Two important precursors to rock 'n' roll feature films were Soundies and Scopitones. Made in the United States between 1940 and 1946, Soundies were short films of popular music and dance performance that played on Panoram visual jukeboxes in bars and restaurants. Originating in France in 1958 and flourishing for a decade, Scopitones were similar short films for jukeboxes; they too featured many forms of popular music, but little rock 'n' roll.

33 The integrated form is best exemplified by Vincente Minnelli's work for the Freed unit at MGM, beginning with *Meet Me in St. Louis* (1944) and culminating in *An American in Paris* (1951) and *The Band Wagon* (1953). But the distinction between musicals in which diegetically and stylistically autonomous discrete numbers interrupt the narrative in the manner of Berkeley's 1930s films and those in which the songs, dance, and other elements are all integrated into it, organically emerging from it and furthering its progress, is not entirely categorical. The many interim degrees of integration have been schematized as follows: (1) those that "are completely irrelevant to the plot" (as when the characters watch an arbitrary nightclub performance); (2) those that "contribute to the spirit or theme"; (3) those "whose existence is relevant to the plot, but whose content is not" (as in show business musicals in which important characters are themselves performers); (4) those that "enrich the plot, but do not advance it, by establishing a situation or atmosphere or displaying character, but that could be removed without causing noticeable continuity gaps (love duets, for example); (5) those that "advance the plot, but not by their content" (as with a successful audition performance); and (6) those that "advance the plot by their content." See John Mueller, "Fred Astaire and the Integrated Musical," *Cinema Journal* 24.1 (Fall 1984): 28–40 (quotes pp. 28–31). Minnelli excelled in numbers in the last category. "Dancing in the Dark," for example, from *The Band Wagon,* in which the discovery that the Astaire and Cyd Charisse characters can in fact dance together transforms their relation with each other and the possibilities of the plot. Mueller also notes that though musicals featuring numbers of the third category are usually designated as unintegrated, if the story concerns the process of putting on a show, then the accumulation of such numbers does integrate them into the plot. This is the case with most rock 'n' roll musicals.

34 Rick Altman developed the notion of the "dual focus" in his magisterial *The American Film Musical,* to which I am fundamentally indebted, here especially

to pp. 16–27. For Altman the gendered dual focus is feature of all musicals, and he curtly summarizes: "No couple, no musical" (p. 103).

35 Astaire cited in John Mueller, *Astaire Dancing—The Musical Films* (London: Hamish Hamilton, 1986), p. 26.

36 Ironically, the big band music instanced by Whiteman is precisely the kind of music against which rock 'n' roll would react, specifically in the first extended rock 'n' roll narrative film, *Rock Around the Clock* (1956). *Strike Up the Band* especially resembles another early rock 'n' roll film, *Rock, Pretty Baby!* (Richard Bartlett, 1956): its hero, also called Jimmy, also comes from a middle-class family, and against his father's wishes aspires to being a musician rather than a doctor, and it too culminates in a contest for high-school bands, though in this case it is broadcast on television rather than radio.

37 "The Self-reflective Musical and the Myth of Entertainment," *Quarterly Review of Film Studies* 2.3 (August 1977): 313–26; rpt., Rick Altman, ed., *Genre: The Musical* (London: Routledge and Kegan Paul, 1981), pp. 159–174, and subsequently elaborated in the book, *The Hollywood Musical*, 2nd ed. (Bloomington: Indiana University Press, 1993). Feuer does not use the term "commodity relations." Altman's term for "backstage" musicals is "show" musicals and he distinguishes them from "folk" musicals in terms similar to Feuer's: see *American Film Musical*, pp. 200–270. Like Feuer, he argues that the folk musical attempts to conceal the commodity relations it involves: "In short, the folk musical preaches a gospel of folk values to an age of mass media. It creates a myth to dissemble the break between production and consumption, between capital and labor, between past and present. Yet paradoxically this folk message, this attempt to reconstitute a national folk, must be carried by the very mass media which represents its avowed enemy" (*American Film Musical*, p. 322).

38 Feuer, "The Self-reflective Musical," in Altman, *Genre: The Musical*, p. 160.

39 Hall and Whannel, *The Popular Arts*.

40 Feuer, *The Hollywood Musical*, p. 3.

41 Feuer, *The Hollywood Musical*, p. 16.

42 An important Hollywood subset of this genre couples the rise of an actress with the corresponding decline of the actor who discovers her. The best known is *A Star Is Born* (William A. Wellman, 1937), remade by George Cukor with Judy Garland in 1954 and adapted to popular musicians in Frank Perry's 1976 version starring Barbra Streisand and Kris Kristofferson.

43 Biopics about jazz musicians continued after the emergence of rock 'n' roll with, for example, *The Gene Krupa Story* (Don Weis, 1959), *The Five Pennies* (Melville Shavelson, 1959) (about Red Nichols), *Lady Sings the Blues* (Sidney J. Furie, 1972) about Billie Holliday, *Bird* (Clint Eastwood, 1988), and *Round Midnight* (Bertrand Tavernier, 1986), a fictionalized composite of Bud Powell and Lester Young. Of the many biopics about rock 'n' roll musicians and tributary forms of music, the most interesting include *Your Cheatin' Heart* (Gene Nelson, 1964), about Hank Williams; *Leadbelly* (Gordon Parks, 1976); *The Buddy Holly Story* (Steve Rash, 1978); *The Rose* (Mark Rydell, 1979), based on Janis Joplin; *Coal Miner's Daughter* (Michael Apted, 1980), about Loretta Lynn; *Sid and Nancy* (Alex Cox, 1986), about Sid Vicious; *La Bamba* (Luis Valdez,

1987), about Richie Valens; *Great Balls of Fire!* (Jim McBride, 1989), about Jerry Lee Lewis; *The Doors* (Oliver Stone, 1991) focusing on Jim Morrison; *What's Love Got to Do with It* (Brian Gibson, 1993), about Tina Turner; *Ray* (Taylor Hackford, 2004), about Ray Charles; *Control* (Anton Corbijn, 2007), about Joy Division's Ian Curtis; *Walk the Line* (James Mangold, 2005), about Johnny Cash; and *Get On Up* (Tate Taylor, 2014) about James Brown.

44 Frank Zappa, "The Oracle Has It All Psyched Out," *Life,* June 29, 1968, p. 85.

45 Again, Frank Zappa: "To deny rock music its place in the society was to deny sexuality. Any parent who tried to keep his child from listening to, or participating in this musical ritual was, in the eyes of the child, trying to castrate him." "The Oracle Has It All Psyched Out," p. 86. The psychoanalysis of visual pleasures has been extensively theorized: pleasure in looking at other people in cinema is supposed to be a variable combination of identification with and symbolic possession of the visible object in processes that are specifically gendered. In general, heterosexual men derive pleasure from visual identification with male ego ideals and visual consumption of female erotic objects, while women are divided by more complex patterns of identification and desire; these scopic regimes are constantly in flux, and any given film may shift and destabilize the dominant patterns of identification. In the absence of any similarly developed psychoanalysis of musical pleasure, it may be assumed that listening and especially listening to music involve similar libidinal transactions operating at an interface between biological sensuality and cultural coding. The production and apprehension of sonic patterns organized in respect to pitch, rhythm, duration, color, and so on and—especially in the case of singing, the timbre or grain of the human voice—create circuits where the drive to hear may, if not realize its object, still circle around it in ongoing pleasure. These processes may be especially rich, realized consciously as well as unconsciously, in the case of popular song, which is so commonly erotically invested, if not so specifically gendered as are scopic relations among people. Religious music, opera, *lieder,* and modern pop are all fundamentally concerned with the pleasures and pains of love, and no less than other music, popular songs typically offer a spectrum of opportunities for identification that multiply across gender roles, especially with the sliding signification of pronouns in the lyrics. In Freud's theory of human sexuality, *drives (Triebe)* are fundamental. Unlike instincts, which reflect purely biological needs, drives are simultaneously somatic and psychic, and hence cultural and symbolic. Jacques Lacan's elaboration of the nature of drives in *The Four Fundamental Concepts of Psycho-Analysis* (New York: Norton, 1978) maintains the distinction, but adds that they can never be satisfied and in fact do not aim at completing a relationship with an object, but rather circle around it, the repetitive movement itself being the source of pleasure. (His phrase, *la pulsion en fait le tour,* contains a pun according to which the drive both tours and tricks the object [p. 168]). These drives are always partial (this reiterating Freud's phrase, "partial drives") in that sexuality participates in psychic life "in a way that must conform to the gap-like structure of the unconscious" (p. 176). The four partial drives are the oral (to suck, located at the lips), the anal (to defecate, located at the anus), the scopic (to see, located at the eyes), and the invocatory (to hear, located at the ears). Though it may be entailed in various forms of attention to the buttocks, the anal drive is not prominent in rock 'n' roll, a conspicuous exception being punk rocker G. G. Allin, as documented in *Hated: G. G. Allin and the Murder Junkies* (Todd Phillips, 1994). But the scopic and invocatory desire are. An unusually lucid explicator of Lacan notes that a drive "originates in an erogenous zone, circles round the object, and then returns to the erogenous zone," all in a circuit "structured by three grammatical voices": active (for example, to see), reflexive (to see oneself), and passive (to be seen); see Dylan Evans, *An Introductory Dictionary of Lacanian Psychoanalysis* (London; New York: Routledge, 1996), pp. 46–8. These scopic and invocatory circuits are fundamental to the phenomenology of concert attendance and of musical cinema.

46 These issues have been addressed by Michel Chion in *Audio-Vision: Sound on Screen*, ed. and trans. Claudia Gorbman (New York: Columbia University Press, 1994). Despite proposing that film should be understood as a combined audio-visual mode of perception (which would appear to imply a union of sight and sound, simultaneously apprehended in both modes), Chion consistently presents sound as subordinate and supplementary; it is an "added value" (p. 5) to the image, and "most cinema" is defined as "'a place of images, plus sounds'" (p. 68). Rick Altman more acutely notes that the "reversal of the image/sound hierarchy lies at the very center of the musical genre" and cites the Busby Berkeley production number as the point at which *"Everything— even the image—is now subordinated to the music"* (italics in original); *The American Film Musical*, p. 71. Astaire's contrary priorities—"Either the camera will dance, or I will"—privileged the single shot, with a virtually stationary camera that kept the singers and dancers in full view through the entire sequence. Berkeley and Astaire exemplify, respectively, what may be thought of as the "Eisensteinian" and the "Bazinian" models of audio-visual musical composition. Between them lies the issue of whether the relation between the image and the music should be one of similarity or contrast, parallelism or counterpoint. Addressing this question in 1944, Theodor Adorno and Hanns Eisler attacked parallelism: "Why should one and the same thing be reproduced by two different media? The effect achieved by such a repetition would be weaker rather than stronger." *Composing for the Films* (rpt. London: Continuum, 2007), pp. 44–45. In Berkeley's sequences, both camera and dancers danced, the sequences were fragmented and kaleidoscopically rearranged in the editing and elaborated with non-diegetic metaphors; but the music directed the visuals' structure. In the earliest rock 'n' roll films, parallelism dominated because it was easier and cheaper, but as the rock 'n' roll film grew in importance, more complex audio-visual images were created and the advent of music videos launched unprecedentedly sophisticated compositions derived from experimental film.

47 Carrie Rickey first raised the possibility that a film could embody rock 'n' roll's aesthetic qualities. In her attempt "to identify the distinctive features of the rock-movie genre, the qualities that make rock roll," she excluded all the obvious candidates—films that represent music, including concert movies such as *The T.A.M.I. Show* (Steve Binder, 1964), cinéma-vérité chronicles such as *Gimme Shelter*, and authorized documentaries, such as Madonna: *Truth or Dare* (Alex Keshishian, 1991)—and instead nominated films that mobilize values equivalent to those that she sees as defining rock 'n' roll's cultural

ethos: "Movies about youthful charisma, narcissism and sex appeal all dressed up (or down, if you prefer) in death-defying, sometimes death-embracing, attitude," which she dates from *Knock on Any Door* (1949), Nicholas Ray's melodrama about a juvenile delinquent. Her canon begins with *Blackboard Jungle,* whose delinquents first manifested a youth culture separate from that of adults, before it divides into "Sexwatch" and "Deathwatch" subgenres. The former was inaugurated with Elvis's sex drive and rebelliousness in *Jailhouse Rock* (Richard Thorpe, 1957) and continued through the Beatles' more blithe sexuality in *A Hard Day's Night* (Richard Lester, 1964); the latter, in which the protagonist is redeemed in death, began with *The Harder They Come* (Perry Henzell, 1973) and continued in similar martyr biopics from *The Buddy Holly Story* (1978) to *The Doors* (Oliver Stone, 1991) that, like *Knock on Any Door,* feature fast-living young men who die young (see "Rockfilm, Rollfilm," quotations from pp. 113 and 114). *Knock on Any Door* does, in fact, make some association between juvenile delinquents and hot jazz—the rock 'n' roll of the time—but it rather looks back to the gangster films of the 1930s, such as *Angels with Dirty Faces* (Michael Curtiz, 1938) in that its celebration of delinquency is more ambivalent than equivalent films of the sixties and after. David Laderman's *Punk Slash! Musicals* is an exemplary investigation of the way films about punk formally internalize musical properties.

48 Cinema studies has an advantage over musicology in possessing a terminological distinction between "film"—the strip of celluloid imprinted with visual and aural information that is communicated to the spectator—and "cinema"—the ensemble of institutions and processes, of psychic and material apparatuses within which films are produced and consumed, and which they reciprocally sustain, the film's mode of production.

49 A schematization of this field would be bounded by the following limit-case examples: industrial films about industrial musical production, such as *A Hard Day's Night*; industrial films about amateur musical production, such as *The Commitments* (Alan Parker, 1991); amateur or avant-garde films about industrial musical production, such as *Scorpio Rising* (Kenneth Anger, 1964); or *Superstar: The Karen Carpenter Story* (Todd Haynes, 1987); amateur or avant-garde films about amateur musical production, by definition not well known, but *The Blank Generation* (Amos Poe and Ivan Kral, 1976) and *The Punk Rock Movie* (Don Letts, 1978), home movies of early punk in New York and London, respectively, approximate them.

50 Between 1963 and 1969, for "the first time record sales surpassed the gross revenues of all other forms of entertainment"; see Richard A. Peterson and David G. Berger, "Cycles in Symbol Production: The Case of Popular Music," Simon and Goodwin, eds., *On Record: Rock, Pop, and the Written Word*, pp. 152.

51 Although it unaccountably omits substantial reference to popular music, Paul Young's study of competition among the media industries, *The Cinema Dreams Its Rivals: Media Fantasy Films from Radio to the Internet* (Minneapolis: University of Minnesota Press, 2006), appropriately asserts the absoluteness of Hollywood's stake in confronting any new media: "the maintenance of the Hollywood cinema as an *institution* that is and will remain distinct from competing media institutions" (p. xxii).

5

The triumph of the musical film

Background and topics

As noted at the end of Chapter 3, between 1930 and 1945 crooners went from being regarded by many as dubious or even dangerous, to being thoroughly beloved by millions. Part of this transformation was due to the work of people like Bing Crosby. His efforts at self-promotion and the promotion of other singers like him succeeded in calming fears and helping to ease the emergence of younger film stars and musical celebrities.

Once such performer was Frank Sinatra. Sinatra is regarded by many music critics to be one of the greatest musical artists of the twentieth century. This is of particular interest to us here because he had many marks against his name, at least from the standpoint of the traditional moralists who spent so much of the last century keeping a very close watch over American popular culture. Sinatra was the son of Italian immigrants and grew up poor in Hoboken, New Jersey. He spent his early life in exactly the kind of cosmopolitan center that some regarded as a hotbed of immorality. His mother had a particular passion for left-wing politics as a suffragette, advocate for women's reproductive rights, and as a very active supporter of the New Deal. Sinatra began his musical career as a crooner as part of various vocal quartets and then sang with big bands before starting his solo singing career. He continually attracted extensive and sometime even aggressive female attention, a notable feature of the first half of his career. Theoretically, all of this should have attracted almost disqualifying criticism. But it did not. Instead, he attracted ever increasing success.

Two markers of that success were two films that can show us the upward trajectory of the crooner, popular music, and the musical film in the 1930s and 1940s. One was a short and modest film called *The House I Live In*. The other was the massive spectacular musical extravaganza, *Anchors Aweigh*. Both were released in 1945. These two films will be the subject of the Focus section below because they can tell us some important things about how the

FIGURE 5.1 *Frank Sinatra publicity photo (1947).*

popular culture that would come after them would be very different than the one that preceded it. The reasons for this will be the subject of the first part of this chapter.

The key reading for Part Two of this book is

James, David. (2015) "Introduction: Rock 'N' Film." In David James (ed.), *Rock 'n' Film: Cinema's Dance with Popular Music*. New York: Oxford University Press, 1–22.

You will need to read this as crucial background to this chapter and the next. For this chapter focus on pages 137–143, as this section provides a concise overview of the era of "the Hollywood musical," which lasted from about 1930 to 1955. It was during this period that new ways to see, hear, and experience music developed through the medium of film. As noted in the Overview to this book, this is yet another example of music, and especially popular music, being an integral part of establishing and maintaining the popularity of a new form of media.

Musical films and film musicals

From the very beginning of film, even during in the silent era, music was a central aspect of the medium and the synchronization between sound and image has always been present to some degree. Just as importantly, musical films have always been an important vehicle for the introduction, distribution, and consumption of new music. The types of films in which music was used in film in this era were numerous. Many early musical films were "revues," or shows that resembled well-known stage shows consisting of dozens of different performers. They relied on what the historian Rick

FIGURE 5.2 *Technicians setting up the turn-table and amplifiers for* The Jazz Singer, *Sydney Australia. (ca. 1928–9).*

Altman describes as "every conceivable musical source: opera, operetta, classical music, military marches, Viennese waltzes, folk songs, gospel hymns, Jewish canticles, Tin Pan Alley tunes, nightclub numbers, vaudeville routines, jazz riffs, and even burlesque favorites." However, there were a wide variety of themes, narrative types, and musical traditions portrayed in these films.

What would become "the musical" and, specifically, "the Hollywood musical" began to cohere in the early 1930s. Among the more popular and influential of the early musical films that led in this direction were *The Jazz Singer* (1927) and *The Broadway Melody* (1929). Both resembled more conventional narrative films that engaged audiences through the potent combination of coherent stories and musical production numbers that were more or less integrated into the narrative. As Altman explains, the success of films such as these saw "every Hollywood studio immediately and repeatedly turned to production of 'musical melodramas' which shared superficial characteristics such as 'diegetic music,' performers as main characters, performance-heavy plots, unhappy love affairs, and an unabashed display of the latest technology." There was also a shift toward a lighter narrative touch in the form of romantic comedies, and a much heavier reliance of increasingly spectacular "showstopping" song and dance numbers.

The technical achievements of these films should not be overlooked. In the late 1920s, early musical films were often little different from existing stage shows recorded with a small number of mostly stationary cameras. While the early shows themselves were spectacular aesthetic and technical accomplishments, by the mid-1940s, the sounds and images audiences consumed were far more sophisticated and all-encompassing. Simply put, the sounds they heard were fuller and louder and of a higher quality than anything available anywhere else (Figures 5.2 and 5.4). The images were carefully synchronized to produce a seamless web of dialogue, singing, dancing, and music. Further, the experience of these films in the movie palaces of the time would probably also represent the best experience of recorded sound and imagery available to most people at the time. Most importantly, these films were part of a broader multimedia experience of the music presented in these films as Altman explains:

> For thirty years Hollywood musicals were inextricably intertwined with the daily lives of a nation of music lovers. With sheet music available in many theatre lobbies and every department store, families regularly gathered around the piano to sing the latest Hollywood hit. Courting couples recreated their favorite Hollywood scene by spooning to a record of the film's music. Every new musical style was instantly turned into a dance craze learnt in Fred Astaire or Arthur Murray Dance Studios and widely practiced in ballrooms around the country. Every potential social use of the musical was reinforced by the omnipresence of the

genre's music, serving as figure for the broader practices championed by the musical.

This succinct summation tells us something very important about the experience of popular culture that we will be exploring in the next chapter as well. It tells us that seeing a film or listening to a record was part of a larger environment of multimedia experience. Far from being isolated experiences, they were instead part of a complex web of cultural experiences and social relationships that were both shaped and exploited by media producers who were guided in turn by the response of a large, heterogeneous, mass public. As we will see in the next chapter this same market persisted and expanded into something called "youth culture" that centered around a new kind of

FIGURE 5.3 *Advertisement for* The Broadway Melody. Screenland. *(1929).*

FIGURE 5.4 The Broadway Melody *at the Fox Theater, Seventh Avenue, Seattle (ca. 1929).*

music called rock and roll. Before we do this, however, it is important to understand the larger context in which this public was formed into a mass consumer market.

While a thoroughly American phenomenon, the Hollywood musical had a significant global impact. Indeed, "Hollywood" more generally was a part of the rise to dominance of the United States as a cultural and political power since even before the Second World War. The period between 1930 and 1945 marks the transformation of the United States from a country wracked by economic depression and repeated recessions to a global superpower with hegemonic ambitions in both politics and culture. As such the rise to dominance of Hollywood after the Second World War cannot be understood as an isolated phenomenon.

For our purposes, it is important to understand how what was called the Hollywood "Studio System" eventually became a central cog in the promotion of "wholesome" and "patriotic" entertainment. As a model of an industry directing its influence of popular culture, it has proven a powerful one. As many historians of film have shown, the studio system was defined by an oligopoly, or a small number of large corporations that dominated the film industry. Further, the corporations that produced the vast majority of films also maintained control over where they were shown by owning chains of movie theaters and distribution networks. This meant that they had a great deal of power over the range and types of filmed entertainment available to the general public. This dominance was not limited to the United

States, but extended overseas as well. Film was a central form of media in the dissemination of what many called "American values" taking the form of newsreels, documentaries, fictional films, and, of course, musicals. Many such productions issuing dire warnings about the threats of foreign systems of government while others offered both the vision and experience of consumerist abundance as the rightful fruits of modern capitalism.

It was in this context that the film musical became a harbinger of a dominant form of American popular culture which extolled the virtues of a particular kind of complacent "normality." As we will see in the next section, a self-imposed regime of censorship called "The Hays Code" gradually enfolded the big movie studios shaping the bounds of what was expressible in film for decades to come. The dominant vision of the world produced in most films of this period was one of aggressive "normalcy." That is, the codes enforced a vision of the virtues of monogamous, heterosexual relationships preferably placed within the bounds of marriage, at least eventually. Race relations were similarly constrained as representations of African Americans in particular, and non-Americans in general were often rife with racist stereotypes shaped by forms of humor indirectly taken from the dark arts of minstrelsy.

While musicals were often impressive in their technical innovation, they were often aesthetically static. That is to say, their narrative styles, characterizations, and emotional appeal tended to be tightly regulated and highly repetitive from production to production. The purpose of some of the form's generic features, having the same kinds of situations experienced by the same sorts of characters, was to more effectively differentiate and highlight the big song and dance routines.

Explore and report: MGM musicals and The Hays Codes

One of the more striking consequences of the control over film production, distribution, and consumption that this small collection of corporations enjoyed was their ability to respond to social and cultural pressure brought to bear on them. This was especially true concerning issues of morality and vice. One of the studio system's most important and persistent responses to criticism was expressed in the voluntary production codes that all of the major American film studios adopted in 1930. Informally called The Hays Codes, after their author Will Hays, the head of the movie studios' trade association, these guidelines set out a wide range of topics and scenes that were to be prohibited from film.

The code is a reflection of the utter seriousness with which many conservative social commentators viewed film. It is important to understand that public concern over the power of new media to whip up the emotions of listening and viewing audiences reached a peak in the late 1920s. Racist and fascist demagogues had used radio and other media to spread their messages and attract large crowds to their rallies and speeches. The code also has strong resonances of the fearful anti-urban, anti-cosmopolitan views used by many to attack the crooners, as noted in Chapter 3.

Our goal here is to understand the values and aspirations that supported The Hays Code. We can read this document, not simply as a form of industrial regulation, but as a coherent and thorough expression of a particular view of the world. The full code is very easy to find, simply enter "The Hays Code" or "The Motion Picture Production Code (1930)" into any search engine.

First, read the first sections of the code which are called "Reasons for the New Code" and "Principles Underlying the Code." Write a critical and analytical interpretation of these sections that provide a plausible explanation for their content. What values were its authors seeking to champion? What values were they seek to repress and exclude from film? Why do you think they chose to censor films in this way? What broad view of the world do these principles imply?

Second, read the main body of the code in which the authors detail the specific sorts of scenes and depictions to be banned from film. Write a short response explaining the extent to which the specific types of scenes banned from film from 1930 to about 1955 or so may have shaped how films were written, produced, and consumed. Compare these to contemporary films and television series. Explain what kinds of entertainment options we would not have access to if these codes were still in force. Find specific examples of currently popular films or television programs that you would not have been allowed to see had these codes be in force. Explain these examples in detail.

Focus: Two films with Frank Sinatra

As noted earlier, crooners were regarded by critics with suspicions that often drifted into outright hostility. The criticism of their singing style and the content of their songs centered around the lack of what many viewed as traditionally "masculine" characteristics, such as strength in their vocal styles, the ability to dominate women in their personal relationships, and an exclusive sexual interest in women. By the early 1940s, however, crooners weren't simply rendered harmless—they had become icons of American patriotism.

Two films in which Frank Sinatra appeared show us how the rehabilitation of the crooner image relied on linking the singer with the dominant ideals of liberal democracy. The films are a short film entitled *The House I Live In* and a classic MGM musical, *Anchors Aweigh*, both released in 1945. The two films could not be more different in style, tone, and execution. The short film only lasts ten minutes, with its centerpiece being Sinatra's performance of the titular song. The latter stretches out to over two hours and presents a series of song and dance numbers that was advertised as "Bigger than the biggest thing you've ever seen." Yet despite these contrasts, both films rely on Sinatra to provide a musical soundtrack to America's emergent ascendance as a global empire as it began a period of unrivaled power and influence around the world.

The story of *The House I Live In* is very simple. Sinatra is singing at a recording session. During a break between songs, he steps out into an alleyway for a smoke break. There, he sees a group of boys chasing and attacking another boy because, as one of them says, "we don't like his religion." When Sinatra expresses astonishment, another begins to say "Now look mister he's a dirty–" but Sinatra cuts him off. While there is no explicit reference to the bullied boy's religion, the fact that the film was commissioned by the Anti-Defamation League of B'nai B'rith makes the central issue of the film fairly clear. Sinatra teasingly calls them a "bunch of those Nazi werewolves I've been reading about" and then sits them down and talks through a civics lesson with them. He explains how America is made up of "a hundred different ways of going to church, but they're all American ways." He regales them with a story of how an Irish pilot and a Jewish bombardier we able to destroy what Sinatra called a "Jap battleship." He then concludes the lesson with a performance of the song *The House I Live In*, with the music written by Earl Robinson, later blacklisted during the McCarthy era, and the lyrics written by Abel Meeropol, also the author of "Strange Fruit."

Meeropol's lyrics ask, rhetorically, if America is merely a flag or a name. Instead, he tells the listener that America is a whole host of things, with the second verse capturing the spirit of the song:

> The place I work in, the worker by my side/The little town or city where my people lived and died/The "howdy" and the handshake, the air of feeling free/And the right to speak my mind out, that's America to me.

The song is fairly understated, easing its way through a brief prelude and three verses before climaxing briefly at the end of the fourth. The version played in the film adds coda that presents a passage from "America the Beautiful" as one of the mob of attackers hands the bullied boy his cap and schoolbooks and they walk off together.

Anchors Aweigh is a different proposition altogether. It is a classic of the MGM musical genre. It is big, bold, comical, romantic, and uncomplicated. Yet, despite the differences in scale and technical accomplishment, the films are both interesting responses to the attacks on the masculinity of various Hollywood film stars, especially those who appeared in musicals.

FIGURE 5.5 *Publicity photo for* Anchors Aweigh *from* Screenland *(1945).*

This film starred Gene Kelly and Frank Sinatra in the story of two sailors on three days of shore leave in Hollywood (Figure 5.5). Even the most genial summary of the film today brings up issues of gender and masculinity that appear to us today to be not entirely anachronistic. Kelly plays Joe Brady, a man seemingly obsessed with pursuing women as a form of sexual conquest in order to satisfy his possibly fragile sense of masculine self-regard. Sinatra plays Clarence Doolittle, a shy, much younger man who was forced to reluctantly admit to Brady that he was a virgin. Doolittle sought out Brady in the hopes of learning how to seduce a woman. Several comical scenes in which Brady attempts to tutor Doolittle establish the dynamic of their relationship. Brady is the popular and charismatic alpha male whereas Doolittle simply feels lucky to have been taken into the more experienced man's world.

As with many such films, the story is little more than a bare bones narrative of the pursuit of monogamous, heterosexual love in which a main character is transformed for the better, morally and psychologically, by its eventual realization. The story does little more than provide some sense of forward motion between one lavish production number, ballad, or light romantic song to the next. Many of those songs and the dialogue that surrounds them are shot through with sexual double entendre and a frankness in the pursuit of women that pushed right to the edge of the Hays Codes. Interestingly, although perhaps not surprisingly, many of the larger showstoppers were also strongly tinged with patriotic music. On several occasions, the noted conductor and pianist José Iturbi directed full strength navy bands through medleys of familiar military tunes. (Multiple scenes are available on video-streaming platforms.)

What is important to understand about these two films is the manner in which the defining musical elements of crooning became so central to mainstream popular culture. There were the performative intimacy of this form of singing, the pleading and almost abject nature of a man's powerlessness in the face of real love, and the nakedly emotional pull of the music itself. This is important because even as late as the mid-1930s, those elements of crooning were still capable of inspiring a degree of harsh criticism that still retained traces of the original censorious force. Yet, by the mid-1940s, crooning was used to represent the highest and most noble of aspirations in both the civic sphere and personal life. This kind of transformation was not the first or last time a new form of music born in controversy quickly matured into acceptability.

INDEPENDENT RESEARCH WORK

The tradition of the MGM musical was a very influential and lucrative one. Films such as *Meet Me in St. Louis* and *Show Boat* were very popular. The MGM musicals made in the 1940s and 1950s have long been regarded as the definitive form of the musical. However, as noted above many different kinds of musical films such as the "backstage musical" and revues preceded their more spectacular descendants. Compare the earlier musicals with their later counterparts. Compare narrative styles, storylines, and characterization. Also, compare the nature of the spectacle. How did the capabilities of the film musical form change over time? Finally, compare how the tone and scope of the stories changed. The older musicals sometimes took more chances and were far more explicit and suggestive about sexuality and gender than the later films. Examine why this might have been the case and what effect it may have had on the film industry in this period.

References and further readings

Altman, Rick. (1996) "The Musical." In Geoffrey Nowell-Smith (ed.). *The Oxford History of World Cinema*. New York: Oxford University Press, 43.

Barrios, Richard. (1995) *A Song in the Dark: The Birth of the Musical Film*. New York: Oxford University Press.

Cohan, Steven. (2002) *Hollywood Musicals: The Film Reader*. New York: Routledge.

Cohan, Steven. (2005) *Incongruous Entertainment: Camp, Cultural Value, and the MGM Musical*. Durham, NC: Duke University Press.

Lahr, John. (1997) *Sinatra: The Artist and the Man*. New York: Random House.

Marshall, B., and R. Stillwell. (2000) *Musicals: Hollywood and Beyond*. Exeter, UK: Intellect.

Thompson, K., and D. Bordwell. (2003) *Film History: An Introduction*. Boston: McGraw-Hill.

Wierzbicki, James. (2008) *Film Music: A History*. New York: Routledge.

6

The "youth" movie and the hit single

Background and topics

In the years following the Second World War, the one country that benefited more than any other from the new forms of economic and political interconnection emerging around the world was the United States. Geographically removed from the unprecedented levels of killing and destruction in Europe and Asia, it was able to impose the terms of the new world order which followed to an unprecedented degree. It should be obvious that a broadly considered American culture has had a profound influence on nearly every region of the globe since this time.

Importantly, in this exact same period, a wide range of new political movements exploded into public consciousness all over the world. In countries such as Ghana, Cuba, Congo, Vietnam, and Indonesia, anticolonial mass movements which had been building for decades finally came to fruition. Similarly, strong well-organized campaigns for civil rights reached a peak of effectiveness in many of the wealthier countries in the world, especially the United States. These movements were built by people who were colonized, marginalized, or excluded from the main currents of political and cultural power in their societies. After the Second World War, they demanded respect, inclusion, and recognition. Many of these movements were led by people whose relative youth belied their media savvy and political acumen. Just as importantly, many such leaders were able to politically mobilize vast numbers of young people in ways that had not happened before.

Intriguingly, young people in all of these countries were also gradually becoming more politically engaged and that engagement flowed across both popular and political spheres in distinctly new ways. One important component of what was an emerging international commercial and popular

FIGURE 6.1 *Close-up of a jukebox (ca. 1950).*

culture was a particular symbolic fascination with youth, hedonic freedom, and personal ambition and achievement that defined the cultural politics of the decades following the end of the war. These values and their appeal to a wide swathe of people in many societies shaped a wide range of debates over almost all aspects of social life in many countries. This was due in part to the fact that, between 1945 and 1965, a generation of young people who were more numerous than ever before came of age. They would become more commercially influential than young people had ever been before.

We need to understand that despite the dramatic changes in the range of allowable forms of public expression, surprising little persistent tangible political change emerged from this period. This was due to the fact that many of the social, cultural, and political changes that were sought or achieved were contained and directed into less threatening forms of social activity. In fact, by the end of the 1960s, while the personal liberation pursued by so many had been achieved mostly by a privileged few, the genuine achievements of an almost utopian promise of a new age of enlightenment that had been a genuinely mainstream preoccupation since the mid-1950s began to be undermined, denuded, and viciously clawed back in the ensuing decades.

In this chapter, we will focus on how complex and often contradictory ideas of social, cultural, economic, and social freedom were translated into the commercial products of American popular culture. What is most important for us to understand is exactly how these "freedoms" were symbolically represented in these products.

The key reading for Part Two of this book is

James, David. (2015) "Introduction: Rock 'N' Film." In David James (ed.), *Rock 'n' Film: Cinema's Dance with Popular Music.* New York: Oxford University Press, 1–22.

You will need to read this as crucial background to this chapter. For this chapter focus on pages 127–137 and 143–150. This first section provides a concise overview of the rise of rock 'n' roll. The second provides us with an analytical basis for rock 'n' roll films.

There are several issues to clarify and understand as you read. First, consider how James describes the meaning and consequences of rock 'n' roll on pages 128–132. He argues that rock 'n' roll was part of larger "fundamental transformations in US society and the music industry." These included new forms of economic and social connection and interaction that were produced and facilitated by new forms of media, such as vinyl records, and old forms of media that had been opened up to new voices, such as the many new kinds of music broadcast on radio. The new experiences these media produced often helped in challenging prevailing social norms surrounding race and gender. James argues that with "rock 'n' roll, musical and social delinquencies were intertwined, each the other's cause and manifestation." What he means by this is that adherents of this music often acted in ways that transgressed the repressive social norms that were intended to govern how they could act. Often this took the form of controversies over what music young people could dance to, who they could dance with, and where they could do it.

On page 137 James notes that this music had many associated forms of expression which were as symbolically important to it as the actual sounds of the music. These included hair and clothing styles, body language and use of new slang, as well as the associated imagery that attended their favorite performers. We will address some of these concerns in the focus section below.

James also argues from page 143 onward that the rock 'n' roll film was a particular kind of reinvention of the Hollywood musical. He claims that, like the musical, the primary focus of the rock 'n' roll film is the spectacle of this music being performed set within an enfolding narrative of the stories of the performers' lives. He further suggests that these films excited their audiences through a visually enticing, narratively engaging spectacle that was produced through the continuously superior sound quality and volume already developed through the classic movie musicals. Before looking at some of the details of these films, we need to understand how they were part of a new environment of music consumption which, while having many continuities, also had important differences with that which preceded it.

A new consumption environment

The Second World War had a marked accelerating and intensifying effect on the technologies that would become central to the lives of billions of people. The war pushed technological development across multiple areas, such as air, land, and sea travel and national and international communications, and established new and more stable routes for international commerce and personal and cultural interactions. All of this had profound effects on popular culture, both directly and indirectly. Developments such as the transistor and magnetic tape recording, for example, resulted from research undertaken by various governments during the war. As we will see in this and later chapters, these two inventions had a particularly important effect on the production of popular music. Further, the infrastructure for such forms of research grew to unprecedented size and scope during the war and persisted long afterward. This led to a great many new technologies which we will look at in later chapters.

What is of particular interest for us here is how the social relationships occasioned through the production, distribution, and consumption of music changed in rapidly evolving social and cultural environments after the war. These changes happened both in public and at home. Two good examples of the changes that happened in public were audio and video jukeboxes. Both had been available since the 1890s. As noted in previous chapters, machines like kinetoscopes operated in public viewing galleries previously. The updated version, called soundies, showed short musical films of the sort one might see in a Hollywood musical (Figure 6.2). Several different types existed, but the technology was very similar to what one would find in a movie theater, except in miniature. The films showed an interestingly wide range of performers from across the spectrum of vaudeville and popular music, including rhythm and blues, jump blues, hillbilly acts from the Grand Ole Opry, as well as holdovers from the era of minstrelsy.

New Slot Machine Shows Sound Films

SOUND-MOVIE cabinets, operated by dropping a coin in a slot, and quickly installed anywhere, offer a new form of entertainment for railroad stations, lunch rooms, and other public places. Sponsors of half a dozen makes, already in use or nearly ready for production, expect them to compete in popularity with the coin-operated phonographs now in vogue. A typical model is shown at right, with James Roosevelt, son of the President, watching one of the reels his film company has made for it. Using sixteen-millimeter film, it presents a three-minute program, the pictures being projected on a small screen at the front. One maker proposes a more ambitious sort of installation. From a suitably located cabinet in a restaurant, a system of mirrors would convey the images so that they could be viewed by occupants of every booth in the establishment.

James Roosevelt viewing pictures on a new "Talkie" automat

FIGURE 6.2 *An article in* Popular Science *about Soundies (1940).*

Audio jukeboxes also operated quite widely since the 1890s. This technological form began when player pianos, pianos operated by rolling sheets of perforated paper, began to appear in bars and saloons in the 1890s. Automatic record players offering about a dozen 78s appeared as early as 1928. However, the popularity of jukeboxes increased dramatically in the 1940s and 50s when various companies developed machines that could store over 100 recordings (Figures 6.3, 6.4, and 6.5). These were played through speakers of greatly increased frequency range and volume. When 45 rpm singles became widespread, these small, light, durable records allowed patrons to access a wider range of recordings more quickly while enjoying better sound quality than what previous machines had provided. The history of jukeboxes is replete with tales of people playing the same records over and over again and of groups of young people holding both spontaneous and formal dances in front of these machines.

The environment for music consumption at home also changed dramatically in this period. The most obvious addition to the homes of many

FIGURE 6.3 *AMI Multi-Horn High Fidelity 200 Play Jukebox (ca. 1959).*

FIGURE 6.4 *Jukebox at Prince Edward State Park, Virginia (n.d.).*

FIGURE 6.5 *Jukebox at a high-school dance in Tallahassee, Florida (1957).*

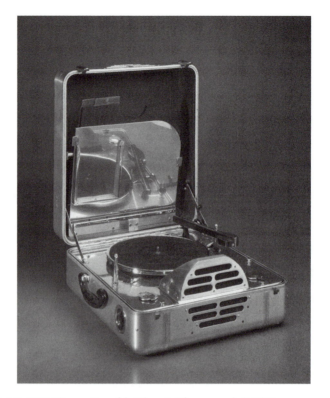

FIGURE 6.6 *RCA Victor, Portable Electric Phonograph (1935).*

people was television. While we will look at television in more detail in Chapter 9, it is important to note its importance to the experience of popular music in the home. Television began to become a common presence in many homes from about 1945. In the early years of broadcast television, a lot of the programming was live music, dance, and vaudeville style performance. Numerous variety programs, some resembling a more technically and theatrically modest version of the revues of the 1930s, began to show regularly. Given the immediate and growing demand for programming, new opportunities opened up for a wide range of popular musicians.

In addition to television, new forms of sound reproduction proliferated. The long-playing record, or LP album, was introduced commercially by Columbia in 1948 (Figure 6.6). RCA Victor responded with the 45 rpm single the next year. The years of industrial rivalry that followed had a complex and lasting effect on how consumers developed relationships with the music industry. Consumers were presented with variously sized records and different speeds at which to play them. The profusion of different kinds of stereos and record players in the late 1950s could be a baffling but also

FIGURE 6.7 *Arthur Fiedler, conductor of the Boston Pops Orchestra, demonstrates the new RCA 45 rpm record player (1949).*

exciting fact of life. As in the early twentieth century, the machines designed to play these new records also came in a wide range of shapes, sizes, and costs. The top of the range models were artisan-crafted pieces of furniture with separate compartments for radios and turntables. The smallest and most affordable were battery-powered, which often came in their own carrying cases, sometimes so compact that children could carry them (Figure 6.7). Many models had slots for storing records inside and some were capable of playing stacks of the 7-inch 45 singles providing long stretches of sound without any attention being paid to the machine. When linked with the other social changes in postwar Western countries, these small inexpensive record players often provided young people with a new sense of autonomy and independence. Many could easily afford the smallest and least expensive machines. Also, singles were deliberately priced extremely low to feed the volume business the music industry had become. As a result, in the 1950s young people grew into a market segment increasingly distinct from all others, and musicians and record labels acted accordingly.

Another important piece of the new worlds of music consumption in this period bridged the gap between public and private. The transistor radio became increasingly popular from the mid-1950s onward. And, with the advent of FM radio in the mid-1940s, and its increasing popularity throughout the 1950s and 1960s, the ability to listen to a wide range of music almost anywhere, anytime was a real possibility. Some radios could fit your pocket and cost less than ten dollars while others were more solid with larger speakers and better sound. As with the new record players, these devices didn't simply symbolize freedom, they embodied it. As you can tell from the advertisements which follow in the next section, they were sold with exactly this image in mind.

One of the most important things we need to understand is how all of these new forms of media created new kinds of social relationships and new kinds of fame. Importantly, these relationships were not simply conceptual, but material and experiential. The actual environment of things that made music come to life had changed dramatically from only ten years earlier. People, and especially young people, could experience their favorite artists and stars through more channels more often than ever before. Young people had more control over a broader range of choices that were more easily accessible than ever before and very often the music industry was speaking directly to them. We will look more closely at how this audience was addressed in the so-called youth movies of this era, but first we should try to understand the new culture of music consumption in a little bit more detail.

FIGURE 6.8 *Radiogrammafon, model Granada III, made by Gyling and CO. Sweden (ca. 1957).*

FIGURE 6.9 *Battery-Powered, Portable Record Player (ca. 1950s).*

FIGURE 6.10 *Battery-Powered, Portable Record Player (ca. 1950s).*

Explore and report: New ways to see and hear

Below are a range of images of home stereo units, portable record players, and transistor radios. Look at the images of the machines themselves first. Make a few notes about their shape and their details. Then, look at the advertisements. Make some notes about who these various ads are directed

FIGURE 6.11 *Battery-Powered Transistor Radio (ca. 1950s).*

FIGURE 6.12 *Akkord Peggie Transistor Radio, First Model Sold in Germany (1957).*

at and what appeals are being made. Then, search for a range of similar ads on various websites, such as Pinterest, Wikimedia Commons, and using Google image search terms such as "RCA Victor 45 advertisement," "RCA Victor record player," "Transistor radio ads," or "Columbia Records ads 1950s."

After bookmarking a range of such advertisements, compare the language and imagery of these ads to similar music-themed ads for contemporary technologies such as Spotify, iPhones, and SONOS home sound systems. You will find their ads on YouTube. Develop an argument based on your critical and interpretive comparison of these ads which explains why they look they way they do and why they make the claims and appeals they do.

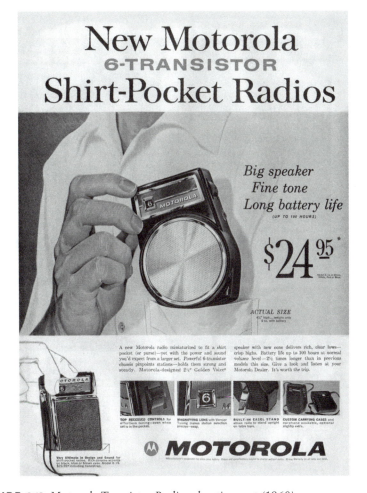

FIGURE 6.13 *Motorola Transistor Radio advertisement (1960).*

Focus: Marlon, Jimmy, and Elvis on film

Elvis Presley made thirty-one films in which he was an actor. The first was *Love Me Tender* (1956), which was made right at the start of his first blush of national fame. The last was *Change of Habit* (1969) made thirteen years later. Apart from his two-year stint in the Army, there was usually an Elvis movie showing somewhere in that period. To a significant extent, the tone, content, and stories of these films are a marked contrast to the moral panics that surrounded the emergence of rock 'n' roll in general and Elvis in particular. As the journalist Mark Feeney suggested, "The Elvis [film] canon

FIGURE 6.14 *Channel Master Transistor Radio advertisement (June 4, 1964).*

has one axiomatic principle: respectful, respectable hedonism (a.k.a. good, clean fun)." Feeney found "no thrill of excess" in them. Instead, they were "flat, mechanical, bored."

This not only sits in direct contrast to the emergence of rock 'n' roll, but also to the very films which have been said to have inspired Elvis's movie career in the first place—films such as *The Wild One* (1953) starring Marlon Brando or *Rebel Without a Cause* (1955) starring James Dean. Presley reflected more than once on his admiration for these two men and his desire to emulate them. Unfortunately for Presley, he was not able to achieve the levels of critical acclaim Brando and Dean received for their roles in these two films. Instead of following on from them in the development of the "rock rebel" persona in his films, Presley was more often saddled with mawkish sentimentality and plots that were mostly thinly veiled vehicles for performances of his music.

What is of particular interest here are the themes of rebellion, delinquency, and authenticity that the "rock rebel" films developed and which Presley's early films, such as *Loving You* (1957), *Jailhouse Rock* (1957), and *King*

FIGURE 6.15 *RCA Victor Portable Radio advertisement (1948).*

Creole (1958), used to start Presley's film career. In both *The Wild One* and *Rebel Without a Cause* the main characters are alienated from mainstream American society and judge it to be rife with a pervasive moral hypocrisy. As the media scholar David Baker has suggested, each character fills out various pieces of the rock rebel persona. Brando's character, Johnny Strabler, seeks freedom in the constant mobility of his motorcycle gang and displays a distinct "the lack of commitment to anything other than intensity of feeling in the present." He strongly resists any form of moral of personal containment. For Baker, Dean's character, Jim Stark "represents a different kind of rebel" in his "unwavering commitment to authenticity and sincerity" and his near-constant search for some kind of truth and honor that he cannot find in the adult world around him.

Importantly, both *The Wild One* and *Rebel Without a Cause* were received with something approaching hysteria in some places, with both being banned outright or receiving the "X" classification. This may have had

FIGURE 6.16 *Portable Transistor Radio advertisement (May 14, 1959).*

some influence on the tone and content of Presley's early films, all of which take great care to make Presley's characters strong-willed, occasionally threatening, but moral and decent. While the dramatic tension in each springs from the fact that Presley's characters all face significant obstacles, each overcomes these to greater and lesser extents due to their innately good

FIGURE 6.17 *Zenith Transistor Radio advertisement (1959).*

characters, the eventual realization of their authentic selves, and the support and love of a good woman. Further, the problems Presley's characters face in these films are rarely their fault, but more often the inevitable result of trying circumstances. Each then seeks the same kinds of freedom and independence that Brando's and Dean's characters sought as well while simultaneously doing so within an implicit code of acceptable behavior and through this a general striving for some kind of respectability.

Jailhouse Rock is of particular importance here not simply because it follows these narrative tropes in a fairly straightforward way, but also because of the inclusion of the titular MGM musical-style production number intended to transform Presley into the film star those around him thought he should be. The song and dance number in *Jailhouse Rock* was not only designed to resemble those of films such as *Anchors Aweigh*; they were

FIGURE 6.18 *Elvis and the Jordanaires (n.d.).*

FIGURE 6.19 Jailhouse Rock *publicity photo (1957).*

FIGURE 6.20 Jailhouse Rock *publicity photo (1957)*.

also produced by the same studio and by even some of the creative talent that produced many of the classic Hollywood Musicals of the 1940s and 1950s. The song and dance number highlights the contradictions between rock 'n' roll as a social phenomenon and as a commercial one. (Please see the film clip widely available on the internet.)

The narrative setup for this number is that Presley's character is asked to perform on a television show. He decides to perform a heavily stylized and tightly controlled version of rock 'n' roll dancing. As the publicity photos below show, the costuming and dance style also had a good deal more to do with the old style musical than the loud, boisterous music that had captivated so many young people. The clothes are a pristine, symbolic approximation of the clothes Presley's character wore in jail earlier in the film. Importantly, the dancing in this number is a similarly symbolic approximation of rock 'n' roll dancing. The steps and poses seen in the images below clearly come from Elvis's well-practiced and widely familiar stage performances. In the film, however, they become a series of stock

FIGURE 6.21 Jailhouse Rock *publicity photo (1957).*

moves deployed within a larger framework into which the attributes of rock 'n' roll, from its sound to its dance moves to its attitude, have been uncomfortably grafted.

In many ways, *Jailhouse Rock* marks a major step in the incorporation of the purported threat that rock 'n' roll once represented to established orders of race, class, and gender into the commercial mainstream of a youth-oriented entertainment culture. While *The Wild One* and *Rebel Without a Cause* had both been strongly sold as films for adults, and taken seriously enough to provoke strong censure, Presley's films were taken far less seriously. While Presley's films did evoke occasional hysteria, it was mostly of the positive kind. Further, this film in particular marked rock 'n' roll's definitive move away from its origins in a complex amalgam of African American rhythm and blues and Anglo American hillbilly and rockabilly sounds. Instead, this film shows us how this musical and social form eventually became a collection of sounds, images, and ideas that could be safely contained and used for a variety of patriotic and commercial purposes much like its predecessors had been.

INDEPENDENT RESEARCH WORK

Elvis Presley made thirty-one feature films between the years 1956 and 1969. While many of his friends and associates from the time claimed that Elvis had the ability to become a great actor, his performances in these films do not bear out such an assessment. Making so many films in such a comparatively short time suggest that at the very least they were financially successful if not artistically so. Explore the making of these films and Presley's film career in more depth. Specifically examine Presley's relationship with his manager, Colonel Tom Parker. He is often accused of preventing Presley's development as an actor. Write an essay that examines both the economic and cultural legacy of Presley's films and how these relate to one another. He acted as both an economic and artistic model for those who came after him, notably The Beatles and The Rolling Stones. Presley was one of the most successful musicians of his era and spending so much time and effort making films transformed his career. They also transformed how business was done in the music industry. Find out how.

References and further readings

Baker, David. (2005) "Rock Rebels and Delinquents: the Emergence of the Rock Rebel in 1950s 'Youth Problem' Film." *Continuum*, 19(1): 39–54.

Brackett, David. (2005) *The Pop, Rock, and Soul Reader*. New York: Oxford University Press.

Dawson, J., and S. Propes. (2003) *45 RPM: The History, Heroes, and Villains of a Pop Music Revolution*. San Francisco: Backbeats Books.

Feeney, Mark. (2001) "Elvis Movies." *The American Scholar*, 70(1): 53–60.

James, David. (2013) *Rock 'n' Film: Cinema's Dance with Popular Music*. New York: Oxford University Press.

Kelley, Andrea. (2018) *Soundies Jukebox Films and the Shift to Small-Screen*. New Brunswick, NJ: Rutgers University Press.

Killmeier, Matthew. (2001) "Voices Between the Tracks: Disk Jockeys, Radio and Popular Music, 1955–60." *Journal of Communication Inquiry*, 25(4): 353–74.

Nash, Amanda. (2004) *The Colonel: The Extraordinary Story of Tom Parker and Elvis Presley*. Chicago: Chicago Review Press.

Palmer, Robert. (1995) *Rock & Roll: An Unruly History*. New York: Harmony Books.

Turner, Fred. (2013) *The Democratic Surround: Multimedia and American Liberalism from World War II to the Psychedelic Sixties*. Chicago: The University of Chicago Press.

KEY READING

Chasing Sound: The Culture and Technology of Recording Studios in Postwar America

Susan Schmidt Horning

After World War Two, developments in audio engineering and sound recording, coupled with the rapid growth of the music industry rendered the recording studio an important site of cultural production. In the 1940s, a typical recording session lasted three hours and yielded four songs; by the late 1960s, a single record might be pieced together from multiple performances over weeks and even months. Through the introduction of tape recording and the technological innovations that followed, the recording studio had been transformed from a functional worksite in which well-rehearsed performances were recorded on the spot, to a creative workplace in which the tools of recording became integral to the creative process itself. At the center of this transformation are the users of recording technology who were actively engaged in modifying, adapting, and pushing the capabilities of their equipment. As a site in which a diverse community of musicians, producers, and technicians come together to work toward a common goal, the recording studio forms an important nexus between culture and technology.

After being drafted into the U.S. Army in 1943, accordion player and bandleader Frankie Yankovic booked time in the studios of the Cleveland Recording Company to record his polka band while home on furlough. In one afternoon session, Yankovic cut thirty-two songs using the standard recording technology of the era: a transcription disc recorder, broadcast control console, and one or two microphones. The band played the songs from beginning to end while they were cut directly to lacquer-coated discs. Mistakes were inevitable, but re-takes were expensive because of the time

"Chasing Sound: The Culture and Technology of Recording Studios in Postwar America" by Susan Horning. *Icon*, 6 (2000), pp. 100–18. Republished by permission of the publisher.

involved and the unreusability of the discs. Consequently, the Yankovic band's initial performances, "clinkers" and all, were recorded for posterity.[1] Twenty-three years later in Los Angeles, musician and producer Brian Wilson booked seventeen recording sessions in five different studios, employing dozens of musicians over a three-month period to complete the recording of a single Beach Boys' song, 'Good Vibrations.'[2] Much of the recording equipment at Wilson's disposal did not even exist when Yankovic conducted his marathon session in Cleveland, and the idea that a song could be edited, layered, shaped, and worked like a kind of aural sculpture, rather than simply transcribed and later reproduced by that equipment was practically unheard of in the early 1940s.[3]

While these two examples represent extremes in studio technique and practice – not to mention musical style and economic circumstance – they illustrate the dramatic changes that occurred in the technology and culture of recording in the decades after World War II. No longer was the musical performance simply captured and preserved by recording technology; the technology itself had become integral to the creative process.

This was neither the result of a single innovation nor a case of technological determinism.[4] Actually, the history of recording studios – particularly in this postwar period – conjures up a Rube Goldberg[5] model of cause and effect rather than a linear history of development. As new recording technologies gave rise to new norms of studio practice, these, in turn, opened up even more possibilities for how sound – indeed *what* sounds – could be recorded and how music was created. At the center of this transformation were the users of recording technology who were actively involved in improvising, modifying, adapting, and pushing the capabilities of the equipment available to them. By users, I refer predominantly to the recording engineers who operated the controls, but also record producers, arrangers, songwriters, and musicians who often suggested new ways of achieving sounds on record. Studio work in this period became more collaborative than it had ever been before. As a site in which a diverse community of artists and technicians came together to work toward a common goal – the creation of a record – the recording studio forms an important nexus between culture and technology.

In the acoustical recording era, the roles of recordist, musical director, and artist were relatively discrete. The recordist, or engineer, was the technical expert who instructed the artist where to stand before the recording horn, how far to move for certain powerful notes to avoid 'blast' on the recording, and in general commanded all but the musical artistry involved in recording. The artist was the creative force, and the musical director, or producer, acted as the interpreter between the two.[6] The limitations of the recording technology dictated that performances be well-rehearsed and that performers follow the recordist's instructions. With little room for creative experimentation or artistic temperament, successful collaboration in the acoustical recording studio required that each member of the recording team stick to what he or she did best.

Producer – Engineer collaboration

The advent of electrical recording in 1925 brought better sound quality and relaxed some of the restrictions on artist placement in the studio, but it was not until after the introduction of tape recording in the late 1940s that engineers and producers began to work in more collaborative and experimental ways. Creating a more 'live' sounding record by use of artificial echo and over dubbing became an early objective of such collaborations. A classically-trained oboist who first recorded with Elisabeth Schumann in 1936 and later became one of the most successful popular music producers of the 1950s, Mitch Miller, worked closely with recording engineer Bob Fine to develop echo and overdubbing techniques for popular singers like Vic Damone and Patti Page. Miller recalled his early work with Fine for Keynote Records:

> I didn't know enough about the technique of recording sound, but . . . every record I heard . . . those that were made in the '30s, it sounds like they're singing through a hunk of wool. Every vocalist, everything. It used to drive me crazy. So when I first began to produce, I said to Bob, 'How can I put a halo around the voice?' . . . And within a day he came up with this idea. . . . He used the bathroom.[7]

It was a simple solution, and although still considered a radical recording technique for the time, Fine was not the first to have tried it. In 1937, unconventional bandleader Raymond Scott had achieved what one listener called 'a big auditorium sound' on his records, simply by placing microphones in the hallway and men's room outside his record company's office (which also served as the label's recording studio).[8] A decade later, Chicago engineer Bill Putnam placed a microphone and a speaker in a bathroom to achieve the same effect for The Harmonicats' recording of 'Peg 'O My Heart.' After this, bathrooms, as well as stairwells and hallways were commonly used as 'echo chambers' because they had helped create records that became huge hits.[9]

Stories of legendary makeshift echo chambers abound: engineers at Columbia Records used the stairwell of their studios at 799 Seventh Avenue in New York City, both Atlantic and Chess Records used men's rooms, and even in the late 1950s, fledgling record producer Lee Hazlewood bought a cast iron storage tank, inserted a microphone in one end and a cheap speaker in the other, to achieve that reverberant quality on guitarist Duane Eddy's records. These people changed the notion of acceptable studio practice, and desirable sound quality on records. They found ways to achieve economically the kind of sound that had previously been possible only in concert halls or on the radio. Echo and reverberation, long employed in motion picture sound and in broadcasting since at least the early 1930s, were nothing new. Their application in the recording studio, however, was novel if not revolutionary.

The engineers: Technicians and diplomats

Mitch Miller achieved fame as a record producer but the name Bob Fine never became a household word.[10] The recording industry, like the movie industry, has always tended to honor its technicians separately from the artists, even as the industry values creativity and unconventionality.[11] Yet many record producers believed, as Miller emphatically stated, that 'engineers were the strongest link in the chain,' and he was among the first to suggest that they be given album credit.[12] Record companies balked at this suggestion, so engineers who recorded prior to the late 1950s, with a few exceptions, remain anonymous. With the founding of the Audio Engineering Society in 1948, recording engineers began to forge a professional identity and much later, wider recognition as part of the creative team. By the mid-1950s, a growing contingent of hi-fi buffs recognized how significant a contribution the engineer made to the final outcome. As record critic David Hall observed,

> Of some recordings, however effective they may be as an end product, it is often difficult to say how much credit goes to the performing artist and how much to the combined efforts of the recording director, recording engineers and tape editor.[13]

Hall's observation pertained to classical music and the increasing amount of editing being done to create a 'mechanically perfect' performance from many different takes of the same piece, or from sections of a longer composition recorded separately and subsequently spliced together. The same could be said for other forms of music, particularly popular recordings. But in those instances, such as Les Paul's 'multiple recordings' from the late 1940s, the primary objective was to create a distinctive *sound* rather than a flawless performance. In Paul's case, the performing artist was also the recording engineer.

As for training in the art of recording engineering, many members of the cohort that entered the recording business after World War II had served in the U.S. Army Signal Corps, several worked on secret projects like radar, and others worked in radio broadcasting or transcription services. But most recording engineers simply learned on the job, as did the mechanical engineers of a century before them and the 'recording experts' of the early years of the commercial record business.[14] Tinkering provided the foundation for many who eventually entered the recording field in these years before recording had become big business, but it was the kind of serious tinkering that characterized many hobbyists of this time, from drag racers to ham radio operators.[15] Interest in sound recording had been growing since the advent of instantaneous disc recording in the 1930s, but the war imposed strict limits on key recording materials like shellac, aluminum, and vacuum tubes, affecting amateur and professional, broadcast and record-company engineer alike. By war's end, the pent-up demand for all kinds of consumer goods and services created a climate in which the record industry flourished. Returning veterans skilled in radio and electronic communications found ready employment in broadcasting and recording studios.

Led by a small but determined group of recording professionals who had broken ranks from the Institute of Radio Engineers, an audio engineering community rapidly took shape in the immediate postwar period. To illustrate how fertile the interest in recording had become since the war, the March 1947 issue of *Radio* magazine, 'the journal for radio and electronic engineers,' ran an editorial on its inside cover explaining the publication's recent decision to change title and format: 'Because there has been no technical magazine devoted solely to this field, all engineers interested in audio engineering have had to gather piecemeal, from a large number of sources, such information on the subject as is published.'[16] The editor went on to proclaim in the first issue of the retitled *Audio Engineering* that the editorial content of the magazine would henceforth be devoted to 'the sadly neglected audio engineering field,' and, he continued, 'because so little attention has been devoted to recording, we are placing particular editorial emphasis on this subject.'[17]

Indeed, the only existing organization devoted to recording interests at that time was the Sapphire Club, a small informal group of record industry leaders which began meeting in New York in 1942, initially to trade materials due to shortages imposed by the war.[18] They were joined in 1947 by the Hollywood Sapphire Group, and together these provided a much needed forum for exchanging information among recording professionals.[19] This 'informal trading of technical know-how'[20] which grew exponentially with the formation of the Audio Engineering Society in 1948 was a catalyst for development of recording technology and practice. By October 1949 the Society sponsored its first annual Audio Fair, displaying the latest technological developments in the recording and reproduction of sound.[21] Four years later, the *Journal of the Audio Engineering Society* began publication, and became the major source of practical as well as theoretical discourse among audio engineers and audio equipment manufacturers. While not every recording engineer joined the Society, the industry as a whole benefited from its existence by virtue of the rising standards of practice that such an association encouraged.

From the early days of the acoustical recording era, the recording expert had to possess a wide range of skills, both technical and interpersonal, to be successful in the studio. In his memoirs, Victor Talking Machine Company recordist Raymond Sooy concluded with five pages of 'Requirements Necessary for a Good Recorder,' ranging from the ability to identify sound vibrations by examining the grooves of the wax, to instilling confidence and trust in the recording artist.[22] In 1996, echoing Sooy's earlier experience, one studio manager succinctly described a recording engineer as 'both a technician and a diplomat.'[23]

But studio engineers possessed personalities every bit as diverse as the musicians they recorded. They ranged from the fastidious and eccentric Rudy Van Gelder, to easy going natural diplomats like Eddie Smith and Tom Dowd. Van Gelder was an optometrist and electronics tinkerer who built his first recording studio in his parents' Hackensack, New Jersey, living room, later moving to Englewood Cliffs, New Jersey, where he built a new studio from the ground up. He became renowned among musicians and jazz fans alike for the unique sound he achieved engineering the legendary Blue Note and Impulse! jazz recordings of the 1950s and 1960s as well as for his quirky and sometimes abrasive personal style. He was so good at what he did, that musicians went out of their way to use his studio rather than one of the many studios in Manhattan, sometimes driving through blizzard weather conditions, only to be told by the punctual Van Gelder that they had arrived too early and would have to wait in their cars until the appointed time.

Eddie Smith was an arranger for bandleader Lucky Millinder in the 1940s before becoming a recording engineer at King Records in Cincinnati, Ohio, in the 1950s, then at Bell Sound Studios in New York during that independent studio's heyday of the 1960s. Smith, who had acquired an amateur radio license at the age of fourteen, possessed a background in both music and electronics which provided the ideal training for a recording engineer, although he didn't know it at the time. When his friend from the Millinder days, trumpeter and songwriter Henry Glover, called Smith in 1951 to ask if he wanted to be the King Records 'A&R' director – which stood for 'artist and repertoire,' or essentially record producer – Smith did not expect that he would soon be operating the recording console. But the King Records operation, as he soon learned,

> [W]as like a community thing – anybody that could sit down would do the date. 'Cause I mean what did you have? Four microphones . . . most of the stuff we did, we had one vocal [mike] for the singers, and the group would use the same mike . . . we'd pick up the whole rhythm section with one mike. You had to! There was no stereo or 2-track.[24]

In its informal and basic approach to recording, King epitomized the independent recording facility of this period, but it was extraordinary in its vertical integration of all aspects of the business – recording, pressing, label and album artwork, song publishing, record distribution – and was therefore an ideal training ground. By the time Smith got a call to work in New York at Bell Sound Studios, he knew nearly every aspect of recording, engineering and record manufacturing, and his arranging and musical ability gave him a talent few other engineers in the United States possessed – he could follow a musical score while engineering an orchestral date. With broad technical experience, solid musical background, and an easygoing manner, Smith became one of the most sought-after recording engineers in New York, working with artists ranging from Ferrante and Teischer to Burt Bacharach and Hal David.

Tom Dowd, who as a college student had worked on the Manhattan Project, got his first engineering job at a small recording studio in Manhattan before becoming chief engineer for Atlantic Records and going on to build that label's first studio in 1958.[25] Dowd had heard about guitarist Les Paul's eight-track tape recorder, built by Ampex Special Products Division and delivered to Paul's New Jersey home studio in 1956, and he convinced Atlantic's owners that this was an essential tool for their business. Working with songwriters and producers Jerry Leiber and Mike Stoller in the 1950s, Dowd recalled that, 'I was their engineer, but at the same time, I could give them input, and it was always a two-way street, an open door, move things around, "What about this?"'[26] When he explained what the eight-track recorder could do, that they could make a record 'sound bigger if they sang that part again, backed up and overdubbed another series of voices,' the songwriters immediately embraced the concept. '"You can do that? Here we go, look out world!" Then they started writing that way, to take advantage of the new technology.'[27]

During the late 1960s, there emerged clear generational and aesthetic differences between engineers and the artists they recorded that mirrored the larger sociocultural changes of that decade. Ironically, as the technology of recording became more advanced, the level of training of the musicians who came into studios declined. More than one engineer who began his career during the big band era and worked with artists like Benny Goodman – himself noted for exacting standards of musicianship from his players – expressed utter despair at the changes necessary after the advent of rock 'n' roll. Frank Laico, who had begun recording in the 1930s for World Broadcasting transcription services, then worked as a Columbia Records engineer from 1946 until 1982, described how he approached recording the new music:

> I tell you, when I first got involved in it, which was a couple years after it really took hold, when the major record companies got into it, I took it on as a challenge. I would listen to whatever the records people said were hits. And you know most of that stuff they recorded was done in someone's basement or garage or whatever. Then the producers,

the people involved would say, 'Duplicate that sound.' Well, it's very difficult to duplicate that sound when it was done in the most meager circumstances and equipment, and here you are in a studio that was built for recording, you have all the modern equipment and all the talent that goes with it, and now you have to go all the way down the ladder and start over. Well, I found it a challenge, and I kind of enjoyed doing it. . . . I did it for a few years, and I finally went to the boss and said, 'I can't do it anymore.' He said, 'Why not?' I said, 'They're driving me crazy. I sit there, day after day and I'm hearing the same bass notes. It's impossible, I can't do it.' He says, 'Well, you got to.' I said, 'Well, maybe it's time we separated, cause I'm not going to.'[28]

Where engineers like Laico once recorded four 'sides,' or songs, in a three-hour session, they now had to learn tremendous patience with musicians who came into the recording studio with just an idea for a song, or perhaps could barely play their instruments, and frequently insisted on going over the same song, or section of a song, repeatedly until they felt they had gotten it right. For the recording engineer who had spent years learning a skill, working with highly polished bands who either came into the studio rehearsed or were such good sight readers that they did not require much rehearsal, working with untrained musicians must have seemed tantamount to deskilling.

The examples noted earlier of Frankie Yankovic and Brian Wilson might offer some clues to the role recording technology played in this. Yankovic's band may not have been as well-rehearsed as Benny Goodman's, but they simply could not afford to re-record every time they made a mistake. The group Laico described recording in the early 1970s was equally unrehearsed, but they could afford to re-record, primarily because they were using tape rather than disc recorders and tape could be reused or edited. Moreover, record companies by the 1960s believed that the sales of records justified whatever amount of studio time was required. In any event, if studio costs mounted, it usually came out of the performers' royalties.

High fidelity – How 'faithful' was it?

Debates about natural versus artificial sound permeated the 1950s, the era of 'high fidelity' and experimentation with what could be achieved on tape. Not every recording professional sought to push the bounds of recording technology. Jazz record producer John Hammond decried the use of echo chambers and other methods of achieving what he called 'phony effects' that he saw record companies 'knocking themselves out to achieve. . . . Fun for the sound engineers, maybe, but tough on the musicians. What's the good of having every instrument in a band sound as if it were being played in the Holland Tunnel?'[29] In the early days of stereo, considered by professionals and the public alike to be mere gimmickry, some of the more adventurous artists, engineers and audiophiles tried to explore the potential for new and better sounds on record. Conductor Enoch Light contributed to the popularization of stereo with his *Persuasive Percussion* album, conceived in 1959 as a vehicle to show the capabilities of stereophonic sound, again with the aid of engineer Bob Fine. The difficulty they encountered in achieving the separation of sound and in making a final master disc led to improvements in the technology. In a 1977 interview, Light recalled that:

> we must have blown fifteen or twenty Westrex cutters . . . we kept getting new cutters and blowing cutters and sending them to California and getting them back . . . no one had a cutter that could really cut a stereo record so our . . . experimentation . . . caused Westrex a lot of trouble but it also caused them to improve their cutter tremendously.[30]

The recording cutters, used to engrave the grooves in the master disc from the original recording made on tape, were not equipped to handle the level of power Light and Fine had managed to achieve on the original recording. Here was a case of improvements in one area of recording technology forcing improvements in another. Two- and three-track stereo were soon followed by four, eight, and sixteen track recording capabilities. Multitracking introduced the concept of physically separating instruments, at first by baffles or 'gobos' – movable partitions – placed between the instruments making it possible to record discrete tracks, which in turn made it possible to remove a single musician's or singer's mistake without rerecording the entire performance. This was considered by many to be the greatest benefit of multi tracking, whereas some noted that it often led to incompetence because of the general attitude that things 'could be fixed later in the mix.' One key quality in records of the pre-tape era and into the 1950s – a quality that began to vanish with the advent of multitracking – was the excitement of live performance and the tension created by the knowledge that one's performance was permanent. There was no opportunity for things to be changed later in the mix. Les Paul felt that the creative tension of having to get it right during the process of tape overdubbing and the overwhelming desire not to have to start over from the beginning made for better recordings. Engineer Mike Dorrough believes in the importance of the 'eyeball-to-eyeball' approach in the studio, how a certain 'symbiotic' interaction between the instruments provides a harmonic quality that is absent when instruments are recorded separately and later mixed together.[31] Both mention the overwhelming desire of each musician not to be the one to ruin a take, thus inspiring tighter, more lively and spontaneous performances.

The built environment of a recording studio was as important as its technical components, endowing records with an acoustic 'signature' that was as identifiable as a name on a label. Several engineers claim they could detect where a record was made by the way it sounded. Some of the most famous studios from the 1930s and 1940s were former dance halls, hotel ballrooms, or churches. Liederkranz Hall in Manhattan, home of the German Singing Society, was transformed into a recording studio in the 1930s and used by every major label to record popular and classical artists alike. Even today the name evokes fond memories among those who worked there, as expressed by conductor Andre Kostelanetz in his memoirs:

> The studio was an unimpressive upstairs room in the home of the old German Singing Society, Liederkranz Hall on Fifty-eighth Street. To have played there is to be spoiled forever as far as acoustical standards are concerned. It was all wood, which is the best material for good acoustics. One mike picked up everything. I was lucky not only to record in the Liederkranz studio but to do the Coca-Cola program there for five years, beginning in 1938. My ear became so sensitive to the acoustical perfection of the room that after a while I could tell just by how the orchestra sounded on a given morning whether the floor had been swept the night before. When CBS decided, in the mid-Forties, to turn it into a TV studio I was frantic; I tried to change Paley's mind but to no avail. I believe the building is gone altogether now, a loss that even today's most sophisticated technical equipment cannot make up for.[32]

The legend of Liederkranz lingered long within the recording community. Twenty years after CBS president William S. Paley destroyed its acoustical perfection, Fairchild Recording Equipment Corporation proudly sold its 'Reverbetron' as a compact means of achieving the classic Liederkranz sound: 'Famous for REVERBERATION . . .' declared the advertisement's bold heading, under which was featured a photograph of the stately facade of the nineteenth-century building:

> For years Liederkranz Hall was world renowned for its remarkable acoustic effects and consequently it was in constant demand for recording. But even Liederkranz Hall had its limitations! Engineers could not always control the reverberation quality and time. However if you wanted to record in Liederkranz Hall today it would be impossible because, as with most old landmarks, it's destined for destruction. But . . . don't fret, don't worry! There's a much more practical, effective, and less expensive method to add controlled reverberation to your sound. Now reverberation comes in a compact, portable attractive and rack mountable package 24 1/2″ high by 19″ wide in . . . THE FAIRCHILD REBERBETRON.[33]

Such appeals to compactness, affordability, and above all, controllability were common features in the marketing of recording studio equipment, a trade that literally exploded during the 1960s. Long before independent studios such as the Record Plant, Hit Factory, and Power Station built custom-designed studios with the latest sophisticated technical equipment, record labels like Columbia, RCA-Victor, and Mercury used large, preexisting facilities like the Pythian Temple, built by the Knights of Columbus; Columbia's 30th Street studio, once a Byzantine church; and the ballroom of the Great Northern Hotel, where performers appearing at Carnegie Hall, located just up the street, once stayed. All of these studios had wonderful natural acoustics for the kind of big band and orchestral recording that was popular into the early 1950s. But as recording engineering advanced, as ensemble sizes shrunk, as the recording equipment became more sophisticated, and as record companies realized enormous postwar profits from record sales, they abandoned older studios in favor of purpose-built facilities in which the engineers could achieve greater control over the sound.

Probably the first large-scale custom-designed recording studios were those incorporated in the Capitol Records Tower completed in Los Angeles in 1956. The first recording facility of its kind, including three specially designed studios and four sublevel reverberation chambers, the Tower studios were designed literally from the ground up. According to the company's vice president of manufacturing and engineering, James W. Bayless, in his account of the studios' design and construction for the Audio Engineering Society's Eighth Annual Convention in September 1956:

> We at Capitol have had a unique opportunity: a chance to start from the ground up and create a recording facility embodying many features which modern recording practice makes desirable. We borrowed the techniques of motion picture sound-stage design and construction to achieve low noise levels and proper diffusion. We employed advances in acoustical materials and constructions to achieve a new concept in studio design: minimized reverberation, but a nearly flat characteristic. We designed compatible reverberation chambers to provide optimal acoustical properties. The result has been a modern, diversified plant, physically attractive, acoustically controllable and electromechanically flexible. The combination provides the fulfillment of the esthetic considerations important to the artist and the practical engineering considerations of concern to the producer.[34]

Unfortunately, the studio did not meet these high expectations immediately. During the first sessions in February 1956, conducted by Frank Sinatra for an orchestral album entitled *Tone Poems in Color*, the musicians were appalled when they first began to play: 'THUD! It was just dead as hell,' recalled clarinetist Mitchell Lurie. 'I think it sounds like shit!' answered cellist

Eleanor Slatkin when Sinatra asked what she thought of the playback.[35] Capitol engineer John Palladino recalled that session and many that followed as disappointing to the musicians and challenging to the engineers, mainly because the studio was so much larger than the Melrose Avenue studio they had grown accustomed to:

> You don't have anything of a constant. You're going into a different monitor room. You don't even know whether you've got a basis for listening to anything. And then you go and you have this big studio, and some of the same techniques [we] used at Melrose didn't seem to work out . . . because of the acoustics.[36]

To be sure, there was a certain level of resistance to the new and attachment to the familiar. Another Capitol engineer recalled that the Melrose studio, which had a tremendous reputation with musicians, 'really set a standard for music at the time.' He grew so tired of hearing the musicians say, 'Let's go back to Melrose,' that he finally played them a recording made at the former studio, 'and they all suddenly realized that the new studio was by far acoustically superior.'[37] But that was only after a good deal of acoustical and electronic tinkering, and considerable additional expense had been invested in bringing the facility up to optimal standards for artist and engineer alike.[38]

It was just such tinkering that appealed to recording engineers, who exhibited their own particular brand of technological enthusiasm that was so essential to the development of recording and the growth of studios. Like the drag racers Robert Post studied in *High Performance,* audio engineers wanted to 'chase sound' for the satisfying emotional experience of tweaking the machinery in search of something better.[39] Les Paul spent years honing his techniques of disc overdubbing and electronic effects in a succession of home studios in which he continued to record exclusively throughout his career. He was just one, albeit among the most famous, of many audio enthusiasts who sought to improve the art and science of recording in the postwar decades. Clair Krepps, who in 1946 built the Capitol Records New York mastering studio and in 1965 built his own eight-track studio, Mayfair Recording, recalled the days in which 'high fidelity' became the watchword among engineers:

> That's why we started the Audio Engineering Society, to improve the fidelity of the phonograph record . . . we all thought we are carrying the torch for Thomas Edison. Really! That was our thing – we were going to advance Edison's art. It was a very exciting period . . . when we were doing this – this is hard for young people to understand – the people we worked for: producers, musicians, they thought we were a bunch of nuts to improve the sound of the phonograph record. They said, 'It doesn't matter, it's the song that counts.'[40]

The song, the arrangement, the artist – these were considered the critical factors in a hit song from the beginning of the commercial recording industry in the late nineteenth century until the middle of the twentieth. By the late 1960s, however, the creation of a uniquely identifiable sound had begun to acquire as much importance as the identifiable melody and lyric, at least within the musical genres that had grown to dominate record sales: pop, rock and psychedelic music. These styles arguably owed their very existence to the use of the recording studio as a creative tool. By 1968, the recording studio had become so integral to the creation of music, it led one pop culture critic to observe:

> A phenomenon of today's music is that much of it can't be heard live, except by a few people, at least not the way it is heard on the records responsible for the music's success in the first place. The methods used to achieve the collection of sounds called rock 'n' roll (and/or psychedelic, jazz-oriented, baroque rock, whatever term you like; it's pretty fluid just now) are so complex that they often can't be reproduced outside the studio. Luckily, fans don't expect the same performance onstage of tunes they play on the phonograph.[41]

Clearly, recording quality had come a long way from the days of the Edison 'tone tests' a half-century before, when the 'faithfulness' of recordings to the live performance was so questionable that the public had to be sold on how 'lifelike' the phonograph record could sound.[42] Indeed, the recorded work in 1968 had surpassed the live performance to such an extent that listeners were more likely to judge the live performance based on how closely it resembled the record, rather than the other way around.

Conclusion

These developments put recording studios among the most important sites of cultural production since the end of World War II.[43] Between 1948 and 1968, the introduction of professional magnetic tape recorders, improved microphones, stereophonic sound, transistors, multitrack recording – all revolutionized the way composers and musicians conceive music, the way engineers and producers work in the studio, and the way we hear music.[44] Although some of these innovations have already entered the hallowed realm of obsolete technologies, their impact on the changing culture of music recording was profound and enduring. It is no single technology, but rather the aggregate effect of a general trend toward greater control and manipulation of sound that shaped the direction of musical style in the postwar period.[45]

The 1940s to 1960s were watershed decades in the history of music recording. Not only had the recording industry grown exponentially, but the number of recording studios expanded so dramatically and globally that *Billboard Magazine* issued the first *International Directory of Recording Studios* in 1970. By then, the number of tracks in state-of-the-art studios had grown to twenty-four, and eventually reached forty-eight. Postmixing became a group effort simply because one engineer did not have enough fingers to manipulate the controls alone, so companies began to introduce automated mixing to cure that problem. But what followed in the 1970s tended toward excess, with an attendant loss of immediacy, spontaneity and excitement that the punk and new wave movements that originated in the United States and flowered in the United Kingdom attempted to reverse. The direction of studio recording, like the record business itself, had changed with the growth of the capital enterprise and the decline of the hobbyist/experimenter. Those pioneers who had spent years chasing sound had made it possible for the ultimate control and manipulation of sound. As one participant neatly summed it up, 'the studio became an end in itself, rather than simply a means to an end.'[46]

Notes

1 F. Yankovic, as told to R. Dolgan, *The Polka King* (Cleveland, 1977), 67.

2 B. Wilson with T. Gold, *Wouldn't It Be Nice: My Own Story* (New York, 1991), 145–7.

3 Disc overdubbing had been attempted, but usually resulted in excessive noise as each overdub led to degradation of the sound quality. One well-publicized and highly successful attempt was made by clarinetist Sidney Bechet for RCA-Victor in 1941. Bechet's 'One Man Band' versions of 'The Sheik' and 'Blues of Bechet' featured Bechet on six different instruments 'recorded by re-recording 5 times.' C. Delauney, *New Hot Discography* (New York, 1948), 23. Similarly, guitarist Les Paul experimented with disc overdubbing and succeeded at creating remarkably clean-sounding multiple recordings by the late 1940s.

4 Although I do not claim to undertake such an analysis in the present article, Thomas Misa's 'meso-level' approach to studying sociotechnological change has influenced my thinking on this subject. T. Misa, 'Retrieving Sociotechnical Change From Technological Determinism,' in *Does Technology Drive History? The Dilemma of Technological Determinism*, ed. M. Smith and L. Marx (Cambridge, Mass., 1994), 115–41.

5 Rube Goldberg (1883–1970) was a trained engineer turned cartoonist in the early twentieth century. His most famous cartoon strips featured, as Goldberg himself put it, 'outlandish complications of inventive effort to accomplish practically nothing' (e.g. 'Professor Butts' Self-Operating Napkin'). Inspired by his love of complex machinery, Goldberg's 'invention cartoons' held such

universal and enduring appeal that any complex mechanism – social, political, technological – requiring more energy than justified by the output became forever linked with his name. P. Marzio, *Rube Goldberg: His Life and Work* (New York, 1973), 177–222, quote from 301. I do not mean to imply that recording inventions resulted in practically nothing, only to suggest that the simplicity of the outcome belied the complex technical effort involved.

6 There were exceptions to this rule, as some early musical directors/producers, such as Frederick Gaisberg, also operated recording equipment. See F. Gaisberg, *The Music Goes Round* (New York, 1977).

7 Mitch Miller, Interview with author, New York, New York, 21 January 1999.

8 Al Brackman recalled the incident in I. Chusid, 'Raymond Scott,' liner notes to *The Music of Raymond Scott: Reckless Nights and Turkish Twilights,* Columbia CD 53028.

9 Although the term 'echo chamber' is most commonly used, the effect generated is often reverberation, and there is a technical difference: reverberation is the prolongation of sound waves by repeated reflection, the sort achieved by reflecting off very hard surfaced walls, such as bathroom tile. But if that reflection achieves a 1/20 second delay, it is then considered an echo. H. Tremaine, *Audio Cyclopedia,* 2d ed. (Indianapolis: Howard W. Sams, 1969, c. 1959), 89.

10 Although eventually identified with his 'Sing Along With Mitch' recordings and television shows, Miller had achieved notoriety long before as concert oboist turned pop producer who raised Columbia Records from last to the dominant position in popular recording sales in the early 1950s. G. Millstein, 'He Calls the Hit Tune,' *Collier's* (January 19, 1952): 20–1, 35–6.

11 Consider, for example, the annual Academy Awards ceremonies, made by the Academy of Motion Picture Arts and Sciences, in which the 'technical' awards are presented at a different location and time than the 'creative' awards presented with much fanfare and publicity on 'awards night.' Thanks to Michael Grossberg for pointing out this parallel to me at an early stage in my research.

12 Mitch Miller, Interview with author, New York, New York, 21 January 1999.

13 D. Hall and A. Levin. *The Disc Book* (New York, 1955), 11.

14 M. Calvert, *The Mechanical Engineer in America, 1830–1910: Professional Cultures in Conflict* (Baltimore, 1967); H. Seymour, *The Reproduction of Sound* (London, 1918).

15 On drag racing and its predecessor, hot-rodding, see H. F. Moorhouse, 'The "Work" Ethic and "Leisure" Activity: The Hot Rod in Post-war America,' in *The Historical Meanings of Work,* edited by P. Joyce (Cambridge, 1987): 237–309; and R. Post, *High Performance: The Culture and Technology of Drag Racing, 1950–1990* (Baltimore, 1994). On amateur ('ham') wireless operators see S. Douglas, *Inventing American Broadcasting, 1899–1922* (Baltimore, 1987), esp. chapter six. Periodicals such as *Radio-Craft* (1929–1948) and *Radio News* (1920–1948) specifically catered to the radio amateur and regularly featured articles on home recording.

16 J. Potts, *Radio* 31 (Feb/March 1947): inside cover page.

17 J. Potts, 'Transients,' *Audio Engineering* 31 (May 1947): 4.

18 The Sapphire Club, named for the use of sapphire corundum as the recording cutting tool or stylus, had its origins when Wally Rose of the Frank L. Capps Company, makers of recording stylii, began to lunch regularly with Vin Liebler, head of the recording department of Columbia Records, Inc., and G. E. Stewart of the National Broadcasting Company's recording division. They soon invited more members of New York's recording community, and eventually began to hold monthly meetings. This by-invitation-only club used printed invitations and designed a group pin, a sapphire on an oval representation of a phonograph record. Donald Plunkett, Interview with author, New York, New York, 9 February 1999; William Savory, Interview with author, 29 November 1997.

19 R. Callen, 'Hollywood Sapphire Group,' *Audio Engineering* (January 1948): 17, 39–41. According to several members, the New York group was always more of a social club than the Hollywood group, but it was significant for initiating the process of communication between competitors in the recording industry, which had a history of secrecy dating back to the days of Edison.

20 E. von Hippel, *The Sources of Innovation* (New York, 1988).

21 W. Temple, 'We Went to the Audio Fair,' *Senior Scholastic* 55 (Dec. 7, 1949): 23T.

22 R. Sooy, 'Memoirs of My Recording and Traveling Experiences for the Victor Talking Machine Company,' n.d., unpaginated, unpublished photocopy of typescript. Copy in possession of author, courtesy Alexander Magoun. Original photocopy in Hagley Museum and Library Collection 2138, 'Files of Nicholas F. Pensiero.'

23 Dave Teig, Telephone conversation with author, July 1996. Mr. Teig was the manager of Bell Sound Studios from 1958 to 1974, then of Atlantic Records Studios from 1974 to 1981.

24 Eddie Smith, Interview with author, New York, New York, 23 January 1999.

25 Tom Dowd, Telephone interview with author, 23 March 1999.

26 Quoted in J. Tobler and S. Grundy, *The Record Producers* (New York, 1982), 25.

27 Ibid.

28 Frank Laico, Telephone interview with author, 13 January 1999.

29 Quoted in 'Talk of the Town,' *The New Yorker* (July 17, 1954), 17–18, quote on p. 17.

30 R. Gradone, 'Enoch Light (1905–1978): His Contributions to the Music Recording Industry' (Ph.D. diss., New York University, 1980): 194.

31 Mike Dorrough, Telephone interview with author, 19 August 1996.

32 A. Kostelanetz, in collaboration with G. Hammond, *Echoes: Memoirs of Andre Kostelanetz* (New York, 1981), 82.

33 Fairchild Recording Equipment Corporation advertisement, *Journal of the Audio Engineering Society* 13 (Oct. 1965), p. A-234.

34 J. Bayless, 'Innovations in Studio Design and Construction in the Capitol Tower Recording Studios,' *Journal of the Audio Engineering Society* (April 1957): 75–6.

35 Quoted in C. Granata, *Sessions with Sinatra: Frank Sinatra and the Art of Recording* (Chicago, 1999), 116.

36 John Palladino, Telephone interview with author, 15 October 1999.

37 P. Grein, *Capitol Records: Fiftieth Anniversary, 1942–1992* (Hollywood, 1992), 21.

38 Granata, op. cit. (35), 116.

39 R. Post, *High Performance: The Culture and Technology of Drag Racing, 1950–1990* (Baltimore, 1994).

40 Clair Krepps, Telephone interview with author, 23 March 1999.

41 A. Geracimos, 'A Record Producer Is a Psychoanalyst With Rhythm,' *New York Times Magazine* (September 29, 1968): 32–3, 55–70; quote from pp. 32–3.

42 E. Thompson, 'Machines, Music, and the Quest for Fidelity: Marketing the Edison Phonograph in America, 1877–1925,' *Musical Quarterly* 79 (Spring 1995): 131–71.

43 The literature on the history of the phonograph and sound recording has grown substantially in the last decade. Books that deal to some degree with the evolution of studio technology include S. Jones, *Rock Formation: Music, Technology, and Mass Communication* (Newbury Park, California, 1992), A. Millard, *America on Record: A History of Recorded Sound* (New York, 1995), and D. Morton, *Off the Record: The Technology and Culture of Sound Recording in America* (New Brunswick, New Jersey, 2000).

44 Studies which explore the effects of recording on the creation and perception of music are M. Chanan, *Repeated Takes: A Short History of Recording and its Effects on Music* (London, 1995), and M. Katz, 'The Phonograph Effect: The Influence of Recording on Listener, Performer, Composer, 1900–1940' (Ph.D. diss., University of Michigan, 1999).

45 Efforts to control the behavior of sound in enclosed spaces by earlier scientists paralleled, and contributed to, the work recording engineers undertook in this century. See E. Thompson, '"Mysteries of the Acoustic": Architectural Acoustics in America, 1800–1932' (Ph.D. diss., Princeton University, 1992).

46 Matthew Barton, Telephone conversation with author, 1 November 1998. Mr. Barton has written for the *Boston Globe* and *Street Beat,* a trade paper for juke box operators. In 1996 he began working with Rounder Records as a technical adviser for *The Alan Lomax Collection.*

Research for this project was made possible by a Doctoral Dissertation Research Grant from the National Science Foundation's STS Program.

7

FM radio and the long-playing record

Background and topics

When sympathetic commentators look back on the 1960s, they often do so through a haze of nostalgia. Many imagine what historian and political commentator Thomas Frank notes is a simple contrast between mainstream culture and the counterculture. The former was grey and dull, the latter colorful and exciting: "Mainstream culture was tepid, mechanical, and uniform; the revolt of the young against it was a joyous and even glorious cultural flowering." The young people born after the war and who came of age in the early to mid-1960s are said to have initiated and realized a cultural revolution specifically by rebelling against their conformist elders. The reality, however, is more complicated.

As Frank explains, the desire to escape the conformist chains of mainstream culture was not confined only to particularly free-thinking teenagers. Instead, it came from a large section of mainstream culture itself. Historians, artists, novelists, psychologists, journalists, business leaders, and academics all counseled the young against simply accepting the world they were inheriting. Young people were told in newspapers, magazines, books, and on television to seek out and find their authentic selves. This was because the changes to the social and cultural realities of many places in the world that defined what we now call "The Sixties" began far earlier than is generally acknowledged. They were also championed by some long thought to be the natural enemy of those changes. Even writers and researchers who focused on such sober topics as the economy and corporate management published critiques of the soul-destroying demands of large bureaucratic organizations. Everywhere one looked, it seemed, one could find a stirring

FIGURE 7.1 *Playing records on the radio (1940).*

call to challenge authority. As Frank argues, "The meaning of 'the sixties' cannot be considered apart from the enthusiasm of ordinary, suburban Americans for cultural revolution." He says that "we have forgotten the cosmic optimism with which so any organs of official American culture greeted the youth rebellion."

The backdrop of this yearning for personal and expressive freedom was the pervasive anxiety of the Cold War. The very real fear of total annihilation through nuclear war inspired a great number of people in many parts of the world to seek out something different, something better. The historian Jeremi Suri suggests that what eventually became known as the counterculture has its origins in the diffuse ideological battle lines drawn between contending forces:

> Ideological competition in the Cold War encouraged citizens to look beyond material factors alone, and to seek a deeper meaning in their daily activities. Many women, however, did not feel freer in the modern kitchens that US vice-president Richard Nixon extolled as a symbol of capitalist accomplishment. Many men did not feel freer as they went to their daily jobs in the large-scale industries that underwrote the costs of new global responsibilities. Many students did not feel freer as they

attended mass institutions of higher education, particularly universities. An international counterculture developed in response to dissatisfaction with the dominant culture of the Cold War.

If the Cold War was a war for people's minds and souls, then this meant that the basic things of everyday life were charged with new meaning. Everything, from clothes to music to hair, mattered. "Politics" was not something thought to occur only in legislatures. It happened on the street, in the home, in the workplace, and in schools. One document captured this collective feeling perhaps more than any other. It is called the "Port Huron Statement." It was written by a group of young people who gathered in Port Huron, Michigan, in 1962 and called themselves Students for a Democratic Society (SDS). They aimed to set down their desires and aspirations for their future.

Their values were very much shaped by the events going on around them. They argued that they were "the inheritors and the victims of a barren period in the development of human values." While they all attended universities they found "little enlightenment there" because "the old promise that knowledge and increased rationality would liberate society seems hollow, if not a lie." However, rather than petitioning Congress for a redress of their grievances, they looked for something much larger and more ambitious: "The liberation of this individual potential is the just end of society; the directing of the same potential, through voluntary participation, to the benefit of society, is the just end of the individual." Their claims and argument almost established a kind of ideological blueprint for the emerging youth movement soon to be called "the counterculture." They sought authenticity and meaning:

> The goal of man and society should be human independence: a concern not with image or popularity but with finding a meaning in life that is personally authentic: a quality of mind not compulsively driven by a sense of powerlessness, nor one which unthinkingly adopts status values, nor one which represses all threats to its habits, but one which has full spontaneous access to present and past experiences, one which easily unites the fragmented parts of personal history, one which openly faces problems which are troubling and unresolved; one with an intuitive awareness of possibilities, an active sense of curiosity, an ability and willingness to learn.

Note the language and the focus. Much of what they sought could not be granted through formal political channels in the form of law or policy. They sought no less than a cultural revolution.

With this background in mind, we now turn to the development of radio and sound recording from the late 1950s to the late 1960s through FM radio and the long-playing record, or LP. Bear in mind that this specific context of cultural change shaped how people would take these familiar forms of media and experiment with them in new ways.

The "new" record and the new radio band

From the late 1950s and into the 1960s, new and influential uses were made of two technologies which had existed for a long time: radio and records. These new uses were only partly inspired by technological innovation and were in large measure a result of larger social changes. So, while we can note the birth date of radio broadcasting as 1920 and find out that the first FM broadcast was in 1940, in the mid to late 1960s some people began to use radio in ways it had not been used before. Similarly, something that we would recognize as an "album" was made commercially available in 1948 and we might date its invention as far back as 1931. Yet, like radio, new uses were found for this familiar technology. In both cases, the new uses for these existing technologies were so different than what had gone before that many people were forced to rethink their potential in fundamental ways.

The first objects we might recognize as precursors to "albums" were produced by RCA Victor from 1931 to 1933. These were based on the discs used in the Vitaphone sound system used for films (see Figures in Chapters 3 and 5). Referred to as "Program Transcriptions," they held more music than any physical format had before. However, their durability and sound quality were limited and RCA's engineers could not find a way to make them last more than a few dozen plays. It wasn't until Columbia introduced the full-length vinyl LP in 1948 that recording formats that could hold more than ten to twelve minutes of music became a permanent feature of the music consumption landscape. Over the next twenty years, long-playing records would take up a social position and status first as a vehicle for "serious" or "adult" music, such as symphonies or Broadway cast albums, and later a symbolic marker of the music of young people.

While it may seem obvious to us that the vinyl long-playing record album was a significant improvement over the formats which preceded it, this was certainly not the consensus at the time. But this had less to do with the quality of the sound or the capacity to hold what was then an unprecedented amount of music in a durable and convenient form. Instead, as the music historian Alban Zak tells us, there were serious disagreements about what the very purpose of sound recording actually was. Some claimed that the studio should only be used to document live musical performances. This, so the argument went, was not "canned music"; it was real—the recording simply translated it to us. Anything else was mere fraud. As Zak explains, "The critical consensus held that sound recording was meant not to invade and manipulate real-world musical experience, but to document it and make it portable; studio trickery was an unseemly affront to musical intelligence." We can see how this sentiment fits in very comfortably with the ideals of music noted in earlier chapters. Music was far too important and influential a social force to allow such "trickery" to occur.

This perspective is what we can call the "documentary" perspective of sound recording. It was a holdover from the era of 78s in which recorded music never really approximated the sound and experience of live music. In the era, the distinction between live and recorded music was always immediately audible. However, most places in which music was recorded were always creative spaces used by musicians and those recording their music in innovative ways. Further, as studio technology, recording techniques, records, and speakers continually improved, innovators came to demonstrate that sound recording was an art unto itself. It did not and could not simply "replace" live music. Its purpose had never been to simply document a sound event. Instead, it could provide a vast new set of tools and techniques for the expansion and diversification of the listening experience. In short, the recording studio became a sphere of creativity and the sound recordings became the tangible outcome of that creative work. We will look at this in more detail in the next chapter.

However, now we need to look briefly at the other key reading for this part of the book:

Horning, Susan. (2000) "Chasing Sound: The Culture and Technology of Recording Studios in Postwar America." *Icon*, 6: 100–18.

In this article, historian Susan Horning examines how "the recording studio had been transformed from a functional worksite in which well-rehearsed performances were recorded on the spot, to a creative workplace in which the tools of recording became integral to the creative process itself." For this chapter we will focus only on the first half of the article, from pages 192 to 200. Here Horning explains how the "documentary" perspective on sound recordings often contrasted with a more creative model. Look in particular at how she explains that innovation was certainly not absent from the recording studio from the beginning. However, what is important to understand is how those working in recording studios often used clever and original methods to realize their aims. Her main claim here is that there is no simple cause and effect relationship between the availability of new tools and artistic or technical innovation on the part of musicians, producers, and engineers. Make sure you understand the key concerns of those Horning describes and how these concerns continue throughout the historical period she examines even as the tools they use change significantly.

Sound recording, DJs, and radio

The changes in the status of the sound recording and the use and purpose of the recording studio also had a strong influence over radio broadcasting as well. As noted above, the idea of playing records over the radio was not as straightforward as we might think. There was a strong assumption that audiences were somehow being fooled and taken advantage of through the use of prerecorded music and programming. However, with the advent of television, most of the core programming on most radio stations moved to television very quickly. This included not just the on-air talent, but the producers, writers, and promoters as well. This had several significant consequences that changed radio broadcasting forever. First, the reliance on centralized network programming declined substantially. The programs that had been the mainstay of most radio broadcasting since the late 1920s had either moved to television or had simply ceased to exist. Second, this opened up new opportunities for local control over programming and led to the emergence of a new kind of cultural presence: the disc jockey. Unlike those who preceded them, DJs played records, lots of them. They were often derided by some in the music industry for simply playing other people's records and not creating anything of their own. Nevertheless, there was no way for record companies to ignore the power that local radio stations and their on-air talent had managed to acquire for themselves. This was the power to make or break a record in a particular city or region. Interestingly, it was at this exact historical moment in which the radio broadcasting industry was expanding rapidly. Hundreds of new stations were licensed and a whole "new" band came into operation, the FM band. Albin Zak suggests that in the 1950s "the country was awash in recorded sound." He continues: "Disc jockeys guided their listeners through the plenitude," he says, by "highlighting records they particularly liked or were, in one way or another, induced to play."

Finally, some of the new records people were beginning to hear on the radio sounded a lot different from the old ones. The new records were in stereo and so was the new radio band. This was a new way to hear music. Instead of a largely flat imaginary aural space, stereo allowed increasingly discriminating placement of sounds in a listener's total field of hearing. This

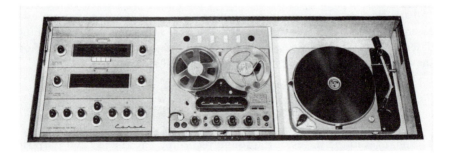

FIGURE 7.2 *Detail of a high-end Carad Pro Arte audio unit (1962).*

meant that sounds could be placed not just on the left or the right, but in the front and in the back. This concept has been referred to as the "Soundbox" and has come to define the modern listening experience of most studio-produced music. Stereo was one of the more subtle and easily overlooked musical revolutions of the 1950s and 1960s. Quite literally, it changed how we heard music, deepening and enriching the experience right when that music was becoming increasingly complex and ambitious. Before we examine one manifestation of that complexity, we need to understand how the album became "the album."

Explore and report: How to listen to an album

Traditionally, the term "album" has meant simply a collection or compilation. However, the term has almost universally come to refer a very historically specific material form. In this version, an "album" is a double-sided vinyl disc, 12 inches in diameter, with about twenty-two minutes of music on each side. Additionally, the contents are meant to have some kind of thematic or aesthetic coherence even when they are contained music produced by multiple artists. However, as the images on the next several pages show, the objects that we could conceivably count as "albums," or at least precursors of "the album," have always displayed a great deal of variability.

There are two goals for this section. First, you need to come to a fairly specific understanding of the very different kinds of albums that have existed over the years. Second, you need to come to an understanding of how the album has had many different kinds of social meaning attached to it, differences stemming from the various types of social relationships albums were intended to create and facilitate. This is a good way to understand how people's listening and buying habits are primed and shaped when new technologies arrive.

First, look at the images below and make some notes about the qualities all of these "albums" have in common and what distinguishes them from one another. Think about what they look like in terms of size and their labels, how many separate tracks they hold, how each organizes music, what kinds of music are on each, and how you are probably meant to use them.

Second, follow up by finding out more about the following: "Program Transcription records," "33 1/3 microgroove LPs," "RCA Victor Extended 45s," and the advent of commercially available vinyl albums generally between 1948 and 1958. Look for advertisements and scour YouTube for instructional and explanatory films about the process of making vinyl records. RCA released a short film in 1956 called "The Sound and the Story" and another called "Living Stereo," which explain the process of recording live music and their final form on vinyl. There are many others you should view as well.

FIGURE 7.3 *Label for an Edison "Transcription" Disc (1926).*

FIGURE 7.4 *Columbia 7 inch 33 1/3 rpm microgroove LP (1948).*

FIGURE 7.5 *Three Sizes of Vinyl Record.*

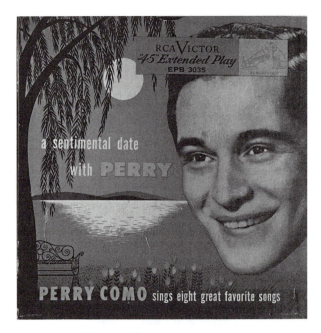

FIGURE 7.6 *RCA Victor 45 Extended Play (1948).*

FIGURE 7.7 *RCA Victor 45 Extended Play (1948).*

FIGURE 7.8 *Poster for KMPK First Birthday Benefit (1968).*

Finally, find out as much as you can about the albums released by Columbia between 1948 and 1958. Focus especially on their classical music recordings, the original-cast album to the musical South Pacific from 1958 and the albums by Frank Sinatra between 1953 and 955. When albums were first introduced, they were sold almost exclusively as "adult" music. Explain why this was the case.

Focus: Freeform radio

The changes in the radio broadcasting industry in the United States in the 1950s created the newly influential figure of the DJ. The greatly increased numbers of radio stations and vast numbers of hours to fill with programming

FIGURE 7.9 *Advertisement for WMMS-sponsored concert (1969).*

created a whole new culture of radio. The on-air voices were dominated by men who played an extremely limited numbers of 45 rpm singles and focused their playlists on a very small number of songs that were very closely related stylistically. They supplemented this with simple, slang-laden "patter" intended to demonstrate their relevance to the culture of teenagers. Between about 1945 and 1960, this new culture became the dominant way music was presented in public in many places. It was called simply "Top 40" radio and it had significant influence around the world becoming a widely used template for radio low-cost, high-engagement radio broadcasting.

However, by the early 1960s there were a number of DJs who were beginning to resist the significant constraints imposed by this dominant form of radio. They wanted to play something other than three-minute singles and do more than simply reproduce the reigning symbols of what was considered cool at any one particular moment. Perhaps more significantly, they wished to avoid using the often rigid formats of radio broadcasting that ruthlessly slotted music into preexisting categories. They wanted to play longer pieces of music, they wanted to juxtapose music from different traditions and genres, and they wanted to talk about things they felt people weren't talking about on radio.

As the journalist and writer Marc Fisher has explained, a new culture of music listening had been building since the late 1950s that expanded with the introduction of FM stereo broadcasting in 1961, FM car radios in 1963, and a demand from broadcast regulators that any broadcaster owning both AM and FM stations had to put original programming on both bands. Fisher also notes that new, more complex hi-fi systems intended to provide the full experience of the new stereo records as well as table-top stereo units had begun to sell in the tens of millions across the decade. Up to this point, FM had been mostly left to those broadcasting classical music, the cast albums of Broadway musicals, and the rich syrupy sounds of easy listening, along with a few small stations devoted to playing jazz. Those broadcasting these forms of music took advantage of the richness of the new technologies and others wanted to do the same.

The first stirrings of what would eventually be called "freeform radio" began at a few commercial AM and FM radio stations spread out around the United States. New kinds of radio started being broadcast mostly from midnight to 6 a.m., a time slot thought to be very nearly pointless, at least in a commercial sense. A few DJs such as Jean Shepherd and Long John Nebel began to gain some attention by expanding their on-air patter to include compact-but-engaging brands of storytelling mixed in with music while others rambled through lengthy improvised monologues. They produced hours of programming that seemed anarchic and could often be very dark in tone and content. Yet each attracted more listeners and influence than anyone in their industry thought possible. These hosts experimented with live call-ins, still unusual in those days, produced aggressive live comedy and satire, and dreamed up stunts that were realized by groups of particularly devoted listeners. As use of the FM band expanded, more and more marginal forms of expression began to find their ways onto the radio. Some hosts began to mix an unprecedented range of materials together in shows that stretched out for several hours on end. Programs such as Radio Unnameable, started by Bob Fass in 1958 at WBAI in New York, were emblematic of this style of broadcasting. Largely freed from the constraints of the program format and managing the demands of organizing musical genres into coherent programming, these programs were often wildly incoherent, but also free, open, and inventive.

By the end of the 1960s, DJs at several commercial FM stations, such as KSAN in San Francisco and WABX in Detroit, began to take the ideas of freedom and autonomy that were all around them and make a new kind of radio out of them. However, rather than the improvisation and random unpredictability of some of their predecessors, those making what was called "freeform" radio tried to speak coherently to their audience. They were influenced by several things. First, many noted that the classical and jazz stations on the FM band often played very long stretches of music without alienating their audiences. Indeed, their audiences expected this.

The producers of freeform radio simply wanted to do the same with "their" music, mostly rock, blues, and folk. Second, they wanted to take full advantage of the album format and play entire sides or even entire albums straight through without interruption. Finally, they tried to craft a diversity of sources melded together through lengthier passages of uninterrupted music that they felt could shape new ways of experiencing and thinking about music, and hopefully, the world.

As broadcast historian Michael Keith has shown, freeform radio stations valued musical eclecticism and allowed their DJs a great deal of latitude in what they played. This included the blues, rock 'n' roll, rock, folk, country music, as well as what would later be called "world music," especially Indian classical music and Indonesian court music, or gamelan. However, it is important to note that most of the time these stations were not the pure, open, on-air free-for-alls of legend. Many had clear programming guidelines, stuck to familiar scheduling rhythms, and many succeeded financially in ways markedly similar to the Top 40 stations they challenged. That is, they established a clear repertoire through a keenly developed relationship with their audience. Then, they managed to stay current and relevant to that audience by engaging with its interests and responding to its demands. Gradually, the cultural momentum pushing freeform radio dissipated and most of the stations eased into becoming fairly straightforward commercial rock stations. A few underground, noncommercial stations remained, such as WFMU in New Jersey, and they continue to embody an ethos of free, open programming that began over fifty years ago.

INDEPENDENT RESEARCH WORK

Freeform radio DJs was an interesting example of a cultural intermediary. In the music industry, a cultural intermediary is a person who facilitates the relationships between musicians and their audience. Freeform DJs were interesting because they were not usually directly a part of the music industry. Their credibility with their audience depended on this. Explore the history of freeform radio and the role of DJs in it. Then, find someone in a roughly comparable position today. Perhaps you could explore the role of playlist curators and compare their roles with those of freeform DJs. Examine the similarities and differences between the two. Specifically, compare their respective relationships with the music industry, with listeners, and with musicians. Come to some kind of qualitative assessment of the roles and value of each. In short, argue which one was better for musicians, listeners, and the music industry.

References and further readings

Elborough, Travis. (2008) *The Long-Player Goodbye: The Album from Vinyl to iPod and Back Again*. London: Sceptre.

Fisher, Marc. (2007) *Something in the Air: Radio, Rock, and the Revolution That Shaped a Generation*. New York: Random House.

Frank, Thomas. (1997) *The Conquest of Cool: Business Culture, Counterculture, and the Rise of Hip Consumerism*. Chicago: University of Chicago Press.

Keith, Michael. (1997) *Voices in the Purple Haze: Underground Radio and the Sixties*. Westport, CT: Praeger.

Students for a Democratic Society. (1962) "The Port Huron Statement."

Suri, Jeremi. (2003) *Power and Protest: Global Revolution and the Rise of Détente*. Cambridge, MA: Harvard University Press.

Zak, Albin. (2010) *I Don't Sound Like Nobody: Remaking Music in 1950s America*. Ann Arbor, MI: University of Michigan Press.

8

Magnetic tape and the recording studio

Background and topics

One of the more remarkable spoils of the Second World War was magnetic audio tape. The intelligence staff in the US military who had been monitoring the movements of various Nazi leaders noticed that some of them appeared to have been in two places at once. This was because the audio quality and length of their recorded speeches was often far higher and lasted far longer than the so-called transcription recordings made possible. However, near the end of the war, American troops occupying the town of Bad Nauheim found several of the sorts of machines pictured below (Figure 8.1). They were called Magentophons. Various versions of magnetic recording existed as far back as the 1890s. Some had even been demonstrated in Germany before the war, but most produced noticeable distortion in both pitch and timing. The inventors of the Magnetophons had solved these problems by developing new capabilities that had been kept a closely guarded secret.

Several of these machines were turned over to a member of the US Army Signal Corps named Jack Mullin who took them home. After spending several years making alterations to them, he made several public demonstrations of his new machines in Hollywood in 1947. As with the Edison "Tone Tests," Mullin engaged in some dramatic sleight of hand, tricking listeners with the higher fidelity of the new machines. The new technology attracted a great deal of attention. It was immediately obvious to many working in the film and music industries that this was a whole new standard in sound recording and reproduction. Bing Crosby, who long harbored great frustration with the inadequacy of transcription recordings of his radio shows, took a strong interest in the new technology.

FIGURE 8.1 *AEG Magnetophon Tonschreiber B. (ca. 1942).*

He was able to arrange financing for the development and manufacture of new machines by what was at the time a very small company called Ampex. They produced a series of new machines and, within a year of Mullin's demonstrations, Crosby was broadcasting tape recordings of *The Bing Crosby Show* on national radio. It is hard to underestimate the consequences of the commercial availability of magnetic tape and tape machines. They changed how music was recorded, how films were made, and how people listened to music at home and in public.

This chapter will provide a broad overview of the changes in how people used recording studios during the twentieth century. It will focus especially on the years after the introduction of tape and multitracking. The goal is to link technological change to the kinds of social changes that have allowed musicians, producers, and engineers to record and use nearly any sounds they can imagine.

Before doing so, however, let's revisit our key reading. Examine the second half of Susan Horning's article, "Chasing Sound" (pp. 192–208). In this part of the article, Horning describes the debates that took place over what was called "high fidelity" sound recording. Note in particular that the ideas and aspirations of the artists and engineers often exceeded the capabilities of their technology. Also, note her description of the use of room dividers or sound baffles in the studio to more effectively manage what are still live recordings and that the "built environment of a recording studio was as important as its technical components, endowing records with an acoustic 'signature' that was as identifiable as a name on a label." Her point here is that the very idea of a "studio" has always been a complex and variable idea that has evolved along with, but sometimes independent of, available recording technology. We can also take from this article that there has long been an uneasy and unresolved relationship between what I called the "documentary model" of sound recording and the "creative" model. As I recount a very broad overview of the evolution of the recording studio, try to bear this relationship in mind.

The historical trajectory of the recording studio

This section will present a very particular overview of how the recording studio has changed over time. It will do so using a series of photographs of people using different studios in different ways at different times in history. You should focus on two things. First, look closely at what the people in the photos are actually doing to make sound. Second, focus on the character of the social relationships implied by these photographs between the various people in them and within the specific material environments these images show us.

The earliest forms of sound recording are referred to as acoustic recording. The sounds were translated directly through a horn to the surface of a wax cylinder or a disc. The recordings were then played back through the same horn. These recordings lasted about three minutes and the lines cut into the cylinder or disc were often uneven and their size was dependent on how much sound reached them. As a result, their sound quality and durability were limited. Importantly, the actual machines used to make these recordings were surprisingly simple. They had no electronics and no knobs or sliders of any kind. In fact, the machines did not allow the user to adjust any aspect of the recording on the machine itself. However, this did not mean that these machines were simply used to document the sounds they were capturing. As you can see from the first five images below, these machines were part of a range of other devices and techniques that were used to shape the sound of the music being recorded. In the first image you will notice the piano is raised several feet of the ground. You should also note that the horn is pressed right up against the back of the piano. Further, the very large wooden box in the background was used to isolate sounds from the surrounding environment. The second image shows you the range of equipment used; note especially the large range of horn sizes. These photos show us that studios were often places for experimentation as much as anything else.

Techniques of instrument and microphone or horn placement as well as sound baffling and isolation were a defining feature of recording in this

FIGURE 8.2 *Phonograph recording in Edison Laboratory Music Room (ca. 1905).*

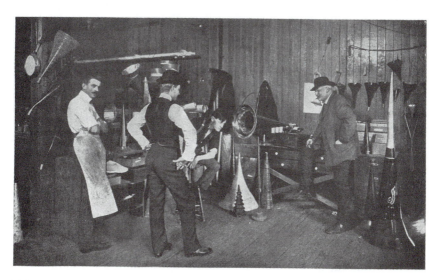

FIGURE 8.3 *Listening session in Edison Laboratory Music Room (ca. 1905).*

era. In the next three images you will notice that the primary performers, vocalists and cellists, are placed closest to the sound capturing horns and the rest of the ensembles are placed around and behind them. Notice too, in all three images, how unusual the arrangement of the musicians

FIGURE 8.4 *Tenor Lucien Muratore and soprano Lina Cavalieri recording in Paris (1913).*

is. These would not have been seen in live performances. One writer explained the arrangement of musicians for one recording session in 1910 this way:

> They would look natural enough if they sat around in a civilized fashion, but they don't. They are perched on stools of varying height, some quite near to the ground and others stuck aloft on little platforms. This is because the carrying power of the instruments differs and has to be arranged for, so that the receiving horn will not get too much of any one thing.

This tells us that sound recording had its own sets of rules and demands and that recordings were not mere reproductions of traditional live performances.

When electrical recording became the standard in the late 1920s and into the early 1930s, the tools and techniques used in studio changed as well. As you can see in Figure 8.7, electrical "disc cutting" machines were very different from the acoustic sound recorders. The sounds were sent through microphones instead of horns and were regulated electronically. Also, these machines were far more precise than acoustic sound recorders. The actual cutting of the sound into the disc was an electrical process that meant the grooves cut into discs were more uniform. As you can see from Figure 8.7, the engineer is looking through a lens at the surface of the disc to monitor the cutting process. Electrical recording allowed engineers to regulate how different levels of sound were captured. As a result, the sound quality

FIGURE 8.5 *Victor Orchestra recording session, New Jersey (1925).*

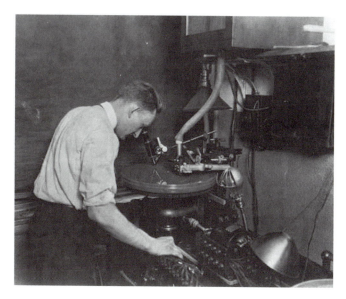

FIGURE 8.6 *Engineer using a Westrex Electrical Recording machine (ca. 1925).*

improved and a wider frequency range could be captured more effectively. Perhaps most importantly, the presence of microphones didn't just change the sound of recordings—it changed how recordings were made and even the music itself. For example, as noted in Chapters 3 and 5, the microphone

FIGURE 8.7 *Waldorf-Astoria Dance Orchestra, Eveready Hour, WEAF, New York (1924).*

FIGURE 8.8 *RCA Victor engineers, Montreal (ca. 1940s).*

became the primary musical instrument for singers. This transformed the role of vocalists from an occasional presence on ballads or quieter numbers to a dominant presence and chief interlocutor with the audience. Even in bands without vocalists, the microphone was still the focal point, especially for ensembles playing on the radio. Notice in Figure 8.8 how the man standing on the left of the picture holding the violin is closest to the microphone. He

FIGURE 8.9 *Typical radio studio (ca. 1940s).*

FIGURE 8.10 *Typical radio studio (ca. 1938).*

FIGURE 8.11 *Frank Sinatra publicity photo (1947).*

FIGURE 8.12 *Columbia Records studio, New York (1952).*

would have acted as a kind of "MC" and bandleader. Also, the arrangement of the musicians is far more traditional and microphones allowed radio bands such as these to play in a far more familiar setup and still produce a reasonable overall sound.

Another aspect of electrical recording that is important to acknowledge was how much more complicated it was than acoustic recording. It was simply more difficult to produce a high-quality sound recording. You also needed more people to do so. One producer from the era of 78 recording was quoted by historian Michael Chanan as describing it this way:

> It was a nightmare. I stood there with a score and began a countdown during the last thirty seconds of a side and then shouted "DROP!" at which point one engineer would fade out the side that had just ended while another, with luck, would lower the pickup on the beginning of the next side. If anything went even slightly wrong there was nothing to do but go back to the beginning, and as every LP had to be cut at least twice in case of an accident during processing at the factory it was a tedious and frustrating business.

Sound recording also required more trained personnel to get a good result. Note in Figure 8.8 that it wasn't even possible for one person to operate the equipment. Perhaps just as importantly, when the division of labor in sound recording changed, the physical layout of the recording studio began to

FIGURE 8.13 *Contemporary Recording Studio (2014).*

FIGURE 8.14 *Contemporary Recording Studio (2010).*

change as well. Figures 8.10 and 8.11 show us older radio stations. The next image is Columbia Records' studios in New York. Note how the performers and the engineers are in separate sealed rooms— one had all of the musical instruments, the other held all of the recording equipment. In this case, the physical layout matches the specialized work that goes on in each room. This is a fairly common setup for contemporary studios and is shown in Figures 8.13 and 8.14.

The introduction of magnetic tape

The introduction of magnetic tape utterly transformed the process and potential of recorded music. There were many reasons for this. First, tape was far cheaper to manufacture and use than any of its predecessors. Second, tape machines were more flexible, more durable, provided better sound quality, and higher fidelity than any other recording technology at that time. This made it more accessible to more people, especially the kinds of small record labels like Chess, Sun, or Motown that helped make forms of music that had a great deal of success regionally easier to record, distribute, and sell. This was especially true of those forms of music originally produced by African Americans. Styles such as rhythm and blues, gospel, rock 'n' roll, and more modern forms of the blues became far more widely recognized

FIGURE 8.15 *Ampex Model 300. Sun Studios. Memphis, TN (ca. 1950s).*

forms of music than they had been previously in part because they sounded much better and were far easier to buy than they had even been before.

In fact, tape had such far-reaching consequences that it eventually changed, in foundational ways, how people thought about the purpose of the recording studio. The primary reason for this was that tape was reusable. Tape machines made it possible to simply erase a version of a recording that was unacceptable and replace it with a new one. This meant that musicians had a lot more scope to experiment in the studio.

Musicians could use early takes of a song as a form of quality control and discard ones deemed inferior. They could try different instruments, techniques, and sounds and see which ones sounded the best on the recording. They could also use the recording studio as a kind of instrument in and of itself. This constituted a basic change in understanding of what a studio was for. When multitrack tape machines became available, this simply intensified the situation. While there are many famous examples of musicians using the new technology to great effect, such as The Beatles'

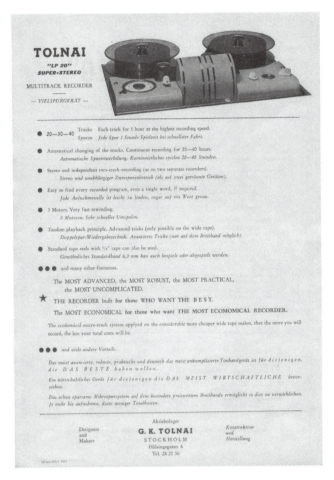

FIGURE 8.16 *Ad for Tolnai Multitrack Recorders, Sweden (ca. 1950s).*

Sgt. Pepper's Lonely Heart Club Band and The Beach Boys' *Pet Sounds,* the practice was widespread as early as the mid-1950s. People such as Mitch Miller assumed positions within the big record labels that we could describe as "musical directors" or simply "producers." This was a relatively new kind of position. Historian Albin Zak provides an excellent capsule description of what people such as Miller actually did:

> Miller was an idea man, not a songwriter or nuts-and-bolts arranger but a conceptualizer and the ultimate authority in the studio. He selected songs with specific voices in mind and coached singers in directions that often led away from habitual comfort zones; he chose arrangers, invented ensembles, and suggested stylistic directions for musical treatment and he edited songwriter's work. . . . In the studio's control room, he collaborated

with the session engineer, selecting microphones for specific singers and instrumentalists and presiding as the ultimate judge on matters of sound and balance.

Clearly, a "producer" such as Miller is not at all synonymous with "recordist" or "engineer." He had to know about the market, the music, and the gear. He had to be well-versed in managing artists as much as managing a studio budget. He also would have accrued a great deal of power over how records sounded, who worked on them, and how they got made. This sort of position within a record label, while not unprecedented, was now a necessity due in large part to the increasing number of variables, technical, artistic, and economic, that now shaped the production of sound recordings.

Shortly, we will look at the career of one recording engineer, Atlantic Records' Tom Dowd, and follow him as he moved from the crucial period from 78 disc cutting to magnetic tape recording. But first, we need to summarize the broad changes in sound recording to put Dowd's career in context.

Explore and report: Summarizing sound recording

At this point in this book, it would be helpful to take a closer look at the broad historical trajectory of sound recording and playback technology by looking backward and forward. The goal is to lay out in a clear and concise way the parameters of change and show how each part of the production-distribution-consumption equation changes in relation to the others.

You need to compare the following for each medium: durability, storage capacity, sound quality, ease of movement, ease of use, and overall effectiveness. "Overall effectiveness" means how people experienced each of these technologies.

Draw up a chart something like this:

	Cylinders	78s	45s	LPs	Tapes	mp3s	The cloud
Durability	–	–	–	–	–	–	–
Capacity	–	–	–	–	–	–	–
Sound quality	–	–	–	–	–	–	–
Ease of movement	–	–	–	–	–	–	–
Ease of use	–	–	–	–	–	–	–
[OTHERS]	–	–	–	–	–	–	–

There are numerous places where you can get the information you need to complete this chart. The first thing to do is to go back through previous chapters of this book and begin there. Second, look at the Wikipedia page called "The History of Sound Recording." This is a strong summary of important developments of strong relevance to this task. But Wikipedia is never, ever enough. A third thing to do is to look closely at many ads for record players, stereo units, and tape players directed at consumers that you can find through Google image searches. There are many reproduced in this book, but there are many, many more available online. Look at what the manufacturers claim their products can do for consumers. How do these claims change over time? What similarities do they have? What do they show consumers doing with these new technologies?

Let's consider just one as an example, the cassette. The audio cassette was one of the most popular formats for several decades. This popularity extended around the world. This was because it was cheap, had decent sound quality, and held up to 120 minutes of music. It was also something someone could hold in their hand.

The cassette is mostly the same technology as reel-to-reel, except in miniature (Figures 8.17 and 8.18). It was portable and reusable for producers and consumers alike (Figure 8.19). Much like every other sound recording technology used in the home, tape came in a variety of shapes and sizes. You can see the similarities between reel-to-reel and cassettes fairly easily. How might this flexible, high-quality, accessible technology have affected how music was produced and distributed, and how people might have listened to it?

FIGURE 8.17 *Sony portable reel-to-reel tape player and recorder (ca. 1960s).*

FIGURE 8.18 *TDK audio cassette tape.*

FIGURE 8.19 *Sony Walkman (1979).*

Focus: Tom Dowd, producer at Atlantic Records

Tom Dowd was born and raised in Manhattan. He was the son of an opera singer and a concertmaster. In school, he was a musician who played trombone, tuba, and bass. By the age of sixteen, he had finished high school and had begun to study physics at Columbia University. Stationed at a physics lab at the university, he also served in the military during the Second World War. The lab contributed to the development of the atomic bomb, although the secrecy conditions meant no one outside the lab was aware of this. Instead of continuing with his work in physics, Dowd took a job as an audio engineer at Apex recording studios in Manhattan. It was there that he came to the attention of Atlantic Records when its founder, Ahmet Ertegün, used the studio to record some of the then-small label's early singles.

In a 2003 documentary about him, Dowd explained that he found some aspects of studio recording in the 1950s limiting. Specifically, the rhythm sections of most recordings were far too subdued to approximate the importance of those instruments in live performance. Ertegün agreed with Dowd. Ertegün explained how he and his brother used to go to see jazz in the 1930s and was always shocked at how different the experience of live music was from sound recordings. Ertegün said that this was particularly true of the music Atlantic wanted most to record—rhythm and blues. Dowd and Ertegün found working together easy as they had the same goals. What also made Dowd stand out was the ways in which he worked the board during a recording session. Prior to the availability of magnetic tape, most of Dowd's recording sessions were fairly short, usually only allowing one take of a live performance. But Dowd suggested that he "was never an advocate of the use of one mic in the studio," as was standard practice at that time. He explained his reasoning:

> There was such a dynamic difference between the intensity of a string bass, we didn't have amplifiers; if you're playing a string bass or an acoustic guitar versus the drums—I didn't need to put a mic anywhere near the drums. He'd come in on the bass mic. So I'd put a mic on the bass. I'd put a mic on the singer. Then when I got in the control room, I would selectively increase or decrease the volume. All of sudden people are saying "Oh there's a bass on the record! How did he do that?"

You can hear the difference Dowd's knowledge and sensitivity made if you compare the 1949 recording of Atlantic's first hit, Stick McGhee's "Drinkin' Wine Spo-Dee-O-Dee," with the 1947 original on Harlem Records. The differences in the clarity and impact of the rhythm section are abundantly clear. (Both versions are available for comparison on YouTube. Be sure NOT to listen to the remastered version of the Atlantic one.) After 1954, Dowd began working exclusively for Atlantic, recording artists such as Ray Charles, the Drifters, and Ruth Brown during the label's first rush of success.

Dowd began to use tape in the late-1940s and he presciently began to record in stereo and mono simultaneously. As a result, Atlantic had begun to build up a library of stereo recordings before it was even possible to sell them on disc. This allowed the label to produce genuine stereo records before any other labels, which had all of their catalogues in mono. Around the same time, Dowd was inspired by the work of Les Paul, who Dowd said was producing multitrack recordings although Dowd presumed he didn't have a multitrack machine. In fact, Paul had built his own and, as Dowd said, it sounded so good because Paul "was storing information on the tracks and then putting it back together." Through his association with Paul, Dowd was able to get Atlantic the second Ampex 200A multitrack tape machine ever produced. Rather than continue to use what he called "hand me down radio equipment," Dowd began to build an 8-track sound board to go with the new tape machine. Notably, he was able to source sliders to replace the large knobs originally used for mixing the various sound sources. This allowed greater flexibility during the recording session and afterward while remixing. Dowd began introducing musicians, such as Ray Charles, and songwriters, such as Mike Stoller and Jerry Lieber, to 8 track, even building a new unit for Charles in the artist's Los Angeles studio.

Dowd is a good example of the first generation of record producers who were able to see the advantages of the new technology very quickly. Dowd no longer had to make his mixing decisions on the fly as the studio session was actually happening. He could "store the information," as he put it, on individual tracks and decide what to do with it later in a more measured and precise way. Importantly, it is this seemingly simple insight that shows us the tremendous impact magnetic tape had on the music industry. First, it extended the artistic discussion about how a recording should sound beyond both the actual recording session and the studio itself. Second, it was now possible to use a far more complex and flexible division of labor in the studio. The role and purpose of the producer had changed as had the idea of artistry. Musicians, producers, and engineers could be seen as genuine collaborators. Third, the location of artistry had changed as well. It was not necessarily just a flash of artistic inspiration to be realized by the technical staff. Instead, a range of people with a range of skills could be brought to bear on a production when needed. Finally, multitracking had changed the very conception of the purpose of recording and recorded sound by changing the idea of what music could be. Instead of simply understanding music as the notes and harmonies of a song, it could be, and increasingly was, thought of as a collection of sounds. These sounds could be created, shaped, and finished entirely within the studio without any reference to any one particular live performance of a work. Music could be constructed in a modular way, piece by piece, section by section, sound by sound. After multitracking, there was no going back.

INDEPENDENT RESEARCH WORK

There is a large literature on music production and music producers. Explore this literature, especially any interviews or detailed profiles you can find. There are three related issues of importance in how making music changed in this time period: the role of technology, the musical knowledge and experience of the producers, and their relationship to the music industry, especially those who ran record labels. Explore these issues and write about how each played a distinct role in shaping the significant and powerful changes in how music was recorded in the 1950s and 1960s.

References and further readings

Chanan, Michael. (1995) *Repeated Takes: A Short History of Recording and its Effects on Music*. London: Verso.

Cohen, Rich. (2005) *The Record Men: The Chess Brothers and the Birth of Rock & Roll*. New York: W. W. Norton.

Milner, Greg. (2010) *Perfecting Sound Forever: An Aural History of Recorded Music*. New York: Faber and Faber.

Moorefield, Virgil (2005) *The Producer as Composer: Shaping the Sounds of Popular Music*. Cambridge, MA: MIT Press.

Moormann, Mark. (2003) *Tom Dowd and the Language of Music*. New York: Force Entertainment. [DVD]

Schmidt Horning, Susan. (2013) *Chasing Sound: Technology, Culture, and the art of Studio Recording from Edison to the LP*. Baltimore: Johns Hopkins University Press.

Taylor, T., M. Katz, and T. Grajeda. (2012) *Music, Sound, and Technology in America: A Documentary History of Early Phonograph, Cinema, and Radio*. Durham, NC: Duke University Press.

Zak, Albin. (2010) *I Don't Sound Like Nobody: Remaking Music in 1950s America*. Ann Arbor, MI: University of Michigan Press.

PART THREE

New forms of media, new kinds of fame, 1960 to 2000

KEY READING

Music, Image, Labor: Television's Prehistory

Murray Forman

Popular music and television are inextricably entwined. When television was nothing more than a dream in the mind of visionaries or a conundrum troubling scientists around the world, there was a clear sense that the sounds and images of musical performance would one day converge in a single broadcast transmission. The widely circulated notion of "radio with pictures" in the 1920s made sense then since much of television's invention, financing, and program planning emerged directly from the radio broadcasting industry. As countless historians have explained since, even though radio was less than a decade old and still developing as a standard facet of daily life at the end of what was termed "the roaring twenties" or "the jazz age," the earliest television broadcast experiments regularly incorporated musical performances (Fisher and Fisher 1996; Koszarski 2008; Magoun 2009; Rodman 2010). Documents show that many radio network executives believed that their approaches to programming and scheduling (with popular music prominently featured) would prevail although they could not forecast what television's content might actually look like. The issue of visualizing popular music consequently presented an early dilemma in TV content development.

When synchronized sound was still relatively new in cinema (having been successfully launched in 1927 following the release of a series of short synch-sound films) musicals quickly won public favor (Gabbard 1996; Mundy 1999; Koszarski 2008). Featuring spectacular imagery structured upon the thinnest of narrative scaffolding and musical performances by some of the era's most popular artists, the early film musicals were indebted to Broad-way's presentational logic. Yet by the mid-1930s there was still nothing that could be described as a *tradition* of film musicals that television pioneers might emulate.

Television's early indeterminacy presented a major conceptual barrier but, of course, the challenges accompanying such indeterminacy can also inspire expansive thinking and lead to incredible innovation. Broadcast executives were expected to project how television might fit within their existing range of services and those in charge of radio programming and content development attempted to predict how abstract audience formations would respond to hypothetical TV shows. Imagining television — what it would be, whom it would be for — necessitated deep and probing analysis of an array of cultural factors encompassing the spirit and conditions of an era.

Somehow, during an economic depression and throughout a horrific war, the television industry continued to grow and evolve even as various other industrial sectors stalled and a great many original ideas withered on the vine. And while television's creators worked to improve the medium, musicians were intrinsically involved in the ongoing television experiment, at times toiling as full-fledged collaborators. After the war there was a remarkable burst of invention with several crucial developments facilitating the convergence of popular music and television.

In each of TV's transitional phases, discussions always incorporated popular music and the broadcast value of musical performances. The dominant discourses and public debates concerning early television and the role of popular music are noteworthy for they often illuminate other important features of the period, revealing a dynamic cultural vortex. By exploring some of the key sociocultural elements at television's inception (involving art and aesthetics, technology, and institutional entities) and the ways in which television was positioned among them, we might generate a better sense of the underlying values that informed the nation's cultural expression and leisure practices and the concurrent stakes for popular music and its performers.

Preparing for television: The 1930s

In a December 1930 corporate memorandum, George Engles, National Broadcasting Corporation (NBC) vice president in charge of programs, wrote that with the emergence of visual broadcast capabilities it would be increasingly necessary to review and vet the physical or *telegenic* attributes of the singers hired by the network. Engles gently upbraided Bertha Brainard of the network's Program Department, reminding her that with "the forecast of oncoming television and the new requirements it would demand in the pictorial quality of our artist personnel" there was intensifying pressure to "revamp" the musical talent under contract "with a view to having when needed a picture that would pass the censors" (1930a). In this context, the "censors" to which Engles refers were internal network executives charged with evaluating the look and comportment of prospective TV talent, ensuring that no one deemed to be of sub-par physical appearance would be hired as television broadcasting progressed.

Brainard was the extremely rare woman in an organizational cadre dominated by men, having entered radio broadcasting in the early 1920s and risen in NBC's Program Department, where she worked closely with senior executives including Engles and John F. Royal (Halper 2001). Memoranda from the 1930s reveal Brainard's firm principles, shrewd mind, and sharp wit, and in her reply to Engles she subtly requested examples of any incidents where she and her programming unit may have failed to adequately assess the visual potential of vocalists, further suggesting that such a process of judgment requires an agreed-upon set of criteria. Noting the apparently subjective nature of such visual appraisals, she writes, "I find, unfortunately, a question of who is and who is not good looking, arising in the men's minds" (Brainard 1930).

As these exchanges indicate, during television's earliest phase no one had a clear sense of how the medium would accommodate the various expressions of art and culture, including musical performance, nor was there a stable notion of a visual standard for musical presentation. The discussions were fully in the realm of abstraction. Those such as Brainard and Engles (as well as countless engineers, directors, and programmers who were tasked with designing television) strived to meet as-yet-undefined broadcasting goals, to predict and then fulfill viewer expectations. Profoundly lacking rules and formal guides, television's first decision-makers — both independents and those working under the aegis of corporate broadcasters — stumbled forward with speculation more than fact at their disposal. In retrospect, theirs seems an almost impossible undertaking.

The dialogue between Engles and Brainard points to an emergent visual strategy at the network. It articulates the beginning of an industrial process that involved TV's appropriation and instrumental attitudes toward popular music and musicians that would only intensify over the next twenty-five years. Their interaction also indicates that the visual regime championed by Engles evolved at the network as a source of pressure and even coercion, challenging the prevailing practices and audio supremacy associated with radio broadcasting. Brainard's push back against Engles should not, therefore, be regarded as insubordination but as an example of two paradigms colliding within the specific contexts of 1930s corporate broadcasting.

Engles further outlined the problem of visualizing music in a lengthy response to Brainard, explaining, "Several rumors had come to me that various members of the Program Department were pushing artists whose sole claim to distinction lies in their voices" (1930b). His barely contained ire was based on the belief that employees in the network's Program Department evidently remained committed to the established talent recruitment and hiring practices of radio broadcasting. In his view, Brainard and her colleagues in the Program Department lacked proper foresight as plans for the network's television broadcasting branch evolved, as well as falling short of NBC's corporate objectives. David Sarnoff, president of NBC's parent company Radio Corporation of America (RCA) and a driving figure responsible for the formation of NBC in 1926, was an early and constant supporter of television. The network's executives and middle management were exposed to a stream of directives and corporate statements from Sarnoff addressing the medium's development. Indeed, Sarnoff staked much of his reputation on television's success. The issue of musicians' image and appearance developed into a central topic as television evolved, creating conflict and debate about visual or aural primacy in musical presentation.

The interaction between Engles and Brainard conveys a pressure that is common within hierarchical, top-down structures of power. As an executive representative, Engles exerted a coercive force extending institutional authority. He communicated NBC's corporate line within a chain of command and as volumes of published records confirm, his emphasis on television reflects Sarnoffs priorities at the time. Sarnoff's corporate support for technical research and his aggressive legal maneuvering pertaining to TV patent issues represent two fronts in an effort to dominate early television; programming represents a third front. Engles and Brainard were not merely encountering an insignificant impasse but, rather, they were engaged in a discussion about the process through which the corporation would integrate music in the manifestation of television.

In urging the Program Department to consider television's particular visual demands pertaining to singers, Engels introduced the terms "salable outstanding radio artists" or "salable talent" to his discourse about musical performances. The implication was that the commercial practicality of any given artist and, by extension, any given television program would eventually be judged according to the combined standards of performers' appearances *and* their musical talent, drawing television nearer to stage performances and cinema than to radio. In one sense, Engles's reference to salability points to a perceived need for musical artists to make a solid impression; to "sell" a song was a common expression among entertainers, referring to a quality performance that registered positively.

Engles implies more, however. He also addresses the need for musical artists to essentially sell themselves to audiences through their engaging performances and innate visual appeal. Here we get closer to the evolving notions of artists' commodified congeniality and television presence that was regularly attached to the concept of television in its nascent period. In yet another related sense germane to the era, the commercially oriented terminology suggests that it is television itself that must be "sold" to a public that was, by the mid- to late 1930s, highly familiar with radio broadcasting and with the performance aesthetics of film musicals and live theater or nightclubs but that was also skeptical of the early TV industry's promise of a fuller, visually enhanced entertainment experience (especially one that necessitated the purchase of an expensive new electrical appliance). Music was going to help sell the concept of television to the public.

The discourse of commercial/commodity value and televised musical performances speaks to the extent to which culture was ensconced within a capitalist logic at this historical moment but it also reflects how deeply invested in commercial media and music industry economics NBC, television's industry leader, was at the time. Russell and David Sanjek (1991) explain how Sarnoff oversaw both the implementation of NBC's nationwide broadcast network and the acquisition of the Radio-Keith-Orpheum (RKO) theater chain and film production company in 1928 and spearheaded RCA's purchase of the Victor Talking Machine Company (creating the RCA Victor phonograph company) in 1929. After the 1930s, popular music lay at the center of each of these sectors and the corporate jockeying for dominance notably affected television's trajectory.

Industry executives injected a pronounced capitalist sensibility into television's development even though the programming structure and content — the medium's main selling point — had not fully congealed. The popular music sector had by this point already proven its strengths and value in relation to the commercial culture industries and radio, too, was confirmed as a valid medium within purely corporate and capitalist ideals. By conceiving TV's programming content in relation to abstract commodity values before any norms or standards existed the industry was operating within a symbolic realm whereby cultural texts are understood as objects with commercial worth. The programs and the musical performances were all oriented toward the logic of commodification and consumption, setting a pattern for the entire future of the medium.

Establishing a workable program schedule and ensuring top-quality performances was a prime objective if the public was to be "sold" on the new medium. In this reading, televised musical performances can be attached to a range of other commercial interests, and, in fact, the whole notion of TV viewer expectation, pleasure, or satisfaction can be linked to commercial and commodity values. Engles and other executives were, thus, dedicated to creating a commercial medium that could deliver consistently engaging and pleasurable shows that featured visually attractive musical performers.

The industry's early deliberations surrounding the role of popular music on television indicate a tendency toward the brute appropriation of musical talent, reflecting attitudes that prevailed throughout the medium's developmental phase and over the next quarter century. Without explicitly declaring that an artist's visual appearance and telegenic qualities trumped his or her musicality, Engles (among others) seems to place these attributes at least on par in the commercial contexts of television broadcasting. Although this position may have seemed contentious to some at the time, the perspective was not unknown in the realm of musical theater or cinema where physical appearances were crucial in casting. Such concerns were also an integral factor in the production of modern icon status; good-looking actors or musicians fared inordinately well in the nascent celebrity culture of the early twentieth century.

The film industry had confronted somewhat similar issues, if in reverse. When synchronized sound technology facilitated the "talkies" in the 1920s (the first feature-length film with synchronized musical selections being *The Jazz Singer*, in 1927), a host of attractive screen actors quickly found that, despite their acting talent, physical attributes, or film experience, their vocal abilities were under close scrutiny and subject to intensified critique as dialogue-laden scripts and musical scenes were popularized. For some (rumored to include the top silent film stars John Gilbert and Norma Talmadge), looking good or moving well onscreen was not always enough; they had to sound good as well in order to "sell" both the individual movie and the concept of the talkies. For artists faced with imminent irrelevance, the enlistment of vocal coaches and elocution lessons was a desperate attempt to maintain a footing in the changing industry. Musicians hired to provide musical accompaniment for the silent films in the nation's movie houses were also summarily dismissed with the advent of synch-sound. With the prospect of television, NBC's Engles expressed an apparent willingness to hire marginally inferior musical talents possessing better-than-average physical traits, urging his staff to identify appropriate-looking singers, especially those already under contract with NBC's radio branch, who could be efficiently plucked from the existing talent roster on the network's payroll.

The rather blunt exchanges that flitted between NBC executives over musical talent and telegeneity in the 1930s align with two of Simon Frith's observations, that "the dominant use of music on television, one might conclude, is to sell things" and "looking good on television has always been essential for success" (2002: 281–84). It is important to acknowledge, however, that the social practices and the discourses informing early television's commercial trends and its visual character also have their own unique histories. Each evolved in a nonlinear fashion as various industrial and cultural factors ebbed and surged. As television progressed through the 1930s, there was never a doubt that it would be anything other than commercial (the balance between culturally edifying content, strictly educational fare, and popular entertainment remained a point of considerable debate), yet in this early instance, television was not a fully realized technological medium *or* a commercially viable broadcast option. Much of the commentary in the 1930s was subsequently hypothetical, projecting various cultural values, hopes, and ideals as much as solid plans for television's future.

TV's song and dance experiments

From the 1920s to the late 1940s prominent inventors (in the United States, Allen B. Du Mont, Philo T. Farnsworth, C. Francis Jenkins, and Vladimir Zworykin among them) or teams of comparatively anonymous scientists in corporate laboratories (A.T.T., General Electric, and Westinghouse were most prominent) worked to construct reliable TV studio production equipment or reception appliances while executives applied themselves to building an efficient television broadcasting system. For the science and engineering wizzes, content was a subordinate concern that served a purpose for the testing of transmission and reception. Jonathan Sterne identifies similar tendencies in sound reproduction experiments of the late eighteenth and early nineteenth centuries (involving recordings on phonograph cylinders), observing that the content of the recordings were "clearly aimed at the middle-class market" (featuring musical pieces that echoed "the range of subject matter in other middle-class entertainment") and that "the recordings were very much limited by the parameters of the available technology" (2003; 244). In reproducing and transmitting sound, simple phrases and familiar musical ditties (or, at least, familiar musical genres such as marches) were the standard for laboratory experiments and for public demonstrations.

According to Richard Koszarski (2008), in their rudimentary broadcasts the engineer-headed experimental TV stations in New York City and the surrounding environs all at one time or another featured children's vocal choruses and adult soloists, piano players and instrumentalists, and the occasional Broadway performer. The CBS network launched its television station W2XAB with much fanfare in July 1931; while still very much an experimental station, the launch featured musical performances by the talented radio and recording vocal trio the Boswell Sisters,[1] the newcomer Kate Smith (her radio and recording career still ahead of her), and the inestimable George Gershwin, who performed the song "Liza," composed two years earlier. With the technological barriers rapidly falling away in the 1930s, television's content and the accompanying issues of visual allure were reprioritized among the broadcast industry's executive decision-makers, who turned their focus toward presentational aesthetics and programming strategies that, like the prior sound reproduction trials, might appeal to middle-class values and middlebrow tastes.[2]

In 1935, NBC's Bertha Brainard again figured in discussions about the intensifying need to define television's programming and refine the visualization of popular music. She received a memorandum from William Fairbanks of the network's Statistical Department, who referred to an experimental demonstration on June 3, 1935, at the NBC television laboratory located in Camden, New Jersey, that, as he explains, included "a very ambitious sight and sound reproduction of Fred Waring's rendition of 'Lullaby of Broadway' as a production number" (1935). The decision to emphasize Waring's performance was surely based in his general popularity as a bandleader and his prior film experience: he and his band The Pennsylvanians had participated in the production of Vitaphone musical shorts in the late 1920s and in 1929 they headlined in the film *Syncopation,* "the first feature-length musical made in New York" (Koszarski 2008: 170).

Fairbanks enclosed a copy of the script from the Camden demonstration detailing a forty-five-minute musical production structured upon a recognizable Broadway theater format featuring music selections sung by the cast (composed of Billy Milton, Sara Allgood, Rose Walker, Reita Nugent, Georgie Harris, Charlie Woods, and a dance chorus aptly called The Eight Good Lookers) with musical accompaniment by Sydney Jerome's seven-piece band. The 1935 demonstration featured typical production numbers and popular songs associated with Tin Pan Alley, Broadway theater, and Hollywood films such as "Rock and Roll," "Zing Went the Strings of My Heart," "Sady O'Grady," "Forty-Second Street," "Sidewalks of Cuba," "Here Comes That Rainbow," "I'm on the Crest of a Wave," "When Love Comes Swinging Along," "Limehouse Blues," "Old Folks at Home," "It's an Old Southern Custom," "The Man from Harlem," "Mood Indigo," and the aforementioned "Lullaby of Broadway."

Though no visual record remains of this television experiment, the script reveals several key production considerations with a pronounced reliance on established theatrical and cinematic performance conventions encompassing repertoire, staging, and (to lesser extent) interstitial dialogue. The show's loosely structured narrative and musical performances portrayed ersatz versions of various New York City locales in all of their cultural and spatial diversity: Broadway, China Town, Harlem, and the swank Rainbow Room nightclub (which had opened less than a year earlier on the sixty-fifth floor of the GE Building at Rockefeller Center, where the NBC corporate headquarters are also housed). Interestingly, the influence of radio is entirely absent in the discussion; the production logic was anchored in visual performance styles that immersed audience members in a fantasy spectacle, promising a generally pleasant experience while virtually "transporting" them to other cultural locales. The TV demonstration also harbored latent similarities with filmed travelogues that displayed exciting or exotic Otherness cohering within recognized cultural sites. We can see here that the aesthetic push-and-pull between the existing communication media and various performance sites and forms was not yet resolved, and TV's early experimental process explored the potentialities of each option for future musical productions.

Script notes explain the character of the studio set designs for each musical number, describing the construction of ersatz urban spaces and props that reflect the highly staged aspect of the broadcast production. Offering basic stage directions with cast entrances and exits, the script also illustrates how, even in 1935, there was careful forethought about television's onscreen action, camera placement, and shot composition, and the communication of presentational intimacy forged in the dynamics between musical talent and the camera. Simultaneity, immediacy, and a sense of presence were as crucial to early television as they were to theater.

Lynn Spigel addresses these representational issues and television's distinguishing characteristics with the observation,

> Television, it was constantly argued, would be a better approximation of live entertainment than any previous form of technological reproduction. Its ability to broadcast direct to the home would allow people to feel as if they really were at the theater. . . . According to the popular wisdom, then, television was able to reproduce reality in a way no previous medium could. Whereas film allowed spectators imaginatively to project themselves *into a scene,* television would give people the sense of being *on the scene* of presentation — it would simulate the entire experience of being at the theater. (1992: 138–39)

Proximity, intimacy, liveness, and an ideal perspective or "perfect view" (ibid.: 140) that privileged the audience member were important features of early TV broadcasting even as the medium experienced programming and technical modifications. Although television had yet to fully mature, by 1935 the conceptual framework and representational principles that eventually came to dominate were already discernible and many of the general qualities inscribed in this early "TV laboratory" trial remained more or less intact when television was finally introduced on a massive commercial scale at the end of the 1940s.

Though the Camden experiment stands out for its detail and complexity, similar experiments involving popular music performances continued throughout the 1930s. In 1936, the television pioneer Philo T. Farnsworth hired the Nick Ross Orchestra to appear on his self-operated experimental station W3XPF in Philadelphia, where he also featured preadolescent amateurs in televised song and dance routines (Fisher and Fisher 1996: 253). Also in 1936, NBC introduced musical artists including the popular radio trio the Pickens Sisters in a promotional demonstration that was narrowly beamed to televisions viewed by invited network insiders, advertising executives, and select members of the press corps.

Later that year, a further demonstration was conducted for the press under what NBC and RCA jointly termed "practical working conditions. . . . It represented the first showing of a complete program built for entertainment value as well as a demonstration of transmission" ("Television Developments" 1936). The network's explicit announcement of "practical working conditions" implies that this was more than a simple experiment, rather, something akin to a product roll-out; its purpose was not merely to titillate reporters with a vision of what TV broadcasting *may one day be* but was a much more grounded presentation asserting what TV *is*. In terms of corporate expediency the demonstration was also an attempt to make good on the promotional promises that had accumulated over the previous several years while serving notice to the competition that NBC was ahead of the pack. Music again figured prominently and the demonstration featured performances by The Inkspots and Hildegarde, a likable if unremarkable chanteuse whose in-house moniker was "The Television Girl" on account of her telegenic qualities and frequent participation in NBC's early experiments.

A young Frank Sinatra, recognized as an emerging star during his tenure with the Harry James Orchestra (and soon to join forces with the Tommy Dorsey Orchestra), was invited to participate in NBC's experimental TV broadcasts in 1939, but he demurred. Broadcast experiments continued without Sinatra in NBC's cramped and overheated studio 3H in midtown Manhattan, with Dinah Shore singing for the closed circuit system well before she reached full blossom as a top recording, film, and television star ("Dinah in Blackface" 1949; Ritchie 1994; Kisseloff 1995: 56). At the DuMont studios, the program host Dennis James (a former radio disk jockey with WNEW in New York who went on to define the role of the TV host) was also tentatively exploring the new medium with a fledgling show called *Television Roof* in 1939. The show featured the vocal group The Pied Pipers, which included Jo Stafford (Kisseloff 1995: 68). In these instances musicians served a primarily functional role since their performances fulfilled the network's demonstration objectives yet demanded minimal scripts or none at all, making them a cheap and effective solution to the medium's content dilemma. Demonstrational presentations at this stage featured popular songs as a rule, not as an exception, and in so doing they primed the public for a visual medium that included popular music as a vital component.

Music's central significance in television development continued when NBC made its grand — and ultimately premature — announcement of regular television programming at the 1939 New York World's Fair (the subsequent broadcasts originated from station W2XBS in mid-town Manhattan). The company introduced the famed Broadway composer Richard Rogers (accompanying the theater singer Mary Wescott on piano), as well as Fred Waring and his Pennsylvanians, broadcasting their well-known dance band selections to those on the fairgrounds and to the roughly 250 television households in the New York area; according to NBC's estimates, this number eventually climbed to roughly 2,000 set owners by the end of the year ("RCA and NBC" 1940). The World's Fair broadcasts were proudly touted as the official launch of NBC's television division, although critics at the time were divided on the achievement: on the one hand there was much excitement and anticipation about the prospect of regular TV entertainment, but on the other hand reporters were generally unimpressed, commenting in exquisite detail about the abysmal quality of the broadcast performances.

In retrospect it was perhaps providential that television's progress was interrupted by the outbreak of war in the early 1940s since the public was not yet fully convinced about TV's value and there was much room for improvement. James Von Schilling (2003) explains how the cost of television sets (around $500) during the 1939 Fair remained prohibitive for many families. Purchasing a TV set was not a priority when fine musical entertainment could be had for free over cheaper radio sets or, for a reasonable cost, at public theaters and nightclubs. Phonograph players and records, too, were both less expensive and already established as a consumer item. The Federal Communications Commission (FCC) also voiced concern that consumers would be enticed to spend on televisions before the technology or the programming reached a standard of acceptability. Though the cost of TV sets was sharply reduced as part of an aggressive marketing campaign, the content still did not justify the expense; according to Richard Koszarski, "The public expected value for money" (2008: 465).

With the buildup to the war, more urgent issues beset all the major players in television development, including the TV set manufacturers, the networks, and the government's policy makers. Philip Auslander writes of this period: "The first television era in the United States . . . occurred between 1939 and 1945, for although programming and the industrial development of television were truncated by the war effort, the discourse on television remained lively during the war years" (1999: 14). Auslander's assessment is generally accurate; broadcasting experiments and demonstrations involving popular music performances did not completely halt during the war years even though the mission and priorities at the networks were seriously altered. Both CBS and NBC briefly suspended their operations in 1942, yet the General Electric studio in Schenectady, New York, and the fledgling DuMont network continued their studio experiments. In fact, television's technical development was assisted by various spin-off benefits from electronic engineering and scientific research oriented toward the war effort. While the greatest progress during the war was in the technical realm, production and programming work also advanced, albeit within a reduced scope and with lesser aspirations.

Photographs published between 1944 and 1945 in the DuMont corporation's monthly newsletter *The Raster* depict musical artists in the network's New York television studio working on performance and broadcast productions while the war raged. The musicians represent a remarkable range of genres, including the celebrity bandleader Waring accompanied by members of his Glee Club vocal group, the "negro" folk singer Josh White, Margaret Johnson (wearing a cowboy hat, singing the western classic "Don't Fence Me In"), and two unnamed Latin music trios. James Von Schilling also cites a 1944 NBC broadcast featuring the wide-eyed song-and-dance man Eddie Cantor, who encountered the first documented case of network censorship while performing "We're Having a Baby, My Baby and Me" that featured arguably suggestive lyrics (Von Schilling 2003: 53). As these examples illustrate, popular music was central in television's ongoing (and very local) broadcast trials while the nation was at war, even though the music industry and many of the top orchestras of the period were rent apart by enlistment, fuel rationing, and other constraints.

The diversity of acts appearing on television through the war years, spanning a musical and cultural spectrum, defies the still relatively common notion that early television was relentlessly homogeneous. The fact that televised musical performances cleaved toward mainstream, middlebrow tastes (Mundy 1999) is not to say that the broadcasts were uniform in their musical content or performance aesthetics. In many ways, television was more consistently varied in its formative phase than it was in later decades. Television producers who were still toiling to perfect the medium tapped into an assortment of musical forms representing an array of cultural sensibilities and ethnic or racial backgrounds. These industry architects were intent on honing their facility with different music and performance styles in the quest to introduce a broad range of musical performances to the slowly growing ranks of television viewers.

Aesthetic ideals and critical predictions

Citing television's promise and predicting its positive cultural influence during the war years, Robert Lee wrote in 1944, "Everybody should know about television, because it's going to be 'everybody's art.' Television belongs to the people — more than motion pictures, or even radio. There isn't one person in the United States who won't be affected by television" (1944: 6). Lee's optimism was rooted in what he believed were television's democratic and artistic potentials as a medium (following the rhetoric of TV's more ardent promoters), although history reveals that, apart from his final remark, his views were rather naive.

In his assessment and predictions specifically about music, Lee curiously undermined TV's distinguishing visual element, stressing that the images should remain secondary to the aural experience of any televised musical performance. His comments reflect an outlook that was likely influenced by the prevailing modes of reception and audience listening demeanor at classical music concerts or the comfort and familiarity associated with electrical home-entertainment appliances: "In presenting music, the sight channel must always be the hand-maiden to sound. When the video screen cannot conceivably add anything to a musical effect, producers must have the courage to leave it blank. This is true of much of the world's music. As a matter of fact, most great music can be best enjoyed in darkness; any activity on the screen would be distracting" (ibid.: 10). As Lee envisioned it, capable musicians would be called upon to perform in their standard manner, but it was, in his opinion, improperly left to the television producers, camera crews, and technicians to coax and shape the performance's compelling elements according to the medium's visual capacity. The studio experiments up to this point showed that musicians' expertise and talent were overwhelmed by the comparatively inexperienced and clumsy efforts of the TV production units. Despite his enthusiasm and support for the primacy of the musical performance, Lee's particular misgivings were soon realized: the visual regime of television proved to be a formidable force and music's aural qualities were regularly subordinated to the scopic pleasures offered by handsome male and beguiling female performers or to the spectacular production numbers that quickly became television staples.

Lee's perspective also seemed to rely on TV sounds being of acceptable, if not necessarily pristine quality, yet the poor-to-mediocre sound of most early television sets (roughly on par with those of the average midprice radio receiver) conspired with the low-resolution images of the tiny screens to produce what were reported to be a less-than-rewarding audience experience (VanCour 2011). Whereas the voice carried reasonably well in early television's dramatic performances (depending on proper microphone placement and related staging aspects) or on sports broadcasts under normal circumstances, musical performances, especially those involving multi-instrumental arrangements and nuanced orchestral presentations, were poorly served.

Lee was more accurate, however, in his predictions when he noted, "Top name-bands — especially when enhanced by interesting camera-handling — are especially adaptable: the solid showmanship of Fred Waring's Pennsylvanians; leaders with singularly visual personalities, such as Kay Kyser and Cab Calloway; or Xavier Cugat, whose talents as a cartoonist can add a whimsical touch to his telecasts of South American melodies" (ibid.: 107). Lee identifies specific musicians whose performance skills and spectacular excesses were already well-established facets of their performance aesthetic, lending them additional cachet as the new industry sought feasible talent-as-content. Each of the musicians Lee mentions did, in fact, go on to active television careers as invited guests or as program hosts. Of those listed, it was the comparatively subdued Waring (who had already performed in front of TV cameras and under the blazing hot studio lights in prewar and wartime experimental broadcasts with NBC and Du Mont) who would enjoy the greatest success, eventually hosting his own show featuring a sixty-member musical agglomeration on CBS from 1949 to 1954 and again, briefly, in 1957.

Anticipating enhanced artistic innovation in the combination of music and images, several commentators in the 1940s focused on the promising experiments in *synaesthesia* (a condition whereby the senses are involuntarily stimulated by a single catalyst; for example, one may experience an overwhelming sensation of visual shape and color while hearing a musical passage). Kay Dickinson defines the condition as "the transportation of sensory images from one modality into another. Synaesthetes claim the ability to see music (usually in terms of color) or to taste shapes, with the former being the most common of its manifestations and the most pertinent to the study of music video" (2007: 14).

Animators and other visual artists (Thomas Wilfred or Oskar Fischinger among them)[3] attempted to merge the sensory experiences of sound and sight, creating free-form nonnarrative films involving abstract electronic images that throb and glow in varying intensities, matching transitions in the musical arrangements. Robert Lee also described such possibilities for television, referring in 1944 to the mechanical "image-organ" — consisting of a cyclorama "upon which appears a kaleidoscopic whirling of patterns and shadows in cadence with the music" (1944: 109).

Seeking a different model for TV emulation, Mildred Steffens (1945) identified *Fantasia*, Walt Disney's animated film released in 1940, as an ideal example of tasteful, artistic musical presentation. She suggested that television's visual artists might create animated accompaniment à la Disney or design abstract and symbolic light and image renderings of classical music performances for television broadcast. Steffens's references to "optical accompaniment" were not, however, entirely accommodating of "popular" music; instead, she framed her preferences within a discourse of musical aesthetics and quality that unambiguously favored classical music. Steffens explained, "When television promotion again goes forward following 'V' day, a maturer, more thoughtful public will demand serious programs of good variety. And it will insist upon music — 'good' music. . . . Although we are limiting ourselves here to a discussion of good music, even 'swing' can be visualized with tremendous effect" (1945: 9). It is worth emphasizing that, like Lee, Steffens regarded musical instrumentation as the dominant element, with TV's visual effects accentuating or otherwise reinforcing the arrangement in a secondary role.

Addressing the artistic creation of what he termed "audiovisual music," Ralph Potter also cited the brilliance of Disney's *Fantasia*, although his interests at the time lay within the wartime development of electronic rather than mechanical technologies, including light response mechanisms such as "the sound spectograph" that "picture musical notes in action . . . with visuals accompanying sound in unison" (1947: 74). Praise for *Fantasia*, with its soaring classical soundtrack, was widespread in this period, and if there were any doubts about the high-art pretensions of Disney's animated extravaganza, these were allayed by the film's narrative voice, provided by Deems Taylor, the composer, music critic, and first radio announcer of the

New York Metropolitan Opera's radio broadcasts (in 1931, on NBC), who added experience and gravitas to the film's renderings of familiar symphonic compositions (Pegolotti 2003: 188–90).

It is striking that, while music is the chief interest in these assessments and proposals, there is little effort to address the portrayal of actual musical performances. The musicians are relegated to the background or, worse, they are merely assigned to the soundtrack while the image-music correlation is achieved via technical or graphic means. Notwithstanding these predictions and appraisals for the visualization of music, the television networks showed little inclination to adopt them or to reproduce *Fantasia*'s animated style for the small screen.

The home television, it was suggested, would eventually provide an entertaining visual appliance that either augmented or surpassed the basic aural experience of listening to radio broadcasts or phonograph recordings. There were also occasional debates about the hierarchy of the human senses, displaying a prevailing set of social values and a latent belief that sight is of a higher sensual rank than hearing. In the music trade magazine *Billboard* this visual privileging produced the interesting term "em-see" (instead of MC or emcee) to describe television program hosts, with the term "fem-see" applying to female show hosts. Through the postwar years, expert predictions, industry proclamations, and media speculation about television accelerated, with many touting the medium as a logical and welcome cultural achievement or an avatar of progress, in the process fanning the flames of public anticipation for television's new pleasures.

Another set of descriptions at the time compared television to public (or nondomestic) entertainment contexts, most frequently relating television entertainment to existing options of the cultural arena, notably the cinema or performances in theaters or nightclubs. This comparison implicitly acknowledged that these leisure pastimes had achieved ritual status within American culture and were, thus, a standard aspect of everyday life for many Americans. Cast in this light, television's most aggressive promoters (including network executives and television set manufacturers) sought to discursively normalize television, aligning it with typical entertainment interests and leisure patterns.

Viewers were promised "the best seat in the house" (reinforcing ideals of individualized reception), or else audiences were assured that the medium would deliver quality entertainment in the style and form of familiar musical showcases while freeing them from the cost and effort of attending actual public events. In the midst of this promotional phase it seems that few people asked the question whether American entertainment was such a priority or if people sought or demanded alternative leisure options. That they did was a largely unchallenged assumption on the part of broadcasting and advertising industries. Indeed, this underlying assumption has been maintained throughout the years since television's introduction and continues to inform the development of many subsequent leisure and entertainment commodities.

While prevailing attitudes invoked the element of convenience, television's development was also explained as a matter of rational economics as the TV industry's executive deliberations and public promotional strategies often framed a TV set purchase as a one-time financial outlay for years and years of home-based entertainment. As one early advertising campaign declared, television was "the greatest free show on earth!" although, by 1953, this same phrase was cynically employed in *Variety* as the industry lamented the rising costs of TV talent and the rapidly increased expense of producing musical programs (Rosen 1953: 1). Such claims for TV's contributions to leisure and entertainment were initially a matter of faith since the early programming schedule did not offer much upon which to form an opinion and what did exist was, as many reviews of the day indicated, of dubious quality.

The TV set manufacturers and networks promised potential consumers and audiences that television would eventually flourish, although the promises had been forthcoming for over a decade and the medium still remained far beneath the praises heaped upon it. Cultural critics and industry watch-dogs reported on each new development and innovation, providing considerable publicity for the burgeoning medium yet granting no quarter to the industry when the actual product lagged so far behind the promotional hype. Slow TV set sales were a major concern for the industry, especially as manufacturers repeatedly fell short of their sales projections and sweated over the corporate costs and the pressure from increasingly impatient investors and shareholders (Baughman 2007). Over time, as the television networks established a track record by offering increased programming (including a shift away from remote broadcasts of sports events or simple roundtable discussions featuring various "experts," community leaders, or authorities) and demonstrating a new production savvy, they could point to their mounting achievements as proof that the medium was indeed able to provide solid musical entertainment and, thus, offer value to viewers.

By the end of the war, television was far more than "an eccentric idea offered by a few esoteric inventors" as William Chafe (1986) and Constance Hill (2000) each claim. After almost twenty years of development and continual technical improvement, it was about to erupt as a full-fledged industrial sector. While there remained substantial doubts about how television might fare, the corporate broadcast networks and TV set manufacturers were gearing up for a concentrated thrust into the market. Given the sheer scale of the industry buildup, there was little to suggest that this was simply an "eccentric idea" but, rather, a major incursion into American business and cultural life. With greater technological consistency and production reliability in the late 1940s, television programming and content issues were prioritized. The specific question of musical presentation rose as a regular topic, spilling into the entertainment trade papers such as *Billboard, Down Beat, Metronome,* and *Variety.* The popular press also weighed in on television's programming developments, and reporters such as John Crosby at the *New York Herald Tribune* and Jack Gould of the *New York Times,* among others, soon emerged as important monitors of the rising television industry, providing astute analysis of policies and technical developments as well as offering keen criticism of TV's musical content.

American Federation of Musicians and James C. Petrillo

During the Depression and the war years, American laborers found solace and support among unions and the steady rise of both union organizing and membership inexorably influenced the country's economic and social character. In this period the American Federation of Musicians (AFM) effectively secured standard wage scales and employee protection for professional musicians, but the changing patterns of radio broadcasting, jukebox production, and phonograph recording in the 1930s and 1940s intensified the AFM's role and enhanced its status.

Throughout the 1940s, the AFM, under the fiery leadership of its president, James C. Petrillo (who took over the union presidency in 1940), confronted a complex scenario in which musical styles, audience tastes, and commercial demand each underwent substantial change. The influences of war presented several serious challenges to musicians and to their union; after the war, the union played a pivotal role in the concurrent evolution of popular music and television as the union battled with the recording, radio broadcast, and television industries. The AFM had always remained attuned to developments across the entertainment and broadcast industries and Petrillo was cognizant of television's significance and its potential consequences for the nation's musicians, especially after NBC's 1939 New York World's Fair debut when the network's premiere broadcasts prominently featured musical performances. Although the union set a preliminary television wage scale as early as 1943, signing a contract with the emerging networks that permitted union musicians to perform on TV programs, the arrangement proved to be premature since television was insufficiently evolved at the time and the war's effects constituted a barrier to its development.

The AFM engaged in heated squabbles with the recording and broadcasting industries during the war years, even going so far as to ban recording altogether in 1942–44 in an attempt to secure a fair and manageable royalty system and to restrict reproduction without remuneration from radio broadcasters. Paul Chevigny recounts that "the ban made Petrillo's name synonymous in the press with 'dictatorial' and 'featherbedding' labor tactics" (1993: 24). Showing a fighter's resolve, Petrillo also rescinded the union's permission for its members to appear on television in 1945, with the pugnacious union man expressing the view that it was ill advised to commit to an industry that had yet to fully mature.

The ban on televised musical performances lasted for three years, just when the television networks and set manufacturers were preparing to launch their ventures in earnest. Chevigny explains, "More importantly, the bans resulted in national outcry against Petrillo, and in legislation directed against organized labor in general and the musicians union in particular" (ibid.). With musicians surging back into society after their military service, the AFM's importance was reinforced and Petrillo wielded his authority and influence with what his critics denounced as imperiousness, sarcastically citing his middle name, "Caesar," as an appropriate character metaphor. Nonetheless, Petrillo proved to be a wily and tireless adversary as he negotiated with government policy makers and with corporate executives from the recording and broadcast sectors.

Petrillo accurately predicted radio's gradual reliance on recorded music, a trend that emerged throughout the 1940s, and he confronted the radio broadcast industry by seeking suitable compensation as "live" musical performances, studio orchestras, and remote dance band broadcasts were scaled back. Among his demands was that radio networks pay musicians on a retainer basis rather than hiring them under sporadic contracts or on a part-time basis. He also expressed serious concerns about the television networks' plans; with kinescope and film technologies at their disposal, televised music performances could, like any record, potentially be stored and replayed at will with virtually no additional cost to the networks and without proper guaranteed remuneration (what came to be termed residual payments or "residuals") for the musicians involved. It was this aspect of television, not the airing of live musical performances, that most irked Petrillo.

In an open letter to the AFM national membership in 1946 Petrillo voiced a three-part rationale for the TV appearance ban, citing the possibility that television could decimate the radio jobs currently available to union musicians; that the medium might ignore active musicians by relying substantially on kinescopes or films featuring prerecorded musical soundtracks; and that television-radio simulcasts should require dual contracts covering musician performance fees on each medium rather than acquiescing to the broadcasters' desire to pay only a single fee (Petrillo 1946). Stating his position, he wrote to the union rank-and-file members: "Television is not going to grow at the expense of the musicians. As television grows, the musician is going to grow with it, or we are not going to assist in its development. The sooner our critics — I should say our 'severe' critics — understand that musicians, who have been exploited for years, studied their instruments for a livelihood and not just to play for the love of it, the better off we will all be" (ibid.).

Notwithstanding the criticism leveled at Petrillo for his clashes with the expanding entertainment industries (including interunion conflicts with the American Federation of Television-Radio Actors/AFTRA and, occasionally, discord with his own union's locals), he was always fiercely committed to his union as well as to fortifying his own strength and authority at the helm of the AFM. In his brawls with the radio and recording companies and, later, the television networks, Petrillo's actions also exhibited shrewdly conceived political agendas that were important to his wider public profile while improving his stature within the union. He benefited in no small way from a close personal friendship with President Harry Truman, who was a piano player of modest talent and considered as someone who might sympathize with the plight of unemployed or underpaid musicians (Petrillo gave the president a gold "honorary lifetime member" union card in 1949).[4]

In a trend beginning almost immediately following the war's end, the market for the once reigning touring orchestras and dance bands dwindled. The demise of several "name" orchestras in December 1946 (including, as Lewis Erenberg itemizes them, those of Les Brown, Benny Carter, Tommy Dorsey, Benny Goodman, Woody Herman, Ina Ray Hutton, Harry James, and Jack Teagarden) stunned the popular music industry, corroding the foundation of the commercial music business. Erenberg summarizes the situation and its dire implications when he explains, "The growing funeral parade of bands sent shock waves through the music world. . . . The end of so many top orchestras ran counter to people's hopes for the postwar music scene. . . . The postwar depression that so many had feared became a reality in the band business; bright hopes turned dark" (1998: 213–14).

The costs associated with maintaining the large orchestras was certainly a factor, as was the reality that audiences were encountering a major case of aesthetic fatigue, growing weary of swing and big band jazz, which had been the dominant musical form for over a decade. Moreover, with the war's end, the music business was flooded with talent, creating a deluge of available musical labor for a limited professional market.

Musicians who had relied on nightclub employment during the 1930s and throughout the war years also faced dire conditions in the postwar period and individuals working in the music industry or in related cultural sectors were understandably fretful about their professional prospects. *Life* magazine cited a 30 percent drop in nightclub attendance in 1947: "Nightclubs are a surprisingly accurate barometer of U.S. luxury spending. Fewer surplus dollars jingled in the public pocketbook and nightclubs were first to feel the pinch. . . . [I]n New York impresarios were suffering from what the trade calls 'snow-blindness,' an occupational disease brought on by staring at too many white tablecloths uncluttered by customers" ("Nightclubs" 1947: 109). Considering the declining economics of the music industry, there was a latent optimism that television broadcasting could evolve as an important source of musical employment. In the view of many struggling musicians, television couldn't have come at a better time since it was beyond comprehension to think that they would not be hired as an essential facet of television's entertainment package.

Along with fluctuations in the band business, the immediate postwar period also saw the rise and entrenchment of a powerful labor base across the nation's production sectors as the gains of a wartime economy were transferred to peacetime prosperity. Marty Jezer explains that membership in the nation's major union organizations was at a historical high and, flush with membership dues, the unions were well positioned to skirmish with corporate employers while continuing to fund organizing initiatives and membership drives (1982: 78). William Chafe explains, "No group had greater optimism at the end of the war than organized labor. . . . Indeed, the surge of labor organization prompted one scholar to suggest that the United States was 'gradually shifting from a capitalistic community to a laboristic one' — that is, to a community in which employees rather than businessmen are the strongest single influence" (1986: 92).

The AFM was similarly strengthened in this period, yet union members were severely affected by the combined flux in the nation's economy and in audience tastes, and in several locals a sense of frustration set in. Despite his steadfastness on their behalf, among struggling union musicians there existed a creeping sense that Petrillo's confrontational approach to the music and broadcasting industries was counterproductive to their employment interests, antagonizing potential employers and narrowing their performance options. His intransigence, based on principle, politics, or personal style mattered little to the union's economically disenfranchised musicians. Petrillo also lost several key battles.

For instance, Petrillo's demand that radio broadcasters maintain studio musicians and orchestra members on a retainer basis whether they intended to use them or not was regarded by broadcasters — and the government — as tantamount to extortion, and Petrillo's critics regarded his actions as little more than criminal racketeering. His attempt to impose a levy on recordings that might be broadcast on the radio was similarly castigated. After extensive hearings of the Congressional House Committee on Interstate and Foreign Commerce under the guidance of Chairman Clarence F. Lea, the U.S. Congress passed the Lea Act in 1946 as an unambiguous response to Petrillo's uncompromising stance toward the radio broadcasting industry (and, as Lea explained in a letter written in 1946 to the National Association of Broadcasters, a handful of other "practices").[5] The congressional action — unofficially known as the "Anti-Petrillo Act" — refuted the AFM's power of coercion in the radio sector and among the act's immediate outcomes was the dismissal of hundreds of musicians from broadcasters' payrolls and the gradual eradication of radio studio orchestras with the end of the union's "standby" contract provision.

The advertising and broadcast industry trade paper *Sponsor* reported in early 1947 that regional radio disk jockeys were also contributing to transitions in the music industry, gaining new ground by spinning records by top artists while the major networks' "live" performance broadcasts of the same musicians often fared less well: "Dinah Shore platters compete with the *Ford Show* with Dinah Shore; Old Gold's Frank Sinatra session on CBS fights a number of 'Frankie' sessions on turntables all over the nation; and so on through the night" ("Music Sells" 1947: 21). The main music industry trade papers, *Billboard, Down Beat,* and *Variety,* described a rather dire set of conditions, acknowledging that a growing number of union musicians faced an indeterminate future. Petrillo saw corporate broadcast practices as being harmful to his union and its collective interests and, accordingly, he attempted to reassert the AFM's power by establishing the Recording and Transcription Fund, a fee charged to broadcasters and transcription companies by the union regardless of whether the recordings were ever actually replayed on radio or not. Petrillo imposed the fees preemptively as a precaution against the broadcasting industry's proven inclination to avoid additional recompense for subsequent or repeat airings of recorded material.

His efforts on behalf of the union were once again thwarted by direct and decisive federal involvement. In August 1947, The Labor-Management Relations Act, known as the "Taft-Hartley Act" (sponsored by Senator Robert Taft and Representative Fred Hartley Jr.), was written into law. The act was a biting piece of federal legislation with the stated intent to protect both employers and workers by ensuring, among other things, that the nation's business productivity would not be interrupted by strikes, picketing, boycotts, or other "disorderly" activities, especially involving secondary strikes by sympathetic unions. The unwritten intent was to curb the power of American labor unions. The act's various clauses also collided with the AFM's practice of collecting fees through its Recording and Transcription Fund as well as tempering Petrillo's constant threat of a nation wide AFM strike against the broadcasting and recording industries. Though Petrillo's old friend President Harry Truman attempted to veto the act, his effort was defeated after an extended Senate filibuster. As the Taft-Hartley Act, section 302, states, it is forbidden to "cause or attempt to cause an employer to pay or deliver or agree to pay or deliver any money or other things of value, in the nature of an extraction for services which are not performed or not to be performed," a ruling that effectively rendered the AFM's Recording and Transcription Fund illegal.

With television's imminent commercial breakout, the instinctive fear within the AFM in 1947 was that any reliance on recorded material could further harm musicians, reducing employment and negatively impacting revenues that traditionally accrued to them from performances. Additionally, the union was concerned that television broadcasting might erode finances deriving from jukeboxes and radio broadcasts if audiences switched to television for their entertainment. Such apprehensions were not unreasonable (as rudimentary audience and consumer research surveys indicated) and though no single factor can be identified as the main culprit, television *did* quickly challenge other established entertainment options by creating new competition for audience attention.[6] Petrillo was keenly aware that, as dues-paying members, working musicians contributed to a stronger and more financially empowered union over which he presided. Television was sure to add to the estimated $25 million that radio already contributed to the AFM coffers by the late 1940s.

Petrillo's staunchest detractors hoped that the governmental edicts would alleviate his renowned belligerence and combativeness; they were to be disappointed. Following the signing of the Lea Act and the Taft-Hartley Act, the angered but unrepentant AFM leader imposed the second recording ban in less than a decade in January 1948. By instating the 1948 AFM recording ban, Petrillo sought to ensure that musicians were not financially compromised as the radio stations continued their trend away from remote or studio music performances by turning toward the nefarious disk jockey; DJS spinning recorded songs were on the cusp of attaining a new and powerful role as sales motivators and musical tastemakers and without a responsive royalty system in place, the AFM regarded them as the enemy. Although in the long run DJS helped to spur music sales among the youth demographic, promoting R & B and the soon-to-emerge rock 'n' roll genre, in the late 1940s the outcomes could not be predicted.

As Russell Sanjek and David Sanjek (1991: 83) recount, the prospect of yet another AFM recording ban sent the major record companies into a frenzy of studio recording sessions. They hurried to produce an archive of unreleased material that would provide a cushion during the ban since songs recorded prior to the ban were not restricted from the market. Whereas the first ban in 1942 had caught the labels shorthanded and, in some instances, without sufficient recorded material to see them through the ban (or reduced to releasing vocal/acappella recordings — vocalists were exempt from the ban), the situation was different in 1948 when the major labels anticipated Petrillo's actions.

With vaults of recordings in place they were better prepared to fight Petrillo while continuing to release new material to the market. Staying the course, the record industry was able to outwait Petrillo with negligible damage. The ban extended almost a full year, until late 1948, when the AFM and recording companies finally agreed to the formation of the Music Performance Trust Fund, through which industry monies were paid into a separate nonunion account and then reallocated to the union to pay musicians to perform in free public concerts and musical exhibitions. The fund differed from the earlier Recording and Transcription Fund in that it was administered by an impartial trustee agreed upon by the record labels and the union (*Music Performance Trust Fund* 1949).

While the recording companies were mostly able to circumvent Petrillo's commanding decrees, television broadcasters were in a fix. With his ban on TV performances by union members, Petrillo held up the broadcasters, who were now certain that their new medium would rely heavily on musical programming. The AFM announcement came just as the nation's industrial manufacturers began to produce electrical home appliances (including radios and phonographs) in unprecedented volume and as the budding television industry hastened its program development and promotions for a nationwide market. The television networks attempted to maneuver around the union's TV ban as numerous extant NBC memoranda reveal. In response to the AFM's music restrictions, a memorandum sent by Ray O'Connell to the NBC national program manager, Thomas McCray, in late 1947 presents an extensive list describing a series of network programs with status reports on their musical material, designating programs within categories, "not affected by strike," "substitute program required," "could be done by using recorded musical background and bridges," "show could be done without music," and "program would require extensive revision."

With no clear sense of when the AFM would relent, the entire 1948 season program schedule was cast into doubt, necessitating alternative musical strategies and in some cases the dissolution of TV studio orchestras or cancellation of shows. In his statements to the House Committee on Education and Labor in January 1948, Justin Miller, the president of the National Association of Broadcasters excoriated Petrillo (a nemesis whom he loathed), explaining, "If as a result of this artificial restriction television is permitted to develop without musicians, musicians may lose potential jobs. If this happens, the result will be ascribable, not to the development of a new technology and not to the desire of employers, but solely to Mr. Petrillo's own ruling." With emphatic clarity, Miller declared, "Mr. Petrillo is educating a generation of television broadcasters in how to program television without the use of musicians" (1948).

These numerous overlapping clashes again revealed Petrillo's stubborn character as a negotiator. Obviously unafraid to confront the large entertainment corporations, major broadcast associations, or the government, he was unapologetic about revoking the networks' access to unionized musical talent. It was by this point inconceivable to either television's advocates or its critics that the medium could advance without featuring popular musical performances, and TV executives and others with stakes in the medium's advancement were justifiably livid. The NAB's Miller explicitly labeled Petrillo "an economic pirate," a leader with "absolute and dictatorial power over his union," accusing the union chief of antidemocratic practices, a serious claim in the era of intensifying anticommunist sentiments. In his conclusion, Miller stated, "Whether Mr. Petrillo realizes it or not, practically every position which he has taken has defied the immutable tides of technological progress and the right of the American people to enjoy the benefits of that progress. In addition, he has obstructed the normal growth of musical employment" (ibid.).

In testimony two days later at the same House Committee hearing, J. R. Poppele, president of the Television Broadcasters Association, seconded Miller's opinion that it was audiences and musicians themselves who suffered most from the AFM's ban on the televised broadcasting of live musical performances:

> The result, while imposing understandable hardships on television broadcasters has not, in itself, deterred the growth of the industry. . . . [T]elevision viewers today have been deprived of the operettas, the musical comedies, the symphony concerts, the first rate film entertainment and multitudes of other forms of entertainment which are naturally integrated with music, and which should normally be expected by the public from this new means of mass communication. In our final analysis, however, it is our thought that the musicians themselves, as well as members of other unions, who normally would be employed for their entertainment value, have suffered the most. (*Weekly Newsletter on Television* 1948: 1).

Despite Poppele's evaluation, the truth is that statistically few U.S. homes actually owned television sets during the immediate postwar years when the AFM music ban was in effect, nor was there yet a sophisticated and expansive programming repertoire to view. The general public did not necessarily miss much at all.

Petrillo knew full well by 1948 that his union was the linchpin in the networks' expanding television operations, and he realized that changes in communications technologies, a gradually growing trend toward industrial synergy across the entertainment sectors, and new cultural performance options required careful evaluation in order to secure the best possible contracts for the union membership. The AFM's obdurate stance may have impeded the industry's progress, yet the union was adamant that it would not lose revenue or member remuneration once television was up and running. In the spring of 1948, the AFM's monthly magazine, *International Musician*, directly articulated the union's views on television's growth potential, noting, "Television may prove for the late 40's and 50's what the radio was in the 20's: a big boom. . . . Television may reach the above-average income group, and at the same time hit the mass market. If television does succeed in reaching the quality market, presumably high caliber live shows will be required, at least for some shows over live video" ("Television Outlook" 1948: 7). The tentative nature of the statement, with its qualifying terms "if" and "may," reflects musicians' cautious approach to television at its inception, although it was very quickly evident that their presumptions were accurate, that it was a medium with mass appeal, and that it would rely on musical content performed by union musicians.

Television manufacturing executives had already seen, if briefly, how solid musical presentations could have a positive influence on television purchase patterns. The advertising agencies also promoted televised musical performances in their attempts to motivate consumers to buy new TV sets. These interrelated corporate structures were important in the industrial strategies developed between the conjoined RCA manufacturing arm and the NBC broadcasting network since the late 1930s and between the Du Mont corporation's TV manufacturing and broadcasting branches through the 1940s. Examples of the promotional links between television set sales and musical programming were not rare.

For instance, an advertisement in *Variety* (November 19, 1947, 35) for Du Mont's flagship New York station WABD reflects the network's emphasis on musical performance for attracting viewers, notably almost five months prior to the end of the AFM television ban. Under headline copy reading "The new look in television" is a close-up image of the actor and singer "honey blond, vivacious Sylvie St. Clair," who it is written, "makes her personal appearance on WABD every Wednesday night at 8:15." The advertisement copy also includes what is described as "an unsolicited letter" that reads: "Last night we saw you on television. *This made me decide to buy a television set.* You have been excellent—full of pep—and I thank you very much for the pleasure you gave me. I hope to see you often as soon as I get my television set." Since vocalists were not required to join the AFM, St. Clair was at liberty to sing to recordings on television while unionized musicians waited out the ban. *Variety* later speculated that securing a contract agreement with the AFM would provide the networks and set manufacturers with additional "impetus to receiver set sales. . . . Many people who've been disappointed in the tele shows haven't been activated to buy yet. There's still a margin for stimulus to set-buyers, consequently, and it's expected that improved programming resulting from the AFM pact will supply that stimulus" ("AFM Action to Hypo Set Sale" 1948: 30).

Robert Leiter writes that, in spite of Petrillo's uncompromising posture in negotiations with various entertainment industry factions, "the year 1948 was one in which major decisions were made by the American Federation of Musicians. At the beginning of January disputes were raging with regard to the manufacture of records, the negotiation of radio contracts, the future of frequency modulation, and the performance of live music over television. Each of these difficulties essentially was adjusted by the end of that year" (1953: 164). On March 18, 1948, Petrillo announced the signing of an initial three-year contract with the television networks (with the additional stipulation of trimonthly reviews as the medium grew and developed). The agreement finally allowed music performances to proceed on television while ensuring parity between the television wage scale and that of radio and fair remuneration in the way of residual payouts.

The union's new television pay scale was based on established radio rates, guaranteeing musicians an additional "duplication" wage of $7.50 over radio scale for performances simulcast on radio and television; other aspects of the pay scale included distinctions between local and national network broadcasts. The issue of film/kinescope taping of musical performances for multiple broadcasts was also addressed with the rules of use stipulating that the networks could air the programs only once over either key or affiliated stations. They were not, however, permitted to freely air performances by AFM members at will, and any repeat broadcasts required the union's written authorization ("Television Pay Scales" 1948: 12).

One of the idiosyncratic considerations that emerged from the negotiations involved what television executives termed "tuxedo rates." This nuanced proviso acknowledged the material realities of the transition from radio to television's visual context, offering supplemental wardrobe expenses to musicians due to the fact that "the visual medium will require the AFM boys to dress" ("TV's 'Tuxedo Rates'" 1948: 31). Similar considerations included enhanced compensation for additional makeup and rehearsal time as well as for participation in nonmusical dialogue or visual shtick before the cameras. Such details explicitly highlight television's emphasis on the image and accordingly compensated musicians for aspects of their preparation as *visual* broadcast performers.

As *Variety* reported, at the conclusion of the TV ban many AFM members (as well as those of the Association of Broadcast Unions and Guilds) felt Petrillo had ultimately "surrendered" to the networks with his television deal ("Petrillo's 'I Surrender'" 1948: 27). The crux of the deal hinged on the television performance rights, musicians' wages, and compensation for repeat broadcasting of filmed musical segments, but critics felt that the networks had provided Petrillo with little room to navigate as they pushed for a final resolution to the dispute. Even with his powerful negotiating position, his options had been quickly constrained when the network executives uncharacteristically closed ranks, collaborating as a single industry force unlike the major record labels (and the vastly greater number of vulnerable independent companies) that had tended to negotiate with the AFM autonomously in Petrillo's previous industry showdowns.

With the AFM television performance agreement finally in place, the networks could advance with their programming strategies. The hurdle behind them, the AFM and the networks officially opened the door for professional union musicians to enter the television domain on March 20, 1948, only two days after the AFM TV ban was repealed. The first AFM-sanctioned musical broadcasts featured Eugene Ormandy and the Philadelphia Orchestra appearing on CBS while, within an hour and a half of the CBS show, NBC broadcast a performance by the conductor Arturo Toscanini leading the NBC Symphony Orchestra.

Optimists within the union and elsewhere in the popular music industry surmised that as the medium evolved, "musicians will get more pay on television as more TV sets are sold and advertisers become willing to pay more for telecasting" ("TV's Musical Math" 1949: 40). Even Petrillo eventually admitted that television offered the "only hope" for finding new jobs for musicians, especially once TV's production patterns and viewer practices settled into more consistent patterns[7] ("TV Only Job Hope" 1950: 18).

In retrospect, there are several ways to consider Petrillo's strategies, objectives, and failures during this period. Displaying his antagonistic style and legendary brio, Petrillo may have been forward thinking in his assessment of television's technical development and the increasing trends of convergence among the distinct sectors of the wider entertainment industry. Petrillo's unyielding force, for example, resulted in the first residual payouts to the members of the AFM in 1951 for music in movies that were screened on television.[8] His aggressive responses to the new industrial realities that radically altered the form and trajectory of the recording and broadcast sectors were in many ways appropriate as his corporate adversaries sought to maximize their own power and economic position through collaboration or collusion. Yet his apparent inability to stare down the networks and to have his way with the TV industry may also suggest that his sense of the AFM's power was misplaced and that his authority in such situations was not beyond reproach (even though he retained leadership of the AFM until 1958 and served as head of the AFM Chicago branch until 1963).

Petrillo may also have been blind to the deeper implications of the postwar shifts that were under way throughout the entertainment industry, misreading America's modified leisure preferences and musical tastes. Paul Chevigny explains that Petrillo "came out of an environment in which all music was played live, in which one did not hear music except when produced by an individual or an orchestra. He was never really interested in player pianos, recordings, moving picture soundtracks, broadcasting or any other form of mechanical production. He was interested in work for live musicians" (1993: 24). Indeed, his postwar battles were the most bruising to his reputation as he endeavored to secure a funding pool for live musicians via his transcription funds. Petrillo also failed to adequately gauge the importance and rising popularity of newer music forms — R & B and the ongoing musical activities among the bebop and jazz artists (uncounted numbers of which were not AFM members) as well as the burgeoning Latin music scene — a potentially debilitating oversight.

His adherence to outdated principles, invested in the belief that the previous prosperity would return to the music sector now seems like a grave shortcoming. Like many executives at the major music labels and the editors of several musical journals (such as *Down Beat*), Petrillo maintained faith that the industry was only experiencing a momentary slump before the traditionally successful and lucrative dance bands reclaimed their market dominance in the nation's ballrooms and resorts. They did not.

Notes

1   The Boswell Sisters exhibited their close harmony vocal style in their first one-reel film, *Close Farm-ony* (Aubrey Scotto, director, 1932), soon after the CBS/W2XAB station launch.

2   Raymond Williams notes that radio followed a similar trajectory in its formative stages: "In the early stages of radio manufacturing, transmission was conceived before content. By the end of the 1920s the network was there, but still at a low level of content-definition. It was in the 1930s, in the second phase of radio, that most of the significant advances in content were made" (1975: 28).

3   There were several noteworthy experiments in the 1920s and 1930s that merged music and image for the screen: Thomas Wilfred designed a "color organ" called a Clavilux, introducing an abstract sound-image art form that he termed "Lumia" (Betancourt 2006). Oskar Fischinger reflected the avant-garde aesthetic of the 1930s with his animated short films (such as the 1936 film *Allegretto*) that consisted of wildly pulsating geometric shapes in brilliant hues accompanied by music in the grain of George Gershwin's "Rhapsody in Blue" and performed in a style consistent with that of Paul Whiteman's symphonic jazz (Moritz 2004). In these cases, however, the music-image dynamic was not reliant on, or inhibited by human presence on the screen.

4   Reflecting the extent of Truman's involvement with the AFM and Petrillo, in mid-June 1954 Truman appeared with Petrillo onstage at the AFM annual convention in Milwaukee, where the two performed a piano-trumpet duet. Petrillo was most polite in a telegraph to the NBC president Pat Weaver, asking that the network arrange to cover the staged event that Petrillo describes as "this matter which is very close to my heart" (Petrillo 1954).

5   Clarence Lea's list of AFM infractions includes the union's recent ban "upon the making of records and transcriptions, the quota system for the employment of musicians, the employment of standby musicians, restrictions on the appearance of members of the American Federation of Musicians on television broadcasts, restrictions on the use of service bans on the air, and disputes between A.F. of M. and NABET concerning platter turners" (1945).

6   A *Good Housekeeping* magazine survey in 1951 reported that among members of TV households, there was a 42 percent decrease in attendance at theater or concert performances, a 50 percent decrease in listening to phonograph records, and an 82 percent drop in radio listening ("TV Set Owners" 1951: 85).

7   On Christmas Day, 1953, ABC-TV broadcast a special feature, *The Musicians' Christmas Party,* described as "the AFM's 17th annual party-benefit for blind musicians." The program offered an opportunity for the union and its incendiary president to demonstrate their understanding of TV. For his part, Petrillo, who it was written, "mellowed for the occasion," introduced his mother on the air ("Musicians' Christmas Party" 1953: 16).

8   Reports suggest that, along with the efforts of unions such as the AFM or AFTRA, artist talent agencies were also important in negotiating for and acquiring residual rights for recorded/filmed screenings. See Glickman 1952.

Bibliography

Primary sources

"AFM Action to Hypo Set Sale, Better Shows." 1948. *Variety,* March 24, 30.

Brainard, Bertha. 1930. NBC interdepartmental correspondence, December 16.

"Dinah in Blackface." 1949. *Modern tv and Radio,* 70.

Engles, George. 1930a. NBC interdepartmental correspondence, December 15.

Engles, George. 1930b. NBC interdepartmental correspondence, December 18.

Fairbanks, William F. 1935. NBC interdepartmental correspondence, July 17.

Lee, Robert E. 1944. *Television: The Revolution.* New York: Essential Books.

Leiter, Robert D. 1953. *The Musicians and Petrillo.* New York: Bookman Associates.

Miller, Justin. 1948. "Statement of Justin Miller, President of the National Association of Broadcasters, before the House Committee on Education and Labor." January 13.

Music Performance Trust Fund Trustee's Regulations. 1949. New York: Samuel R. Rosenbaum, Trustees' Office, July 1.

"Music Sells . . . When a Disk Jockey Spins Records." 1947. *Sponsor* (February), 20.

"Nightclubs." 1947. *Life,* December 15, 109–15.

Petrillo, James C. 1946. "Why Members of the American Federation of Musicians Are Not Working for Television and Frequency Modulation Radio." *International Musician* 44, no. 10 (April), 1.

"Petrillo's 'I Surrender.'" 1948. *Variety,* March 24, 27.

Potter, Ralph. 1947. "Audivisual Television." *Hollywood Quarterly* 3, no. 1 (Fall): 66–78.

rca *and* nbc *Present Television.* 1940. New York: Radio Corporation of America.

Rosen, George. 1953. "Greatest 'Free' Show on Earth: TV Talent Costs at Record Peaks." *Variety,* October 7, 1.

Steffens, Mildred. 1945. "The Case for Visualized Music in Television." *Telescreen* (Spring): 8–12.

"Television Developments Demonstrated for Press by NBC and RCA." 1936. Press release. New York: National Broadcasting Company, November 6.

"Television Outlook." 1948. *International Musician,* April 7.

"Television Pay Scales for Musicians." 1948. *Down Beat,* August 23, 12.

"TV Only Job Hope." 1950. *Broadcasting-Telecasting,* June 5, 18.

"TV's Musical Math." 1949. *Broadcasting-Telecasting,* April 18, 40.

"TV's 'Tuxedo Rates.'" 1948. *Variety,* March 24, 31.

Weekly Newsletter on Television. 1948. New York: Television Broadcasters Association, *January 15.*

Secondary sources

Auslander, Philip. 1999. *Liveness: Performance in a Mediatized Culture.* New York: Routledge.

Baughman, James L. 2007. *Same Time, Same Station: Creating American Television, 1948–1961.* Baltimore: Johns Hopkins University Press.

Chafe, William. 1986. *The Unfinished Journey: America since World War II.* New York: Oxford Books.

Chevigny, Paul. 1993. *Gigs: Jazz and the Cabaret Laws in New York City.* New York: Routledge.

Dickinson, Kay. 2008. *Off Key: When Film and Music Won't Work Together.* New York: Oxford University Press.

Erenberg, Lewis A. 1998. *Swingin' the Dream: Big Band Jazz and the Rebirth of American Culture.* Chicago: University of Chicago Press.

Fisher, David E., and Marshall Jon Fisher. 1996. *Tube: The Invention of Television.* New York: Harvest.

Frith, Simon. 2002. "Look! Hear! The Uneasy Relationship of Music and Television." *Popular Music* 21, no. 3: 277–90.

Gabbard, Krin. 1996. *Jammin' at the Margins: Jazz and the American Cinema.* Chicago: University of Chicago Press.

Halper, Donna. 2001. *Invisible Stars: A Social History of Women in American Broadcasting.* Armonk, NY: M. E. Sharpe.

Hill, Constance Valis. 2000. *Brotherhood in Rhythm: The Jazz Tap Dancing of the Nicholas Brothers.* New York: Oxford University Press.

Jezer, Marty. 1982. *The Dark Ages: Life in the United States 1945–1960.* Boston: South End Press.

Kisseloff, Jeff. 1995. *The Box: An Oral History of Television 1920–1961.* New York: Penguin Books.

Koszarski, Richard. 2008. *Hollywood on the Hudson: Film and Television in New York from Griffith to Sarnoff.* New Brunswick: Rutgers University Press.

Magoun, Alexander B. 2009. *Television: The Life Story of a Technology.* Baltimore: Johns Hopkins University Press.

Mundy, John. 1999. *Popular Music on Screen: From Hollywood Musical to Music Video.* Manchester, UK: Manchester University Press.

Pegolotti, James. 2003. *Deems Taylor: A Biography.* Boston: Northeastern University Press.

Ritchie, Michael. 1994. *Please Stand By: A Prehistory of Television.* Woodstock, N.Y.: Overlook Press.

Rodman, Ron. 2010. *Tuning In: American Narrative Television Music.* New York: Oxford University Press.

Sanjek, Russell, and David Sanjek. 1991. *American Popular Music Business in the 20th Century.* New York: Oxford University Press.

Spigel, Lynn. 1992. *Make Room for tv: Television and the Family Ideal in Postwar America.* Chicago: University of Chicago Press.

Sterne, Jonathan. 2003. *The Audible Past: Cultural Origins of Sound Reproduction.* Durham: Duke University Press.

VanCour, Shawn. "Television Music and the History of Television Sound." In *Music in Television: Channels of Listening.* Edited by James Deaville. New York: Routledge.

Von Schilling, James. 2003. *The Magic Window: American Television, 1939–1953.* New York: Hawthorn Press.

9

Music on television in the 1960s and 1970s

Background and topics

In this section of this book, we will focus on slightly different themes and ideas than in the previous sections. We will start to focus more directly on the character and qualities of the kinds of musical fame and celebrity that began to emerge in the 1960s and took full form by the 1980s. These forms of fame and celebrity emerged through different forms of media, such as television, but also in a very different context, a context in which the music industry expanded to become a global phenomenon. (Reread pages 38–43 of the Garofalo article for a helpful summary.) First, we will examine that context, and then we will focus on how music was presented on television in the 1960s and 1970s. We will look in particular at how artists were presented on this medium.

One crucial aspect of the changes experienced by the music industry in these decades was the increased prominence and pervasiveness of popular music, especially when performed at large, high-profile events. There had been a few such events in years prior to 1960 that caught the attention of the wider public. The frenzied reception of Frank Sinatra performing at the Paramount Theater in New York in 1944 is a good example. These so-called Columbus Day Riots happened several years into a long series of shows the singer performed intermittently at the Paramount beginning in December 1942. While the reception of these shows had long been exultant, and occasionally disruptive, the shows on October 12, 1944, attracted an unusually large crowd of young people estimated to be around 30,000 strong. The theater held no more than 4,000 at any one sitting. The crowds on this particular day were far too big and active to control and they could

FIGURE 9.1 *Radio and TV Store, Sweden (1961).*

not be accommodated in the theater itself. Audience members of the early shows refused to leave when the next sitting made their way inside and what began as jostling for limited seating ended in the wholesale destruction of the ticket office and a few windows as well. News coverage at the time carried a distinct tone of disbelief at the sheer numbers of fans who turned up to hear Sinatra sing such standards as "Old Man River," "I'll Walk Alone," and even an arrangement of the famous "Lullaby" by Johannes Brahms. These young people, often derided as primarily female "bobbysoxers" for their distinctive rolled down socks, were said to be in the throes of a kind of mass sexual delirium.

Another event of similar size was Elvis Presley's performance at The Texas State Fair on October 11, 1956. The year 1956 saw Presley go from a very successful performer in regional auditoriums to a national celebrity and it is not hard to see why. He had signed to RCA records in late 1955 and by March of the following year he had completed his first album from which came multiple hit singles. In April, he had stirred up a hornet's nest of both excitement and condemnation with his aggressive hip-grinding performance of "Hound Dog" on the nationally televised "Milton Berle Show." By October he had already completed work on his first film which was eagerly anticipated by his growing fan base. It is not surprising then, that instead of playing a 2,000-seat auditorium, he played in The Cotton Bowl, a sports stadium usually reserved for football. The show attracted over 25,000 people and one journalist jokingly said that it was so big that must have registered on the Richter scale.

Perhaps two of the more influential of these kinds of events were the shows The Beatles played at New York's Shea Stadium, a then-new baseball stadium in the borough of Queens. The concerts occurred in 1965 and 1966. Videos of the 1966 concert are widely available through a simple internet search. The crowd for the first show was estimated at over 56,000 while the crowd for the second was somewhat smaller. These events followed the template established by Sinatra and Presley. The Beatles were widely available via records, films, television appearances, and live shows. Their presence in the media throughout the world was certain to attract a great deal of attention. And similarly, the reaction of the crowd, again dismissed as primarily consisting of slightly hysterical teenage girls, was a dominant theme of the news coverage.

What is important to understand here is that The Beatles, Sinatra, and Presley were all multimedia musical celebrities at the times of these respective events. They appeared in films, on radio, and in near-constant live performance as they toured around various countries. Also, all appeared regularly on variety and music programs on television. It was this very accessibility that fostered the seemingly unprecedented passion and intimacy that defined their relationships with their audiences. This is what brought these avid fans out in such large numbers. These kinds of events had a strong influence on the development of the music industry in the decades that followed.

One of the reasons for this was, as noted in Chapter 7, the generation born in the late 1940s and early 1950s became the biggest and one of the most influential of the twentieth century. These "baby boomers" were able to shape the politics, culture, and economics of their time to a tremendous extent. They also lived in a time of new ideas about society, about families, about sexuality, and about the ideals by which their societies should be governed. These ideas were widely debated and expressed through books, magazines, films, and television, as well as through the visual, literary, and music arts. Popular music in particular took on an economic and cultural importance it did not previously have. This was in part due to the new importance placed on all forms of artistic expression in the 1950s and 1960s as well as the increasing presence of popular music in everyday life. As the communications scholar and historian Fred Turner has shown, a wide variety of art forms were thought to act almost as models of new forms of human interaction. Art, music, and literature were imagined to be able to realign people's perceptions in new and exciting ways.

One of the more famous and memorable iterations of these ideas was the free music festival. Events such as the Monterey Pop Festival in 1967, the Woodstock Music and Art Fair, or simply "Woodstock," in 1969, and the Altamont Free Concert (1969), were meant to be open to all. Organizers of each event imagined creating a kind of forum for a new kind of culture and, by extension, a new kind of society. These kinds of events tended to be free and open to anyone who wanted to attend. Often, such events included performances by musicians from India, such as Ravi Shankar, and the

FIGURE 9.2 *Swami Satchidananda opening Woodstock (1969).*

FIGURE 9.3 *Music Festival, Yokohama, Japan (2009).*

South African musician Hugh Masekela. In fact, Woodstock opened with an invocation by Swami Satchidananda, a well-known religious figure.

These events also included multiple performances that became legendary, such as Jimi Hendrix burning his guitar on stage at Monterey or performing a sharp and biting version of the "Star Spangled Banner" at Woodstock.

They were often chaotic and complex events with thousands of people trekking sometimes long distances and camping for days on end, often indulging in the fabled trio of sex, drugs, and rock and roll. Altamont, in particular, was marred by highly publicized violence that marked a symbolic end to the "hippie revolution." While the politics of the free festivals of the 1960s did not last, their influence was still significant. They marked the beginning of an era in which concerts would grow in size and scope. The most successful artists would no longer play theaters or auditoriums. They would play sporting venues. The "stadium concert" would become routine by the mid-1970s and artists would commonly play dozens of such venues all over the world on massive months-long tours that would often see total attendance in the millions.

The image of the artist

One of the central themes of the four chapters in this section of the book is how the images, ideas, and representation of musicians changed in this era. They changed in a lot of different ways, but one of the central aspects of these changes was that the activities of musicians were regarded as increasingly important. Events such as those described above were not merely fanciful curiosities—they were newsworthy events. Musicians were taken seriously both in terms of the praise bestowed upon them and the criticism leveled at them. They were regarded as important and influential figures if for no other reason than for their ability to repeatedly assemble massive numbers of fans at stadiums around the world.

However, alongside the expansion of the music industry on a global scale was also a change in how musicians were regarded as artists. As we will see in this and the next three chapters, from about 1965 onward musicians were increasingly written about and represented in the media, not simply as "performers" or "entertainers," but as "artists." Their work was analyzed with increasing complexity and respect. Their achievements were regarded as significant and influential, not only within the music industry, but within the broader culture and society. Documentaries and news features were made about musicians and these kinds of productions gradually became a way of explaining wider social phenomena in the arts, society, and politics. Musicians were increasingly asked for their views on contemporary issues and topics, and their engagement in such issues ranged from the symbolic to the pragmatic. However, it is important to understand how the presence of musicians on television set the stage for the kinds of importance and influence, artistic and social, that popular musicians would experience in subsequent decades. Television was able to create distinct kinds of social relationships with a uniquely large audience of young people, many of whom were prosperous and comfortable enough to translate their experience of music on television into a long-term attachment to their favorite artists in particular, but also to popular music more generally. This acted as a template for similar kinds of social relationships that persist to this day.

Explore and report: Analyzing music on television

As with film, music was an integral part of television right from the beginning of the medium. However, one obvious difference between the advent of film and television is that film didn't have television to compete with. When television arrived, it could not really compete with film. Films would draw huge audiences to large movie palaces and theaters to experience a sensory experience that television simply could not match. The television was in many ways a lot like radio, but with pictures. Given this, television took over much of the cultural terrain occupied by radio. Large numbers of radio producers and on-air talent moved over to television and helped to shape early programming. In this section, you will look closely at the kinds of music that was presented on television in the 1960s and 1970s. In the next chapter we will look at how music videos became a staple product in the 1980s and 1990s, and we will bring the music on television story into the twenty-first century in Chapter 15.

First, we need to look at our key reading. It is:

Forman, Murray. (2014) "Music, Image, Labor: Television's Prehistory." From *One Night on TV Is Worth Weeks at the Paramount: Popular Music on Early Television*. Durham, NC: Duke University Press, 17–35.

Forman argues that it is important to realize that no one involved in early television really had any firm idea of what the medium would eventually be like. This lack of certainty, he says, "presented a major conceptual barrier but, of course, the challenges accompanying such indeterminacy can also inspire expansive thinking and lead to incredible innovation" (p. 246). The executives in this new industry then set to work trying to establish some basic rules and ideas that might shape the music and musicians that would appear on this medium. The most obvious idea was that they had to begin to consider the appearance of the musicians as much as the quality of their work. As Forman says, "The issue of musicians' image and appearance developed into a central topic as television evolved, creating conflict and debate about visual or aural primacy in musical presentation" (p. 248). Eventually, it was "the commercial practicality" that won out and "any given television program would eventually be judged according to the combined standards of performers' appearances and their musical talent, drawing television nearer to stage performances and cinema than to radio" (p. 249).

Importantly, Forman notes that musicians would be asked not simply to perform well or look a certain way. They would also be asked to "sell themselves to audiences through their engaging performances and innate visual appeal." He calls this "commodified congeniality" and he explains that, from the very beginning, music on television was "oriented toward the logic of commodification and consumption" (p. 249). This defined the worth and value of any musical performance that might be considered for broadcast and definitively shaped how those performances looked and sounded. The promise of television was that viewers were offered "quality entertainment in the style and form of familiar musical showcases while freeing them from the cost and effort of attending actual public events" (p. 259).

With these arguments in mind, you need to view and analyze examples of music on television from the years 1950 to 1980. The goal here is to develop clear and effective analytical tools to understand the presentation of music on television.

- First, you need to develop a solid understanding of each of the programs listed below. All have clips available on various video-streaming platforms. All have been written about extensively by academics, historians, and enthusiasts. You need to research and consult a range of credible sources to develop a clear understanding of when each was broadcast, who produced it, who the intended audience was, what kind of musical content was offered, and how each was generally received.

- Second, you need to use the key concepts put forward by Forman to analyze them. Develop you own list of concepts and apply them to an example from each program. Think of his terms such as "commodified congeniality" or "visual appeal" and use them to assess the purpose and importance of each program.

- Third, write an essay that will provide an overview of the development of music on television between about 1950 and 1980 and which focuses on how music was made appealing to a wide and varied audience. Focus on how musicians and their music are made to appeal to the audience.

Your Hit Parade (1950–59)

Your Hit Parade began as a radio show in the 1930s and moved to television in 1950. It was broadcast by NBC until 1959. As the scholar Gary Burns has shown, this program acted as a forerunner for later programs that claimed

FIGURE 9.4 *Regular Cast Members of* Your Hit Parade *(1955).*

to match the popular music charts, such as *American Bandstand*, *Top of the Pops*, and *Countdown*. Burns also shows how strange this program appears to us today. It features moderately theatrical backdrops with props and settings drawn from the old variety show formats in film and vaudeville theater productions.

Analytical Focus: This show was unlike more recent music-centered television shows. Instead of having well-known artists appear to perform their own work, it had a regular cast performing their own versions of well-known songs. Also, instead of performing in a traditional setup with an ensemble, the instrumentalists were off-camera and the singers were placed in slightly corny theatrical tableaux. Explain why this show appears to be so different than the ones that followed it.

The Ed Sullivan Show (1948–71)

The Ed Sullivan Show was one of the most prominent and genre-defining programs of its time. While it was a variety show and not only a music program, it regularly featured some of the most popular musicians performing at key moments in their careers. Many of their performances are still remembered as both important and widely influential. Sullivan had

FIGURE 9.5 *The Supremes on* The Ed Sullivan Show *(1966).*

ground-breaking performances by artists such as Elvis Presley, Sam Cooke, The Supremes, The Beatles, Nina Simone, The Doors, Sly and the Family Stone, The Rolling Stones, and Stevie Wonder.

Analytical Focus: The artists that appeared most often on *The Ed Sullivan Show* were The Supremes. They appeared fourteen times. Their appearances were widely influential as very few African American performers had appeared on national television with the regularity of this group. Sullivan was a strong advocate of African American performers. However, he was also notably sensitive about how musicians performed, routinely asking artists to change the style and content of their work to suit the show. Bob Dylan even refused to perform rather than be prevented from playing his song "Talking John Birch Society Blues." Examine the political and expressive constraints a program such as this imposed on performers.

American Bandstand (1950–89)

This show was one of the most powerful and influential of its time. Its longevity alone suggests this. From 1950 to 1957, it was produced in Philadelphia and aired regionally. In 1957, it began to be broadcast across the United States. After some changes in scheduling, it took up a customary afternoon slot which it held for decades. The program was recorded live

FIGURE 9.6 *The Beatles with Ed Sullivan (1964).*

and featured well-known artists miming to their most recent hits, usually pretending to play their instruments as well. It also featured a studio audience of teenagers dancing along with recorded versions of hit songs, with a camera that routinely sought out specific dancers to feature.

Analytical Focus: As the historian and scholar Matt Delmont has pointed out, *American Bandstand* had "an extraordinarily high level of promotional activity, even by the standards of commercial television." He continues, "Almost every minute of American Bandstand was dedicated to selling products. From paid advertisements for consumer goods to promotions of records and musical guests". See if you can work out why this show was so lucrative for so long.

Top of the Pops (1964–2006)

Top of the Pops was produced and aired by the BBC. It was a standard countdown show in which the entire show would build up to the number one song in the United Kingdom. Most episodes featured a youthful studio audience dancing to a familiar mix of recordings and mimed performances from performers whose work had been in the charts that week.

FIGURE 9.7 *Dick Clark, Host of* American Bandstand *(1963).*

Analytical Focus: Compare a video clip of *Top of the Pops* to a clip from *American Bandstand* from the same year. What similarities and differences can you find?

Soul Train (1971–2006)

This program featured African American artists performing mostly soul, rhythm and blues, funk, and some dance music. The creator and host, Don Cornelius, wanted to use the program explicitly as a platform for the positive reflection of African American life and culture through music. The program featured a live audience dancing to recordings, artists miming to their recordings, but it also featured live performances by artists such as James Brown and Ike and Tina Turner. The show remains perhaps most famous for its efforts to highlight the often flamboyant and demonstrative dancing and fashion of its audience members.

Analytical Focus: Given that the show's purpose was to positively reflect African American culture, what does this entail? For example, the program initially resisted allowing hip-hop artists to perform over concerns that the genre would not support the show's purpose. Explain what opportunities the show allowed its audience members and performers, but also what constraints it tried to impose on them.

Countdown (1974–87)

Countdown was a program produced by the Australian Broadcasting Corporation, Australia's public broadcaster. The show featured the

FIGURE 9.8 *Jackson 5 on* Soul Train *(1974).*

FIGURE 9.9 *Family watching television (1958).*

standard chart countdown format with musicians miming their hits to a small studio audience. The host, Ian "Molly" Meldrum, became a national celebrity, a status he retained long after. The show featured Australian artists as well as international artists touring Australia. It also made extensive use of music videos in its programming, at the time an unusual feature. The show was known for its encouragement of flamboyant and often ridiculous performances by well-known artists singing along with recordings.

Analytical Focus: Even though this program had many of the same features as the others listed here, the producers often favored and encouraged extremely colorful and extravagant performances by acts such as AC/DC and Skyhooks. Look for particular examples of these kinds of performances and compare them to the shows listed above.

Focus: The global telecasts of *Our World* and *Elvis*

The invention of television inspired a great many people to imagine a whole host of utopian possibilities for the new medium. Not unlike radio, television was thought to have power to unite all of humanity into a single harmonious whole. However, it was also viewed as an unprecedented opportunity to access consumers in the home, an environment presumed to be comfortable and intimate. Two broadcasts from 1967 and 1968 respectively can reveal for us these two contrasting views of the medium.

One was called *Our World*, a global satellite television broadcast which took place in 1967. The second was simply called *Elvis*, but has since become known since as the *Elvis 68 Comeback Special*. These two television events are similar in form, but very different in purpose and attitude. *Our World* was meant to present the ideals of international communication and cooperation guided by the idea that talking to people and seeing their art and hearing their ideas would make the world come closer together. *Elvis* was motivated by a very different set of ideas. It presented backward-looking values, heavily tinged with nostalgia for the recent past. Presley was a performer who was seen by many to have been passed by the momentous events of the 1960s. This was a television show that recast rock and roll as wholesome family entertainment, hollowing out a form of music which had only a few years before caused a moral panic. We will look briefly at both broadcasts and examine their meanings and implications.

Our World was a two-hour live program broadcast around the world on June 25, 1967. Fourteen countries participated and around 500 million people were estimated to have watched. The content was high-minded, including a performance by the opera singer Maria Callas and extensive reflections on technology and history by well-known scholars as well as by a sober voiceover that traced a variety of technological achievements over the preceding centuries. According to the television scholar Lisa Parks, *Our World* was founded on "the cultural legitimacy of public broadcasting, the benevolent paternalism of Western liberals, and the space age utopianism of satellite communications."

Somewhat remarkably, the final act to perform was The Beatles. Preceded by a double piano recital from Lincoln Center in New York City, the band premiered their song "All You Need Is Love," the first time it had ever been played in public. They performed at Abbey Road Studios in London. The studio was populated by a large crowd of their friends, fellow musicians, and a solid group of hippies. Most of the attendees wore colorful clothing and flowers in their hair. The broadcast included a fairly lengthy explanation of the recording process, with scenes of George Martin offering advice and asking for another take. The performance has long been viewed as a defining moment in the symbolic event that was the "Summer of Love."

On December 3, 1968, NBC broadcast *Elvis*, in which Presley performed a series of set piece, theatrical production numbers, loosely following his personal biography, and a series of live performances of the songs he made famous. The latter were recorded in a television studio before an audience which sat around a small square within which Presley and his most trusted band mates played.

Before the "comeback," Presley had reached a comparative low point in his career with his movies no longer commanding the fees and audiences he was used to and the world of popular music having passed him by as artists such as The Beatles, James Brown, and Jimi Hendrix having taken their own roots in rock 'n' roll and rhythm and blues in directions no one had suspected. But instead of challenging these artists on this new terrain, Presley reminded his fans of what he once was. He also proved he could still command a hefty fee, albeit in a new medium. The program revitalized his performing career and he went on to produce a series of live television specials that redefined his late-career legacy. It also became a template for the future use of the medium by a wide range of stars, far more so than the worthy idealism of *Our World*. Presley's ability to use his importance and prominence to command a national television broadcast to offer what was, essentially, a lengthy remembrance of himself points us toward the kinds of musical fame and celebrity that would become dominant in the ensuing decades.

INDEPENDENT RESEARCH WORK

B etween the years of the "classic" television concert special, such as Elvis' comeback (1968), and the increasing prevalence of music videos up to and after the founding of MTV (1983), a large number of high-profile music programs were broadcast on television. Many were intended to feature the work of well-known and established musical celebrities such as Johnny Cash, Andy Williams, and Tina Turner. Others were variety show formats and others were simply live concert especially made for television. Still other mixed musical performances with sitcom-styled shows in which the musicians acted as themselves. Explore and research a range of television shows produced in this time period. Examine and report on how each type of program intends to create different kinds of relationships with its viewers. Here are some titles:

- US: Solid Gold, Soundstage, The Monkees, The Partridge Family, NBC's Midnight Special, In Concert (ABC).

- UK: Check It Out, The Old Grey Whistle Test.

- Australia: Hitscene, Sounds Unlimited, Night Moves.

References and further readings

Burns, Gary. (1998) "Visualising 1950s Hits on *Your Hit Parade.*" *Popular Music*, 17(2): 139–52.

Delmont, Matt. (2012) "'They'll Be Rockin' on Bandstand, in Philadelphia, PA': Dick Clark, Georgie Woods, and the Value of Rock 'n' Roll." *Journal of Popular Music Studies*, 24(4): 457–85.

Kitts, Thomas. (2009) "Documenting, Creating, and Interpreting Moments of Definition: Monterey Pop, Woodstock, and Gimme Shelter." *The Journal of Popular Culture*, 42(4): 715–32.

Kooijman, Jaap. (2002) "From Elegance to Extravaganza: The Supremes on The Ed Sullivan Show as a Presentation of Beauty." *The Velvet Light Trap*, 42: 4–17.

Parks, Lisa. (2003) "Our World, Satellite Televisuality, and the Fantasy of Global Presence." In L. Parks and S. Kumar (eds.), *Planet TV: A Global Television Reader*. New York: New York University Press, 74–93.

Sewlall, Harry. (2015) "'The Grain of the Voice': Elvis Presley's 1968 NBC-TV Special." *Journal of Literary Studies*, 31(4): 56–70.

10

MTV and the evolution of the short musical film

Background and topics

As we have seen, the short musical film has taken a variety of forms since the invention of the motion picture. The first were short films featuring artists such as Bing Crosby, Bessie Smith, or Duke Ellington. Musicians often appeared live as part of short narrative films in which they would perform a thematically appropriate song. Audiences would see these films at the movie theater when they were presented before longer feature films. Another form of short musical film was the so-called soundies, presented to audiences through video jukeboxes. With the advent of television, shows such as *Your Hit Parade* featured short performances of the latest hit songs complete with theatrical backdrops and costumes.

Building on this history, but within a very different context, the American pay television channel Music Television (MTV) transformed the purpose and status of the short musical film. In this chapter, we will first look at how MTV helped make short music films, now called "music videos," central to the music industry at large. Then, you will be asked to analyze how musicians are presented in a few videos regarded as important and influential from MTV's first decade. Then, in the Focus section we will examine how this company created new ways to link popular music with a seemingly endless range of consumer products, forms of publicity, and marketing opportunities.

MTV began broadcasting on cable television in the United States in 1981. At the time, its availability was limited to the relatively small number of subscribers of pay television in that country. Within a decade, however, its reach extended around the globe, establishing channels and outlets in

FIGURE 10.1 *MTV "Moonman" and logo statues (2008).*

multiple countries and languages in every region of the world, including the former Soviet Union, then only a few years removed from communism. By the turn of the century, the company had expanded its reach to over 300 million subscribers and its video content included a wide variety of musical genres that had expanded a great deal from its very limited early offerings. The channel also produced content dedicated to linking musical celebrities to fashion, film, politics, sports, animation, reality television, and regular live music events.

MTV was created by a group of people who had been involved in the television industry for many years. Several of them saw a series of new opportunities opening up for them in a music industry that, despite being mired in a downturn, still had enormous potential for profit. The vehicle they chose was cable television which was expanding its subscriber base as new services became available in the mid to late 1970s. New channels offering programming not available on free-to-air broadcast television included dedicated movie channels, sports channels, and children's programming. For the television executives responsible for creating MTV, a dedicated music channel seemed obvious. As one of the founders of MTV suggested at the time, despite plans for a shopping channel and a games channel, "MTV was the easiest to do because it was the cheapest and we could get it going quicker." There was plenty of material available in the form of promotional music videos that were already being produced in the music industry and it was "a body of work that had never been exploited."

Clearly, the founders of MTV were able to build on previous models of music television. As we saw in the previous chapter, shows such as American Bandstand devoted almost their entire programming content to selling products. MTV would do the same, as we will see below. As Murray Forman argued, the presentation of music on television was defined from the beginning by the ability of musicians to sell themselves and their music through their appearance and what he called their "commodified congeniality." It was the job of producers to translate these qualities into successful, profitable sponsorships. MTV was no different in this respect. However, it was a 24-hour television channel dedicated to music. At first, the creators explicitly imagined it to be a form of visual radio that would provide the basis for the channel to assume an expansive presence in popular culture. This made its relationship with its audience very different from those of its predecessors. It was literally on all of the time and the sheer scale of the material it made available was simply overwhelming for that time. Also, the idea of an audience that could be expected to use the channel, not once a week or every evening at a set time, but all the time, appealed to advertisers, especially those seeking to access a younger market. Moreover, the channel was something new and different in comparison to its most obvious competitor, radio. Unlike most radio stations which were deliberately focused on limiting the range of music they played in order to establish a clear musical identity, MTV's content was not determined only by genre, but by also visual appeal. Despite the fact that they were initially seeking only what they called "the rock audience," which was almost an exclusively white audience at the time, the artists they presented were still more varied than most radio stations.

Just as important was MTV's ability to establish itself as a central gatekeeper in the music industry. The era in which MTV was founded was defined by a smaller and smaller number of large corporations controlling larger and larger numbers of television channels, record companies, and radio stations. This was due to changes in the laws governing media ownership in many countries around the world, led by the United States. This facilitated the ability of media companies such as the one that owned MTV to buy their way into markets around the world allowing them to expand their audiences. The expansion of their audience enabled MTV to begin to exert more power within the music industry. They did so by signing contracts with the major record companies that sought to have their videos played exclusively on the channel. These contracts established MTV's sole right to play selected videos and deny this right to their competitors. As the communications scholar Jack Banks has explained, these "mutually beneficial

FIGURE 10.2 *Mark Knopfler from Dire Straits on stage (1983).*

arrangements allowed MTV to pick video clips featuring hit singles and major recording stars for its exclusive use that would probably increase its ratings, while record companies could get guaranteed exposure for their artists that might not otherwise get airplay." In return, MTV "provided cash and advertising time to the major labels" (1997, 297). These anticompetitive arrangements even allowed the channel to start to influence how videos were made and what they might look like. Further, this influence shaped the contracts artists signed with record labels, with most specifying new terms for the compulsory production of videos, usually with the costs borne by the artists themselves.

By the mid to late 1980s, most music videos that made it on to MTV had become extremely expensive, spectacular, and visually exciting. This in turn started to change how artists were viewed by their audiences. While it was a new and exciting experience for many television viewers to see an occasional live performance by their favorite artists, MTV expanded the scope of music videos to include unique inflections on an artist's work, including distinct types of costuming and fashion, unique choreography, and expansive visual imagery not available elsewhere. Far from the straightforward capture of an ersatz live performance, MTV helped directors to push music video to spectacular and flamboyant heights few thought it could achieve in the previous decade. This, along with an expanding market for music, helped push the music industry into a significant period of prosperity of the type it had not experienced before.

Explore and report: Top video artists of the 1980s

There are simply an enormous number of music videos from the 1980s available on various video-streaming platforms. This offers you a significant analytical opportunity. Below is a short list of artists and songs whose music videos are widely regarded as important and influential in this time period. Each entry has some annotation as background. Your task is to analyze three videos of one artist. You can do your own research and find a different artist if you like. Either way, the analysis should work as follows. First, do not simply describe or explain what you see in the video. This is not analysis. Instead, analysis is an attempt to produce distinct and specific interpretive meaning from these materials. Second, this analysis must be based on research. You need to establish who each artist is and where each of these songs fits within their overall career. Third, all of these artists and their videos have been written about extensively. Find sources such as *Billboard*, *Rolling Stone*, *Fader*, or websites such as Pitchfork or Pop Matters. Find articles and interpretations of music video generally and these artists and their videos specifically. You need to be able to write a concise summary of the overall critical assessment of these videos. Finally, develop an argument or interpretive claim about what you think the influence and importance of the artist and his or her work is specifically as expressed in these videos. Be specific. Here are some of the key questions to ask: Why are most of these videos based solely around the existing recordings of each song? How is the artist positioned and portrayed in each? What implicit values does the video explicitly express or implicitly reject?

- Michael Jackson: "Billie Jean," "Beat It," "Thriller."

These three videos are regarded as representing a significant change in how MTV approached its programming. MTV started with a pronounced bias toward the rock tradition. However, Jackson's videos were so popular that they have since been regarded as opening a door for much greater diversity in MTV's programming. Central to all three videos is their narrative coherence linking to the lyrics of each song, the display of extensive group and solo choreography, and the high quality of each production. On a sidenote, Jackson later altered "Billie Jean" for use in a Pepsi television ad in 1984. It might be interesting to compare this ad to the original video.

- David Bowie: "Let's Dance," "Modern Love," "China Girl."

David Bowie was already a globally renowned and influential artist before MTV arrived. The various personae he created through his various albums were striking for their periodic reinvention of Bowie as an artist. These

FIGURE 10.3 *Michael Jackson with President Ronald and First Lady Nancy Reagan (1984).*

three videos represent one such persona. What visual themes link these three videos together?

- Madonna: "Holiday," "Like a Prayer." "Material Girl."

Madonna's career mirrors that of MTV. Her early hits coincided with the channel's rise to prominence after its early formative years. Each video is notable for the singer's fashions, all taken from different spheres of social life, a strongly visual theme, again each taken from different reference points, and clear links to the music. On a sidenote, "Like a Prayer" was launched through a multimillion-dollar deal with Pepsi. What influence do you think this might have had on the song and its video?

- Duran Duran: "Rio," "Hungry Like the Wolf."

Duran Duran's early videos in many ways established a new standard in terms of imagery and spectacle. Each was set in what were then regarded, somewhat condescendingly, as "exotic" locations. Also, each was shot as if

FIGURE 10.4 *David Bowie and Madonna on stage (1983 and 1987).*

it was a miniature film, that is with a large crew and at great expense. Also, look at how each acts as little more than a flamboyant vehicle for the band members to simply mime their parts.

- Tina Turner: "What's Love Got to Do With It?," "Private Dancer," "Simply the Best."

Similar to Duran Duran, each of these videos foregrounded Turner lip-syncing to her recordings. However, each has its own visual theme that surrounds the singer. How does each visual theme link to its respective song?

- Prince: "1999," "When Doves Cry," "Kiss."

Prince's videos from the first third of his career very often appear to be simple performance videos. "1999" and "Kiss" are good examples of this. However, despite the obvious similarities, examine the style of each. There is a coherent set of fashion symbols and iconography for each that marks each out as a self-contained world of images and ideas. This is also true of "When Doves Cry" which, while not a performance video at all, also creates a seemingly self-contained and complete world of images and symbols unique to this artist.

- Run DMC: "It's Tricky," "My Adidas," "Walk This Way" (w/ Aerosmith).

Run DMC were one of the first hip-hop acts to feature regularly on MTV. As a result, they had a far broader appeal than many within the music industry

FIGURE 10.5 *Prince performing (1990).*

had previously imagined possible. Specifically, the rock-based samples on "It's Tricky" and their collaboration with Aerosmith both helped to fix hip-hop videos on MTV from the late 1980s onward. Examine these videos, specifically comparing the physical deportment and presentation of these artists with their rock and pop counterparts. How is their use of symbolism and iconography distinct?

Focus: From playing music videos to branding musical fame

One of the defining features of MTV is how the channel has continually altered and expanded its offerings across nations, regions, cultures, and subcultures that were defined socially, culturally, and economically. As noted above, MTV has produced a wide range of programming far beyond its seemingly originating purpose of broadcasting music videos. However,

FIGURE 10.6 *RUN DMC concert poster (1984).*

the idea that its only interest has ever or should have ever been showing videos is something of a misnomer. Instead, its originating purpose was to create new kinds of relationships with music consumers and to profit from doing so. The form these relationships took had always been extremely open and flexible. Given the links popular music has always had across a wide swathe of consumer culture, this was always going to be a complex and varied mission. As one executive put it on the channel's twentieth anniversary, "Music is a 360 degree experience." He claimed that as a result "we have to have MTV on as many platforms and possible—all offered in a complementary way." In practice, this has meant creating a multitude of consumer relationships simultaneously.

Perhaps the most important thing to remember about MTV is that nearly everything that they broadcast is a commercial for something. In fact, the network predicated its existence on being able to make every piece of content they produced earn revenue in some way, either directly through sponsors or indirectly through brand associations. MTV's goal has always been to develop consequential, influential, and profitable associations with brands, the success of which was dependent on a wide range of constantly evolving types of audience engagement, engagement which is then sold to sponsors and advertisers as the core of the channel's effectiveness and continued existence. Crucially, while some have argued the MTV's evolution has proceeded from a channel defined by its engagement with music to that of a "lifestyle" network, the fact of the matter is that the channel has pursued its expansive vision of being a wide-ranging lifestyle network almost from its earliest days. We can helpfully survey a few of MTV's efforts in this regard.

New channels

From the very beginning, MTV sought to be more than just a music video "channel," but instead aggressively pursued its goal of becoming a suite

FIGURE 10.7 *MTV logos (1990s).*

of channels that were part of a global network of interlinked entities. For example, less than two years after MTV went to air, the channel's parent company started VH-1, a new video channel originally intended to present a range of music not presented on MTV, such as softer pop and rock, notably by many African American artists who were generally denied access to MTV. This marked the first of many efforts to create channels defined by their content, such as MTV Latino founded in 1992 and MTV Tr3s, a similar effort started in 1998. MTV's parent company also created channels devoted to slightly different demographic and consumer groups, such as with M2 (later called MTV 2) in 1996, which was originally devoted to playing nonstop music videos with a 24-hour "No Repeat" policy. The "relaunch" as MTV 2 in 1997 resulted in sharply genre-segregated and artist-specific programming. Its executives regard the audience for this channel "more musically advanced" and saw the channel's goal as "taking more chances" than the rest of the network. In 1998, the company created VH-1 Smooth, which was quickly rebranded to VH-1 Classic in 1999. In 2016 it was rebranded again as MTV Classic. It was as VH-1 Classic that the channel began to produce and air its influential *Classic Albums* documentary series in 1992 and the *Behind the Music* documentary series in 1997. Another content-based effort was a channel devoted to live music, originally called Palladia on its founding in 2006, and later MTV Live. This channel grew from earlier efforts to produce live music through MTV Unplugged, beginning in 1990, where famous artists would perform a new acoustic version of their work live, and MTV Live in 1997, where artists would perform their regular stage shows in MTV's studios.

Beyond this, the company has continually pursued the establishment of new channels around the world such as MTV Europe in 1987, MTV Brasil in 1990, and MTV Asia also in 1990.

Brand/product associations

A mere twenty months after MTV established itself in 1981, one of their more interesting product placement efforts was completed. MTV established a relationship with the producers of the film *Flashdance*. This film was about a young female dancer trying to juggle the demands of her job as a welder with her ambitions as a professional dancer. Scenes of her rehearsing her various dance routines were accompanied by hits such as "Maniac" by Kenny Loggins and "Flashdance (What a Feeling)" by Irene Cara. The film's producers excerpted complete scenes from the film, which exactly resembled music videos in form, length, and content, and MTV showed them uncut and unedited in their regular rotation. The success of the film and its soundtrack proved such relationships to be economically viable and shaped future efforts by the channel to pursue these sorts of efforts. These eventually resulted in MTV Films which began producing full-length feature films in 1996. MTV's relationship with the film industry has always been apparent, with the film program The Big Picture airing from 1988 to 1997 and the MTV Movie Awards beginning in 1992.

New programming

Unsurprisingly, as the channel grew into a global network, its programming varied dramatically. However, a few key themes can help us make sense of some of their efforts. One of the central kinds of programming MTV has pursued is programming which seeks to establish a limited canon of "great artists" whose work is considered to be superior if not transcendent. Their first efforts in this regard were the regular event the Video Music Awards which started in 1984. These shows featured daring and often controversial performances, as winners carried home the iconic "Moonman" statues. A range of pop chart countdown programs have featured off and on since Top 20 Video Countdown aired in 1984. Perhaps most important have been the series of short music documentaries that the company began to produce beginning in 1989, including VH-1's *Classic Albums* and *Behind the Music* documentary series. MTV's first feature-length music documentary, *Tupac: Resurrection*, was released in 2003. These productions mark a clear effort by the network to place a definitive stamp on how the history of popular music is to be produced and understood.

Importantly, the channel often produced programming that went well beyond any of its initial plans, such as when it broadcast every moment of the first Live Aid concerts in 1985. This is still regarded as the channel's "coming of age."

Types of music/news/current affairs programming

MTV also specialized in producing regular weekly programs that clearly sought to place the channel's stamp on how various areas of popular music evolved, specifically by using its scale and visibility to champion some artists over others. Programs such as *120 Minutes* featured so-called "underground" and alternative rock and punk acts from 1986, the heavy metal-themed *Headbanger's Ball* from 1987, and a series of hip-hop shows such as *Yo! MTV Raps* from 1988 and *MTV Jams* from 1992 worked in precisely this way.

The network applied the same logic to its news programming, such as its daily, hourly and weekly news content which began when the channel itself did, as well as its coverage of politics and culture with its Choose Or Lose election coverage starting with the 1992 American presidential elections

FIGURE 10.8 *Live Aid Stage in Philadelphia (1985).*

and *The Jon Stewart Show*, MTV's first talk show which began in 1992. Fashion and sports were not exempt either, as the channel featured links to a variety of "youth-oriented" sports which evolved into the extreme sports or X Games phenomena. The brand associations and commercial sponsorships of these kinds of programs should be obvious.

Types of engagement

Perhaps the most important aspect of this survey of programming is the kinds of audience engagement they were supposed to produce. These are most obvious in a few specific program types MTV has sponsored or created. One of the most popular was its request shows. Beginning in 1986 with *Dial MTV*, and continuing with *Total Request* and *Total Request Live* in 1996 and 1998 respectively, the channel created opportunities for its audience, ostensibly its "ordinary" viewers, to call in and request a video to be played. While this sounds innocently straightforward, these programs were actually created to give record companies a way to leverage the enthusiasm of the fan bases for various artists into airtime for their products and, through this, to manufacture a sheen of popular support for their music. Often, the official fan clubs of different artists would be organized to flood the phone lines (and later websites) of MTV with requests for specific videos. It became a kind of unrecompensed, informal PR work for the music industry.

Perhaps one of the more symbolically notorious forms of programming MTV has produced are its various "reality-based" programs. Beginning with its Spring Break broadcasts in the United States in 1986, and up to its many different forms of reality TV, such as *The Real World* from 1992, as well as *Punk'd* and *Pimp My Ride* from 2003, the channel most clearly fulfilled its aspirations to become a "lifestyle" network. These programs often reflected music only indirectly, as part of a larger set of events, some organic, some manufactured. However, these kinds of programs did not simply present "ordinary people," but musical celebrities and their lives behind the scenes. Throughout the existence of this channel-cum-network, those producing the programs have long recognized that it is their ability to understand how the multitude of social relationships music creates can be exploited was the only way they could survive or thrive.

INDEPENDENT RESEARCH WORK

Explore the kinds of links popular music has had with other brands from the mid-1980s to the mid-1990s. The linking of artists, labels, and brands is usually called "brand association." Some of the most profitable of these in this time period were between artists such as Michael Jackson and Madonna and Pepsi. Both artists sold their songs to support global advertising campaigns for this soft drink manufacturer. These campaigns caused controversy among those who believed this devalued the music these artists were making and the messages their music presented to the public. Others argued that it merely offered artists a neutral platform to reach a larger audience. Research these controversies and report on the contending arguments about them.

References and further readings

Banks, Jack. (1996) *Monopoly Television : MTV's Quest to Control the Music.* Boulder, CO: Westview Press.

Banks, Jack. (1997) "Video in the Machine: The Incorporation of Music Video into the Recording Industry." *Popular Music*, 16(3): 293–309.

Denisoff, R., and W. Romanowski (1990) "MTV Becomes Pastiche: 'Some People Just Don't Get It!'" *Popular Music and Society*, 14(1): 47–61.

Hay, Carla. (2001) "Billboard Salutes Twenty Years of MTV." *Billboard*, 113(30): 52–70.

11

The popular music documentary

Background and topics

The popular music documentary emerged from a historical context of great social, cultural, and political change. As noted in Chapter 7, the late 1950s and early 1960s marked a turning point in many societies around the world in which a powerful desire to escape what many saw as the conformist chains of mainstream culture was widespread. As the scholar of American history and culture Barry Shank has argued, this desire represented not simply a thirst for personal development. It represented a new model of personal and collective subjectivity. Shank argues that it was "a paradoxical longing for both authentic connection and autonomous freedom." When translated into a tangible movement to transform society, Shank claims that many firmly believed that "any truly effective collective must consist of healthy, personally authentic individuals. These individuals should feel connected to their past and their present, but they must not concern themselves with the good opinions of others. Their interactions with each other should be as fully independent, as free of the constraining ties of status competition or the struggle for distinction." This was a new model of personal subjectivity positing a model of an authentic self that was part of a larger set of social structures. The sole purpose of those social structures was supposed to be to facilitate this ideal self. This new ideal emerged over several decades and remains with us today in many different forms.

One particularly relevant manifestation of this new understanding of an authentic self was the ways in which popular musicians began to be represented in print and on the screen in this period. Instead of being portrayed as entertainers, musicians such as Bob Dylan, The Beatles, Janis Joplin, and Nina Simone began to be portrayed as artists, not in exceptional circumstances, but as a rule or tacit assumption. Music journalists such as Ralph Gleason and Ellen Willis wrote for both young and old audiences

FIGURE 11.1 *Bolex H16 Reflex. Among the first portable movie cameras (1956).*

about the complexity, power, and importance of popular music in ways that had rarely been done before. Filmmakers such as Americans Albert and David Maysles and D. A. Pennebaker set off to document such events as the Monterey Pop Festival and Bob Dylan's tour of the United Kingdom in 1965 with a frankness and directness that came to define a new style of documentary filmmaking, so-called direct cinema. Similarly, British filmmaker Peter Whitehead made more complex, experimental, and loosely constructed music-centered films set in London in the late 1960s. Both groups of writers and filmmakers were part of a larger system of representation which emerged in this period that remains with us today. It is a system that set out to show how this new model of individual subjectivity was reflected not only in the work these artists produced, but in their very beings clearly manifest in the ways in which they talked and acted in the wider world.

In this chapter and the next one, we will examine how different examples of popular music documentaries sought to produce images and representations of popular musicians as authentic beings with important things to say. We will confine ourselves to documentary film in order to pursue a kind of analytical consistency and to see how this specific form of representation has clearly been marked over a long period of time with a particular mode of representing a very specific model of authentic artistry as a model for others to follow. Importantly, we will also focus on what was called "direct cinema," or a form of documentary filmmaking which purported to show an objective truth by using lightweight, handheld cameras to follow subjects closely and intimately revealing their daily lives and experiences. Most often, filmmakers sought to reduce or remove what were regarded as extraneous elements of film, such as lengthy narrative voiceovers, extensive editing, or staged lighting and theatrical effects. It should be clear that this specific idea of an "authentic" representation of an "authentic" subject forms the conceptual basis for the films we are examining in this chapter.

The model of artistry we will use in this chapter and the next has been developed and gleaned from a range of writings on the purpose and value of music and art. Writers and scholars such as Allan Moore and Bernard Gendron have written about these ideas. This model has three basic analytical assumptions or underlying rules about what these films are trying to tell us:

- First, the artist has a genuine and unmediated relationship with their art. The "true" artist does not let anything get between them and their art.

- Second, there is a similarly direct relationship between the artist and their public. This relationship is defined by the direct and honest expression by the artist to the public.

- Finally, the artist "stands for something," something other than just themselves. They represent larger ideas and values that are meant to act as models and ideals for others.

This chapter also draws from wider understandings of a model of artistry that grew from the tradition of German romanticism in the nineteenth century to the present. In a short essay entitled "What Is a Classic," the poet T. S. Eliot concisely encapsulated this tradition of thought by explaining a range of attributes that great art must possess. Paraphrasing Eliot, we can conclude that "great art" is defined by this very particular tradition of thought as having some range of the following characteristics:

- Possess gravitas or a kind of metaphorical weight of meaning;

- Have an inherent seriousness of intent;

- Reflect the intellectual maturity of a particular civilization;

- Reflect the intellectual maturity of the artist;

- Represent the maturity of its own particular artistic form;

- Endure and be subject to imitation; and

- Possess a superlative form of emotional expression and impact.

While these characteristics have their origins in an intellectual culture born well over a century ago, it is simply remarkable how many places we can find exactly these characteristics attributed to contemporary popular music and musicians.

It is very important to understand that these are not checklists of conditions that when met define a given artist and their work as "real" or "authentic." Instead, these are themes that are widespread within a larger system of representation that takes many forms. This means that these three attributes in part define this system of representation and help to establish its purpose and boundaries. Our goal is to critique and analyze these boundaries and the implicit values and ideals they work to uphold. Importantly, these tools are interpretive tools. They are not meant to determine a fact, but to support an interpretation. Therefore, when you use them in these chapters you will have a fair amount of flexibility in the arguments you make and how you support them.

We need to have a brief analytical example in order to see the ways in which these ideas are often expressed in music writing. In an article published in the *Sydney Morning Herald* in 2006, Nick Hasted describes how the British band The Arctic Monkeys emerged into prominence that year. (see http://www.smh.com.au/news/music/record-it-and-they-will-come/2006/07/20/1153166508649.html or type "nick hasted arctic monkeys 2006 record it and they will come" into a search engine.) In short order, Hasted hits all three marks of artistic authenticity. First, he describes the band members' seemingly simple approach to fame. They were school friends who formed their band when still teenagers. Their excitement at playing live and having people listen to their music inspired them to hand out free demos at their gigs. Their reaction to the ensuing fame was understated to say the least. Hasted quotes a band member as saying, "What's the point of talking ourselves up? We know we're not the best band in the country." Hasted described the band as so humble and so intensely focused on their music that they were completely unaware of the online fan communities that had been trading their demos and spreading the word about them. He describes their shock when huge numbers of people turned up at their shows and sang along. Hasted eases from the band's authentic relationship with their art to their authentic relationship with their fans. Hasted describes the fans as the heart of their success story, taking it upon themselves to shore up the band's gigs and contribute to "hysterical scenes outside of oversubscribed venues." The success was due to the band's devotion to its music and to its direct and honest relationship with their fans. Beyond this, Hasted claims that the Arctic Monkeys stand for something much larger than themselves. They stand for nothing less than a more democratic music industry where success is not defined by obscure music industry machinations, but by breaking down the barriers between musicians and fans by bypassing the music industry altogether. Instead, Hasted links the band to iconic acts from the 1980s such as The Smiths and New Order, who also avoided the mainstream music industry at the start of their careers. Beyond this, the band are representatives of a whole new world of music, linked to the best of the past, but looking to the future: "They have proved rock 'n' roll, and its fans, are in rude health once more. And, perhaps, they always will be."

We can apply these same ideas and tools to the popular music films that emerged out of the direct cinema movement and those that eventually transcended it. Look for the details of how musicians are presented and framed by the films we discuss across these two chapters. Pay close attention to how they are talked about, not only in the films, but in the writing about them as well.

FIGURE 11.2 *Paul Anka meeting fans in Sweden (1959).*

The emergence of direct cinema and the popular music documentary

One of the earliest films about a popular musician to use at least some of the techniques of direct cinema is *Lonely Boy*. It was made in 1962 by Wolf

Koenig and Roman Kroitor and produced by the National Film Board of Canada. It sought to document the everyday experience of a young pop star, Paul Anka. Despite the supposedly direct and objective methods, the film's agenda is clear. The directors did not seek to portray Anka as an artist or person. Instead, they portrayed the phenomenon of pop star fandom itself. This is effected through scenes of excited fans displaying Anka merchandise and frank discussions with Anka's managers about how they planned to sell the young singer. This film is far more about a notable and, for the time, very topical phenomenon captured in a manner more akin to a social affairs or news documentary rather than a portrait of an artist. As film writer David Hanley suggests, the content of the film clearly suggests that the filmmakers regard Anka almost as just another piece of merchandise. The film does not seek to attribute too many of the qualities of great art to Anka, but instead seems to suggest he is somehow being prevented from realizing them.

Another direct cinema documentary from 1964 shows us a more complex and intricate portrait of musicians. Entitled *What's Happening: The Beatles in the U.S.A.*, the film also presents the social phenomenon of intense popular music fan experience, but does so with a far more specific focus on the artists themselves. Extensive scenes show the various members of the band routinely expressing astonishment and wonder at their reception in the United States. The filmmakers widened their conceptual scope to show how each of the Beatles found the United States to be a strange and fascinating place. This film marks a subtle, but discernible shift in films of this type toward a close, intimate, and complex portrait of musicians within a world of intense public adulation and media attention that is rendered strange, if not alienating. The filmmakers focus very closely on the musicians themselves and regard their comments and response worthy of constant and often intense attention. As we will see later in the Focus section, this is precisely the sort of portrait of Bob Dylan that D. A. Pennebaker created in the film *Don't Look Back*. Each of these films, however, does suggest that each of these artists is superlative in some way simply for the attention lavished upon them, including the attentions of the filmmakers. This is important to bear in mind.

Another type of direct cinema representation of popular music and musicians is the concert film. Two films in particular provide an analytical window for us to see into some of the values and assumptions that lie behind these seemingly factual and unadorned representations of the often sprawling events that were the free music festivals of the 1960s. *Monterey Pop* (1968) and *Gimme Shelter* (1970) both implicitly and explicitly affirm the esteem and importance with which such events were regarded in the late 1960s. Each film includes extensive scenes of the contrasting contexts of each festival, with Monterey Pop capturing the easy generosity of the crowd experiencing the beginning of the Summer of Love. *Gimme Shelter* includes closing shots of a long, bedraggled parade of attendees leaving the festival by walking under massive power lines and alongside a highway jammed with traffic. This invests each event with a sense of social and historical importance, a sense supported by the ways in which people are caught on camera extolling the social and political virtues of the free music festival.

In each film, many of the performances are presented with a kind of reverent awe. In *Monterey Pop*, for example, many of the lengthy scenes of concert footage are shot from below very close to the stage while other scenes are shot from the side of the stage to capture the audience in the shot as well. The filmmakers also juxtapose the performances with long shots of audience members caught in rapt and unvarying attention. The ability to place the film viewer both in the place of an audience member and in the place of the camera has a powerful effect. Given that we are able to see both the performers and the reaction to them almost simultaneously, the two merge. The audience affirmation of the performances becomes part of the performances themselves. This confirms and legitimizes the adulation and attention directed at these artists suggesting they are talented enough and important enough to deserve it.

Huge swathes of the film *Gimme Shelter* focus intently on a series of performances by the Rolling Stones during their 1969 tour. Many of the scenes are joyous and enlivening until the tour winds up in the shattering chaos and violence of the Altamont Free Festival, much of which is captured on film. The performance scenes are shot in a very similar manner to *Monterey Pop*. However, this film captures more of the raw, unbridled chaos of some of these shows. Audience members repeatedly rush the stage and the closeness of the cameras to the action make otherwise innocent actions look violent or even dangerous. The scenes shot from the back of the stage capture a heaving mass of fans which is always inches away from the musicians. Given that any one of could make a mad dash for the stage at any time, this instills a sense of palpable energy in the attentive viewer. Given that many such viewers at the time already knew the ending, so to speak, this also tells the viewer that the events they are witnessing are serious and consequential. By extension, the music at the center of the film takes on these same qualities.

While some aspects of the direct cinema style have persisted and others have ebbed away, these well-known films of the 1960s had a long and influential afterlife as we will see in the next chapter. In many ways they shaped the culture of rock films that was to come. However, by the mid to late 1970s, many music films took on an explicitly heroic cast with little left to the vagaries of a series of constantly running cameras. A good example of this is *The Song Remains the Same* from 1976. The film is said to have captured Led Zeppelin's three performances at New York City's Madison Square Garden in 1973. However, the three performances were supplemented with staged performances on a movie sound stage in the United Kingdom. The band members watched their performances in New York and mimicked them for the reshoots. The film uses many of the techniques of its predecessors, including similar kinds of shots of live performance as

FIGURE 11.3 *Jimmy Page, Madison Square Garden (1973).*

well as preconcert footage that includes the arrival of the musicians at the airport, a police escort to the venue, as well as shots of a large crowds waiting in anticipation. Remarkably, the film also includes the notorious "fantasy sequences" in which the film leaves the confines of the live concert and follows each member of the band through a brief fictional narrative said to express the essential character of each of them. In many ways, these films established a kind of high water mark in portraying musicians as important, if not transcendent figures.

Explore and report: Direct cinema

You will now examine four of the music documentaries mentioned above that used the techniques of direct cinema to create a portrait of their respective artists. All of these are available on various video streaming web platforms such as YouTube, Dailymotion or Vimeo. (Note: The Beatles film is sometimes called *The Beatles: First US Visit*.) Your goal is to provide an interpretation of the agenda of each of the filmmakers. You want to present this interpretation in the form of a clear claim or argument about each film supporting by evidence drawn from the films themselves as well as the many, many types of essays, analyses, and scholarly interpretations about them. Some of these sources have been listed for you at the end of this chapter. They are many more easily found online. You are looking at multiple films to try to develop an understanding of the repertoire of images that are present across a number of films. You want to be able to understand what types of scenes are characteristic, not just of one film, but of this type of film more generally. For example, many of the films we discuss in these chapters have scenes of musicians arriving at airports as fans wait for them elsewhere. It seems simple, but what purpose might such scenes serve?

First, you need to find a solid collection of writing about these films. Look for factual descriptions, remembrances of participants, explanations of the filmmakers themselves, and interpretive essays. Note down at least three themes that emerge from your research. Second, you need to examine these films in detail. Watch them through keeping a chart of the timings of the various scenes. Note which ones seem particularly important or intriguing to you in specific relation to the themes you drew out of the existing writing about them. Third, carefully review three or four scenes of about 5-minute duration each as analytical examples. Look at each very closely for evidence of the filmmakers' agendas, editorial choices, and how these may reflect a set of preexisting values and ideas that have shaped how these films were made. Remember, while these films may look effortlessly improvisational, they are very carefully filmed and edited to reflect an agenda and set of goals.

Lonely Boy (1962)

This film has several of the types of scenes that were to become characteristic of popular music documentaries. There are scenes of mostly female fans screaming "We Want Paul" and telling the filmmakers why they think Anka is so wonderful. There are behind-the-scenes footage of Anka preparing to go on stage and long shots of him performing, many of which switch back and forth from the singer to fans to capture their reactions.

What's happening: The Beatles in America (1964)

This film features a very common scene to start—the band's arrival at the airport with associated fan reactions and a press conference. This film excludes any voiceover narrative and shows most of the scenes from a perspective close to the band, if not from their perspective. There are long shots on handheld cameras of the band chatting with each other. The film feels very loosely structured, candid, and intimate. How is it both similar to and different from *Lonely Boy*?

Monterey Pop (1968)

The film begins with scenes of people setting up chairs and sound systems for the festival. These are accompanied by the song "San Francisco (Be Sure to Wear Flowers in Your Hair)" by Scott McKenzie which was a kind of Summer of Love anthem. This film includes a lot of the behind-the-scenes organizing that went on. Much of the film also includes long shots of the filmmakers walking through the crowds and documenting the attendees. Compare the performance footage and how it is shot with similar scenes from the previous two films. The film ends with a performance by the Indian musician Ravi Shankar and the very long-standing ovation he received. Why might this film end this way given the other performers that we are shown throughout? Can we see some of the attributes of "great art" emerging from this film?

Gimme Shelter (1970)

This film set out to document the Rolling Stones tour of the United States in 1969. However, the entire film is framed by scenes of violence between members of the Hell's Angels motorcycle gang and audience members at the Altamont Speedway Free Festival. The film cuts back and forth between Mick Jagger and Charlie Watts watching raw footage the filmmakers had shot previously and reacting to it on camera. Their reactions are poignant and bewildered. The film clearly proceeds with the assumption that viewers will know what happened and the film goes through the series of events that led up to the inevitable failure of the concert. There are scenes of the Rolling Stones performing in various venues across the United States, many of which are joyous, but several of which hint at the chaos to come. Look closely at how the filmmakers construct their narrative of these events after the fact. What is their agenda? How are we being asked to see and understand The Rolling Stones?

Focus: *Don't Look Back* and the "Great art" of Bob Dylan

The people who made *Don't Look Back* followed Bob Dylan as he toured the United Kingdom in 1965. It was an important time for Dylan and his

FIGURE 11.4 *Bob Dylan on stage (1963).*

fans because his music was changing significantly in the first of many shifts of emphasis, style, and repertoire. Many of his fans who embraced his first three albums of traditional and original folk songs were confounded by his shift to more personal topics and idiosyncratic expression. The film captures some measure of this disquiet by sympathetically presenting long stretches of Dylan performing his newer material in juxtaposition to the work that preceded it. While some of the distinctions between the various songs maybe lost on many modern listeners, this issue is a central narrative device of the film. It is exactly within such debates over repertoire and performance style that the filmmakers seek to portray Dylan as a great artist. We can see this in several scenes in the film, which we will look at closely here. The first scene is the opening of the film, a section which lasts about fifteen minutes. It includes Dylan's arrival at the airport, a press conference, and several scenes in his hotel with friends and members of the media. The second includes Dylan speaking to several young fans about his music. The third includes a lengthy and tense scene of an interview with a report for *Time* magazine, followed by scenes of audience member entered the Royal Albert Hall, scenes of Dylan backstage, and finally long shots of him on stage. Each tells us how this film presents Dylan as authentic artist who has an honest and direct relationship with his art and his fans, but also stands for something larger. We are also encouraged by the filmmakers to see Dylan's work as important and superlative in the ways in which great art has often been presented to the public. We can see this by looking closely at each of these three scenes.

Don't Look Back starts with an unremarkable scene. A few people get off a bus in front of an airport at night. From the small crowd emerges a youthful Bob Dylan. No one seems to take much notice of him. One of the group then starts to sing "London Bridge is falling down" in a high-pitched voice. They are confronted by an excited crowd of fans with journalists mixed in. A journalist asks Dylan why he thinks there is so much more attention being paid to his arrival on this trip than in previous years. Dylan responds, saying, "I have no idea." The next scene captures a press conference in which Dylan patiently and charmingly answers a series of fairly dull and condescending questions. These opening scenes set the stage for the rest of the film. They confirm Dylan's importance and his willingness to endure the trials of fame in order to produce his work and share it with his public. These scenes also begin to hint at several themes that emerge throughout the film. One is the intense attention that is paid to him throughout. The filmmakers show us the very mechanisms of the fame Dylan seems to be confronted with, in scenes that supply us with the details of how journalists ask questions and several which show journalists reading their stories into pay phones to their editors on the other end of the line. One scene shows us Dylan reading out several newspaper stories about him to his friends and travelling companions, all of whom laugh heartily at the content. A second theme is Dylan's role, however reluctant, as a kind of generational spokesperson. He is continually put in the position of having to explain to journalists that the young people who listen to his music do understand it and that what is being said in those songs matters to them. He is placed in this role as spokesperson for his peers, despite his obvious reluctance to perform this role consistently. The third is the role of Dylan and his art more generally in society. We repeatedly see the young musician speaking forthrightly and strongly both on stage and off. He words express a complex array of insights, reflections, and emotions. The filmmakers want to be absolutely certain that the viewer of the film cannot simply dismiss this art the way many within the film seem to want to do.

The second scene starts about twenty minutes into the film. Dylan meets up with a small group of fans who had been filmed standing outside his hotel whistling to get his attention. He has a particularly direct conversation with a young woman who is not as pleased with his newer music. He gently chides her for suggesting that he shouldn't be playing with other musicians and that "it doesn't sound like you. It sounds like you're having a good old laugh." Dylan says, "Well isn't that okay? Can't I have a laugh?" His tone is suggestively close to annoyance. These kinds of scenes are meant to show us Dylan's willingness to engage directly with his fans in a simple and honest way.

The third scene begins at about the 1 hour and 13 minute mark. Dylan is being interviewed by a journalist from *Time* magazine. The interview begins with Dylan aggressively asking the journalist a series of questions, questions which imply that this journalist, like many others, doesn't really have any idea of what Dylan is singing about. Dylan bristles as he attacks the journalist's employer as irrelevant and incapable of reflecting the world truthfully which then merges seamlessly into a critique of the mass media and mass society more generally. The journalist smiles uncomfortably and responds by asking a series of clarifying questions, one of which sets Dylan off. After a lengthy and calculated pause, the journalist tersely asks: "Do you care about what you're saying?" Dylan responds: "How can I answer that if you have the nerve to ask me? I mean you've got a lot of nerve asking me a question like that. Do you ask the Beatles that?" Dylan is dismissive of the journalist's profession, industry, and what Dylan calls his "class of people," saying, "I'm not questioning you because I don't expect any answers from you."

What follows this awkward interview is just as important as the interview itself. We see crowds calmly filing into the Royal Albert Hall for the final shows of the tour. We see a pensive Dylan carefully preparing to go on stage. Once on stage, the filmmakers present us with a precisely edited montage of a central portion of the show. We see a very simple and clear image of a very young man using only his voice, guitar, and harmonicas to perform the music which has been responsible for everything that has preceded it in the film. Dylan is shown singing "The Times They Are a-Changin'," "Talking World War III Blues," "It's Alright Ma (I'm Only Bleeding)," and "Gates of Eden." The songs included in this montage are by turns, earnest, funny, and grim and this performance montage, along with the interview that preceded it act as a kind of powerful climax to the film as a whole.

When taken together these three scenes encapsulate all the traditional attributes of great art and artists suggested above. The filmmakers have very carefully constructed a very deliberate portrait of the artist from a complex whirl of events through what they chose to capture on film and their precise skill at manipulating what they captured through skillful editing. Indeed, this film is as much a product of editing as anything else. In their film, Dylan is not simply speaking in a powerful and forthright way. He is actually demonstrating the new model of subjectivity I cited at the beginning of this chapter. He continually speaks openly and candidly to everyone he encounters. He refused to accept the authority of the media and mocks them privately and publicly. He winds his way through a series of complex events of which he is the center with an insouciant calm and humor that seems to define his very character. The filmmakers present the viewer with a long, gradual, very carefully constructed narrative of a young musician working to present a truthful picture of his world to an ever-expanding audience with whom he has a direct relationship. This is clearly shown to have earned him the right and duty to stand for something larger than himself. The art at the heart of all of this possesses the requisite weight of seriousness and meaning and is intellectually and artistically mature enough to possess the required degree of emotional expression and impact. We are shown the ripple of meaning that follow in its wake in nearly every carefully selected scene of this film.

INDEPENDENT RESEARCH WORK

Examine and explore the history of "direct cinema." The origin of this form of filmmaking was based in a desire to show the world "as it really was," so to speak. The idea was based on a vision of using film to expose and correct what many regarded as social wrongs. Examine and critique the assumptions and implications of this model of filmmaking. What is the ideal relationship between the filmmakers and their audience? What characteristics and attitudes do they assume their audience possess? Also, what did they think film could accomplish? After answering these questions, apply them to direct cinema films made about music.

References and further readings

Beattie, Keith. (2005) "It's Not Only Rock and Roll: 'Rockumentary,' Direct Cinema, and Performative Display." *Australasian Journal of American Studies*, 24(2): 21–41.

Brody, Richard. (2016) "When the Maysles Brothers Filmed the Beatles." *New Yorker*, April 15.

Chanan, Michael. (2011) "Shooting Star: Peter Whitehead and 1960s Documentary." *Framework: The Journal of Cinema and Media*, 52(1): 324–31.

Edgar, R, K. Fairclough-Isaacs, and B. Halligan. (2013) *The Music Documentary: Acid Rock to Electropop*. New York: Routledge.

Eliot, T.S. (1957) *On Poetry and Poets*. London: Faber and Faber.

Gendron, Bernard. (2002) *Between Monmartre and the Mudd Club: Popular Music and the Avant Garde*. Chicago: University of Chicago Press.

Hanley, David. (2011) "*Lonely Boy*: Documenting the Manufacture of a Pop Idol." *Off Screen*, 15(7), http://offscreen.com/view/lonely_boy.

Moore, Allan. (2003) *Rock: The Primary Text*. Basingstoke: Ashgate.

Pennebaker, D. A. (1967) *Don't Look Back*. New York: New Video Group.

Schowalter, Daniel. (2000) "Remembering the Dangers of Rock and Roll: Toward a Historical Narrative of the Rock Festival." *Critical Studies in Media Communication*, 17(1): 86–102.

Shank, Barry. (2002) "'That Wild, Thin Mercury Sound': Bob Dylan and the Illusion of American Culture." *Boundary 2*, 29(1), 97–123.

12

Rock film at the end of the twentieth century

Background and topics

This chapter will focus on a small number of music documentaries made in the 1990s and early 2000s. These have a particular set of themes and stylistic elements which began to develop in the late 1980s and early 1990s and became a widespread set of characteristics by the early 2000s. These characteristics are very similar to those found in the films in the previous chapter. These films construct portraits of their subjects as authentic artists who maintain direct and honest relationships with their art and their fans while also standing for that elusive "something larger." Further, these artists and their art are presented to us as important, enduring, and worthy of our attention because they embody that which is artistically and culturally mature. Again, please remember that this kind of analysis does not attempt to prove that these portraits are truthful or accurate. Instead, they are meant to offer you a set of tools to help you critically analyze the ways in which these portraits are constructed and the implicit values and ideals they promulgate and express.

The films we look at here accomplish the same tasks as those discussed in the previous chapter, but through slightly different means. First, these documentaries are far less indebted to the techniques of so-called direct cinema. They are instead shaped by the techniques of news reporting and topical documentary filmmaking. For example, most do not have any of the very lengthy shots characteristic of direct cinema. These are replaced with more concise and directed shots that are clearly meant to capture a specific set of events. This is in large part due to the fact that most were commissioned by television networks. They were not films made independently and then

FIGURE 12.1 *Experience Music Project Museum Display (2011).*

shopped by producers to movie theaters. Second, direct cinema tended to use strong, purposeful editing far less often than these more topical documentaries. You can see in each of the films examined in this chapter that the edits happen most often to move from one scene to another or to change perspective within a scene. Third, the films examined here use a great deal of footage drawn from direct interviews with the participants involved in the events that are chronicled within each film and from outside commentators who can contextualize those events. Also, most of these films use voiceovers to inform viewers of key background information that does not appear elsewhere in the film. The cumulative effect of these techniques is a far stronger imposition of a specific and progressive narrative arc onto the events these films present. This is in contrast to direct cinema and its reliance on ambiguity and context to present a story. Finally, the biggest difference between the films we examine in this chapter and those of the previous chapter is how they treat their subjects. These more recent films are less purely celebratory of their subjects. Instead, these films chronicle the struggles, obstacles, and outright failures their subjects encounter and experience. Nevertheless, these films use these struggles and difficulties to present very similar conclusions about these artists as the earlier more celebratory films did. We are still guided to view these artists as authentically pursuing their craft *despite* the obstacles that lie in wait for them or in some cases *because of* those very obstacles. This only enhances their perceived

FIGURE 12.2 *The Who performing in Hamburg (1972).*

authenticity and more completely confirms the value and importance of their art. These films mark a different kind of inflection of this system of representation. It reflects a different, somewhat darker world.

First, we need to briefly account for these differences by examining the broad historical background that shaped the music documentaries of the 1990s and 2000s. Then we will look more closely at a few specific films.

From the late 1970s into the early 1980s, the most prominent music documentaries tended to reflect more traditional styles and attributes, such as those noted above. A good example is *The Kids Are Alright* from 1979. This film is about the English rock band The Who. It is a perfect encapsulation of the techniques of topical documentary noted above. It moves a clear narrative forward, telling the story of this band from the beginning through old footage of the band performing as well as extensive interviews with band members, those associated with the band, as well as outside commentators. The film explicitly upholds a narrative of rock being a form of rebellion against a dominant social order, a revolt embodied in the actions of musicians considered to be outrageous in one form or another. For example, there is extensive footage of guitarist Pete Townshend and drummer Keith Moon destroying their equipment at the end of their shows, scenes presented as a form of symbolic destruction. Another scene features Moon being interviewed in a bondage mask while a scantily clad woman lightly flogs him. This reflects a wider understanding of a particular kind of hedonistic "freedom" often linked with some forms of popular music at this time. A key theme of the film is how the band members' perceived candor and honesty about their lives and music imbues that music with an enduring importance and marks them as reliable holders of the legacy of so-called classic rock.

Two years later, a very similar film with remarkably similar themes was released. It was called *The Decline of Western Civilization* (1981). The film chronicled the emergence of punk in Los Angeles. It consists of almost exactly the same kinds of content as *The Kids Are Alright*, such as extensive interviews with participants in the events the film presents and a large number of performances by the bands who are the main subjects. The crucial difference is that this film's content was not retrospectively acquired and edited, but shot to directly capture the events it portrays. This made the filmmakers much more part of those events. Another difference is that the film sets out to capture, not simply a kind of music, but an entire music scene. As such, it has a much broader scope. The musicians and fans speak openly and candidly about the impact family breakdown and poverty have had on them. The film's implicit narrative suggests that these musicians embody the often serious problems other members of this music scene face. Nearly all of the bands are shown performing a violent, visceral music in very close proximity to their fans, who all fight and wrestle with one another throughout the performances.

A film that is very stylistically similar to this is *Style Wars* from 1983. As with *The Decline of Western Civilization*, this film also closely links music with the wider social phenomena of poverty, violence, and social breakdown. However, this film examines the graffiti artists of the South Bronx in New York City in the late 1970s and early 1980s. The filmmakers engage in very similar kinds of social advocacy as those who made *The Decline of Western Civilization* did. Both films present music and musicians as offering a constructive response to difficult circumstances. Importantly, both forms of music examined in these films were at first ignored and later heavily criticized by social authorities at the time. These films were clearly aimed at dispelling widespread misunderstandings about punk and hip hop. They aimed to do so by presenting musicians as offering an honest and authentic response to their circumstances.

By the mid to late 1980s, music documentaries began to become more and more common and easily accessible. They received widespread theatrical release but, just as importantly, were more regularly shown on the expanding range of pay television channels that were more and more widely available as well. The various channels of the MTV network were important facilitators of this phenomenon. A common format for such films was for filmmakers to follow an artist on tour, much like the films we examined in the previous chapter. This allowed filmmakers to record behind-the-scenes content as well as high-profile performances. The films capitalized on the enormous amount of publicity inherent to world tours and extended the profitable range of these lengthy events.

Two films that did this were *U2: Rattle and Hum* (1988) and *Madonna: Truth or Dare* (1991). Both films are almost identical in their purpose. They both sought to take some of the most prominent artists of their time and show what they were "really like" behind the facades of their fame. In the case of U2, this meant following the band on their tour of the United States for *The Joshua Tree* album. The film begins with concert footage that immediately shifts to the coast of Ireland. After the credits, the first time we hear the band address the camera has them stammering distractedly and inarticulately to the filmmaker's questions. The film focuses on the band performing, not just on stage, in heroic rock star fashion, but also at Sun Studios in Memphis and in a public square in San Francisco. They repeatedly hold court backstage, in press conferences, and in a range of other circumstances. They seek out and meet, on camera, other famous musicians. The same is true of Madonna's film. It is also meant to provide us with an honest portrait of the "real" artist. We see her telling her anxious father that she will not tone down the expressive sexuality of her stage show as she did not want to "compromise" her "artistic integrity." She is also shown in a remarkably similar range of situations, the cumulative effect of which is to again show us an artist who is at one with her work and her public, just like U2. Strangely, both films are shot largely in black and white, perhaps in an effort to confer a superficial "classic" feel to each. In each film, what is meant to be candid access to the artists, merely acts to confirm that their "greatness" extends far beyond the stage and into their very beings.

We will now focus on a very specific kind of music documentary that emerged in the late 1990s and early 2000s. It was a kind of film that focused mostly on those within one branch or another of rock and each film focused intensely on the difficulties involved in being a rock star. Those films are *I Am Trying To Break Your Heart* (2002) about the band Wilco, *Dig!* (2004), about The Dandy Warhols and The Brian Jonestown Massacre, and *Some Kind of Monster* (2004), about Metallica. Each film examines the often terrible problems faced by each group of musicians from mental illness to drug addiction and violence to band members being abruptly asked to leave and record companies dropping them from their labels. Yet, in every case, each film uses the same ideas of artistic value and authenticity to provide an explanation for the full scope of the events they present.

The makers of *I Am Trying To Break Your Heart* (2002) were confronted with far more than anyone involved say they expected. The original idea of the film was to show how Wilco's 2001 album *Yankee Hotel Foxtrot* was made. However, the making of the album included arguments between band members that were so serious that one member left the band during the making of the film. Further, the band's record label refused to release the album and subsequently dropped them from the label, only to see them brought back under the auspices of a subsidiary label of the same record company. The album ended up being Wilco's most successful to that point.

Along the way, the viewer sees the musicians struggle with mental and physical health issues as well as with the music itself. The content of the film consists of the same kinds of things all of the other films in this chapter have consisted of, such as candidly shot behind-the-scenes footage in rehearsal and the studio, formal interviews with participants and commentators, and extensive scenes of live performances by the band. All of this is framed by what is presumed to be the essential greatness of their work. In fact the first thing we hear about Wilco is that their new album is a "masterful, dense artistic statement." The various trials that follow are all presented to confirm this initial assessment.

Dig! is constructed out of the same materials for the same purpose. The film presents the audience with two bands, The Dandy Warhols and The Brian Jonestown Massacre. It follows each as they struggle to make some kind of living from their music. The film has a strong narrative structure and a voiceover presented by a member of The Dandy Warhols. The filmmakers move back and forth from one band to other, showing how they each start their careers, meet up and play together for a few months and then take entirely different paths through the music industry. The Dandy Warhols sign on to Capitol Records and see their first two albums sell far below expectations, until one of their songs is picked up for a mobile phone commercial in Europe. Early scenes of frustration and lost promise are redeemed by triumphant scenes which see them playing sold-out venues and in huge music festivals. The Brian Jonestown Massacre, by contrast, suffer bouts of intense and violent conflict within the band, much of it initiated by the songwriter and lead singer, Anton Newcombe. His actions are portrayed throughout the film almost entirely as those of a self-sabotaging artistic

FIGURE 12.3 *The Brian Jonestown Massacre on stage (2012).*

genius, as opposed to the result of a potentially serious, undiagnosed mental illness. Harrowing scenes of assault against bandmates, friends, and family are presented alongside extensive praise for Newcombe's artistic vision. His vision is portrayed as simply too expansive and ambitious for the mainstream music industry to accept.

One of the main characters in both films is the music industry. In each, multiple examples of both success and failure are presented through the struggle to realize one's ambitious artistic aims. When a band is successful, the viewer is shown how their unswerving dedication to their art and their public has made their inevitable triumph possible. Yet, when a band fails, the viewer is told that this same kind of dedication has resulted in work that is not yet understood well enough to succeed.

Some Kind of Monster from 2004 takes a slightly different tack. It shows Metallica's success as eroding the very things that made it possible in the first place, such as productive collaborative relationships between the band members and the drive and ambition to make music that is an honest form of self-expression. In order to confront these problems, the band essentially goes into group therapy. They hire a performance coach to talk them through their problems, a good deal of which is captured on film. This film is distinct from the previous ones discussed here, in that Metallica's success is never threatened nor is their place in the history of popular music questioned. Instead, they are portrayed as artists so desperate to meet their own expectations and demands as artists that they put themselves and those around them through an intense period of personal, emotional struggle. They do this in the full public view of a lengthy and self-indulgent documentary film. Like the other films mentioned here, this one predicates all of its complex scenes on the band's authentic and direct relationship with their art and their public. Their work is so important and powerful that they submit to all manner of challenge and argument just to be given the opportunity to continue to make it.

The major "character" in all of these films is, of course, "the music." The scenes of musicians making music are clearly the most important, yet often the most ambiguous. We see musicians sitting alone working through a stubborn passage that won't come right. We see lengthy and arduous rehearsals and studio sessions. We see live performances in front of massive adoring crowds. Yet to some extent, the power and meaning of the music in these films often remains paradoxically elusive. We see a great deal of it, but it remains opaque to us if it were not for all of the surrounding content that makes it meaningful in specific ways. We will now focus on one series of music documentaries that makes familiar music meaningful in specific ways. We will look closely at the *Classic Albums* documentary series and see how the role of artists and their art has become fortified with extensive reflections and discussions of its meaning, value, and historical importance.

FIGURE 12.4 *Metallica on stage (2008).*

Explore and report: *Classic Albums* series

The *Classic Albums* documentary series began showing on American television in 1992. The goal of these comparatively short documentaries was to take apart albums already regarded as "classics" and explain how they were made in an attempt to make viewers see what makes them "great art." These are nostalgic and reflective films, by definition. Most episodes work their way through the album of choice track by track. The producers interview the musicians, engineers, producers, and music industry personnel involved with the album. Often, the engineers and producers remix and replay the original tracks on camera in order to highlight parts that confirm the larger narrative of the film.

The films also feature outside commentators such as music journalists, biographers, and other well-known musicians who may have a particular interest in the album under examination. Their purpose is to affirm the general quality of "greatness" by compiling many, many smaller examples of artistic or technical inspiration and innovation that contribute to it. Another key theme is to have authority figures explain what made the album important at the time of its release. (Important note: Many of these documentaries are available on various video-streaming platforms. Many are also available from the iTunes Store for a small price.)

It is useful and important to think about why these films present their subjects in a particular way. The goal of these films is to place the albums under examination in the special and exclusive category of "important works." The term for this is "canonization." Important works are those that have made a difference to the history and tradition of their art form. These decisions don't simply have artistic consequences, but social and political ones as well. When a canon is constructed and maintained, the clear and unavoidable implication is that if you wish to be literate within a specific tradition of artistic practice, you will have to know these works. Popular music didn't always have a canon of standard important works, but it does now and these documentaries have been part of the process of building one.

We will focus on the episode about Nirvana's 1991 album *Nevermind*. This episode was produced in 2005. We will focus on the section that examines the songs "Something in the Way" and "Smells Like Teen Spirit." The goal is to find specific ways in which the filmmakers construct a portrait of Nirvana as "great artists" and the album *Nevermind* as "great art." This clip is about fifteen minutes long and it adheres to all of the criteria for constructing a portrait of an "authentic" artist who makes "authentic" art we have looked at so far. Throughout, we are both told and shown that these musicians had a genuine and unmediated relationship with their art and their public and that they stood for something larger than themselves. One music industry executive even says, "It wasn't just an album. It was a movement." Further, the people who tell this story claim in a variety of ways that this work of art reflected both the maturity of Nirvana's work and the pinnacle of rock at this time. We are also told that it was a serious, enduring, and important work. The question for you is this: how does this film tell us all of this?

Your task is to examine this clip and compare it with excerpts from a different episode of this documentary series. First, examine the clip from *Nevermind* and list all of the various qualities attributed to these two songs, to the album as a whole, and to the band. First, listen to kinds of things the people being interviewed tell us. They use terms like "emotional truth," "messianic," and "universal truth." Kurt Cobain, in particular, is described as follows: "He was like a reporter," "It was like he was singing about you," and he was said to be the voice of his generation. Second, find out who is interviewed in this section of the film. Why did the producers choose these people? What authority do they have? Third, look closely at the images used throughout this section of the film. What is their purpose? Fourth, examine very closely how all of these various pieces of sound, image, and spoken word are linked together. What is the story the producers are trying to tell us here? Carefully plot it out. Finally, repeat these steps with an excerpt from another film from this series and compare the two. Write an essay that explains the conclusions of your analysis and research.

Focus: *Meeting People Is Easy* and the "Great Art" of Radiohead

Meeting People Is Easy: A Film About Radiohead (1998) is a very strange and unusual film when considered in comparison to all of the films we have examined in this chapter and the previous one. While most of the films we have looked at tend to portray their subjects as heroic and important in some way, this film does not. Instead, it presents the band members with what is at times an imposing distance and detachment which is often contrasted with an unsettling closeness and intimacy. There are several ways this film does this. First, it departs from the kinds of techniques and content of previous films in its use of sound, imagery, and storytelling. Second, instead of imposing a strong narrative on the hours of footage the filmmakers shot, they simply follow Radiohead on their world tour after the release of their album *OK Computer* in 1997. The scenes are only linked through chronological proximity. Third, instead of clear audio and visual elements, viewers are confronted with an audiovisual maze that often demands close attention to understand. The sounds the viewer hears are often not directly linked to the images we see. Often, the filmmakers overlay text and graphics on the events they filmed in order to complicate their meaning. Fourth, the music is not presented as any kind of special event in relation to other events. In some scenes, the performance of music happens in small television studios or empty auditoriums. In one scene, Thom Yorke, the lead singer, looks mirthfully disengaged as he holds the microphone out to an enormous crowd to allow them to sing his part. In another scene, the camera gradually backs out of the venue completely while the performance continues without us being able to see it.

The purpose of the film is not simply to capture the events of this tour. Instead, the film is a sharply critical portrait of the wider society and the ways in which fame and celebrity are conferred on people such as musicians. Importantly, the imagery from the film often resonates with the themes from the album. The album is pervaded by themes of fear and dread. The lyrics suggest a terrifying loss of personal and social control over the machines

FIGURE 12.5 *Radiohead in concert (2012).*

that shape so much of our lives. The film recalls these ideas in images of things such as airports, train stations, and hotels. The music on the album is a very subtly crafted soundscape that lacks the clarity of structure, melody, harmony and lyrical sentiment of Radiohead's previous albums. The film presents us with analogous forms of ambiguity in its soundtrack and its imagery. We will more closely examine just a few minutes of the opening of the film to clarify these interpretations.

The film begins with the image of a satellite floating above the earth and the soundtrack is comprised of a computerized voice flatly exhorting us to live better, more healthy lives. It does so over an out-of-tune piano being played in irregular rhythms backed by the white noise of a crackling communications system. After a brief interval, it is clear that the soundtrack is taken from the song "Fitter, Happier" which is the seventh track on OK Computer. The track continues as the camera takes us into a train station. The passing train cars are nearly empty, as is the station itself. The image begins to twitch and we hear Colin Greenwood from Radiohead repeating the multiple radio identifications the band members have been asked to record. We then see the members of the band in entirely mundane situations, walking down hotel corridors, posing in an empty courtyard for publicity photos, and speaking to journalists. This bears more than a passing resemblance to the opening scenes of Don't Look Back. In both films, we see more or less the same sequence of events. However, the mood of this film is profoundly different. The jumpy edits between the various scenes feel dark and confining in their insistent repetition.

A few minutes later, after the band play the opening verse of "Lucky" at the tours first show in Barcelona, the music briefly stops. When it resumes, the background imagery is a sharply edited montage of the band playing. Overlaid on top of this are transcripts of an interview the band was doing during their tour. The soundtrack mirrors this. "Lucky" continues to play in the background while an audio montage of interviews with journalists plays over top. The questions are striking in their bland strangeness—"What is music to you?" "What did you want to achieve when you started the band?" and so on. We don't hear the band's answers under the visual and audio tide of questions. Again, as with Don't Look Back we are shown the machinations of the media throughout the film. Yet, whereas Bob Dylan was shown contesting the terms under which his voice and image were relayed to the world, this film shows the band members reacting with discomfort, nervous laughter, and failed attempts to redirect the flow of events down a path that might be more amenable to them. When we briefly consider this film as a reflection of the circumstances in which it was made, we find little of the optimism and power attributed to music that we might see in earlier rock documentaries. Instead, we find a jittery, complex world in which our very senses seem to be disconnected with one another and sense can only be made of events in the exception.

INDEPENDENT RESEARCH WORK

Music documentaries after the year 2000 began to routinely exhibit qualities that, while not new, had always been marginal to the form generally. These qualities were those that showed musicians struggling with mental and physical health issues, and showed musicians acting rudely, obnoxiously, arrogantly, and aggressively. As noted in this chapter, these kinds of scenes became characteristic of factual films about musicians. Explore the larger changes in the areas of factual film and television from the mid-1990s to about 2010. Writing about these trends and innovations might help us account for the changes in this genre of film and television that we have seen in this chapter.

References and further readings

Regev, M., and J. Toynbee. (2006) "Special Issue on Canonisation." *Popular Music*, 25(1): 1–2.

Stahl, Matt. (2013) *Unfree Masters: Recording Artists and the Politics of Work*. Durham and London: Duke University Press.

Williams, Alan. (2010) "'Pay Some Attention to the Man Behind the Curtain'— Unsung Heroes -and the Canonization of Process in the Classic Albums Documentary Series." *Journal of Popular Music Studies*, 22(2): 166–79.

PART FOUR

Clouds, crowds, and idols, 1980 to 2015

13

New ways to connect

Background and topics

The final four chapters of this book will examine a period of tumultuous change in the music industry. We will examine the changes faced by musicians, record labels, and consumers from 1980 to 2015. We will focus most closely on the transition from analogue media, such as vinyl discs and magnetic tape, to digital media. Most importantly, we will see how this period, especially the years 1995 to 2010, saw the transformation of all of the central social relationships between producers, distributors, and consumers. In short, the ways in which musicians and producers made music, the ways record labels promoted, sold, and distributed music, and the ways in which consumers chose, acquired, and listened to music all changed drastically in a relatively short period of time. Beyond this, the nature of the music industry changed not simply in terms of what they sold and how they sold it, but who was doing the selling. Technology firms such as Apple and others, which had historically not been involved in the buying and selling of music, became a dominant presence in the music industry.

There are four broad topics areas we will look at in these final chapters. This chapter will look at how the file format known simply as the "mp3" was created and how it developed. The next chapter will look at the battles over copyright and intellectual property rights that results from the widespread practice of illegal mp3 downloading and file sharing. While this story is often dominated by the brief existence of the original Napster file trading service, the issues are much broader than that. Chapter 15 will examine one of the most remarkable success stories of this era: music-based reality television. We will examine how television shows such as *Pop Idol*, *The Voice*, and *X Factor* could be so successful while much of the music industry was suffering dramatic drops in sales and revenues at the same time. The final chapter will examine the advent of music streaming. It should be noted

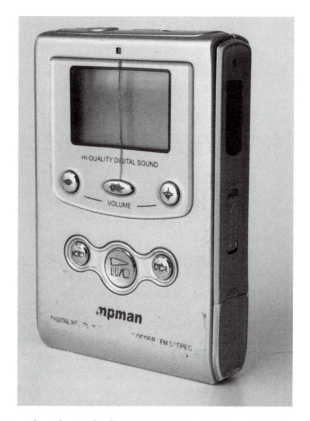

FIGURE 13.1 *Before the iPod: The MPMan F60 mp3 player (1998).*

that all of these topics are far more complex than we can fully cover here. It would be best to think of these chapters as a broad overview of the central issues of this time period.

We will begin with an overview of the final key reading for this book. This article is called "The Heavenly Jukebox." It was written in 2000 by Charles Mann and it was published in *The Atlantic*, a topical magazine examining politics and economics. It would probably be best to save it as a PDF to use for future reference. You can find it here:

https://www.theatlantic.com/magazine/archive/2000/09/the-heavenly-jukebox/305141/

It is important to remember that this article was written in 2000 which places it right in the middle of some very significant changes, many of which were only just starting to have an impact at that time. This was before any of our more familiar devices, such as the iPod and the iPhone, existed and before the idea of music streaming existed in any commercial form. Despite this, much of Mann's analysis and conclusions suggest many developments that later came to pass.

Mann begins by recounting one of the more high-profile events of the music piracy debates, the legal contest between Metallica and Napster. He uses this story to explore what seemed at the time to be a completely intractable problem. On one side, the very structure and function of the internet not only encouraged the free flow of information, but demanded it. On the other hand, the music industry depended very heavily on profiting from the copyrights on their intellectual property. If record labels could not secure the exclusive use and benefit of these, it was hard for many people at the time to see any future for this industry.

In the second and third parts, "Legislation, Litigation, Leg-Breaking" and "Joe Average Becomes Jane Hacker," Mann explores the historical background of copyright disputes over music and compares these past conflicts to the present. He explains that similar conflicts happened in the past and composers and publishers had to fight for years to have laws passed to establish new rights to their work and then to have these rights protected. Mann notes that, while this seems similar to the issues surrounding digital file trading, there are significant differences. The most obvious and important difference is the nature of the internet itself. As internet use became increasingly widespread, the volume of traffic through its ever increasing numbers of channels grew exponentially. Some in the music industry saw the scale of the problem very early and suggested that record labels and artists find some way to use it to their advantage. Mann explains how few realistic solutions there actually were at the time to prevent individual computer users from ripping CDs and sharing the digital files that resulted. According to Mann, part of the explanation for the impossibility of this task is how "Joe Average Becomes Jane Hacker." He explains that the tools those knowledgeable in computer programming (Jane Hacker) use to find and extract information from various sources can usually be made useful to people who do not have that training (Joe Average). In practice, this meant that most attempts to control the movement of mp3 files failed, and often that failure was realized very quickly. Communities of programmers always found ways to extract the important information they wanted from any attempt to encrypt it.

In the next section, "They're Paying Our Song," Mann switches topics and looks at how illegal file sharing affects musicians. Importantly, he finds that the vast majority of musicians were not necessarily harmed by the practice in large part because of the way the music industry acquires and safeguards music as intellectual property, or in this case the royalties paid out to those who write, record, and perform music. This section is very important because it shows us two things. First, it shows us how dependent the music industry was on controlling the royalties that came from music. Second, it shows us how this made them vulnerable to exactly the kinds of changes that were happening in the 1990s. Not only did the major labels control over 85 percent of the market in music in this period because of their ability to acquire intellectual property, they would have a hard time surviving without this kind of overwhelming dominance.

In the final two sections, "Elton John Gets Mad" and "Fear and Greed," Mann cogently lays out what was at that time a vision of the future that he and those he interviewed in order to write this article were largely correct in anticipating. As we will see in later chapters, the fact that recorded music is universally popular means that someone, somewhere will find a way to make money from it. He notes that musicians and record companies can find new ways to link the attention people pay to the music they love to some kind of profitable transaction. We will see this most directly in Chapter 15 when we look at music-based reality television. As we move forward, be sure to think about the kinds of social and economic relationships that people continue to make through music. They are numerous, but they are often quite different that the ones that preceded them. First, however, we need to get a clear sense of how the music industry evolved in this time period.

The music industry from 1980 to 2000

There were several important changes that made the music industry particularly vulnerable to the changes brought about by digital technology. These were a very strict focus on selling very large numbers of albums by only a small number of artists, a focus almost exclusively on distribution rather than artist development, and a heavy reliance on the exploitation of the intellectual property rights they owned over the music they sold.

At the start of the 1980s, the music industry was in a severe recession. Profits had stopping growing and in many cases fell substantially. The reasons for this were many and complex, but had a great deal to do with a global recession that had affected many people and industries. However, by 1983 the global economy had experienced an upturn and the music industry was carried along with it. But the music industry soon left most others behind. It began to grow steadily and sometimes spectacularly and, despite predictions to the contrary, continued to grow very strongly until 1999. In fact, despite one or two small steps backward, the music industry grew more in these years that it ever had before or since. There are a few reasons for this. First, by the early 1980s, almost every major record label had been bought by those transnational corporations Garofalo talked about in his article at the start of this book. Transnational corporations took advantage of new kinds of laws and regulations as well as new forms of financing to buy large numbers of smaller companies. This wasn't only true of the music and entertainment industries. It was true of many industries. These corporations changed how the music industry worked. Given that most had to go into a good deal of debt in order to become so big, this pushed them to cut costs by getting rid of "underperforming" artists and getting rid of staff regarded as unnecessary. Whereas previously, many record labels hired staff to seek out and convince new artists to sign contracts with them, these roles were gradually cut back or were simply eradicated altogether. Smaller independent labels started to act as an informal way of discovering new and exciting music that the major labels could then acquire.

The new forms of ownership and operation pushed many within the music industry to seek out new kinds of financial opportunities. Rather than spending money seeking out and developing new artists, most big record companies focused instead on acquiring very large catalogues of music which they could economically exploit to the greatest extent possible. As Mann explained, allowing record companies to own the rights to music is the main purpose of the record contracts musicians sign with major record companies. Exploiting these rights was also an increasingly profitable thing to do. Importantly, this was a practice that started as early as the 1950s when record companies began to buy back the publishing rights to the music they sold as recordings. As we have seen in previous chapters, the presence and use of music on television and film expanded greatly in the 1980s and these uses of music always had a price. It is not too much to say that the intense attention paid by the music industry to the exploitation of intellectual property and licensing became the defining feature of the music industry by the early 1990s. One profitable way in which this was done was the introduction of the compact disc in 1982. The music industry was able to convince large numbers of people to "repurchase" a lot of the music they already owned but in the new format. As we will see shortly, however, the CD was a double-edge sword that eventually allowed consumers to make and distribute perfect copies of their music.

The strong pressure applied by investors and shareholders in the service of ever increasing revenues and profits changed other aspects of marketing and distribution as well. For example, from the late 1980s, most major records labels stopped selling singles. Instead, they focused primarily on selling full albums. This was despite the popularity and profitability of singles. Also, instead of spending money to market a wide range of artists, most of the big record companies put most of their resources into trying to sell as many copies as possible of only a small range of albums. Further, when an album became an unexpected hit, companies would do everything they could to strike when the iron was hot. This in turn led to a concentration of wealth at the very top of the overall pool of artists. In turn, this led to an unhealthy dependence on big hits. This made record companies far more vulnerable to high-profile failures.

The most important idea to take away from these points is that some areas of the music industry were unusually vulnerable to sudden changes in the market or in the technological base on which they survived. As we will see in the next chapter, this sudden change arrived in the form of a small group of people who decided they could invent a new way of sharing music by creating Napster. But first we need to understand more about the invention, use, and development of the mp3.

Explore and report: Mp3 players

It might seem remarkable to us today, but when mp3 players first went on sale, some parts of the music industry were afraid of what they might do to the ways in which listeners consumed music. The fear was so deep that several record companies instructed their industry organization, the Recording Industry Association of America (RIAA), to sue the producers of Diamond Rio PMP 300 mp3 player in order to prevent its sale. The lawsuit failed and the device was allowed to be sold to consumers. While we will address the issues that provoked this lawsuit in the focus section below and in the next chapter, first we need to look more closely at these devices, especially the earliest ones, most of which are long gone. When we understand what these devices were like and what they could do, we can understand the controversy over them more completely.

Your task is to find and examine at least four or five of these devices that were offered for sale between 1995 and 2002. Importantly, choose only mp3 players. Do not look at phones or digital home audio equipment. Some of these devices are

- AT&T Flash Pac portable digital music player (1996)
- MPMan F10 mp3 player (1997)

FIGURE 13.2 *The AT&T Flash Pac portable digital music player (1996).*

FIGURE 13.3 *Diamond Rio PMP 300 (1998).*

- The Diamond Rio PMP 300 (1998)
- Sony Walkman MP3 (2000)
- Apple iPod (2001)

There are several ways to do this. First, find as many research resources you can about these devices. Choose reliable sources about consumer technology such as CNET, Ars Technica, and Wired. They often publish articles about "forgotten tech." You can also find videos about them on various video-streaming platforms. You will find old advertisements for some of them as well as the original and more recent product demonstration videos. Make sure you use fairly broad search parameters to start with, such as "early mp3 players" and "ads for mp3 players," etc. Second, find out everything you can about what these devices could do. What were their capabilities? What was their capacity? Did they connect with personal computers? If so, how? If not, how did you load them with music? A very good resource for this kind of information are websites that have PDFs of old product manuals such as manualslib.com and others. These old documents will give you all of the specifications you need to understand what they were designed

FIGURE 13.4 *First-generation iPod (2001).*

to do. Fourth, compare these devices with the current smartphones. How are they both similar and different in terms of capacity, user interfaces, and capabilities?

Finally, write an essay about the evolution of digital music devices. You will need to organize your essay around an argument or interpretive claim that has been generated by your research. Don't simply describe a collection of devices and what they could do. Make an argument about how they have evolved and why they have changed the ways they have. They have not evolved in a neutral way. They have been very carefully designed to appeal to users for specific purposes. For example, early iPods were effective in large part because they were very simple and elegant objects that many people found very easy to use. They could be linked to iTunes on any Apple computer and users could organize their music in ways that were useful to them. Examine these objects and report back about how they have shaped the ways in which we listen to music at the present time.

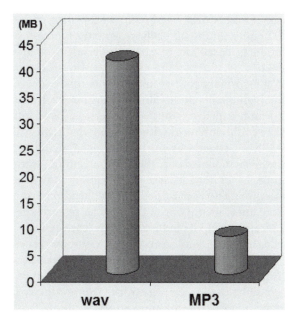

FIGURE 13.5 *Comparison of wav and mp3 file sizes after compression (2011).*

Focus: The invention and spread of the mp3

The mp3 has proven to be one of the most useful, popular, and controversial consequences of the advent of digital consumer technology. This section will look at how and why it was invented and how it spread from a small research project at a collection of German universities to a worldwide default standard for digital sound. It is rare that any seismic shift in popular culture can be traced to the specific acts of a limited collection of identifiable individuals. But in the case of the escape from the bottle of the bedeviling genie known as the mp3, we can get about as close to a date of birth as we are likely to get.

If you reread the section of the Mann article about the invention of the mp3, we can see that it was a kind of historical accident born from the most ordinary of intentions. He tells us that the mp3 was created by a working group put together by the International Organization for Standardization, the body charged with determining what he describes as "conventions for everything from the dimensions of letter paper to the size of screw threads." The working group, called the Motion Picture Experts Group (MPEG), first met in 1988 to establish standards for the compression of digital and audio files. One existing compression and decompression program, or codec, that proved useful had already been under development by a research team acting under the auspices of an umbrella organization called the Institute for Integrated Circuits, an institute whose primary function was to develop commercial products based on research undertaken at a consortium of German universities.

One of the file formats that resulted from this codec was originally intended to send high quality audio files over ordinary telephones lines. One piece of what Mann called its "buffed-up version" was intended for use on machines that could only deal with data slowly; it was called MPEG-1, Layer 3. The MPEG-1 codec was the first to make digital audio files small enough to be usefully circulated over the communications infrastructure that existed at the time. Layer 3 made large audio files up to twelve times smaller by stripping away frequencies most people can't hear in most circumstances, but retaining key aural identifying features. The research group created a free sample program to help its industry clients learn how to use the codec. The source code, however, was stored on a less than secure computer at the University of Erlangen from which it was downloaded by a hacker called SoloH. SoloH and several hacker colleagues developed the code into software that could be used to convert tracks from ordinary CDs into mp3 files. After they circulated these original efforts within a larger network of apparently highly motivated hackers, Mann reports that "an active digital-music subculture was shoehorning MP3 sites into obscure corners of the Net" only a few years later.

It is important to understand that the initially quiet revolution of the mp3 seemed at first to be just one more skirmish in the rich history of struggle between the entertainment industry and its consumers. As the music industry became more and more dependent on amassing profitable stores of "intellectual property," that is the right to the publishing, recording, and playing of music in public, the more they came into conflict with their own customers. For example, the RIAA launched a campaign in the 1980s against people making tapes from their vinyl and CD copies of their music. The tagline was "Home Taping Is Killing Music." The legal conflicts and advertising campaigns against illegal filesharing on the internet were very similar to their anti-home taping efforts. These struggles have long been fought out through the social lives of various audiovisual technologies in order for the music industry to maintain a medium amenable to its primary goals: making money by establishing and maintaining the exclusive use of their intellectual property. But the battle over the mp3 was the first to be fought on the substantially new and unfamiliar terrain of the internet. The main beneficiary of the internet has been the very large, wealthy, and increasingly influential computer industry and, secondarily, computer users, many of whom have extolled and embodied exactly the kind of attitude toward technological development that SoloH and his compatriots exhibited in letting loose the seemingly innocent technical standard of the mp3 upon the world.

In the years since the emergence of widespread file sharing, it has become very clear that the music industry hasn't been fighting a technology, or the distribution of a technology, or even the existence of particular kinds of file formats. They have been combating particular uses of technology. More specifically, they are fighting particular users of technology. As the noted scholar of the history of sound Jonathan Stern has explained, the mp3 was specifically designed for ease of use, universal compatibility, and freedom of transport. It is what he calls a "container technology" whose shape and function are skewed toward free circulation, not defiantly, but by design. What Mann refers to as the "burbling, self-organizing spontaneity" of the internet has been responsible for its widespread circulation and use.

However, there are two more very important questions to address. First, why did most of the music industry try to fight a technology that made their products easier to find, distribute, and listen to than ever before? Second, how did this new distribution technology seem to nearly destroy the music industry? The answers to these questions seem straightforward. The main reason the music industry fought the transition to digital was because by 1995, it had grown into little more than a distribution and marketing system. In a report issued by the Science Policy Research Centre in the United Kingdom, the authors had this to say about the music industry's main interests:

> For many years the music business has had very little to do with music. It essentially consists of fastmoving, unit-led production, marketing, licensing and distribution functions. How much product will sell in which territories, how quickly can they ship, how fast can they re-stock and so on. With the World Wide Web as a potential high-speed digital distribution channel, record companies will no longer be in a position to control the distribution chain.

The lengthy and destructive battles over illegal downloading were about far more than simple questions of ownership and theft. The music industry had no choice but to try to maintain control over the distribution of its products by exercising all the legal, economic, and political power it could muster. The problem was that a perfect convergence of technologies had occurred by the mid to late 1990s that meant this goal was all but impossible to achieve. This was because the CD, which the music industry had spent so much time and money developing, was actually a double-edged sword that allowed consumers to make and distribute perfect copies of their music. Personal computers began to arrive in peoples' home all over the world in such numbers that they quickly became the kind of appliance that few who could afford them wanted to do without. They were the kinds of machines that allowed everyone from computer experts to people with absolutely no knowledge of computer programming to use and benefit from them in various ways. Further, almost all of them eventually had optical disc drives. These read CDs perfectly. Given that the software to allow these drives to transfer the information they read to an individual's hard drive was easy to find, install, and use, everyone could digitize their music collections. The files that resulted, usually mp3s, but also wav files, were usually so small that people could store a large number of them at little cost. Finally, given that home computers were designed to be hooked up to normal phone lines, these files could be posted, traded, and downloaded with comparative ease. In short, an entirely new infrastructure for the distribution and consumption of music had seemingly sprung up overnight, built from some of the most easily accessible technologies that many people already had in their homes. This complex set of circumstances would prove to be influential.

INDEPENDENT RESEARCH WORK

For about ten years, music piracy was one of the most high-profile political debates in many places around the world. The debate was strong and consequential. Many countries passed laws to combat filesharing. The literature on this topic is very large. Use it to write a report explaining the outcomes of these debates. What laws were passed? How were they drafted? Who supported them? Why? Who opposed them? Why? Make a claim about who the "winners" were in these political debates.

References and further readings

Burkart, P., and T. McCourt. (2006) *Digital Music Wars: Ownership and Control of the Celestial Jukebox*. Lanham: Rowman & Littlefield Publishers.

Burnett, Robert. (1996) *The Global Jukebox: The International Music Industry*. London: Routledge.

Cummings, Alex Sayf. (2013) *Democracy of Sound: Music Piracy and the Remaking of American Copyright in the Twentieth Century*. New York: Oxford University Press.

Gillespie, Tarleton. (2007) *Wired Shut: Copyright and the Shape of Digital Culture*. Cambridge, MA: MIT Press.

Kernfeld, Barry. (2011) *Pop Song Piracy: Disobedient Music Distribution Since 1929*. Chicago: the University of Chicago Press.

Sterne, Jonathan. (2012) *MP3: The Meaning of a Format*. Durham: Duke University Press.

14

The catastrophe of Napster, the opportunities of digital

Background and topics

As suggested in the previous chapter, the music industry has had many conflicts with consumers over what the public would and would not be allowed to do with the music they buy. The conflicts over the sharing of mp3 files over the internet were part of this history, but were far more intense and potentially damaging that any that preceded them. It is important to acknowledge that at the time of these conflicts no one really knew what the real scale of change and disruption was going to be. Until this became at least somewhat clear, the music industry was forced to both explore the potential of the new technology and fight legal cases against specific uses of that technology while still trying to develop its own digital capabilities. They were not particularly successful in any of these efforts at first and eventually had to learn how to make deals with the computer industry. In doing all of this, they were able to insert themselves into the larger processes of change and make themselves far more relevant to those changes than they were initially. It is helpful to understand how this happened.

In the 2015 VH-1 documentary about Napster called *Downloaded* (available from various digital movie sales outlets), the filmmakers interview multiple music industry executives. Nearly all of them expressed their complete shock the first time they saw "their music" being traded online at Napster as they recounted their roles in the legal battles that followed the appearance of the online file-trading program. Their shock was symbolic of the extent to which the widespread development and use of digital technologies in the mid-1990s caught many in the music industry off-guard. This was in part due to the fact that the music industry had been doing

FIGURE 14.1 *Advertisement from the* New York Clipper *(1906).*

very well for a very long time. It is fair to say some of those at the top were somewhat complacent. The reasons for this were not too hard to see. The music industry had been making a lot of money for a long time. It was selling a lot of fairly expensive albums on CD, which was usually the only way most fans could buy music. The outlets that promoted their music, such as commercial radio and MTV, were very selective about which songs and videos they played. Similarly, big retail outlets also followed the model and focused on selling as many blockbusters as possible. As films such as *The Way the Music Died* from 2004 have shown, it was simply very difficult to get the music of lesser known or new artists heard by large numbers of people in the 1990s. Despite this, the big record companies were still making a lot of money, but it was mostly from a very small number of artists selling very large numbers of albums. The international music industry of the 1990s was a tightly controlled, highly profitable machine. Not many people within it at that time had any particularly strong reason to seek out and understand the new ways in which people were beginning to share music digitally at that time.

But this did not stop people trying. As journalists such as Bruce Haring and John Alderman described in books written in 2000 and 2001, there were many within the music industry who had long been pushing their superiors to explore what was to many of them a strange new world of computers and software. As early as 1992, several major record labels began to commission consultants to explore the digital world and report back. The advice they received was clear. The consultants all thought that it would be a good idea for the major record labels to start to figure out how to produce, distribute, and sell music through the digital networks that were then emerging, first on American college campuses, and later in the wider public. As with many high volume businesses, these seemingly distant threats usually took a backseat to the more immediate demands of marketing and selling music. They did however take the time and money to sue anyone they saw as violating their rights in any way. While Napster was the most prominent, it is helpful to look at a few other cases.

Early legal cases over internet music piracy were those directed at unauthorized fan websites on which people posted songs. These were not necessarily lawsuits, but often more like legal threats. The other kinds of early lawsuits were more substantial cases which were brought against other companies. Part of the purpose of these suits was to test the idea of "fair use" under US copyright law and to try to scare away anyone who might want to invest in these companies. The concept of fair use establishes that some uses of copyrighted material are acceptable while others are not. It has not always been entirely clear which was which. One use of copyrighted music the music industry objected to was placing music files on portable mp3 players. In 1998, the RIAA sued Diamond Multimedia, the company that produced and sold the Diamond Rio PMP 300 mp3 player. The Rio was a pocket-sized device that could store up to an hour of music and play it back for the user. The user could load files they had downloaded from the internet or use files from their own computers. The RIAA claimed that the device made illegal copies and, since they regarded it as a "recording device," they thought previous laws would prohibit users from putting any files on it. But as the device had no output, the people who made the device claimed it merely allowed people to listen to their own music wherever and whenever they wanted. The producers won the case are were able to sell their devices. The RIAA complained that the decision legitimized illegal file sharing by allowing people to make use of mp3s which, according to them, were all illegal.

A third type of lawsuit was cases brought against the websites that stored mp3s for users. The website mp3.com was a good example of this. In 1997–8, the website allowed users to upload and store their own mp3 files on the company's servers. The goal was to allow users to listen to their music from wherever they could access the internet. However, there were two problems. First, the website was supported by advertising and it was the website itself that made the copies for later use. This allowed the music industry to argue that the website was an entirely commercial service. This was too much to be supported by any existing conception of fair use and the court ruled against mp3.com. It is important to note the consequences of both the Rio case and the mp3.com case. The Rio case established very clearly that personal use of mp3 files was not illegal, while the mp3.com case established that any commercial use of those same files without a license from the copyright owner was illegal. While there were a large number of other cases that went through various courts at this time, these two went a long way in establishing the practical boundaries of the permissible uses of this new technology. One of the more important things to understand about these cases is the fact that the music industry worked extensively to try to exert control over how new technologies were used and through what channels music would move through the digital world. Between 1999 and 2003, they tried the most obvious solution to this problem—they tried to create their own digital channels.

While their lawyers were attacking various uses of mp3s in court, the big record labels were simultaneously working to create their own download services. They were called MusicNet, sponsored by Warner, BMG, EMI, and the digital media company Real Networks, and Pressplay, sponsored by Sony and Universal. Both debuted in 2001. While both services were complete failures, it is important to understand why they failed. The most direct reason for their failure was their design. Both charged $9.95 per month and allowed consumers access to a set number of streams and downloads of individual songs per month. However, most of the downloads were temporary, expiring after about a month. Also, some songs could only be streamed, not downloaded, and users could only download two tracks from the same album to burn onto a blank CD. Remarkably, the songs could not even be transferred to a portable mp3 player. They could only be listened to on one's home computer.

The second reason for their failures was the limited song catalogues for each service that proved unattractive to potential customers. These catalogues were limited because the big record companies behind each service came to informal agreements with each other to only cross-license each other's music. They often refused licenses to record smaller companies outside these informal agreements, or sometimes demanded that they pay hundreds of thousands of dollars to gain entry. As a result of this, these smaller companies formally accused the major labels of colluding to establish artificially high prices for their downloads by secretly agreeing with each other not to undercut a set price and collectively refusing to do business with anyone who didn't agree to these terms of service. The most striking feature of these accusations was

FIGURE 14.2 *An image from the hacker group Anonymous (2010).*

that the major record labels were trying to impose abnormally high prices on digital downloads at the very time free illegal downloads were at their peak. When industry observers said at the time that the music industry "didn't get it," this is a pretty good example of what they meant.

However, despite the failure of these attempts to establish legal digital downloads of music, they did eventually result in the necessary forms of cooperation between the music industry and the technology and computer industries that pushed the music industry toward facilitating the availability of legal digital music and toward the acceptance by the music industry of letting others sell their music online. This gradually paved the way for services such as the iTunes store and Spotify. Before we take a more detailed look at Napster, we will first look at some of the rules and laws that have developed around copyright and digital music. These rules and laws have had a significant influence on the entire digital economy in relation to music.

Explore and report: Fair use, "safe harbors," or free flow of information?

The conflicts over illegal downloads and file sharing were complex and difficult. While much of it took place in court, a good deal of conflict took place in public forums such as the media and the US Congress. There are three general claims about the trading of mp3 files on the internet that were made between about 1995 to 2005 that are of importance here. The first was that some of the use of mp3s were "fair use." This meant the consumers could do some things with them as long as these uses were not seen to be preventing copyright owners from making use of them as well. Another claim applied to websites. By the early 2000s there were a lot of commercial websites which hosted materials posted by users. These websites claimed that they should not be blamed for the actions of their users and that copyright owners were responsible for telling these websites about any illegal uses of their materials that they might be hosting. This idea was adopted into law. It was called the "safe harbor" provision and applied to websites such as YouTube. The third position was taken by groups such as Anonymous and others who demanded that the internet remain open and free from any copyright enforcement that might restrict the free flow of information. If you reread the last section of the Mann article you will find a helpful discussion of some of these arguments in relation to the music industry.

Your task is to research each of these three positions. There is an enormous amount of material about them online and in books as well. Please see the references at the end of this chapter for a starting point for your research. Confine your research to materials that examine the time period 1995–2005. One useful source would be the Wikipedia pages for the following legal cases. (Be sure to look at the references in each of these Wikipedia pages and follow them to their sources.):

- UMG Recordings, Inc. v. MP3.com, Inc.

  https://en.wikipedia.org/wiki/UMG_Recordings,_Inc._v._MP3.com,_Inc.

This lawsuit successfully stopped mp3.com from allowing users to store their music on the company's servers for future use.

- *Recording Industry Ass'n of America v. Diamond Multimedia Systems, Inc.*

  https://en.wikipedia.org/wiki/Recording_Industry_Ass%27n_of_America_v._Diamond_Multimedia_Systems,_Inc.

This case resulted in the personal use of mp3 players being declared legal.

- *Lenz v. Universal Music Corp.*

  https://en.wikipedia.org/wiki/Lenz_v._Universal_Music_Corp.

This case ruled that individuals can have a valid fair use claim to post copyrighted materials on websites.

- *Viacom International Inc. v. YouTube, Inc.*

  https://en.wikipedia.org/wiki/Viacom_International_Inc._v._YouTube,_Inc.

This case established that YouTube was a safe harbor for the posting of copyrighted materials.

Finally, find various papers and articles by people such as Professor Lawrence Lessig, John Perry Barlow, or organizations such as the Electronic Frontier Foundation. The position of "free flow" has been articulated and examined by them very extensively.

Your goal is to examine each of these three sets of arguments about what are "good" and "bad" uses of copyrighted materials in digital form. This is important because these and other debates, claims, counterclaims, and legal judgments have had a significant influence over how we access music through our computers, tablets, phones, and digital audio players and devices. Those who have shaped these decisions, regulations, and constraints on the development of digital music culture have included representatives of the music and technology industries, their lawyers, the judges who decided these cases, but also politicians, lobbyists, and millions of internet users who "voted with their feet" so to speak, by embracing some ways of using technology and rejecting others. Write an essay about who has benefited from the new technology and how. There are several groups to examine closely to see who has benefited the most from the decisions made in this time period—users, corporations, or musicians.

Focus: Napster v. the music industry

Napster was created by a few individuals who were part of a larger community of computer programmers who primarily interacted with each other online. Most met each other through a service called Internet Relay Chat (IRC). In the late 1990s, Shawn Fanning, credited as the inventor of Napster, had experienced a range of frustrations trying to download mp3 files of music and set himself to work on solving the problem. While he didn't explicitly share much of what he was working on with those in his IRC community, he did repeatedly ask for their help solving the various problems he faced. One of his peers said that he and others took this as a challenge. It was this collaborative/competitive environment that was eventually responsible for the innovations that Napster represented.

There are several aspects of Napster that can help us understand why it was this program, and not one of the many, many others available at the time, that captured the time and attention of so many users so quickly. The first aspect was that Napster was not simply a computer application that allowed people to download individual files. It was a "distributed file system" or a decentralized file-sharing program. In short, Napster was different. Users didn't simply download or trade complete files. Instead, users would use the program to contact a Napster server and search that server for the file names of songs they wanted. Then, Napster would connect the user asking for a particular file with every other personal computer operating on the network at the moment that had that file. Then, those computers would connect directly to one another. Pieces of the file would be gathered from all these sources at the same time. The file would then be reassembled on the computer of the person making the request. This is now called peer-to-peer (P2P) file sharing. The implications of this are important to understand.

First, people could get using Napster complete files much faster than by using any other program available at the time and the connections users made with each other were more reliable that those found through other

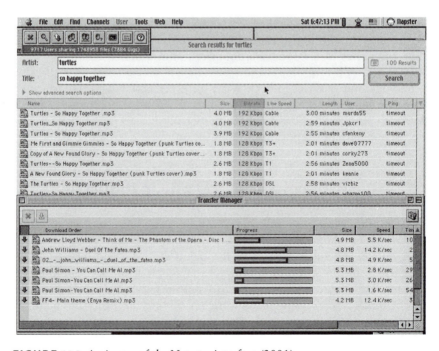

FIGURE 14.3 *An image of the Napster interface (2001).*

programs. As the home page of the application itself once said: "No more broken links, no more slow downloads." Second, the strength, speed, and usefulness of the application depended entirely on how many people made their digital music libraries available to it and were routinely connected to it. In other words, the more people used Napster, the better and faster the program became. Second, Napster was much more than just a file-sharing program; it was a very "social" computer program. It had a chat function that allowed users to speak directly to each other and it also allowed them to play their newly acquired files using an mp3 player that was embedded in the program. This added an immediate, social element to the network that was novel at that time. In fact, the creators of Napster have long claimed that the chat function was far more important to users than has been generally known. Creators Shawn Fanning and Sean Parker said at the time that much of the usefulness of Napster was to be able to "meet people through music." It was the kinds of social interaction people enjoyed through Napster that made it so popular. Third, the other key factor that made the social basis of Napster so appealing was that most of the users could only make effective use of the program if they were on large, powerful computer networks. At that time, the most likely place for Napster users to use such a network would be at their colleges and universities. The implicit social cohesion of most of Napster's users didn't just stem from their shared interest in music, but also from the fact that most were in the same age bracket and shared similar social circumstances. The effectiveness of the program was obvious simply from the number of users it had, reaching about eighty million in 2001, dwarfing the user numbers of far more established services such as Yahoo or Hotmail.

It didn't take too long for established artists and their record companies to try to stop Napster. The program went from complete obscurity to an international news story in only a few months, often due to various universities trying to ban the program to prevent their digital networks' capacity from being overwhelmed by students trading music with one another. A high profile lawsuit was filed by Metallica with the help of the RIAA in July 2001. Metallica claimed that Napster was violating laws of the type more often used to stop organized crime. Metallica member Lars Ulrich became a kind of figurehead for the case against the program, arguing that its

FIGURE 14.4 *The Napster logo (2001).*

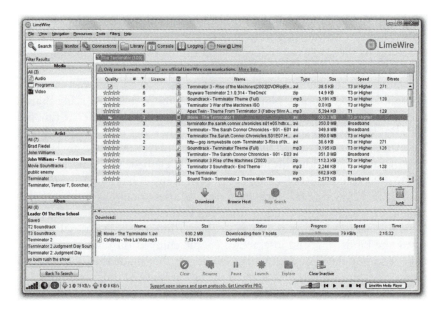

FIGURE 14.5 *An image of the Limewire interface (2008).*

success was based entirely on stolen property. The debates between Napster and the music industry were particularly difficult in large part because there was simply no previously existing relationship between the two. The people who created and developed Napster had no connections with anybody in the music industry and no one who worked for them had ever worked there. In fact, company founder Sean Parker readily admitted that he knew next to nothing about how the music industry even worked. On several occasions, Parker and Fanning claimed to be willing to turn the program over to the major record labels through some kind of licensing deal to become a digital download service for them. However, given the hostility to the youthful outsiders who were causing them so much trouble, it is unlikely that any such offer would have ever been accepted. Many executives at the major record companies viewed Fanning and Parker as criminals.

After a period of deliberation lasting nearly nine months, the court ruled against Napster. The circumstances of the case left Napster with no other option than to file for bankruptcy and sell off all of its assets. However, there was no going back. The consequences of Napster's remarkable rise to prominence had pushed the music industry past a symbolic and practical tipping point. The music industry had to confront the fact that the very people who formed the core of their business, music consumers, had very happily engaged in countless acts of what the music industry viewed as intellectual property crime. It was unlikely that the clearly expressed demands of so many of their customers could simply be ignored. Further, by 2001 there were many other industries carefully exploring how to get into the business of selling music digitally. Given the collaborative and collective nature of the kinds of independent software development that produced Napster, other programs were not far behind once a Napster-shaped hole appeared on the internet. Programs such as Gnutella and Limewire picked up where Napster left off and file sharing continued without much hindrance. The music industry had always had supporters of digital technology working within it and after the Napster case was resolved, these people were finally having more and more influence. It seemed clear to most people in the music industry by about 2005 that they would simply have to find a way to succeed in the face of the widespread presence of free forms of music. Whether or not "free music" was found on underground file-trading networks or on public and popular websites such as YouTube, the simple fact of the matter was that music was now firmly embedded in a digital world that so many had sought to hold off for so long.

INDEPENDENT RESEARCH WORK

The music industry has two "industry associations" that represent it in public and debates and political arenas around the world—the Recording Industry Association of America (RIAA) and the International Federation of Phonographic Industries (IFPI). Explore the purpose and powers of these organizations. How were they established? Who created them? Why were they created? Who are their members? What consequences to they have on the ability of people to make, distribute, buy, and share music? Explain the values these organizations say they support and compare these to the policies they advocate and activities they engage in?

References and further readings

Alderman, John. (2001) *Sonic Boom: Napster, MP3, and the New Pioneers of Music.* Cambridge, MA: Perseus Publishing.

David, Matthew. (2010) *Peer to Peer and the Music Industry: The Criminalization of Sharing.* London: SAGE.

Haring, Bruce. (2000) *Beyond the Charts: MP3 and the Digital Music Revolution.* Los Angeles: OTC Press.

Hardy, Phil. (2013) *Download: How the Internet Transformed the Record Business.* London, Omnibus Press.

Kirk, Michael. (2004) *The Way the Music Died*. Boston, MA: WGBH Educational
    Foundation.
Kot, Greg. (2010) *Ripped: How the Wired Generation Revolutionized Music*.
    New York: Simon and Schuster.
Knopper, Steve. (2009) *Appetite for Self-Destruction: The Spectacular Crash of the
    Music Industry in the Digital Age*. New York: Simon and Schuster.
Rogers, Jim. (2013) *The Death and Life of the Music Industry in the Digital Age*.
    London: Bloomsbury.
Winter, Alex. (2013) Downloaded. VH1 Television.
Witt, Stephen. (2015) *How Music Got Free: The Inventor, The Mogul, and the
    Thief*. New York: Vintage.

15

Music-based reality TV

Background and topics

By the end of the 1990s, the music industry was a very different kind of business than it had been twenty years earlier. Instead of being mostly focused on local or regional markets, large record companies were part of large transnational corporations. (Reread pages 38–46 of the Garofalo article for a summary.) In every case, these corporations produced music, movies, television programs, and more. Not only did this allow for easier integration of music with the film and television industries, it also created larger and larger markets to sell that music to. As a result, while record companies made unprecedented amounts of money from selling albums in the 1980s and 1990s, their range of revenue sources had also expanded tremendously in this period. The industry's increased focus on collecting and exploiting their stores of intellectual property ensured this. Artists and record labels successfully pursued a wide range of very lucrative deals to use music to sell a wide range of products, especially clothes and soft drinks. This also enabled record companies to sell their artists as global "products" who were recognized all over the world and link them to other similar products that were also familiar to a global audience of consumers. As the media scholar Bethany Klein has shown, the use of music to sell other products became a very important source of profit for the most famous artists and their record labels, especially during those periods when the music industry was struggling. Importantly, using music to help create a brand image and brand associations between music and other products also created strong and enduring links between the music and advertising industries.

One of the most successful manifestations of these changes to the music industry was music-based reality television. Programs such as *Pop Idol*,

FIGURE 15.1 *A global map of* Idol *franchises.* (Black and grey areas denote the territory of Idol franchisees.)

X Factor, and *The Voice* took advantage of the potential global reach of the music industry, its connections to the television and advertising industries, and a focus on the licensing of the industry's intellectual property to produce remarkably profitable television shows that were cheap to produce while also reaching a very large audience. More remarkable is the fact that these programs succeeded at precisely the same time as most of the music industry was in very deep trouble. In this chapter, we will look at the most influential of these programs, *Idol*, in order to understand how and why music-based reality television shows have been so successful. We will start with some historical background of *Idol*.

Idol was not the first music-based reality television show. The first was called *Popstars*, a show that began in New Zealand in 1999. The program was presented as a documentary of the process of creating a pop singing group, in this case the female singing group TrueBliss. The program was franchised to fifty countries and while most franchises were canceled after two or three years, a few lasted much longer.

Idol was created by artist manager and television producer Simon Fuller. While *Popstars* is often cited as an "inspiration" for *Idol*, the two shows are very different. *Idol* was a very carefully structured and controlled show. It had clearly defined stages, all of which contributed to each show's overall narrative. While we will examine this aspect of the show in the Focus section below, it is important to get an overview here. The first stage of the show introduces the audience to the hundreds of contestants individually. It shows a broad range of performers from the highly skilled to the truly awful. These auditions tend to take place across a wide geographic range of towns and cities. The purpose of this stage is to highlight the very small number of contestants that succeed and enter the far more exclusive second stage of the competition. The second stage moves the competition to a main center, such as Los Angeles or London. The contestants are asked to rehearse and perform in a range of settings and ensembles. The judges determine who will continue on in the show. This is followed by the semifinals. These take place in a purpose-built television studio and is the first time viewers have a chance to vote. These shows are followed by a series of live shows consisting of a small number of finalists. These shows take place over a number of weeks, each of which is dedicated to a special theme or musical style. In each week of the semifinals and live shows, the lowest vote getter is eliminated. The final consists of two singers performing live, usually in a high-profile venue for a very large audience. The winner is the one who gets the most votes from the public.

While these shows and their supporters often made fairly flamboyant claims about their uniqueness, innovative design, and financial success, they were fairly familiar from the start. For example, Fuller had a great deal of experience in attracting, shaping, and marketing musical talent. He managed the Spice Girls, directing them to their widespread global success largely through manufacturing a network of merchandising and sponsorship tie-ins, all filtered through the Spice Girls brand. Similarly, he created and managed the pop group S Club 7, creating their television show as the primary showcase for the various manifestations of their music and brand. These skills were easily transferable to *Idol*. *Idol* was also strongly influenced by *Big Brother*, the international television franchise that started in the Netherlands in 1999. As with *Big Brother*, those appearing in *Idol* were contestants. They competed directly with one another for the right to continue on the show. The task of *Idol* contestants was to perform for both a live and a television audience who would then vote for their

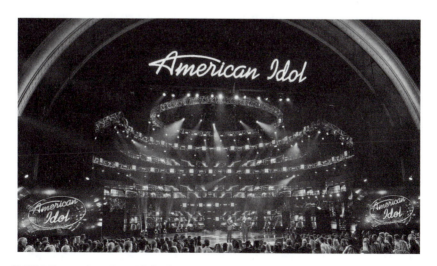

FIGURE 15.2 American Idol *television set.*

favorite performers based on their musical abilities, but also their overall attractiveness and personalities. This process resulted in far more intimate relationships between the audience and the contestants than the *Popstars* audience experienced. One of the keys to *Idol*'s success was the show's ability to draw viewers into close relationships with contestants based on the tension and drama of live musical performance.

A few of these television programs have been extraordinarily profitable. For example, *American Idol* was a top-rated television program for well over five years and had the highest advertising rates of any American television program for almost as long. This often translated into hundreds of millions of dollars in ad revenues each year. Spin offs and competitors like *The X Factor* and *The Voice*, as well as music-centered dramas such as *Glee*, have also found sustained success by attracting large audiences and launching, or relaunching, the careers of contestants, judges, and guests alike. There were many reasons for their success. These shows established new alliances with the very profitable television and computer industries. They made piracy a practical irrelevance by turning the use of digital media into economic and market-building tools. They crafted multiple revenue streams that managed to share out the extensive risks of these long-running, expensive projects. They also cleverly used existing intellectual property to their benefit and established their brand as the navigator of the many sales environments in which they thrived. Importantly, these shows were integrated into a range of online social media forms long before the idea was fashionable, not as ancillary add-ons, but as central forums for fan engagement that included voting for contestants as well as participating myriad contests and publicity campaigns that sustained or enhanced knowledge of and interest in the shows.

Instead of simply trying to sell albums, these television shows instead successfully exploited the environments in which people watched people perform music on television. These environments were then used to create brands whose content can effortlessly and invisibly slip across any existing or emerging media channel and produce profit in any of the multiple guises in which they might appear. These guises only seem to multiply whether they appear as part of a live show, a one-off performance, a soundtrack to a film, television show or advertisement, a promotional appearance, a television or film documentary, a fictional film, television miniseries, and the seemingly endless opportunities for advertising and merchandising.

Explore and report: The successes and failures of music-based reality TV

The assumed purpose of music-based reality television shows is to choose "the best" singer from among a very large group of contestants. The excitement and drama are produced by the competition between them. But how do we as viewers assess the contestants' talent and their performances? Why do some contestants get more votes than others? Do the musical characteristics of their performances matter? What about the singer's "personality"? As noted in this chapter, these contests are intensely commercial enterprises. How does this fact shape who succeeds and who fails?

Your task is to compare several closely paired performances from music-based reality television shows and explain why some contestants succeeded and others did not. It would probably be best to choose one franchise of *Idol* or *The X Factor*. Materials for these shows are widely available. There are many, many performances from these shows available on a range of streaming video platforms. First, choose the program you want to examine and get as much background as you can. You need to understand how it worked, how it was structured, and what the rules were. Second, you need to choose one season of the show to analyze. One of the most useful things to do is to do a series of browser searches of the names of contestants for the show who made it to the later rounds, if not the final round. You need to make sure there are videos available for analysis. Third, compare a range of performances from roughly similar rounds of the program and explain why some performances were lauded as successes and other were criticized as failures. Consider all aspects of the performance including vocal performance, costuming, choreography, song choice, stage setting, and the perceived relationships between the singer and the audience. Write a short analytical essay accounting for both the success and failures of the contestants.

FIGURE 15.3 *One Direction,* X Factor Live *(2011).*

Focus: The *Idol* journey

One of the most important aspects of the *Idol* phenomenon has been of its most overlooked characteristic: the coherence of its narrative. This narrative, or "The *Idol* journey," as it was often called, was meant to show us the transformation of a talented, but raw performer into a "real" pop star. The purpose of the show was not simply to crown a winner, but to show audiences in tremendous detail over a long period of time, exactly how much work and emotion went into that transformation. As with most television shows, it is the story a show produces which is most often responsible for its success. While music-based reality television programs appear to be merely documenting events as they happen, this is rarely the case. Instead, shows such as *Idol* mostly consist of tightly scripted events that are presented to viewers with all of the excitement and unpredictability of a sporting event. However, as with sporting events there are rules and constraints that reduce uncertainty to a significant degree. Further, when considering the ways in which contestants are judged, even the final outcomes of these programs become a great deal more predictable and far less risky for producers. We will work our way through a generic *Idol* journey to get a better sense of the show's defining characteristics beyond the hype and drama.

The standard *Idol* journey began with the auditions. Viewers were shown hundreds, if not thousands, of young hopefuls turning up and waiting for their chance to catch the ears of the judges. They did so at multiple locations around the country or region in which the contest took place. It is important to recognize what went into this introduction to each season of the show. First, these auditions were a huge undertaking. The producers needed to send out several portable camera crews to capture the full range of activity at these events. For example, camera crews routinely captured dramatic shots of long lines of contestants, interviewed dozens of those seeking to audition, and in many cases encouraged impromptu performances by many of them. The auditions themselves became famous in many countries for showing viewers very talented young performers, but just as much for showing very bad performers. Perhaps the most famous of these non-*Idol*s was American William Hung who sang an off-key version of Ricky Martin's "She Bangs" in his first *Idol* audition in 2004. The immediate juxtaposition of good singers and bad has two effects. First, it highlights who the "good" singers are by showing how vastly outnumbered they are by those who just aren't as good as they think they are. Second, it shows us that the show itself is serious enough to sift through the assembled thousands to find out potential finalists.

There are several aspects of these initial mass auditions that are important to understand. One of the most important purposes of these initial auditions is to create a kind of storehouse of raw footage that will be used and reused throughout the entirety of the program. This is crucial to the success of the show because this careful use and reuse of the defining moments of the show that establishes the story will help viewers make sense of the many months of auditions and performances. This tells us something important about the problems faced by the producers at these initial auditions. One of the more subtle purposes of these mass auditions is to make sure that there is good footage of all of the eventual semifinalists. Scenes of their initial auditions needed to be captured and shown to viewers at the later stages of the program to show how much these performers have changed and grown because of their participation in the show. Yet the camera crews are faced with thousands of contestants and without some form of strategy and organization, it would have simply been impossible to capture useful scenes of every possible contestant who might potentially make it to the finals.

Therefore, while viewers are subtly led to believe that these auditions were simply the chaos they appeared to be, this isn't the case. With most versions of *Idol*, the producers of the show were very careful to recruit singers they already knew to be talented enough to succeed. They also used what were called "producer auditions," which were not televised to offer advice to contestants believed to have some potential to get through the mass auditions. The camera crews could then be sure to focus on these singers.

The second stage of *Idol* took those who got through away from home and put them together in a kind of "boot camp" for young singers. Here, the contestants rehearsed their chosen songs, were challenged to "get out of their comfort zones," and tasked with trying new styles of singing and performance. It was this round, between the often bewildering mass auditions and the very specific demands of the semifinals, that performers were often said to have "discovered themselves" as singers. One crucial theme that had to be developed here was that those who made it through deserved their success. This had to be demonstrated to viewers through a cunning paradox. The singers who deserved success were those who could both do the hard work of self-transformation and experience the confirmation of self-realization. The judges decided on a small number of contestants who would be allowed to go through to the far more exclusive performance rounds.

The two performance rounds that followed were usually the first time contestants were allowed to perform live for the judges and viewers. While these performances were sometimes broadcast in prerecorded form, the contestants were still performing live and had only one chance to succeed. Most importantly, this was the first time viewers could vote a contestant in or out of the show. There were several important aspects to these two rounds that made them probably the most consequential of the entire enterprise. First, the relationship between the judges and the contestants became far more important and direct than it had been previously. It may seem contradictory to suggest that the judges became more important as their ability to decide who stayed on the show was taken away from them, but it isn't. In the two performance rounds, the judges acted as the bridge from the small television studio to the big stage. That is, they drew on the credibility they earned through their knowledge and experience to tell the audience who is good enough to make it and who isn't. The guidance and approval of the judges is crucial for the contestants at this stage because it was these assessments that shaped how a contestant was perceived throughout the many weeks of live performance that may or may not get them to the final.

The other important aspect of the performance rounds was how the contestants begin to become more and more surrounded by all of the trappings of pop stardom. One defining feature of the live shows was their themes. Each show had a musical theme that centered around genres or time periods, such as "The 60s" or "Motown." This allowed the performers to present well-known songs in a range of styles that placed different demands on their musical abilities. The stage settings also became increasingly elaborate and spectacular in these rounds. The contestants stopped wearing their own clothes and begin to wear costumes. These were usually thematically appropriate costumes and often were meant to evoke some element of relevance to the song. The contestants also begin to perform with larger ensembles, often small orchestras, and occasionally they worked with other well-known musicians and choreographers. Part of the challenge was working with those who are already highly successful and "rising to the occasion." This was a crucial moment in the process of transformation as the contestants had to do more than simply singing or performing effectively. They had to start to command both the stage and "the moment" with their presence and their abilities. In many respects, it was the live rounds in which the imitation of pop stardom facilitated by the show started to become the real thing.

The final is perhaps the most straightforward of all of the rounds. These events present the fewest possible number of contestants and all of the themes developed throughout the entire run of the season—the joy, the drama, the tears, the triumph—could all be presented without any further need for elaboration or development. There is far less strategy involved with the presentation of the conclusion to the show. Instead, the final event and vote brought to a stirring conclusion the story of the show itself as presented through the transformation of its contestants. The task of the final was to confirm for viewers that this was a special kind of transformation, one borne of innate talent brought to fruition through hard work.

Throughout the show, we were continually reminded that the *Idol* journey was always moving and evolving through thousands of passing moments which are constantly being recontextualized through a process of re-narration present throughout the program. The producers relentlessly collected footage at every stage of the contest and reused it at every available moment during the life of the program. Given the inherently transitory nature of the program and the events it contains, these constant efforts at reestablishing and reshaping these events ease them into conformity with the expected narrative contour they both create and satisfy. The stirring story produced by the contest was the heart of the entire endeavor. It held everything together, keeping the audience interested and engaged. Given the extraordinary number of avenues for audience participation, "*Idol's*" success has been cleverly and carefully achieved and strategically maintained through a series of events that continuously offer us new products that never seemed to stop appearing.

INDEPENDENT RESEARCH WORK

Music-based reality television sparked a lot of heated debate in the 2000s. People claimed that the shows damaged music and musicians, Some claimed that the shows did not value the creation of new music, but instead exploited those who competed in these contests simply to make money off the rehashing of existing music. Supporters argued that the shows were incredibly successful commercially and that this was good for everyone who made music. Examine these debates. Publications such as Rolling Stone, NME, Billboard, and others presented many years worth of articles on this subject. The debates mirrored very closely the debates about the use of popular music in advertising from only a few years earlier. In both cases, the debates overshadowed the consequences of the phenomenon people were arguing about. Write a report about the consequences of music-based reality television. Who has benefited the most from these programs? Did they offer a new path to stardom as their producers argued? Were they the open, democratic contests some said they were?

References and further readings

Fairchild, Charles. (2008) *Pop Idols and Pirates: Mechanisms of Consumption and the Global Circulation of Popular Music.* Aldershot, UK: Ashgate.

Klein, Bethany. (2009) *As Heard on TV: Popular Music in Advertising.* Farnham, UK: Ashgate.

Meizel, Katherine. (2011) *Idolized: Music, Media, and Identity in American Idol.* Bloomington, IN: Indiana University Press.

Zwaan, K., and J. de Bruin. (2012) *Adapting Idols: Authenticity, Identity and Performance in a Global Television Format.* Farnham, UK: Ashgate.

Streaming, clouds, and the dematerialization of music

Background and topics

Between the years 1995 and 2015, the music industry probably changed more than any time since the era of sound recording began. To bring this book to a close we will focus on the three primary social relationships examined in this book and see how they have been transformed in this twenty-year period. These relationships are between the music industry and consumers, between the music industry and musicians, and between musicians and their fans.

One of the more prominent themes in discussion of the music industry during this period was that it was said to be "dying." Musicians said it, observers said it, and even some industry insiders said it. However, it is important to understand what people meant when they said this. Generally, they didn't mean that no one would be able to make money selling music anymore. What they meant was that the specific version of the music industry that had been so successful right up to the turn of the twenty-first century was disappearing and it was unclear what might replace it. In short, the relationships that linked the music industry to its consumers were said to be broken. This was largely because ways in which people experienced music before the existence of digital technologies were less and less useful to people. Buying albums on CD or vinyl was a habit that was not central to the digital world of social media and smartphones that emerged in these years.

While this change did not happen overnight it did happen relatively quickly. If you think back to the early chapters of this book, you might remember that sound recording was invented in the 1870s, but listening to

FIGURE 16.1 *The iPod "Family" of Devices (2009).*

music on recorded discs or cylinders did not become a standard or habitual practice until at least twenty-five years later. The creation of the two most used websites and applications for listening to music, YouTube and Spotify, did not even exist until 2005 and 2006 respectively. Yet, in less than ten years both had become arguably the most important mediums through which most people listened to recorded music. This rapid growth in usage and popularity tells us that it was not so much the music industry's survival that was at stake, but their ability to economically exploit the new and dynamic social relationships being created by the new experiential contexts for music that mattered. If they couldn't do it, somebody else would.

Despite the years of challenge and chaos that caused so many problems, there were people within the music industry who had some insight into where some measure of future stability might lie. Despite the fact that at that time the music industry was in crisis, one industry consultant named Jim Griffin had been advising the record companies who sought his advice to accommodate the new technology rather than fight it. In 1999, Griffin told *Wired* magazine that one seemingly straightforward option had been under consideration since the mid-1990s: digital streaming. He argued that it wasn't consumers who were the problem, but the character of the internet itself. He argued that mp3 downloading simply wasn't containable. However, it could be viewed as a transition technology to a music industry defined by flat-fee, subscription-based audio-streaming services. He suggested that the "economic model behind streaming and ubiquitous access obviates piracy. Intellectual property gains value as it is widely distributed, much like television or radio." Like many observers, Griffin recognized that the trajectory of the internet was toward increasing speed, bandwidth, and ubiquitous access which meant that the value of digital content was "plummeting towards zero." He argued that "unless we stop letting people listen to music, we have no way to control the quantity and the destination of those digits." Griffin, like a few others in and around the music industry, saw the industry's future as a content provider to those companies that would organize and funnel music to consumers, "whether from portable devices, home stereos, or desktop PCs. By aggregating content, the major labels could offer music services that let consumers customize channels in whatever fashion they like, and pay a monthly, all-you-can-eat fee similar to the broadcast models used by AOL and HBO." According to Griffin, "The distribution chain [was] being wasted on delivering digits on a plastic disc. . . . Once freed up, we can sell items associated with music that have higher margins. It's actually a better business to not sell the content. Selling items associated with the music is where it's at."

While it is easy to read these kinds of comments now and take them for granted, his explanation did not fit very well with the prevailing attitudes in most of the music industry at that time. There were a lot of problems that had to be solved before these new ideas could be pursued. In 2002, Charles Mann of *The Atlantic* told readers that the music industry would have to find ways to dramatically alter its business model very quickly, something he didn't think could be done. He argued the music industry would have to find a way to make a profit by selling individual tracks, not albums, make recordings cheaper to produce, change the ways in which artists are contracted to reflect these changes, and make legitimate online services easier and more reliable than illegal file sharing. To do all of this they would have had to do the one thing they did not want to do: go into partnership with the technology and computer industries.

Despite significant opposition to these plans, this is more or less what happened between about 2003 and 2015. Digital streaming was gradually built around new alliances with different parts of the media, computer, and internet industries, with companies such as Apple and Google; it made piracy a marginal concern, it helped to sell a good deal of music in many different forms, it sold a good deal of music that was already widely available, it made profitable use of the music industry's existing intellectual property, and it installed its own brands (the artists) at the heart of the consumer experience.

It is important to understand that music streaming was made possible by the profound change in the music industry noted in earlier chapters: its evolution from an industry concerned primarily with producing and selling recorded music to an industry that is just as concerned on balance with the exploitation of intellectual property rights. This allowed digital streaming to be accepted both conceptually and practically within the mainstream of the music industry far earlier than is often acknowledged. The first efforts toward creating large-scale streaming services began as early as 1994–5 with the development and diffusion of Real Network's RealAudio tools for webcasting and podcasts. As early as 1995 the music industry in the United States began working to establish the laws and contracts that would allow streaming services to operate on a mass scale. Two laws, the Digital Performance Rights Act of 1995 and the Digital Millennium Copyright Act of 1998, made it possible for the music industry to collect royalties from those playing music over new kinds of services such as satellite radio services and webcasters.

This in turn allowed the creation of a number of new streaming services such as Pandora, Last.fm, Rhapsody, and Spotify. Gradually, the music industry worked to establish the kinds of relationships with technology industries that would eventually lead them to decide to establish digital streaming as the new standard in music distribution and consumption. First, record companies began licensing their catalogues to an increasing range of streaming services. Second, the music industry worked to integrate its own services with those of the most used online platforms such as YouTube. They have learned how to license various systems of rights and royalties to profit from rather than strangle new businesses that want to sell music in new ways. Third, the major record labels have begun to link their own digital storefronts with different social media platforms. Social media generally seems to offer the kinds of relationships with consumers that seem well-suited to the exploitation of what musical experience affords people online. The goal is to transform these experiences into tangible transactions. Social media platforms have been able to do this because of their intensive surveillance of their users. Social media measures the kinds of relationships users have with other users by tracking the kinds of things they share, such as comments, photos, video files or links, and how the value of what they are sharing changes over time. Buying into this mass of data gives the music industry the ability to track and analyze a whole range of users' habits in order to exploit their interests and relationships to their benefit.

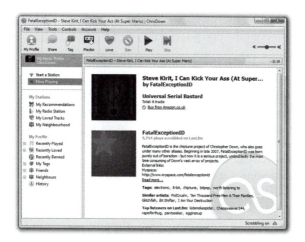

FIGURE 16.2 *Last.fm interface (2006).*

The relationships between the music industry and musicians have also changed significantly, but these changes have not been particularly positive overall. One of the most prominent issues surrounding the introduction of the many different kinds of streaming services has been the levels of compensation paid to artists. Given that these payments are the streaming services' greatest costs, there have been protracted negotiations and legal battles between the major labels and the streaming services over these rates. As is often the case, the place of musicians in these new negotiated systems of power is precarious at best. As I reported in 2015, one music industry analyst explained the problem over a decade before these issues began to make headlines: "As more contracts are being drawn in the Internet age, lawyers working on behalf of the labels have come up with more rigid and unavoidable contract clauses to hold against artists. . . . The norm has been that, with new technology, the labels try to pay the artist less."

Streaming has also transformed the relationships between musicians and fans. As we will see shortly in the Focus section below, the ways in which streaming services organize and present music to listeners has a powerful effect on what songs become hits and which artists become superstars. They shape listeners' habits and tastes. Beyond this, however, the ways in which many people listen to music and discover new artists has become as much a part of the digital world as their social media avatars. Streaming sells access to a range of music that dwarfs anything even the largest record store once offered. It also sells access to the knowledge, expertise, and social status of catalogue "curators." These mediators use the data listeners produce through their phones, apps, and browsers to try to anticipate what we will all want to listen to next. As we will see in the rest of this chapter, these relationships are central to the new digital economy is music.

Explore and report: Musical relationships in the digital age

Who does streaming benefit most, listeners, musicians, or the music industry? This is a difficult question to answer simply because it is hard to determine what exactly a "benefit" is. There are a lot of articles and analyses about these issues that have appeared in a wide range of publications since digital streaming services began operating. Your task is to make a claim about who digital music streaming benefits the most based on evidence drawn from strong sources of information. Look for articles about streaming in *Billboard*, Pitchfork, The Quietus, Music Ally (NOT musical.ly), *The Guardian*, Fader, Vox, *Wired*, *The New Yorker*, and other music or tech-related publications and websites from 2005 onward. (Following the Music Feed on Ref Def can often let you know about relevant articles also.) Then, gather as much as you can about the debates about the influence of streaming companies, how they treat musicians, and how listeners use these services. Further, establish a strong base of knowledge about several of these services by using them and making notes on your experiences. Compare your own experiences with those of others. Then, set out the debates that have taken place among those who work for record companies and streaming companies, musicians, and commentators. Set out as many of the arguments as you can find. Finally, write an essay making the case for one position offered by the representatives of the different groups involved in these debates. There is no "right" answer here. It depends on what you value and what you think is important.

Focus: Curating music in the playlist economy

There is little question that playlists have become important ways for people to find and embrace new music as well as trawl through almost all of the music they have ever known on demand from almost anywhere they can get internet access. So far, they can even do it for free if they can stand the ads. It should be clear that the relationships between musicians, fans, and the music industry created by digital streaming would be very different than any such relationships that preceded them. This section will look at these changes to see what they might mean for the future of music.

One prominent change has been the people who make the playlists listeners find on streaming service. They are often called "curators," and their job puts them right where musicians and record companies try to find their listeners. Those making playlists put them together by drawing on vast databases of existing music as well as new music that might be pitched to them by people working for record companies. Those creating playlists try to both mirror and anticipate listeners' expectations about what music might become popular. Whereas in the past, this might have been done through listener surveys or record store sales, streaming is based on the careful analysis and use of endless amounts of data the actions of listeners produce. They keep careful track of how listeners respond to playlists, seeing how many listen to a track all the way through or skip ahead. User data is also linked with assumptions about who listeners are and what music they might like based on their age, gender, and geographical location. They also use various social media platforms to alert them when a relatively unknown artist might be trending and try to monitor as many of these as possible.

Playlists are not simply organized through musical characteristics that are presumed to make sense to people, such as genre conventions or stylistic attributes that links different artists to one another. Instead, streaming services often focus on what people are doing when they listen to music, where they are, and what moods might be matched to specific

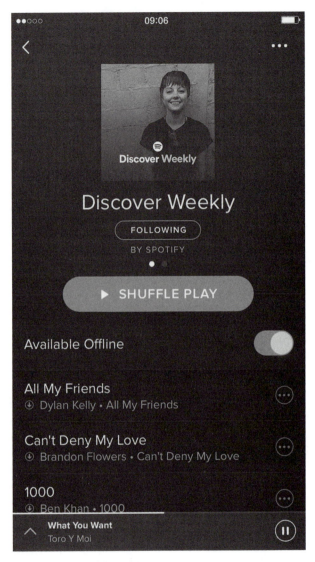

FIGURE 16.3 *Spotify "Discover Weekly" playlist (2018).*

songs. In some ways, the intended experience of music is the focus rather than a song's sounds, affects on people, or the skill with which it has been produced and performed. The uses to which music is put in everyday life is an explicit part of how music is presented by streaming companies. One writer for Pitchfork explained that "one vision of playlists' future has moved beyond recommending music based on what people like already and toward songs tailored to each user's exact present circumstances." The goal of any playlist is to amass followers and subscribers and to do so there has to be an inherently social aspect to its construction and presentation. There is also a crucial element of real-time response by people making playlists. As some analysts have observed, adding a new song to a prominent playlist at exactly the right time can determine its success. The ability to capitalize on something as vague and elusive as "buzz" is sometimes the difference between a hit and a failure.

There have been robust debates about the possible consequences of the power and influence amassed by companies such as Spotify and Apple Music. They do not simply find music that they think might be popular soon and try to present it as advantageously as they can. They also work with companies such as Shazam and Soundhound who produce song identification apps to try to predict what songs are most likely to become hits before anybody else knows about them. Shazam allows its clients to use their data to literally map where songs are becoming popular. A writer for *The Atlantic* described it this way: "The map amounts to a real-time seismograph of the world's most popular new music, helping scouts discover unsigned artists just as they're starting to set off tremors." This affects where record companies devote their promotional resources and informs where artists decide to tour and even which songs they might play in a given place.

Importantly, the ability to predict which songs might become hits based on the kinds of data that these companies collect is shaping how songs get written as well. For example, the data these companies produce and use tell them which songs people listen to and how long they listen. An enormous amount of this data piles up and appears to offer the music industry significant insight into how people are reacting to the music they are trying to sell. Industry insiders and observers have shared with music journalists their anecdotal impressions of how this has changed mainstream pop songwriting. As one writer for Pitchfork explains, "With tens of millions of songs just a few taps away, artists must compete or be skipped." This has resulted in songwriters trying everything they can to capture the listener's attention within the first thirty seconds of a song. Many songs are structured so as to place what they see as the most attractive and catchy section of the song right at the beginning. Often this leads to a rapid succession in musical changes as the listener is offered as much as possible as quickly as possible. Beyond individual songs, streaming has shaped how an artist presents a collection of songs to the public. Whereas albums used to be regarded as commercially and artistically important as unique, complete entities, streaming demands that artists and record companies rethink this assumption. Given the flexibility users are offered with most streaming services, many within the music industry think that few if any listeners will think about a collection of songs by an artist the way they used to think about albums, that is, as a complete, fixed work, much less listen to them that way. In response, some artists have presented collections of their songs released together not as albums, but as playlists. Listeners can rearrange and reimagine the work in any way they want, even deciding, collectively, which song should be the hit single.

The public debates about streaming among musicians and companies trying to sell and profit from their music have been important in identifying how the power over music is changing. They have shown us the power that digital streaming companies have over what music gets made and sold and what that music sounds like. These arguments have revealed that the first decade or so of music streaming has given a small number of companies a great deal of power of whose music will reach the most people and who will make the most money from it. The companies that have been the most aggressive in doing so are some of the biggest and most profitable on the planet. They have been able to make mutually beneficial deals with the biggest players in the music industry, which have allowed both to exploit the ability of music to shape the personal and emotional lives of millions of people. The book has tracked the many different kinds of struggles people have engaged in over this most social of one of our most important collective cultural resources. Hopefully, this is work you will continue.

INDEPENDENT RESEARCH WORK

Those who "curate" playlists for streaming services such as Apple Music and Spotify have been written about a great deal. For many, they represent how the digital economy in music works for musicians and consumers alike. Examine playlist curators and compare them to other music industry cultural intermediaries from the past such as radio DJs, television program hosts, and bandleaders. Write about the characteristics they all have in common.

References and further readings

Burkart, Patrick. (2010) *Music and Cyberliberties*. Middletown, CT: Wesleyan University Press.

Fairchild, Charles. (2015) "Crowds, Clouds, and Idols: New Dynamics and Old Agendas in the Music Industry, 1982-2012." *American Music*, 33(4): 441–76.

Johansson, S., P. Aker, and G. Goldenzwaig. (2018) *Streaming Music: Practices, Media, Cultures*. New York, NY: Routledge.

Jones, Christopher. (1999) "Digital Music at the Crossroads." *Wired*, April 19, http://www.wired.com/culture/lifestyle/news/1999/04/19171.

Kretschmer, Martin. (2001) "Music in Electronic Markets: An Empirical Study." *New Media and Society* 3(4): 417–41.

Sullivan, Jennifer. (1999) "MP3: Flash in the Pan." *Wired*, April 19, http://www.wired.com/culture/lifestyle/news/1999/04/19189.

Thompson, Derek. (2014) "The Shazam Effect." *The Atlantic*, 17 November.

Wikström, Patrik. (2009) *The Music Industry: Music in the Cloud*. Cambridge, UK: Polity.

INDEX